CW00329067

BLUE DIAMONDS

BLUE DIAMONDS

The Exploits of
14 Squadron RAF
1945-2015

MICHAEL NAPIER

Pen & Sword
AVIATION

First published in 2015 by
Pen and Sword Aviation

An imprint of
Pen & Sword Books Ltd
47 Church Street
Barnsley
South Yorkshire
S70 2AS

Copyright Michael John William Napier © 2015

ISBN 978 1 47382 327 3

Design and artwork by Nigel Pell

Printed and bound in India
By Replika Press Pvt. Ltd.

Pen & Sword Books Ltd incorporates the Imprints of
Pen & Sword Aviation, Pen & Sword Family History, Pen & Sword Maritime,
Pen & Sword Military, Pen & Sword Discovery, Pen and Sword Fiction,
Pen and Sword History, Wharncliffe Local History, Wharncliffe True Crime,
Wharncliffe Transport, Pen & Sword Select, Pen & Sword Military Classics,
Leo Cooper, The Praetorian Press, Seaforth Publishing and Frontline Publishing

For a complete list of Pen & Sword titles please contact
PEN & SWORD BOOKS LIMITED
47 Church Street, Barnsley, South Yorkshire, S70 2AS, England
E-mail: enquiries@pen-and-sword.co.uk
Website: www.pen-and-sword.co.uk

Contents

This book is dedicated to the proud memory of

Flight Lieutenant Alan George Grieve BSc

Killed in a flying accident, aged 28, on 13 January 1989
while serving as a Tornado navigator with 14 Squadron, RAF Brüggen.

A loyal and generous friend, still missed today

FOREWORD

by
Air Marshal Sir Timothy Anderson, KCB, DSO

It was with the greatest pleasure and a deep sense of gratitude for his efforts that I agreed readily to Mike Napier's flattering request to write a brief Foreword for the second instalment of his detailed, enthralling and authoritative history of No.14 Squadron RAF. Whilst Mike undoubtedly enjoys the role of author, detective and archivist, penning a comprehensive and richly-illustrated history such as this companion volume to *Winged Crusaders* is nevertheless a time-consuming endeavour and there must have been many times when he, or his close family, wondered what on earth had prompted him to come back for a second bite of this particular cherry! Notwithstanding, without his commitment, stamina and conscientious research, not to mention his refined powers of persuasion, a relatively small but highly-significant component of Royal Air Force and air-power history would have presumably been lost to time, along with the many voices that Mike has amplified for us throughout the pages of his treatize. All who love and are proud to have been associated with 14 Squadron over the years owe him a debt of gratitude for assuming the responsibility and taking the time to formulate this distinctive account of our squadron and I am happy to highlight that here as a matter of record.

As the world reset in the years after the Second World War, 14 Squadron began another prolonged period of overseas service that was to culminate in 2001, by which time it was the longest serving of all of the RAF flying squadrons based in Germany. Even to those of us who may be forgiven for viewing the squadron, its activities and people, through rose-tinted spectacles, it is remarkable how frequently during this extended period the squadron was at the forefront of operations, or was distinguished by its operating performances, rich sprinkling of indomitable characters and enduring spirit – and also, how often history appears to have repeated itself. In 1946, 14 Squadron Mosquitoes were part of the Air Forces of Occupation and carried out shows of force in direct support of ground forces – a tactic used to excellent effect by the squadron's Tornados over Iraq and Afghanistan over sixty years later! The squadron was selected to deploy Canberras to Malaya at very short notice in response to the Indonesian Confrontation. Similar short-notice deployments of Tornados, with 14 Squadron again in the van, took place in later years to the Middle East, as they did too for operations over the Balkans at the turn of the century. Operating the Hunter in the day-fighter role and maintaining QRA to police the central Europe ADIZ, the squadron was the RAF's last pure Day-Fighter Squadron when it gave up its Hunters at the end of 1962. With the Jaguar, 14 Squadron was the RAF's first and last single-seat strike squadron and, with the help of the Tornado GR1, spent 25 years holding QRA (N) as part of NATO's tactical-nuclear deterrent; it also won the Salmond Trophy, awarded for operational excellence, for three consecutive years (the only unit to have done so) and it pioneered HAS operations for the RAF.

By any measure, the squadron has provided much more than a footnote in the development and delivery of UK airpower and this record is a fittingly detailed testament to the its achievements and to the men and women who made them possible. The structure of the book follows the highly-successful format employed in *Winged Crusaders*, with a plentiful supply of photographs of aircraft and personnel – most of them previously unpublished – illustrating the text, underpinned by a rich body of original research. But, inevitably, it is the primary evidence provided by the host of interviews, letters and e-mails, painstakingly collated and exploited for the reader's benefit in bringing the story to life, that marks this book as worthy of particular attention, not least in dealing sensitively with poignant views expressed by contemporary crews engaged in the distinctly unglamorous realities of armed conflict and the taking of life.

More recently, operations by 14 Squadron Shadow aircraft in Afghanistan are almost 'full circle' back to the Senussi campaign of 1915, in which a small number of unarmed BE2c aircraft operated directly for the army commander, providing critical real-time intelligence, reconnaissance and target information. And with the Shadow and whatever comes after, I feel confident that the current and future members of this illustrious squadron will continue to uphold the traditions, values and high-professional standards set by their forebears. Nevertheless, for now, I encourage the reader to examine and enjoy the compelling narrative and respectful witness borne to the squadron's endeavours to date, available through the carefully polished lens of this book.

Air Marshal Sir Timo Anderson, KCB, DSO
November 2013, London

INTRODUCTION

Formed in 1915 and still operational today, 14 Squadron is one of the RAF's longest serving and most senior squadrons. Paradoxically, it is also one of the least-known of the RAF's flying squadrons because its service has largely been based overseas, ignored by the parochial British press and invisible to the British public. The unit's formative years through the First and Second World Wars, and the period between them, have been covered in *Winged Crusaders*; this volume, *Blue Diamonds,* continues the story through the Cold War years and on to the squadron's participation in conflicts in Iraq, Kosovo and Afghanistan. In the seventy years since the Second World War, the squadron has operated in the light-bomber role with DeHavilland Mosquito FBVI, BXVI and B35, the day-fighter/ground-attack role with the DeHavilland Vampire FB5, Venom FB1 and Hawker Hunter F4 and F6, the strike/interdictor role with the English Electric Canberra B(I)8, the strike/attack role with the McDonnell Phantom FGR2, SEPECAT Jaguar GR1 and BAe (Panavia) Tornado GR1 and the attack/close-air support roles with the BAe Tornado GR4. For much of this time the squadron was based in Germany at the front line of the Cold War; in its centenary year, equipped with the aptly-named Beechcraft Shadow R1, the squadron operates in the Intelligence, Surveillance, Target Acquisition and Reconnaissance (ISTAR) role.

For the period from 1945 until 1983, I have been able to refer to official documents, which have been declassified, for the basis of my research. Unfortunately, the relevant documents for more recent years remain classified and instead I have relied upon log-books, contemporary diaries, maps and photographs, as well as oral and written accounts from a large number of ex-squadron members. The result is as complete an account as is presently possible of the operational history of 14 Squadron in the second half of the last century and the opening years of this one.

I have tried to mention by name as many people as I can and on first mention individuals are identified by rank (at the time), initials and surname; thereafter rank and surname are used. Appendix 1; gives further biographic details of all those squadron members mentioned in Chapters 1 to 7. Appendix 2; lists the aircraft operated by the squadron since 1945 and Appendix 3; supports the colour plates elsewhere in the text, and describes the markings used on those aircraft. Unfortunately it has proved impossible to tell the squadron's story without using at least some of the many abbreviations and acronyms that litter the vocabulary of military flying, but I have tried to minimize their use. Technical terms are explained in footnotes to the main text and I have also included a Glossary of Abbreviations and Acronyms.

Times are given in 24-hour clock with the suffix 'hrs'. In most cases the time zone (i.e. local time or Greenwich Mean Time) is not specified because the original records do not specify which time zone is used. Some of these timings are in local time, which in Germany would have been one hour ahead of GMT (i.e. GMT + 1) in winter and two hours ahead in summer.

If there is an omission in this book, it is that it contains little detailed description of the work of the ground crew. To an extent this is inevitable in a work covering seventy years of operational history in just a few pages. The analogy is of a cinema blockbuster which is remembered by its audience because of its storyline and cast of actors, rather than the labours of the production staff, without whom, of course, the film could not have been made. Thus the operational history of a flying squadron will tend to be recorded mainly through the perspective of its aircrew. However, there must be no doubt in anyone's mind that the many accomplishments described in this book could not have been possible without the incredible dedication, loyalty and sheer hard work of the squadron's ground crew: the exploits of the aircrew are merely the visible manifestation of the endeavours of the ground personnel. Nor should anyone underestimate the justified feeling of ownership and pride that the ground crews have in the achievements of their own squadron.

The views and opinions expressed in this book are those of the author alone and should not be taken to represent those of Her Majesty's Government, Ministry of Defence, the RAF or any other government agency. Crown Copyright photographs are released under the terms of the Open Government Licence v2.0.

ACKNOWLEDGEMENTS

Like *Winged Crusaders*, this second part of the history of 14 Squadron is very much a collaborative effort. I have been greatly helped by the enthusiastic support of many ex-members of the squadron who have patiently answered many questions about their experiences. They have provided me with a fantastic archive of material including photographs, logbooks, documents, contemporary diaries and later reminiscences. Relatives of former squadron members have also been extremely supportive and I have received invaluable material from relatives who are keen to see the efforts of their loved ones properly recorded. I have also been greatly helped by a number of other researchers who have gladly shared their work with me in order to get the story of 14 Squadron told.

I am very grateful to the following former members of the squadron for their support and help: *Mosquito*: Derrick Coleman, Don Bond, Mike Levy, Eric Owen, Geoff Perks, Denis Russell. *Vampire & Venom*: Bob Broad, Mike De Torre, Ron Burgess, Don Headley, Peter Peacock, Brian Pettit, Sandy Sanderson, Smudge Smith, Geoff Steggall. *Hunter*: Hugh Cracroft, Andrew Cawthorne, Tim Barrett, Frank Davies, Jock McVie, John Marriott, Derek Morter, Rod Moon, Patrick O'Connor, David 'Snip' Parsons, John Preece, Hartmut Uhr (GAF Radar Controller). *Canberra*: Stew Airey, Mark Anderton, John Galyer, John Hanson, Rod Hawkins, Bill Hedges, Derek Jordan, Jeremy Lane, Roger Moore, George Morris, John Newland, Malcolm Pluck, Peter Rogers, Jim Sewell, Patrick Shiels, Hugh Skinner, Phil Wilkinson, Doug Wilson, Johnnie Wilson. *Phantom*: Robin Adams, John Cosgrove, Ted Edwards, David Farquharson, Peter Goodman, Bob Honey, John Malone, Ken Rhodes, Jock Watson. *Jaguar*: David Baron, 'Raz' Ball, John Bryant, Steve Griggs (Staneval), Den Harkin, Mike Hill, Nigel Huckins, Tim Kerss, Bob McAlpine, Dusty Miller, David Needham, Brian Newby, Kev Noble, Jerry Parr, Frank Turner. *Tornado*: Timo Anderson, Stan Boardman, Tom Boyle, Matt Bressani, J. J. Burrows, Nick Bury, Steve Cockram, Iain Cosens, Chris Coulls, Ian Davis, Trevor Dugan, Andy Fisher, Paul Francis, James Freeborough, Paul Froome, Keven Gambold, Andy Glover, David Hales, Tom Hill, Jameel Janjua, Andy Jeremy, Jim Klein, Darren Legg, Mike Lumb, Duncan Laisney, Paul MacDonald, 'Gus' MacDonald, Ryan Mannering, Tim Marsh, Douglas Moule, Jeremy Payne, 'Stu' Reid, Steve Reeves, Richard Robins-Walker, Pete Rochelle, Phil Rossiter, Kev Rumens, Mark Sharp, Doug Steer, Chris Stradling, Bev Thorpe, Ian Walton, Sam Williams, Martin Wintermeyer.

The following relatives of ex-squadron members have also been generous in their support: Peter Turnill (photographs & films from brother Roger), Andy Perks (details of father Geoff), Stuart Manwaring (photographs from grandfather Ray Cox), Sheila and George Grieve (photograph of son Alan).

I am extremely grateful for the generosity of the following researchers who shared the fruits of their work with me: Malcolm Barrass (whose excellent website Air of Authority is a must for anyone with an interest in RAF history), Jocelyn Leclercq (138 Wing records), Peter Caygill (author, *Jet Jockeys*), Geoff Lee (photographs of 14 Squadron's Jaguars and Tornados), Andy Thomas (who kindly provided a number of photographs of aircraft), and David Watkins (author, *Venom – The Complete History*).

The present 14 Squadron has also embraced the Centenary Project and I am very grateful to Wg Cdr Rich Moir and his successor Wg Cdr Roger Bousfield for their support; also Fg Off Paul Andrews, Flt Lts Kevin Fyfield, Alex Thompson and Sqn Ldr James Nightingale, who hosted me during visits to the squadron headquarters, where I was able to work through the squadron's unofficial crew-room diaries.

Thanks are due, too, to Peter Elliott at the RAF Museum for his great support and for making documents available for research and Andrew Renwick also at the RAF Museum, for photographs. Also to Jean-Paul Dorchain of the Royal Belgian Film Archive Cinematik.

Thank you to Pete West for the superb colour artwork and to my son Tom for drawing up the maps (and for providing inspiration for the cover). Also many thanks to my editor Jasper Spencer-Smith for his enthusiastic support for the project and for doing such a superb job in editing and producing this book. Finally, a huge thank you to my wife Shani for her love, understanding and support – and for sharing her house and husband with 14 Squadron's history for the last ten years!

Mike Napier
Great Rollright, 2014

1

1945-1951
THE MOSQUITO

Peacetime

By early 1945, it was clear that victory over Germany was inevitable and the RAF had already started to reduce in size from its peak strength of over 500 squadrons. By VE Day in May, there were only 479 squadrons in the RAF and the rapid contraction continued apace: by mid-1946 just 140 squadrons remained. At RAF Chivenor in the southwest of England, this general drawdown was reflected in the disbandment at the end of May 1945 of the two resident Vickers Wellington XIV anti-submarine squadrons, numbers 14 and 407; meanwhile, in north-east Scotland, all but one of the four DeHavilland Mosquito FB VI squadrons of the Banff Strike Wing were also disbanded or dispersed. On 1 June the remaining squadron at Banff, 143 Squadron, was renumbered 14 Squadron, thereby acquiring one of the most senior 'number-plates' in the RAF and with it the prospect of a future in the post-war RAF.

For the Commanding Officer of the newly renumbered 14 Squadron, Wg Cdr C. N. Foxley-Norris, DSO, 'the immediate postwar weeks were a difficult time at Banff.' Without any operational flying to give them purpose and with the mass departure of the Dominion personnel for repatriation, those left at Banff were at something of a loose end. According to the squadron's Operational Record Book the situation was not helped by the 'general confusion…consequent upon the disbanding of 14 Squadron at Chivenor and re-forming of 14 Squadron at Banff.' One break from routine which provided some interest was the task to accompany a Wing of Supermarine Spitfires deploying to Norway. The Mosquitoes, with their two-man crew and specialized navigation equipment were ideal escorts for the Spitfires during the long and potentially hazardous transit across the North Sea. On 20 June 1945, Flt Lts Brown and H. Graham led eighteen Spitfires from Dyce to Kristiansand, Wg Cdr Foxley-Norris and Flt Lt J. A. Selka led twenty-four Spitfires from Sumburgh to Trondheim[1] and Flt Lt R. G. Crocker, DFC, led two more Spitfires from Sumburgh to Trondheim[2].

A rare photograph of a De Havilland Mosquito FB VI belonging to 14 Squadron, probably at Banff, in late summer 1945. (Andy Thomas)

On his return from Norway, Wg Cdr Foxley-Norris was tasked to select the best crews on the Wing to join his squadron for service with the British Air Forces of Occupation (BAFO) in Germany. 'A better way of losing friends I never encountered…' he later wrote, 'but in a few days had sorted out the best twenty crews available.' He now commanded an elite squadron of anti-shipping crews – but they would now have to be moulded into a light-bomber unit. Routine training started immediately and continued through the summer of 1945. On 29 August, the squadron left Banff bound for Gatwick, landing there on a grey foggy day. They remained at Gatwick throughout the next month, continuing their role conversion before deploying on 1 October to Landing Ground A75 at Cambrai/Epinoy. Here they joined the two other Mosquito FB VI squadrons of 138 Wing, which was part of 2 Group. The training continued, but in November Wg Cdr Foxley-Norris discovered that, '…the routine training (we of course as ex-coastal pilots had a lot to learn) was to be interrupted by some flying for a film. The film was to be based on the famous attack on Amiens Prison by the great Pickard, himself one of the few casualties of the raid, and was to be called…Jericho. I was invited to lead, somewhat unrealistically, a close formation of twenty-four Mosquitoes [from 14 and 268 Squadrons]; the cameras were sited on the perimeter of the airfield and, amongst other manoeuvres, we were to do a mass dive on them as if they were the walls of the prison. I wheeled my formation into position about five miles away, opened to nearly full throttle and the mock attack began. At about one mile from the target, with my faithful co-stars close around me, I sustained a complete seizure of my right engine, resulting in very sharp deceleration. The effect on the formation was startling: we went over the cameras in as tight a bunch of flying objects as could be seen outside a swarm of bees, only less organized. The French

Mosquito FB VIs of 14 Squadron fly low over the film set for Henri Calef's film Jericho, *a dramatized account of the Amiens Prison raid, in November 1945.* (Sacha Gordine Films via Cinetematek)

director (Henri Calef) was ecstatic. Never had he seen such superb precision flying. How did we do it? The whole group seemed as if locked together (they damn nearly were). We adopted a traditionally British attitude of modesty, and accepted a great deal of free champagne; which we needed.'

During the summer of 1945, HQ BAFO had established an Armament Practice Camp (APC) at the ex-*Luftwaffe* airfield on the German resort island of Sylt. The APC was intended to help squadrons maintain some level of proficiency in weapon delivery by detaching in turn to Sylt for a two or three week period of intensive practice. In December, it was 14 Squadron's turn to use the newly-opened firing ranges there. Sqn Ldr A.G. Deck, DSO, DFC led the squadron formation to Sylt on 3 December, ready for fourteen days of practising low-level bombing, air-to-air firing and ground strafing. Unfortunately, the first few days of the detachment were marred by poor weather and by two accidents. In the first of these, W/Os B.J.F. Barlow and Madison were slightly injured when they attempted to go-around from a baulked approach: both engines did not respond and they crashed landed on the airfield. Two days later, Flt Lts M.J.C. Gooch and M. Holme were killed when the left wingtip of their Mosquito hit the sea while they manoeuvred at 50ft after a low-level bombing pass. However, the remainder of the APC went well, earning the comment from Headquarters 2 Group that, 'although [the squadron] only recently commenced training in air-to-ground and air-to-air firing, results compared not unfavourably with those of other squadrons in the Group…[which] speaks well for the determination and enthusiasm of this squadron'.

The first peacetime Christmas was celebrated with a four day stand down, and the New Year saw co-operation with the 7th Battalion, Cheshire Regiment during a 'show of force' in Essen. After a practice run by Sqn Ldrs Deck and R. H. Golightly on 2 January, six Mosquitoes carried out a flypast and dummy attacks as the Cheshires made their regimental march past two days later. By now Foxley-Norris' hand-picked team was being diluted: some crews were posted to other units, while others were demobbed. Amongst their replacements were two new crews who came directly from the Operational Training Unit (OTU). Sgt A. J. Bonsoni, with Flt Sgt Brewer, and Sgt J.F. Barrett, with Fg Off C. Hoole, arrived in the first week of January and made their familiarization sorties on 14 January. Three days later, both crews took-off for a navigation exercise. Unfortunately the weather clamped in while they were airborne and with the VHF radio homing and the 'Gee' navigation facilities in both aircraft unserviceable, neither crew could find the way back to Cambrai. Both crews subsequently crash-landed when they ran out of fuel, one near Dunkirk and the other near St Pol-sur-Ternoise, writing off two Mosquitoes, but luckily doing so without injury.

There followed a brief interlude when snow stopped all flying. When training continued it included a 'synthetic operation' – another initiative from HQ BAFO to maintain proficiency on their squadrons by tasking them with simulated attack missions. On the night of 12 February, four of 14 Squadron's Mosquitoes, again led by Sqn Ldr Deck, carried out simulated attacks on road convoys and barge traffic on waterways in the area between Dortsen, Munster, Hamm and Gladbeck. It was later reported that, '…in clear weather with bright moonlight all crews enjoyed 'snorting-up' trains, MT and factories…'! This was the last major sortie by 14 Squadron's Mosquito FB VIs: the planned move by 138 Wing to Wahn, near Köln, later in the month was cancelled and personnel were informed, instead, that the Wing would disband at Cambrai. During the remainder of February and March the aircraft were transferred to the Gutersloh Wing or returned to Maintenance Units (MU) in the UK. Meanwhile the squadron's personnel were also dispersed, although a significant number of them were posted to Wahn were they were absorbed into a new 14 Squadron.

Germany

The post-war contraction of the RAF continued through 1946, a major consolidation of BAFO's flying squadrons took place on 1 April with numerous disbandments and renumbering of squadrons. One such development was the disbandment 138 Wing, whose squadron numbers were assumed by units from 139 Wing, which was already at Wahn. Amongst these, 128 Squadron, a Mosquito B XVI unit commanded by Wg Cdr R. I. Jones was renumbered to become 14 Squadron: thus 14 Squadron arrived in Germany, which would be its home for the next fifty-five years. The large outflow of personnel being demobilized from the RAF continued unabated and by early 1947, 14 Squadron's total strength was less than a hundred personnel. It had only ten aircraft against an establishment of sixteen. This fall-off in strength was reflected in the squadron's participation in the group's synthetic operations during 1946: six aircraft participated in an operation against Nienburg marshalling yards in April, five against Gleidingen transformer station in May, and only four aircraft in July's operation.

Any lack of flying was counterbalanced by a steady programme of organized sport which kept the squadron members from being idle, but in any case a number of external

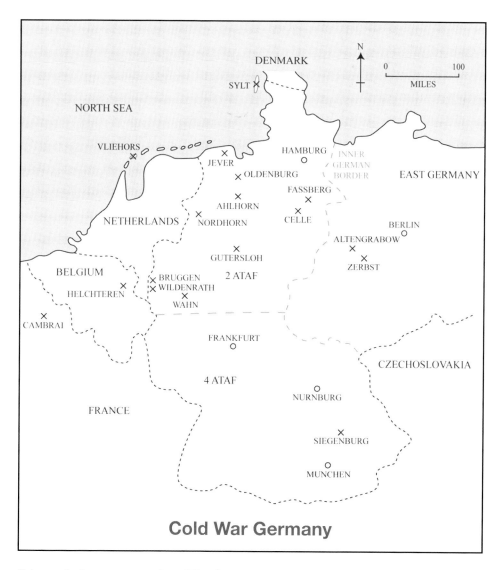

Cold War Germany

flying tasks kept everyone busy. The first was a mass 'show of force' on 9 May over the Ruhr, in which 14 Squadron provided nine aircraft. Two days later, four crews were detached to the war trials courier service. In autumn 1945, when the Nürnburg War Trials had started, BAFO was tasked to provide aircraft to maintain a daily-courier service between Nürnburg and London so that documents and press reports could be easily transferred. Initially, the service was provided by 305 (Polish) Squadron, but from the beginning of March the task was taken over by 138 and then 139 Wings. Two aircraft, one of which was positioned as a spare, were based at Blackbush (between Camberly and Basingstoke) and another two at Fürth (just to the west of Nürnburg) in order to fly a Blackbush to Fürth leg at 07:30hrs every morning and a Fürth to Blackbush leg at 13:30hrs each afternoon.

A formation of 14 Squadron's Mosquito B XVIs set out for a MRCP bombing sortie from Westonzoyland in mid-August 1946. The aircraft nearest the camera still carries 128 Squadron's 'M5' code letters dating from before that unit's renumbering on 1 April. (Denis Russell)

Now under the command of Wg Cdr G.R. Magill, DFC and Bar 14 Squadron deployed to Manston on 1 June 1946 to participate in the 'Victory Flypast' over London on 8 June. Each of the six BAFO Mosquito squadrons contributed a box of four aircraft which flew over central London as part of the main stream just after midday. The formation theme continued into July when 14 Squadron won the 139 Wing formation competition and was selected to give a demonstration of Mobile Radar Command Post (MRCP) bombing in England the following month. The MRCP system of ground-based radar units provided aircraft with guidance for blind bombing of targets which were obscured either by clouds or darkness. The system could be highly accurate, enabling high-flying aircraft to drop within a few hundred yards of their target. The MRCP bombing detachment flew to Westonzoyland (near Bridgewater) on 2 August and spent the next fourteen days practising their techniques. On 20 August, four crews[3] carried out the demonstration successfully, dropping four 500lb bombs each on the 'West Down' range on Salisbury Plain.

All of the 139 and 140 Wing squadrons carried out intensive formation flying through late August and early September, in preparation for the RAF's 'Battle of Britain Flypast' over London on 14 September. Unfortunately, a catastrophic mid-air collision occurred within the 140 Wing formation on 3 September when the tail of a 21 Squadron Mosquito was sliced off by another aircraft and it dived vertically into houses in Bonn, instantly killing the crew. The pilot, Flt Lt W. Moffatt, DFC, had previously served with 14 Squadron. Two days later, the squadron was well represented at Moffat's funeral near Munster. Meanwhile, the formation practices continued and on 7 September four aircraft from 14 Squadron, led by Flt Lt Lowe, flew to Manston, ready to take part in the flypast seven days later.

In contrast to the summer months, 14 Squadron was able to fully participate in three synthetic operations during October, with four aircraft each flying against Uelzen on 11 October, Verden a week later and Stade a week after that. The busy programme of organized sports also continued and the Uelzen task gives a good indication of the lifestyle of squadron personnel at that time: Sqn Ldr Ellis and Flt Lt Tuhill led the sortie and the following day both of them turned out to play rugby for the Wing against the King's Hussars. 'Sports was a great palliate,' wrote AC1 E. Owen, a Flight Mechanic (Engines), 'I indulged and together with a good friend, Ken Bushell, a radar technician, we both represented 14 Squadron, 139 Wing and the air force in Germany, in both football and cricket Inter-Services games. Another good friend was LAC Wilf Parfitt. Wilf was the epitome of the squadron LAC that tutors in technical training camps warn you against. "Never have dealings with these men; they will lead you astray," was the warning. Wilf also played rugby for Wales and the RAF. I am unsure if any of these honours were much appreciated by our squadron's NCOs as we often had to travel away from Wahn to participate in these games.'

From November, two more flying exercises were introduced by HQ BAFO to ensure the proficiency of their crews: 'Operation Daisycutter' involved low-level navigation to another base while 'Operation Roundabout' was a medium-level navigation exercise, invariably involving further distances. Each squadron was expected to carry out a number of 'Roundabouts' and 'Daisycutters' each month. In addition, from June 1946 another new task had been taken on by 139 Wing: the disbandment of 1401 Meteorological Flight that month meant that the 'Met climbs' they had carried out at 05:00hrs and 12:00hrs each day would instead have to be done by the Wing's Mosquito squadrons. Each unit took turns to carry out the 'Met' flights for a two-month period and with intense inter-squadron rivalry at Wahn, there was much pressure on crews to complete the task whatever the weather conditions. Each flight lasted between 1 hour and 1¼ hours and involved taking the temperature readings from 500ft and then at 50 millibar (mb) intervals to 300mb (approximately equivalent to 30,000ft). The 'Met climb' was not popular with the ground crew who, as AC1 Owen pointed out, '…besides having to check and refuel the aircraft after the flight, had to arrive very early at the dispersal location to ready the planes.' From 1 November, 14 Squadron assumed responsibility for the daily 'Met' climb and the first one was carried out by Flt Lt J.C. Stead, DFC and Fg Off F.J. Harper, DFM. Daily 'Met' climbs and routine training flights kept the squadron busy for the next two months until flying was brought to a sudden halt at the beginning of January. The first reason for the cessation of flying was the issue of Air Ministry instruction which required the checking of the landing flaps on all Mosquito aircraft. With much reduced strength among the Wing's engineering personnel, the result was to ground the entire Wing. As if that was not enough, 14 Squadron's dispersal hut, which housed all the unit's engineering facilities, burned down on the evening of 6 January 1947, destroying a large amount of engineering equipment as well as three sets of flaps and all the Form 700 engineering records for the squadron aircraft. The new CO, Sqn Ldr F.C.StG. O'Brien, DFC and Bar, must have wondered what he had taken on when he arrived on 25 January, but six days later the squadron was able to provide two aircraft for the Wing synthetic operation against Gluckstadt.

By now the squadron manpower was less than 50 percent of its established strength and it was being run as a single Flight. As a measure of the difficulties of the times, the 34 hours flown in January 1947 was less than a sixth of that achieved in the January a year earlier. Nevertheless, 14 Squadron was able to provide two aircraft, flown by Flt Lt P.W. Cook with Fg Off Anderson and Flt Lt G. E. Davies, DFC with Fg Off Smith, for the Wing synthetic operation on 7 February. Two aircraft also exercised with the MRCP: Flt Lt Davies and Flt Sgt Cope achieved a creditable 500yd error from 20,000ft on 3 February and Fg Off J. A.G. Slessor, again with Flt Sgt Cope, achieved similar results a week later.

The lack of personnel meant that the ground crews were kept busy: AC1 Owen recalled that they, '…were expected to arrive early at the squadron's Nissen hut location to ascertain whether their aircraft would be flying that day. This information was posted on a chalkboard in the crewroom and ground crews were expected to carry out the daily aircraft inspections accordingly. With no hanger facilities available on the dispersal locations servicing the aircraft was carried out in the open or under canvas field equipment. That made for a bloody rough time, as the 1946 winter was believed to be one of the coldest on record. Everything fell into place and maintenance work on the planes, though perhaps monotonous, some said boring, was never shirked, as the aircrews trusted their lives to the ground staff. The station's administration personnel were also never remiss in their duties and it was the squadron's ground crews that suffered. Every week new rosters were posted detailing which airmen would take over the camp's guard and fire station duties. Bluntly put, this used to upset ground crew personnel who, after working all day servicing and maintaining aircraft, then reported to designated posts to act as overnight camp guards. Following this overnight fourteen hour guard duty, tired airmen immediately returned to their squadron to carry out their regularly scheduled maintenance duties.'

When Wahn had first been inspected for possible use as an airfield in late 1945 it was in an appalling state. Although, according to AC1 Owen, '…the accommodation was first class having previously housed the Waffen SS and other Panzer troops,' the airfield buildings had been taken over by 'displaced persons' who had wrecked them completely. Much of the local infrastructure, including for example the gas mains, had also been destroyed by the Wehrmacht as it retreated eastwards in the closing days of the war. A lot of work was still needed to make the airfield habitable and Wahn remained something of a construction site throughout 1946 and 1947. A major improvement from the operational perspective came in April 1947 when a 2,000yd long concrete runway had been opened: until then temporary runways made from Pieced Steel Planking (PSP) had been used. Wg Cdr O'Brien had the honour of being the first pilot to take off from the new runway in one of the station's Airspeed Oxford aircraft. Another significant enhancement followed a month later with the completion of the dispersal buildings, allowing the squadron to be housed in one place for the first time; previously, the squadron headquarters had been located more than a mile away from the dispersal.

A new system of ranks for NCO aircrew had been introduced during 1946 and, despite the system being desperately unpopular, these were now adopted in BAFO. Sergeant (Sgt) aircrew became Pilot (Plt) II or Navigator (Nav) II depending on their branch and Flight

The 14 Squadron detachment to West Malling in October 1947. Despite having to gather all the ground equipment from other units, 14 Squadron's crews enjoyed a useful three weeks' practice at MRCP bombing. Wg Cdr P.StG. O'Brien, DFC and Bar, OC 14 Squadron, is seated 7th from left and AC1 E. Owen is in the row immediately behind, standing 8th from the right.

Sergeant (Flt Sgts) became Plt I or Nav I; aircrew III and IV ranks were also introduced reflecting lesser-experienced aircrew. These ranks remained in place until 1950 when the system was abandoned, to the great relief of everyone.

Meanwhile, two crews were lucky enough to take part in a welcome diversion from the routine at Wahn when they were tasked to participate in 'Operation Sunshine', a deployment to North Africa. Two aircraft flown by Fg Off Nichol with Flt Lt I. P. Bishop, DFC and Fg Off A. deL. Greig, DFC with Flt Lt F. Belfitt, DFM (the squadron navigation officer), left Wahn for El Adem on 22 April. Alas, the squadron suffered its first accident to a Mosquito B XVI three days later when Greig and Belfitt crashed their aircraft after an undercarriage problem on take-off at El Adem: fortunately neither of them was injured. Routine flying, including the 'Met climb', continued through the summer months. Sports continued, too, and the squadron's efforts in this area were rewarded by winning the CO's Cup for sport. Pairs of aircraft also deployed to Malta in August, this time as part of 'Operation Roundabout', and five aircraft detached to RAF Gatow, Berlin from mid-August to mid-September. Much of the Berlin detachment's time was spent flying as a four-ship formation over and around the city, demonstrating their presence to both the German civilians and the Russian army.

The squadron was again called on to give a MRCP demonstration in the autumn for the School of Land/Air Warfare. This time the team[4] deployed to West Malling where they were dismayed to find themselves in accommodation that had just been vacated by German prisoners of war! There was no ground engineering equipment at West Malling, either, so parties were sent out to beg what they could from other stations. Bomb trolleys were borrowed from Tangmere, Middle Wallop provided practice bombs, while 500lb live bombs were sourced from an MU in Norfolk. They started the MRCP practices on 2 October and were scheduled to give the demonstration on 10 October; unfortunately cloud that day meant that the event was delayed for six days. On 16 October, cloud again covered the target, but the weather was deemed fit enough for the demonstration. The crews took off with 500lb bombs in case the weather cleared completely and 25lb practice bombs for safety reasons in case it had not. Despite a late gap in the clouds, they were already committed to dropping the practice bombs, which they did with an impressive bombing error of only 70yd.

A New Mark of Mosquito

In November, after eight months in command, Wg Cdr O'Brien handed over 14 Squadron to Sqn Ldr G. E. Goode, DFC. Shortly afterwards heavy snow brought flying operations to a halt, heralding the start of three months of poor winter weather. But if the weather was less than cheerful, the squadron did at least have new aircraft to look forward to: during December the first few Mosquito B35s arrived to replace the B XVIs. This latest version of the Mosquito was fitted with more powerful engines, which in turn gave the aircraft an improved performance and a higher operational ceiling than its predecessor. In fact the crew which carried out an altitude test on a new B35 on 21 January reported that it reached 37,000ft with ease; while during a 'Met climb' on 12 March, Fg Off N.O. Cornwall and Nav II G. Read, found that the aircraft was 'still climbing through 38,000 ft.' Another improvement to life at Wahn was the re-opening of the bombing range at Nordhorn.

Apart from the usual 'Met climbs', the Spring of 1948 was spent with routine training, including regular 'Roundabouts' to Luqa, Malta, via Istres and practice on the bombing ranges at Nordhorn and Butzweilerhof. This latter weaponry work was disrupted by problems with the bomb gear on the B35s, but even so the squadron was able to deploy the usual MRCP detachment to West Malling on 13 May in readiness for the demonstration on West Down range on 1 June. The weather was poor over Salisbury Plain on the two demonstration days, so the detachment returned to Wahn early in June without having completed the demonstration. During early 1948, tensions between the USSR and its former western allies had been steadily increasing and in mid-June the Soviets cut all land links between West Germany and Berlin, triggering 'Operation Plainfare', the Berlin airlift. The airlift itself did not directly affect 14 Squadron since the operational area was well to the east of Wahn, although Flt Lt Lewis was sent to Gatow to help organize aircraft movements.

Undoubtedly, the highlight of the year for the 14 Squadron crews was 'Operation Dagger', which ran over the weekend 3 to 5 September. It was the first major exercise to test the UK's air defences since the Battle of Britain. The aircraft of Fighter Command were tasked with defending the UK from attacks by 'Southland' whose attacking aircraft were provided by Bomber Command and BAFO. Participation by 14 Squadron began on 3 September at 14:40hrs when Sqn Ldr Goode and Flt Lt D. E. Coleman led four aircraft[5] to attack the airfield at Middle Wallop (between Andover and Salibury). They carried out their attack from 200ft without being intercepted and came back with film which confirmed the success of the sortie. The following day

'Operation Dagger': taxiing out for a low-level attack on Horsham St.Faith on 5 September 1948. Wg Cdr G. E. Horne (OC Flying Wing) in the foreground and behind him is Gp Capt D. J. Eayrs, CBE, DFC (Station Commander) in the silver aircraft, leading (left to right in the camouflaged aircraft) Plt Off M. H. Levy and Flt Lt D. E. Coleman, Fg Off N. Cornwall and Nav III M. Saxby, Flt Lts J. C. Stead, DFC and I. P. Bishop, DFC, Plt II Jacks and Nav II G. Meredith, Plt II Ridland and Nav II A. A. Fulker.

another four Mosquitoes[6] took off for London. Their target was the Victoria Bridge, which they were to attack from 25,000ft. This time, shortly before reaching the target, they were intercepted by two Gloster Meteors, but the Mosquito crews were still able to claim a successful attack.

Sunday 5 September, was the final day of 'Operation Dagger' and 14 Squadron launched six Mosquitoes against the Meteor fighter base at Horsham St.Faith, near Norwich. 'It was a beautiful sunny afternoon', recalled Plt Off Levy, 'as six 14 Squadron Mosquitoes took off to fly in two vic[vee] formations led by the Wahn station commander. Flying almost a direct route we were not intercepted before we arrived at Horsham on the deck. The Meteor wing had just landed from an interception as we swept over, bomb doors open, dropping our weapons. Our weapons were toilet rolls stamped with 'Government Property' which our ground crews had painstakingly unrolled, inscribed with rude messages for the fighter ground crew, re-rolled and suspended from our bomb racks. Many of these weapons were posted back to us with further rude messages written by the Meteor ground crews!

'One Meteor was still airborne in the circuit and this promptly attacked the Mosquito leader. As we crossed the airfield we took low-level rear-view oblique photos of the hangars, fighters being refuelled and their pilots queuing at the NAAFI van. Instead of exiting quickly back across the coast, we routed across the Wash to Skegness before turning out over the North Sea. As we continued over East Anglia, the refuelled Meteors took off in hot pursuit!'

'We arrived over Skegness still on the deck. I was flying No.2 in the second vic. My leader, John Stead, who was my Flight Commander and an ex-wartime pathfinder pilot, hugged the road along the promenade. No.3 was weaving between the Butlins helter-skelters and I was over the beach, lifting to clear the lampposts on the pier. Meanwhile a dozen or more Meteors were carrying out high quarter attacks on us. The place was packed as it was about 5pm on a warm September Sunday. That was in the days before low-flying complaints!' On returning to Wahn, the formation found their base under a thick mist which made the landing somewhat challenging. So ended 'Operation Dagger' which had been notable by the incredible efforts of Flt Sgt Baird to ensure that all the squadron aircraft were available for the exercise.

The squadron resumed responsibility for 'Met climbs' the following month and other routine tasks continued, such as 'Operation Roundabout'. On 27 October, two crews[7] stood by for an improvement in the fog before they could set off for Istres; eventually the weather cleared and they reached Luqa successfully. They were due to return to Wahn on 30 October, but shortly after take off from Luqa, Cornwall's aircraft suffered a fire in the starboard engine, and it dived into the sea near Gozo, killing both crew members. Another incident occurred exactly a month later when Plt I Goodyear suffered an engine failure during an air test and carried out an exemplary single-engined landing in poor visibility. This was Goodyear's second engine failure in flight and it was noted that on both occasions his airmanship and flying had been of the highest standard.

The aircraft were briefly grounded in January 1949 because of a problem with fuel-injector pumps, but all were serviceable once more in time for two synthetic operations which took place at the end of the month. On 24 January, Plt Off Levy with Flt Lt Coleman, with the callsign 'Otter 23', were leading Plt II Brockbank with Nav II Cooper ('Otter 16') and Plt III R.R. Harding with Nav II Meredith ('Otter 14') to the range at Heligoland. They were due to take off to rendezvous at 09:30hrs with an escort of four Supermarine Spitfires provided by 80 Squadron. Unfortunately all did not go smoothly. The first problem was that 'Otter 14' had problems on start-up and had to be left behind. The rendezvous went well, but then half an hour later the starboard engine failed on 'Otter 23'. As Plt Off Levy left the formation to return to Wahn he realised that the failure was due to fuel starvation and after remedying the problem he was able to rejoin 'Otter 16' and fly as Number 2. Just afterwards the formation was intercepted by four De Havilland Vampires which attacked in pairs from high above the Mosquitoes. Once over Heligoland the cloud cover thickened, making bombing impossible and the formation set course for Celle at 10,000ft. By now the Spitfires were running short of fuel, so they left the Mosquitoes who were almost immediately attacked by five more Vampires. Another attack by four Hawker Tempests was carried out as the Mosquitoes reached Köln (Cologne). Another synthetic operation on 28 January met with a little more success. This time three aircraft were led by Sqn Ldr Goode with Flt Lt Bishop and although they had an engine problem and had to return to Wahn, a spare aircraft flown by Plt II Ridland with Nav I Read was available to take their place. This time the weather was good with no cloud. Four Tempests attacked the formation, which carried out a gentle weave to simulate evasive manoeuvring, before the Mosquitoes carried out bombing runs from 12,000ft on the range at Heligoland. The bomb scores were not very impressive though, caused by bombsight problems. As the Mosquitoes returned via Brunswick and

Munster they were intercepted firstly by four Vampires and then by another five Vampires. They then diverted to Gutersloh because the runway at Wahn had been closed. Both synthetic operations had provided valuable experience of fighter tactics, but the second one also showed a weakness in the squadron's medium-level visual bombing techniques.

A major push to improve the squadron's bombing scores started in Spring 1949 with a record number – over 1,000 – bombs dropped in April. By the end of the month the problems seemed to have been ironed out and, as an example, Plt II Brockbank and Nav II Cooper broke the squadron record for medium-level night bombing with an error of only 55yd.

April 1949 was an eventful month for Plt III R.L. Cocks. On 2 April, he was carrying out the 'Met climb' with Nav II Bolton; as they reached 15,000ft the ground-radar station became unserviceable and Bolton was instructed to use the 'GEE' navigation system to continue the climb. As Bolton switched on the set, a spark caused petrol fumes in the cockpit to ignite, filling it with flames. Both crew members abandoned the aircraft. Cocks landed safely and 'hitched' a lift to Wahn in a passing car, but Bolton landed on a roof and broke his back when he fell off. Three weeks later Cocks crashed another Mosquito while practising a single-engine approach on the airfield at Wahn.

On 6 May, the squadron deployed to West Malling for the now 'traditional' MRCP detachment this time for No.7 Special Senior Course. Despite total cloud cover over the target on 31 May, the formation dropped practice bombs from 12,000ft under the radar control of Flt Lt F.N. Ramsey and achieved an impressive accuracy of 100yd.

After the success of 'Operation Dagger' in 1948, two more major air exercises were planned in UK airspace in the following year. The first, 'Operation Foil' in June, was a fourteen-day defensive exercise mainly for the benefit of fighter squadrons, while the second, 'Operation Bulldog' held in September, was designed primarily to meet the needs of the bomber force. The exercises were run respectively by Fighter and Bomber Commands, but they included the RAF squadrons of BAFO as well as aircraft from the US and Dutch, Belgian and French air forces.

Just prior to 'Operation Foil', on 20 June, two 14 Squadron Mosquitoes participated in a Close Air Support exercise with the army on the Vogelsang training area in the Eifel. Using radio instructions from an RAF controller on the ground they made simulated attacks on troops, transport and tanks which were deployed in the training area. The full 'Operation Foil' started five days later, beginning with a low-level six aircraft attack on the airfield at Thorney Island (near Chichester). The formation was not intercepted on the way to the target and achieved a complete surprise attack. They claimed hits against the runways, hangars and dispersed fighters and, had they been armed with guns, they would also have claimed the single Vampire which attempted to attack the formation over Odiham as they returned home. The next day, four aircraft made another unopposed low-level attack on Manston. Crews much preferred to fly at low-level: in the words of Plt Off Levy,'…medium-level attacks were not particularly interesting as the squadron felt that these simply provided interception exercises for the Meteors, Vampires and Spitfires, which tended to have considerable advantage in performance over our Mosquitoes at such heights. We preferred low-level attacks, particularly if these were against the defending fighters' own airfields!' So it was without much enthusiasm that on 28 June six aircraft set out to attack the Daimler works at Coventry from 25,000ft. Before it reached the target, the formation was intercepted by three Royal Netherlands Air Force (RNLAF) Gloster

Meteors and if it had been a real 'war sortie' four of the Mosquitoes would have been shot down. Nevertheless all six aircraft carried out their attack above extensive cloud cover, but when the strike photographs were developed they showed that the aircraft had actually 'released' their bombs over Birmingham. The next day, six aircraft took off in three pairs for medium-level attacks against Daimler at Coventry, North Weald airfield and the Victory Docks, London. None of these aircraft were intercepted by fighters. The first two pairs attacked blind over complete cloud cover using 'GEE' to locate the dropping point and the third pair prepared to do the same. However, when the leader switched on his 'GEE' set it caught fire and both aircraft promptly returned to Wahn. On 30 June, the Wahn Wing mounted a twelve-aircraft formation, with six aircraft each from 14 and 98 Squadrons, against the Birmingham Small Arms (BSA) factory in Birmingham; despite the size of this large formation the fighter forces did not find it and the only excitement in the flight was when Plt II Brockbank suffered an engine failure and had to divert into Manston.

'Operation Foil' continued into July with a welcome return to low-level for two aircraft tasked against Tangmere on 2 July. After a successful attack they were intercepted by a Vampire which made a series of attacks on them. A further pair of Mosquitoes attacked Coltishall and they too were intercepted as they left the target area by two Meteors. For the finalé of the exercise, six aircraft left Wahn on 3 July as a single formation and flew at low-level to Southend. The squadron Operations Record book noted drily that for this sortie 'all the targets were bombing ranges because the harassed citizens of England apparently did not like the noise of Merlin engines over their houses!' Over Southend the formation split into three pairs, each of which carried out practice attacks on one of the three air-weapons ranges at Fenns Moss, near Whitchurch in Shropshire, Otmoor, between Oxford and Bicester, and Idlicote in south Warwickshire.

With the successful conclusion of the Berlin Airlift in July 1949, BAFO was able to put on a large-scale air display at Gutersloh the following month. It was 'perfect summer sunshine,' reported *Flight* magazine, 'crowded with aircraft and decorated with allied flags, the airfield presented an attractive picture to a visitor from the UK. He could scarcely be blamed for feeling that this was a station in Britain, for, on first inspection, the differences were few. On closer scrutiny there were the parked Volkswagens, the *Luftwaffe*-designed buildings, and the 'Bafs'[8] [sic] which – in lieu of silver and copper coinage – passed between Service spectators and attendant NAAFI vans.' All of BAFO's squadrons participated in the show on 16 August, the climax being an attack on a dummy factory that had been built in the middle of the airfield. For this event 14 and 98 Squadrons each provided a two-box formation each of four Mosquitoes.

Meanwhile, back at Wahn the 'Met climbs' continued, but as Plt Off Levy noted, 'with two rival squadrons doing the met climb alternately it was a matter of intense squadron pride that the sortie was completed, as failure would draw derision from the other squadron. Hence scant regard was paid to weather minima for the duty pilot's instrument rating.' The price of this rather cavalier attitude to the potential hazards of the weather was paid on 30 August when Flt Lt Lewis and Nav I Fulker flew into a hill some 4 miles east of the airfield in poor visibility. Both crew members were killed and the aircraft was destroyed.

Gloster Meteor fighters caught on the ground at Manston by Plt II P.J. Clarke and Nav II W.D.R. Bond during 'Operation Foil' on 26 June 1949. (Don Bond)

Move to Celle

Apart from giving good reason for an air show, the completion of 'Operation Plainfare' freed up the airfields close to the Inner German Border (IGB) which were in a better tactical position than Wahn. As a result the four Mosquito squadrons (Nos. 4, 11, 14 and 98) based at Wahn were moved to Celle in mid-September. Once again the squadron found itself indebted to Flt Sgt Baird's organizational abilities for a problem-free move. The move to a new home coincided with a new squadron commander in the person of Sqn Ldr E.J. Greenleaf, DSO, DFC. Although the squadron was reasonably pleased with its new home, the location caused some difficulties with weapons ranges, as the nearest one, Nordhorn, was over 30 minutes flying time away. This problem would be resolved in mid-January 1950 with the opening of Fassberg range. In the meantime the squadron concentrated on the completion of 'Operation Quebec', a photographic task for the army in Austria and on its participation in 'Operation Bulldog', the RAF's bomber exercise in the UK.

To the great satisfaction of 14 Squadron aircrew, all of the sorties tasked on 'Operation Bulldog' were flown at low-level. At dusk on 24 September, three aircraft attacked the naval dockyard at Portsmouth, returning with excellent photographs of the harbour installations and ships. To add to the excitement they were intercepted by Meteors over Thorney Island as they made their escape. Early the next morning, a Sunday, four Mosquitoes made individual attacks on the fighter airfields of North Weald, Manston, Biggin Hill and Martlesham Heath. On the final day of the exercise, a pair of Mosquitoes successfully attacked Tangmere before being attacked in turn by a Mosquito night fighter.

The exercise season continued into October with 'Exercise Agility' which took up the first half of the month. However, the squadron considered it to be of little value since it was mainly flown at medium-level with almost total cloud cover in the target areas. Immediately after 'Exercise Agility' one crew, Fg Off Levy and Flt Lt Coleman, was selected for a clandestine operation. This was to take vertical reconnaissance photographs of Soviet airfields within and outside the Berlin corridors. Between 18 October and 2 November nine sorties were flown, with the direction of flight up and down the corridors being varied and with landings at Gatow made on some flights. Excellent photographs

The line up of 14 Squadron's Mosquito B35s at Celle in late 1949. All the aircraft have a silver-painted finish and the squadron's identifying code letters 'CX'. Note that the surface of the dispersal is made from Pierced-Steel Planking (PSP). (Geoff Perks)

were obtained of vast numbers of Russian fighters at several airfields, but fortunately the only Russian aircraft seen airborne was a single-engined biplane trainer. The reason for the photography was not explained to the crew but they surmised it to be to check on whether any Soviet jet fighters had yet been introduced into their zone. Later in November, the squadron sent two formations on short detachments to Berlin in order to exercize the British right of access along the Berlin air corridors. In January 1950, thirteen sorties were flown in 'Exercise Upshot Primer' to evaluate the airfield defences at Gutersloh.

1950 – A Year of Demonstrations and Displays

January 1950 was also notable for the opening of the bombing range at Fassberg, a much-needed facility. The squadron spent much of its time practising formation bombing on Fassberg over the next month in preparation for a fire-power demonstration at Sennelager and a low-level bombing demonstration on Salisbury Plain. Nav II Cooper was responsible for organizing both of these demonstrations which were due to take place in March. A rehearsal for the fire-power demonstration was held on 12 March and the event itself took place four days later. Four aircraft from 14 Squadron, followed by four from 98 Squadron, each dropped four 500lb bombs from 500ft. The bombs overshot the target slightly due to a 20kt tailwind, but the results were nevertheless very impressive.

Six aircraft detached to West Malling on 24 March for the low-level bombing demonstration. After several practices the Mosquitoes carried out the demonstration, each aircraft dropping two 250lb bombs from 500ft with an 11 second delay fuse. Once again the results were impressively accurate. Back at Celle the sports programme ensured that everyone was kept busy: the squadron football team trounced both 98 Squadron and the RAF Regiment during March.

Bombing practice continued through the next months with the squadron's Armament Practice Camp (APC) at Sylt during April and May, and a detachment by five aircraft to Leuchars. The Leuchars detachment, which was led by Flt Lt M.O. Bergh, was a task for the army's Scottish Command. It involved a medium-level and a low-level attack by a formation of four aircraft, each dropping 25lb practice bombs as a demonstration of close-support bombing. Flt Lt Bergh was also chosen to lead the 14 Squadron participation in the 1950 BAFO Air Display. For this display Celle's four Mosquito units, Nos. 4, 11, 14 and 98 Squadrons were to flypast in wing formation led by the wing leader Wg Cdr R.W. Cox, DSO DFC, AFC and then spilt up for individual squadron attacks on an 'enemy HQ' which, as in the previous year, had been built on the airfield. The Mosquitoes were instructed to use 60lb bombs, which none of the crews had seen before. 'Whoever sent them to us,' recalled Fg Off Levy, 'did not send the instructions and we had no idea how to drop them safely. It seems incredible now, but we decided that the only way to find out was to do our own trials. On 10 June, two aircraft took off for Nordhorn range to suck it and see. The leader was Oelof Bergh, ...I flew line-astern behind him and we dropped four 60lb bombs each in formation, starting at 250ft and reducing our height on each run. With instantaneous fusing, the bombs exploded directly under the aircraft, the blast giving a strong jolt and the bang clearly being heard over the sound of the engines. In fact we returned unscathed, perhaps because of the marshy surface of the range. A few months later during a demo at West Malling, 98 Squadron damaged three out of four aircraft making the drop – perhaps they were a bit low, or perhaps it was just a harder surface on the airfield! Incidentally, they missed their target just as four of us from 14 Squadron had done just a few moments before! We used the 60lb bombs for the BAFO Air Display carrying four bombs in each of our four aircraft.' The air display was originally planned for 15 June, but had to be postponed by 5 days because of bad weather. After flying past in squadron boxes of four, then in echelon and finally in line astern, the Mosquitoes cleared the area for displays by Vampires, Meteors and the Republic F-84E Thunderjets of the USAF's 'Skyblazers' display team. The Mosquitoes then returned for the finale of the display, a series of attacks on the enemy HQ. Fg Off Levy reported that, '...all sixteen bombs were dropped in one salvo from the 14 Squadron formation and we obliterated the dummy factory which had been built on the Gutersloh airfield. No. 98 Squadron came in last, and I'm not sure what was left for them to aim at.' 'Jolly exciting it was to watch, too!' agreed the correspondent from *Flight* magazine.

The Rt Hon Aidan Crawley MP, Under-Secretary of State for Air meets Plt Off M. H. Levy and Nav II F. Suskiewicz at Celle on 6 June 1950. Mike Levy was a later flight commander on English Electric Canberra B(I)6s with 213 Squadron; originally from Poland, Felix Suskiewicz had flown Mosquitoes during the war and changed his name to Sanders after becoming a naturalized Briton. (Mike Levy)

The display season continued through the month: 2 days after the BAFO display the squadron detached to West Malling to take part in the RAF Display at Farnborough. This event, which recreated the popular pre-war RAF Displays at Hendon, consisted of events and displays involving representatives from the whole of the service. Despite poor weather in the days immediately beforehand, the sun shone on 7 and 8 July for the display and the 200,000 spectators, including the King and Queen, who attended over the 2 days, were rewarded with a magnificent spectacle. One event towards the end of the display was a re-enactment of the famous Amiens Prison Raid of 1944. A mock-up of the prison had been built on Farnborough airfield and the part of Gp Capt Pickard's Mosquitoes was played by twelve aircraft from 14 and 98 Squadrons, with a force of Spitfires painted in German markings to represent the *Luftwaffe* fighters. Fg Off Levy flew as Number 3 in one of the 14 Squadron sections: 'For the sake of authenticity our attacks were made by echelons of three aircraft and this raised a

With its bomb-doors open, a 14 Squadron Mosquito B35 is seen at low level near Hameln on 27 September 1950 during 'Exercise Broadside'. The photograph was taken by Plt II R.L. Cocks. (Stuart Manwaring)

certain problem. We were dropping practice bombs on the target, although explosive charges detonated from the ground were fitted in the target. Naturally we wanted our bombs to hit the target but its small size made this difficult for an attack in echelon. The target was an excellent representation of the original prison, but it was scaled down and was only about 100ft wide. As the wing span of a Mosquito was 54ft 2in, it will be realized that three aircraft could not be fitted into this width. We therefore flew our echelons with the aircraft well stepped back with wingtips overlapping. Even so, as a Number 3, I could not get lined up on the target. I therefore decided to slide across and below the other two as we approached the target. As they were flying at about 50ft and the target was about 30ft high this got quite exciting, particularly as I was in the slipstream of the leading two aircraft! I tended to cross the target with rapid control movements to full travel in either direction.'

After the summer air displays came more exhibitions of the squadron's bombing skills. From West Malling the squadron was able to support the School of Land/Air Warfare with the almost traditional MRCP bombing demonstration on West Down range. The last demonstration was given on 1 August, after which the squadron flew up to Linton-on-Ouse. From Linton they mounted low-level attacks as part of two fire-power demonstrations, one at Catterick on 8 July and another at Fylingdales the next day. By 10 July, the whole squadron had reassembled at Celle.

Whereas the 'Operations Foil' and 'Bulldog' the previous year had been RAF-run exercises within UK airspace, 'Exercise Cupola', which was held from 25 to 27 August 1950, was organized over France, Belgium and Hollands by the Western Union Defence Organization. From the BAFO squadrons' perspective there was little difference in that they would once again be used as 'enemy forces' but at least their targets were nearer to their bases! On the opening day of Exercise Cupola, three Mosquitoes attacked Coulommiers near Paris, while three more attacked Leeuwarden and Valkenburg airfields in Holland. The Mosquitoes flew at 15,000ft, making them vulnerable to fighters and, indeed, the fighters were ready for them: the former three were attacked by two Vampires as they crossed the Dutch border, and the latter were intercepted by four RNAF Meteors. The following day also saw the launch of two formations of three aircraft. One section was tasked against Luxeuil in eastern France and was unopposed; the other revisited Coulommiers and was attacked by two Vampires as they returned towards the Belgian border. Another mission against Luxeuil the next day was also unopposed, but the four-strong formation which toured Gilze Rijn, Koksijde and Beauvechain was met by repeated interceptions.

There was a reprise of display flying in September with the Battle of Britain flypast over London. The squadron moved to West Malling on 8 September and flew in practices on 12 and 13 September. Unfortunately, the weather was below limits on 15 September and the flypast was cancelled. By way of consolation the squadron put on a four-aircraft low-level bombing display at the West Malling Open Day on 16 September. The remainder of the month was taken up by 'Exercise Broadside', a large-scale army exercise in Germany, where 7 Armoured Division moved from Hanover towards Paderborn, and joined with 2 Infantry Division which had advanced from Dusseldorf. The combined force then moved towards Hameln. The RAF squadrons were tasked to hamper the movement of the army formations, which they did both in daylight and at night. For the night attacks, the squadron developed a novel means of carrying out low-level dive attacks: the leader set-off ahead of the main force which followed in a loose two-minute stream. Once the leader had found the target he dropped a flare and the second aircraft attacked under the light. The second aircraft then climbed over the target and dropped a flare for the third aircraft and so on. On the last day of the exercise, as Flt Lt Perks and Flt Lt B.J. Fry, DFC took off from Celle they hit the slipstream of the aircraft ahead. 'His slipstream caused my right wing to drop,' recalled Flt Lt Perks, 'the navigator had selected the undercarriage up a little too soon so the undercarriage was partly retracted and the braked wheel hit the runway, this caused the undercarriage to jam half retracted. I was instructed to abandon the exercise and fly around to use up fuel, this I did for 3 hours and was then instructed to land on the grass to the left of the runway, with the undercarriage selected down. I did a shallow approach and made a good landing on the port wheel. The wing was kept up as long as possible, as lift was lost the wing dropped and the aircraft swung to the right about 90° when the port undercarriage collapsed and the aircraft slid sideways. Both propellers came adrift, the starboard propeller embedded itself in the starboard wing,

the port propeller chopped up the nose. At this stage my left leg became trapped, but at the last moment the a/c [aircraft] moved backwards and my leg was released. The navigator was uninjured, but I could hobble and was in hospital for a couple of days with damage to my lower left leg, I was very lucky.'

In October 1950, 'Exercise Emperor' proved to be the 'swansong' for the Mosquito. The daylight raids in 'Exercises Foil', 'Bulldog' and 'Cupola' had all highlighted the Mosquito's vulnerability to jet fighters and BAFO's ground-attack units had already started to re-equip with the De Havilland Vampire FB5. Furthermore, the increased tension between West and East in central Europe after the blockade of Berlin and the outbreak of war in Korea in late 1950, all drove the need to expand and re-equip the RAF. However, at least 'Exercise Emperor' gave the Mosquito the chance to operate in the role it could still play successfully, as a night intruder. From 7 to 10 October, night attacks were flown against West Malling, Coltishall and Tangmere and some daylight raids were also flown against Biggin Hill, Middle Wallop and Odiham.

A sad-looking Mosquito TK617 after a take-off accident at Celle on 28 September 1950. The crew Flt Lts G.D. Perks, DFC and B.J. Fry, DFC were both lucky to escape serious injury.
(Geoff Perks)

BAFO's two Mosquito B35 squadrons moved to Fassberg on 1 November, while the FBVI squadrons, 4 and 11, remained at Celle for conversion to the Vampire. In February 1951, seven pilots from 14 Squadron were detached to 93 Squadron at Celle to convert to the Vampire and the navigators started to be dispersed. Meanwhile, the Mosquitoes were ferried back to the UK for disposal. For the navigators, particularly, it was a miserable time. Nav III W.D.R. Bond recalled, '…had just got engaged to a Sergeant WAAF [Women's Auxilliary Air Force] who worked in SHQ, and was on leave with her, showing her off to my parents. The phone rang, and it was Ron Harding (one of the pilots) who had just come over on leave, and he was bragging about the beautiful shiny Vampire on the tarmac at Celle. My wife and I were not too happy about that, as apart from my having to leave the even more beautiful Mosquito, it meant that we would be split up when I was posted.'

On 21 February, Sqn Ldr R.A. Sutherland, DFC and Bar assumed command of 14 Squadron and oversaw the start up of the squadron as a Vampire unit.

NOTES

1   In Mosquito FB VI RS606 and RF646 respectively.

2   In Mosquito FB VI 'E'.

3   Sqn Ldr P.C. Ellis, DFC with Flt Lt P. J. Tuhill, DFC; Flt Lt H.H. Lowe with Fg Off Hoole; Flt Lt D.M. Clause with W/O D.H. Russell; Fg Off Nichol with Fg Off H.R. Smith.

4   The detachment was led by Wg Cdr O'Brien with Flt Lt Tuhill and the other crews comprised Flt Lt J.R. Cassells, DFC and Bar with Nav II Hammond, Flt Lt E.G. Lewis with Flt Lt Guy, Fg Off Slessor with Nav II Meredith, PII Jacks with Nav II T.W. Cooper and Pilot II Clarke as a spare pilot.

5   The other crews were: Plt I.S. Goodyear with Nav I. Read, Flt Lt G.D. Perks, DFC with Nav II A.A. Fulker and Plt II P.J. Clarke with Nav III M. Saxby.

6   Flown by: Flt Lt Stead with Flt Lt Coleman, Fg Off Cornwall with Nav III Saxby, Plt II Jacks with Nav II Meredith and Plt Off M. H. Levy with Nav I Read.

7   Fg Off Cornwall and Flt Lt R.L. Williams, DFC in Mosquito B35 TJ141, Plt II Clarke and Nav III Saxby in Mosquito B35 TA714.

8   British Armed Forces Vouchers (BAFVs), which were used as currency in the British Occupied Zone.

2

1951–1955
THE VAMPIRE
AND VENOM

Into the Jet Age

As the world settled into its new order after the Second World War, a clear schism had opened between West and East. Diplomatic relations between both sides steadily deteriorated throughout the late 1940s culminating with the blockade of Berlin by the Russians in 1948. This proved to be an omen of things to come and when the Korean War broke out in June 1950, Europe descended into the 'Cold War'. Developments in the RAF in Germany over the next few years reflected those in the rest of the British armed services: the steady contraction of the immediate post-war years was reversed and units, which so recently had been reduced almost to cadre strength, were re-equipped and expanded. Recruiting increased and the extension of National Service from eighteen months to two years in 1949 helped to provide the manpower for the services to grow. Reservists were also recalled to duty; among them was Sqn Ldr R. A. Sutherland, DFC and Bar an experienced wartime fighter pilot and squadron commander who was chosen to lead 14 Squadron into the 'Jet Age'

The aircraft selected to re-equip the light-bomber units in Germany was the De Havilland Vampire FB5, a single-seat, single-engined jet aircraft which had a greatly improved performance over the Mosquito. Its simple rugged construction also made it a much more reliable machine, while its agility gave pilots the ability to fly in both the day fighter and ground-attack roles. In the Spring of 1951, 14 Squadron's aircrew comprised just nine Vampire pilots, but in the following 3 years that number would increase to twenty-five. Of the squadron's Mosquito pilots who had been detached to 93 Squadron at Celle for conversion to the Vampire, some were posted on to other units but Flt Lt J.L.W. Dunn and Sgts Harding, W.M. Crellin and K. Sharp all

Sqn Ldr R.A. Max Sutherland, DFC and Bar (right) briefs Flt Lt S.A. Barrett (left) next to a 14 Squadron De Havilland Vampire FB5 at Fassberg in 1951. The colour of the lightning-bolt insignia on the Vampire, the 'Fassberg Flash,' denoted the unit: 98 Squadron was red, 118 Squadron black and 14 Squadron was blue. (Sam D'Arcy)

returned to 14 Squadron. The balance of Sqn Ldr Sutherland's pilots came either from other squadrons, or, like Plt Off D.J. Checketts and Sgt A.H. Sinclair, directly from the flying training system. Blessed with good weather throughout the summer of 1951 and with reliable aircraft, the squadron easily exceeded its flying task each month of some 200hrs. Much of this flying time was taken up with routine training as pilots honed their skills on the new aircraft. Vampire sorties typically lasted around 45 minutes and provided pilots with an opportunity to practice battle formation at both low-level and medium-level, as pairs, fours, or even, on Saturday mornings, as an eight-ship. With a half-half mix between the day fighter and ground-attack roles there was an even spread of air-to-air combat exercises in upper airspace and air-to-ground weaponry on the nearby Fassberg range.

The squadron also participated in the numerous exercises which punctuated the year. The first of these, 'Exercise Ombrelle' which took place from 23 to 26 May, involved over 500 aircraft from six member countries of the newly-formed North Atlantic Treaty Organization (NATO). It was designed to test the effectiveness of the air defences of the Low Countries and France, which were bolstered by RAF Vampires operating from Vokel and Soesterburg. However, 14 Squadron's Vampires remained at Fassberg throughout the exercise to act as 'enemy' bombers. The aircraft were painted with black bands across the wings and tailbooms to identify them as 'enemy' forces and in the four days of the exercise simulated ground-attack sorties were flown by 14 Squadron aircraft against the airfield targets of Soesterberg and IJmuiden in North Holland. None of these missions were intercepted before they reached their target – probably a measure of Sutherland's aggressive leadership as anything else! In an era before strict rules controlled low-level flying, pilots were free to fly at whatever height they felt to be appropriate, which for most was around 100ft. But 'Max' Sutherland, whose views were shaped by his hard-won wartime experience, believed in flying much lower than that; in fact some people suspected that he had never really come to terms with the fact that the war was long over.

As might be expected with such an intense flying programme, a number of minor incidents occurred through the summer; these were predominantly birdstrikes, a hazard inherent in low-level flying. However, a major tragedy occurred on 8 June when Flt Lt P.F. Wingate, DFC the popular commander of 'A' flight, was killed on Fassberg range. Wingate, with the callsign 'Whippet 26' was leading Sgt Harding, 'Whippet 24', for a rocket detail using an old tank[9] as the target. 'Flt Lt Wingate had carried out one dummy run' reported Harding, 'and was breaking away from his second live attack as I was lining up to commence my second attack. My height was 3,500ft and I was 3,500yd from the target. My attention was drawn by the sun glinting on the wings of Flt Lt Wingate's aeroplane[10]. The aeroplane was breaking away from the target to the left, the roll was rapid and violent and the aircraft appeared to be out of control.' After rolling inverted, Wingate's Vampire dived into the ground. Investigation later showed that the port ammunition door had become detached and smashed into the canopy, shattering it and probably knocking Wingate unconscious as he pulled off the target.

The squadron was honoured by an informal visit in August 1951 by AVM T.C. Traill, CB, OBE, DFC (Director of Personnel) who had commanded the unit in the mid-1930s. AVM Traill was introduced to all the pilots and took great interest in his old squadron. Meanwhile, the busy schedule of flying exercises continued, including a Wing interception exercise, in which the Fassberg Wing fended off airfield attacks by the Gutersloh Wing, and, during 'Exercise Spica', a high-level transit by six Vampires to Oslo via Sylt. Additionally, the squadron's personnel spent 2 weeks under canvas as part of the Wing's 'Exercise Bertram Mills'. Fassberg's Vampire squadrons were mobile units which, in the transition to war, would deploy away from their vulnerable base on the border with the Russian Zone and move to airfields in Holland. Thus, exercises to test their ability to deploy (even to the other side of the airfield!) and to operate with only rudimentary facilities were part of the routine. This particular exercise included participation in a major army exercise, 'Exercise Stopgap', which involved flying twenty ground-attack sorties each day against army targets in the Soltau training area. Maj Gen C. P. Jones,[11] CB, CBE, MC, general officer commanding 7 Armoured Division was so impressed with the squadron's performance during 'Exercise Stopgap' that he visited the squadron and joined Flt Lt S.A. Barrett on a sortie over the exercise area in a De Havilland Vampire T11, two-seat training aircraft.

The squadron was away from Fassberg for much of the autumn. The first Vampire APC took place at Sylt in September, a month in which the unit flew an impressive 321 hours, easily the most monthly flying since the end of the war. At the end of the month 'Exercise Cirrus', which was a larger-scale version 'Exercise Ombrelle' in May, gave the opportunity to carry out high-level attacks against targets in Holland. Then came 'Exercise Surprise Packet' for which the squadron detached as a composite unit with 98 Squadron to Aston Down in Gloucestershire from 10 to 19 October. This was an army-run exercise in which the UK was divided up much like Korea, with an authoritarian and aggressive 'Fantasia' to the north of a border running from Bristol to London and a democratic and peaceful 'Southland' to the south. Sadly the weather was not very good for most of the exercise and 14 Squadron flew ground-attack sorties on only 3 days. From Aston Down the squadron moved to Wattisham on 24 October where it was temporarily attached to Fighter Command to practice high-level intercepts. This latter detachment was part of a programme that 2 Group had started the previous year in order to give each of its Vampire squadrons a short period of intensive training in the pure fighter interception role. However, the detachment also provided some air-to-ground practice in the form of a firepower demonstration on West Down range on 7 November for the benefit of the School of Air/Land Warfare.

Back at Fassberg, the hazards of a busy flying programme with relatively inexperienced pilots came into focus during a practice intercept over north Germany on 26 November. Fg Off S.H.R.L. D'Arcy had joined the squadron 2 weeks earlier and, '...was flying Number 2 to the Boss on battle flight. We were vectored at 14,000ft to another Vampire formation; they broke and a dogfight ensued. In a steep starboard turn I noticed our Number 3[12] ten yards away just under my port wing, following the same 'enemy' aircraft. Too late to avoid the collision, my port leading edge hit his starboard aileron. He flew back to base, did a high-speed flapless single aileron landing and was flying again 2 hours later. I had one damaged drop tank which would not jettison and an engine that had ingested a lot of aileron. After panicking a bit over the R/T and talking about bailing out, I settled for glide descent and landing at a nearby base'.[13] According to the Board of Inquiry the mid-air collision had nothing to do with poor lookout, training or briefing; they blamed the leader of the other formation for breaking and mixing!

Fg Off D'Arcy also wrote off another Vampire the following month. Tasked on his sixth sortie of the day with simulated attacks on the RAF Regiment positions on the airfield, he discovered that the Vampire's elevator control, '...allowed one to whack the stick back and do an almost right-angled manoeuvre from horizontal to vertical flight at low-level; very impressive from the ground.' Unfortunately, the manoeuvre also imposed an instantaneous 11g on the airframe and the aircraft landed with buckled wings! No one was hurt in this incident, but a few days later three armourers were injured when a rocket fired while it was being loaded onto an aircraft. D'Arcy summed up the atmosphere of the time: '...it was quite unique in RAF flying history. We were in the 'Cold War' a few miles from the border. Everything was new: the aircraft, the propulsion system, tactics, flight envelope, etc. The rate of accidents caused by technical failures and pilot error was high; fatalities were common. With all that it was a very exciting time for everyone, particularly of course for the pilots. I do not believe one could say we felt lucky to be alive, but that spirit was in the background.'

The squadron's second jet APC at Sylt ran from 2 to 26 January and this time the emphasis was on gunnery, both air-to-air firing on a towed flag and strafing ground targets. Air-to-air firing was carried out against a 30ft long banner (known as the 'flag') towed in a gentle circle by a Hawker Tempest tug aircraft. The Vampire started from a 'perch' position above and well behind the tow, then dived across the circle, to fire a short burst at the 'flag' from a few hundred yards range before pulling back up to the 'perch' position and repeating the procedure. The exercise called for high levels of concentration while both firer and tug manoeuvred in three dimensions, and it was easy to become disorientated. Unfortunately, that is exactly how Plt Off E.R. Harbison lost his life on 21 January. Flying in marginal weather conditions, he became disorientated during an air-to-air gunnery pass, lost control of his aircraft and spun into the sea. Harbison had joined the squadron just 5 days earlier. But for this accident, the detachment was deemed to have been successful and most pilots achieved creditable scores on the 'flag'.

A month of consolidation and routine training followed before the squadron detached to Schleswig on 5 March for 'Exercise Skandia II', a joint exercise run for the British, Danish and Norwegian armies. At Schleswig, 14 Squadron joined 274 Squadron Royal Danish Air Force (RDAF) and one flight each from 2 and 16 Squadrons. For the next week, the aircraft flew intensive ground-attack sorties against army units in Schleswig-Holstein, completing 195 sorties during the exercise. The return to Fassberg was made in Wing formation led by the station commander Gp Capt E.M. Donaldson, DSO, AFC and Bar.

By the Spring of 1952, the first National Service pilots had graduated from the flying-training system and the first two, Plts Offs D.V. Finch and R.A.E. Goode, joined the squadron in April for a 6 month tour. Others followed throughout the year as part of the general influx of new pilots that would bring the squadron strength up to seventeen pilots by the end of the year. Despite the increased number of pilots and aircraft, the number of ground crew under the supervision of Flt Sgt 'Pop' Sewell remained almost constant around eighty.

One routine duty allocated in turn to each of the squadrons at Fassberg was to maintain a Battle Flight of four or sometimes six aircraft at immediate readiness. This measure was not so much a precaution against surprise attack by the Russians, but rather a means of keeping the 2 Group air controllers in practice. On most days the Battle Flight was scrambled three or four times and tasked either with an air-to-ground sortie on the range, or with air-to-air work, for example intercepting the Battle Flight from another Wing. 'When it was our turn to be on duty,' recalled Plt Off D.G. Headley, 'we used to sit in a Nissen hut at the end of the runway alongside the ORP[14]. If a scramble came the duty bod would fire a Very cartridge into the air and everyone then dashed to their aeroplane, which had been left with the straps all ready, so that we could leap in and start the engine. It really was a case of every man for himself…and on take-off you missed slipstream as best you could.'

Apart from the four 20mm cannon in the nose of the aircraft, the armament of the Vampire comprised bombs and rocket projectiles. While these weapons were extremely effective against most ground targets, a weapon with a wider footprint would be more effective against massed Soviet armour. In April and May 1952, Sqn Ldr Sutherland and his flight commanders, Flt Lts Barrett and J. Timilty, joined officer commanding flying wing, Wg Cdr W.A. Smith in a secret trial dropping napalm at Fassberg range. The attacks were made from 350kt flying as low as the pilots dared, which was typically about 20ft (though one pass was measured at 10ft)! The napalm was carried in standard Vampire overload tanks and as they approached the tank target, the pilots released the tanks by pulling the jettison lever. Despite the lack of any sighting, all four pilots achieved good accuracy in their attacks, thus proving the concept, at least, of using napalm.

The exercise season was in full-swing again as summer approached. In April, 'Exercise Terrier' involved simulated attacks as part of a formation of forty-eight Vampires at high-level against the Staines reservoir [very near to Heathrow] (refuelling afterwards at Odiham) and in May four aircraft carried out simulated attacks from low-level against Lakenheath as part of Fighter Command 'Exercise 12', this time via Horsham St.Faith. The squadron was again temporarily attached to Fighter Command for the first half of June. Operating from Duxford from 3 to 19 June, the highlights of this detachment included a Wing attack against a formation of fifty Boeing B-50 Superfortress, interception of Avro Lincoln bombers, low-level fighter sweeps of UK airfields from the direction of France and plenty of fighter-versus-fighter combat. The pilots were particularly pleased that no restrictions were placed on the dogfights that invariably resulted on the latter occasions! From Duxford the squadron moved across the Channel to Gilze-Rijen for 'Exercise June Primer'. For this exercise the squadron concentrated mainly on the ground-attack role with simulated attacks against the airfields at Wunstorf, Celle, Fassberg, and Gutersloh and HQ 2 Group at Sundern.

Meanwhile, the 'Cold War' expansion continued and the squadron's unit establishment of aircraft was doubled from eight Vampires to sixteen during June. The airfield at Fassberg was the product of a military expansion of earlier times: it had been built by the Nazi government in the 1930s as part of the clandestine build-up of the *Luftwaffe*. Fassberg's remote location was ideally suited to this secret activity, surrounded as it was by trees on the edge of the Lüneburg Heath, many kilometres from the nearest large town. However, for the RAF personnel two decades later, this isolation meant that those who lived at Fassberg were virtually confined to the base. Fortunately, the Germans had left spacious and comfortable accommodation, including a cinema and an Olympic-sized swimming pool. Since very few of those serving at Fassberg were married, the social life inevitably revolved around the various messes. 'Fassberg had a large bachelor population,' recalled Flt Lt R.N. Broad, 'and the Mess was the centre of social life. The bar was very active and if you have ever watched the sit-com Cheers it had that sort of atmosphere. So much so that a USAF F-84 [Thunderjet] pilot who diverted into Fassberg was so taken by the place that he stayed for nearly a week until frantic signals from his home base dislodged him.' Apart from a welcoming bar, the officers' mess boasted bedrooms with attached sitting rooms and bathrooms, serviced, according to Plt Off Headley, '…by German Fraus who treated us like their own children!' The airmen lived in the squadron's own barrack block, which, though not as luxurious as the officers' mess, nevertheless provided a comfortable living. 'Our Squadron House had ground and first floor rooms, fully double glazed with central heating and beautiful shower rooms and toilets,' remembered LAC R.E. Burgess. 'The roof space was our lounge with three-piece suites, comfy chairs and a non-alcoholic bar, with soft lighting.' The block was also blessed with a games room which was opened in May 1952 with a very successful party attended by all ranks from the squadron. The loft space in the block was also turned into a bar which was decked out like a pirate ship and given the name HMS *Crusader*.

Relations with the German population in the local area around Fassberg were generally very good, but this was not the case on all British military bases: elsewhere small acts of sabotage had been carried out, leading to a fear that there might be an underground movement of disaffected Germans. Because of the possible threat, from early 1952 all officers were issued pistols and hangars and other airfield buildings were guarded by armed airmen at night. Being alone in a dark hangar could be a frightening experience as AC1 D. Sanderson found out: Hangar guard duty …was an all-nighter, patrolling inside the hangar with a Lee-Enfield .303in rifle loaded with a clip of five rounds, which had been issued by the orderly officer at the start of the duty… All was going well: he had his overnight rations from the cookhouse, the aircrew crewroom had the coffee and their armchairs were very comfortable. Then he heard a banging noise coming from the far end of the hangar. This was where the squadron kept their transport vehicles in a large area that had access via an outside door. He thought someone was trying to gain an entry via this door.

Cautiously, he crept down the side of the hangar wall until he reached the room where the banging noise was coming from. He looked into the room, could see nothing untoward, but the noise continued so he shouted, 'Halt who goes there?' The noise still continued so he said loudly, 'I have a loaded rifle and I'm coming in.' With this he loaded a bullet rather noisily. He crept in down the side of the room looking for signs of legs or feet between the wheels of the vehicles. No sign, so he went in further. By this time his heart was thumping and he was getting very tense. At that moment there was a loud bang behind him – instinctively he turned very quickly and fired his rifle. His ears were ringing from the noise in the enclosed space. As the bullet then ricocheted around the room (fortunately missing him) he realized that all the noise had all been caused by an airlock in a radiator on the wall! When he had regained his composure he went back to the crewroom and made himself a mug of very strong coffee.

On 13 July four Vampires from 14 Squadron, operating out of the newly-opened RAF Wildenrath, took part in a flypast at the first NATO air display in Brussels. The impressive line-up included forty-eight F-84s of the USAF, forty-eight F-84s of the French AF, sixty-four Meteors and thirty-six F-84s from the Belgian Air Force, and eight RDAF Meteors; the RAF contingent comprising twelve Meteors and sixty Vampires. The squadron then detached to Sylt for the semi-annual APC, a detachment that was notable for two reasons. The first was that another record for flying task was set in July with over 400hrs flown. The second was an unfortunate incident with a German taxi driver which led to Sqn Ldr Sutherland leaving the squadron two months later.

The whole squadron was sent to Wunstorf for 'Exercise Holdfast' on 14 September for a week under canvas. In a scene reminiscent of the squadron's war-time days everyone was accommodated in tents out on the airfield, with slit trenches dug to provide cover against air attacks by Dutch, Belgian and USAF F-84s. The Vampires were painted with black bands on the wings to indicate that they were part of the 'enemy' forces of 'Greenlandia'. The flying mainly comprised close air-support missions flown against army units deployed in the exercise area bounded by the towns of Munster, Iserlohn, Beverungen and Hameln.

The newly-promoted Sqn Ldr R.H. Benwell, who had been a flight commander with 3 Squadron, arrived at Fassberg to take command of 14 Squadron in October

Post-flight debrief during 'Exercise Holdfast' at Wunstorf in late September 1952. Left to right: Fg Off D.G. Headley, Fg Off L.C.M. Stoate, Fg Off R.W. Bustin, Fg Off D.J. 'Bizz' Checketts. (Don Headley)

1952. The squadron had just participated in 'Exercise Ardent', the largest air-defence exercise in the UK since the war, which ran from 4 to 5 October. The squadron's role had been to act as high-altitude bombers attacking the UK. 'Exercise Ardent' would be the last major exercise involving the squadron for nine months. At Fassberg, routine training concentrated on rocket firing and air-to-ground strafe on the range and air-to-air ciné attacks until the appalling winter weather of 1952 struck in November.

Flying at Fassberg was severely limited for the next four months by low cloud and snow. To an extent the snow and ice caused less of a problem than the clouds: parties of airmen armed with shovels could clear snow and the ingenious technique of pushing a Vampire backwards over the taxiways with its engine running and the jet pipe pointing slightly downwards ensured that surfaces were cleared of ice. Low cloud posed a particular problem at Fassberg because of the very basic radio aids available to allow pilots to find the runway in poor weather. There was no Precision Approach Radar (PAR) or Instrument Landing System (ILS), either of which would have provided pilots with a way to land in all but the very worst weather conditions. Instead, pilots relied on the QGH procedure whereby the aircraft was homed to overhead the airfield using ground-based radio direction finding (RDF) and then a timed 'teardrop' descent designed to line up with the runway was flown as the aircraft headed back towards the airfield. On days with a westerly wind this pattern involved descending in the Russian sector, the border of which lay not far to the east of Fassberg. Although it was an effective enough way to find an airfield on a murky day, it was not sufficiently accurate on days when there was fog, or when the cloud base reached the ground. On these days, the aircrew amused themselves with lectures and sports activities while the ground crew took the opportunity to catch up on the inevitable backlog of aircraft maintenance.

One new pilot was welcomed into the squadron over the winter when Maj Gen Jones arrived for his first flying instruction on 8 December. After giving his eager student a brief ground school, Flt Lt R.C. Simpson collected a De Havilland Tiger Moth from Celle and gave the general his first dual sortie the following day. The Christmas festivities and the January weather caused some disruption to the syllabus, but Jones flew his first solo on 7 February, an achievement which he celebrated with a bottle of champagne in the company of the squadron pilots.

Despite 4in of snow falling and continuing low cloud, a reasonable flying programme started again in February 1953. Tactical sorties were flown whenever possible and during one of these, on 23 February, Fg Off K.D. Howe suffered an engine failure while manoeuvring at 35,000ft. With the airfield under low cloud, Howe opted to attempt a forced landing in open country. He broke cloud at 1,500ft some 15 miles east of the airfield, near the village of Wrested, near Uelzen. Here he found a suitable landing ground and set up for a copybook forced landing pattern. Unfortunately, it seems that Howe's Vampire iced-up badly as he descended through the cloud and that the pitot head froze, robbing him of accurate speed readings. At any rate, he landed

Snow and ice disrupted operations at Fasberg throughout the winter of 1952/53. Two armourers LACs R.E. Burgess and Wibberley pose in front of a Vampire FB5 on an icy dispersal. (Ron Burgess)

The Vampire FB5s of 'A' flight on the line in spring 1953. By then all of the squadron aircraft had been camouflaged; the squadron badge is painted below the cockpit, just above the pale-blue 'Fassberg Flash'. (Sam D'Arcy)

much faster than he had anticipated and after touching down on its belly at around 160kt, the Vampire ballooned back into the air, before stalling. The port wing dropped and the aircraft hit the ground heavily, disintegrating on impact. Howe survived the crash, but he died later in hospital. Howe's story illustrates the human tragedy behind such accidents: apparently he had been ribbed a few days beforehand for not 'pulling his weight' in the bar, but it was discovered after his death that he had very little money to spend because he was sending all his pay home to support his widowed mother. LAC Burgess was at his funeral in Hanover three days later: '…four armourers were detailed for the ceremonial funeral in the local cemetery. I was one of them. We stood in our best blue uniforms with our backs to the grave in each corner, no hats and our rifles reversed with the muzzle on our right shoe and heads bowed, both hands on the rifle butt end. After the burial we fired two rounds of blank ammunition on command from the officer in charge over the grave. It was a sad day.'

A glimmer of hope on the day of Howe's funeral was the prowess of the squadron's boxers in the 2 TAF Boxing Championships. LAC Lee won the light middleweight competition and SAC Dunlop was runner up in the lightweights. Back at Fassberg, the remainder of the month and the beginning of March were taken up with Battle Flight and practice intercepts. On 13 March, the squadron deployed to Sylt, for an APC which ran until 15 April, followed by a detachment to Filton (near Bristol) from 21 April to 5 May. The squadron had been sent there to exercise the fighter controllers in the southwest of England. With most of Fighter Command based in the east of the country, the controllers in the West Country had relatively little 'trade'. For squadron pilots the detachment provided an opportunity to practise interception tactics an air-to-air combat. The relatively quiet airspace also attracted various exotic aircraft carrying out trials flights and these aircraft made interesting targets for practice intercepts: on one practice intercept Fg Off Headley was closing in on (what he thought was) a Transport Command Handley-Page Hastings, only to discover it was an Avro Ashton, an experimental jet-engined airliner. Away from the flying the squadron's personnel also enjoyed a vigorous leisure time filled with activities, including looking around the Bristol Brabazon prototype, which was still at Filton, and attending the theatre in Bristol. In fact the pilots booked a box at the theatre for the entire detachment, almost certainly to the dismay of the cast who had to endure a rowdy audience every night. The chorus girls cannot have been impressed, either, to find that the flowers thrown at them from the 14 Squadron box were attached to lengths of cotton so that they could be pulled back to the box if anyone tried to pick them up!

At the end of the month Sqn Ldr Benwell's tenure as squadron commander, which was always going to be a short term stop-gap arrangement, came to an end and Sqn Ldr J.T. Lawrence took the reins.

The Venom

The arrival of the new CO almost exactly coincided with the arrival of a new aircraft. The squadron's first De Havilland Venom FB1 arrived at Fassberg on 30 May. Although superficially similar in appearance to the Vampire, the Venom was a completely new aircraft with a more powerful DeHavilland Ghost engine and a thin-profile swept wing. Throughout June and July pilots flew familiarization sorties in the Venom between their routine Vampire flying. The conversion was almost minimal: 'The squadron had been 'given' a 'red-banded' Venom a couple of months earlier for pilots to get familiar with,' recalled Fg Off B.D. Pettit. 'For some reason we were severely rationed with flying hours, and I had my turn, 20 minutes, on 22 June. The red bands painted on the wings were to denote that the aircraft was limited to a very low 'g' limit, probably about 6g. The aircraft also had no wing tanks fitted, which changed the handling characteristics considerably…my next trip in a Venom was on 24 July, in a brand-new aircraft, with tip tanks fitted and full'.

On the whole the pilots liked their new machine and Flt Lt Broad found, '…the Venom was a simple aircraft with the same primitive electronics of the Vampire; the only noticeable differences were the transposing of the R/T and RP firing button, and a rear engine bearing temperature gauge cunningly installed by your right foot – effectively it had two positions OK and engine failure. What the Venom did have was a good rate of climb and one could get to 50,000ft easily; it also had with its two tip tanks a useful amount of fuel (just under 500gals). In level flight, one could get up to about .82 Mach but should you exceed .86 Mach (which was actually not all that easy and required a dive from altitude) then all control was lost and the Venom whirled round the sky until you hit thicker air and slowed up. It was easy to fly and to land and all in all should have been a robust inexpensive ground attack fighter. It also was a useful interceptor and was far more capable than the elderly Meteors. The Venom's main weakness was poor serviceability. The problem was, I think, quality control at the manufacturers. Our Venoms were not well made and we had terrible maintenance problems – quite apart from wing failures and engine fires… . We tried running a planned flying schedule, but it foundered because if you flew a flight of four aircraft they were quite likely to land apparently OK and then all have to go back to the hangar.'

The transposition of the transmit and firing buttons on the Venom, as compared with the Vampire, did cause some embarrassment. 'When we re-equipped with the

Vampires,' recalled Fg Off A.S. Carder, 'we were still flying the Vampire and often would get out of one type and, next sortie, directly into the other. This caused the odd incident, particularly when on air-to-ground sorties. The press to transmit button was on the control column of the Vampire but in the Venom it was on the throttle – the armament button being on the control stick. You do not need a vivid imagination to know what sometimes happened, much to the chagrin of the range safety officer, when calling 'Turning Live' in the Venom: four rockets would depart heavenwards!' However, in the more relaxed attitude to health and safety which pervaded at that time, no-one was overly concerned with this inconvenience.

On 2 June 1953, the squadron participated in the Coronation flypast by the Fassberg, Jever and Ahlhorn Wings over Hamburg before the station was stood down to celebrate the Coronation. There were parties and entertainment during the day and more parties including a Coronation Ball in the officers' mess followed in the evening. On 15 July, four of the squadron's Venoms were at RAF Odiham for the Queen's Coronation Review of the RAF. Then it was back to routine flying and the summer's 'exercise season,' which included two detachments to Gutersloh, firstly from 6 to 8 June for rocket firing on Sennelager range and then again from 24 to 31 July for 'Exercise Coronet'. The latter was a major NATO exercise which involved a four-way fight between the forces of 'Westonia' (2 TAF area of northern Germany and the Low Countries), 'Fantasia' (4 ATAF area of southern Germany and western France), 'Franconia' (the rest of France) and 'Wessex' (the UK). With 1,800 aircraft taking part the exercise was a massive undertaking, but from 14 Squadron's perspective the flying was limited by the weather and consisted mainly of intercepting Republic F-84 Thunderjets and North American F-86 Sabres. For Fg Off Pettit, the deployment to Gutersloh was his second flight in a Venom: 'I was flying Number 2 to the Boss, a formation take-off, and had not sat in the aircraft for a month. After take-off, the Boss throttled back so that the rest of the squadron could catch up. At that time I was having problems with the pressurization, blowing hot, and my hand did not automatically go to the control wheel. By the time I found it and turned it to fully cold and could get my hand back on the throttle, I was way ahead of the Boss! Eventually I got back into position by looking over my left shoulder, but by this time the cockpit was filling with snow! The aircon in the Venom was quite effective! I believe the incident was mentioned after landing, but guess who got the blame? By this time though, there was another problem. Eight brand new Venoms landed at Gutersloh, but Gutersloh had just camouflaged their runway with a coating of what turned out to be thinned down tar…still wet. Our nice new birds had had a pale blue underside, which was now dark brown to black, and high-pressure tyres that were coated with tar. I seem to remember that we spent most of our off duty time trying to clean them up.'

The following month's 'Exercise Momentum', which ran for 10 days from 14 August, was more satisfactory. This time the squadron deployed to Ouston in Northumbria; the ground party travelled by train via Zeebrugge while the advance party flew to Ouston in a Douglas C-47 Dakota. The squadron was one of two 2 Group units (96 Squadron who had deployed to Leuchars was the other) whose role in this exercise was to act as home-based fighters in this exercise of the UK's air defences. Enemy forces were provided by Bomber Command, and for the first time the English Electric Canberra force was not

A Venom FB1 pulls up from a strafing pass at a firepower demonstration at Sennelager in October 1953. The destructive force of 20mm high-explosive (HE) shells was made to look even more impressive by packing the target with 'jerrycans' filled with petrol!

limited by speed or altitude for its attacks. As a result most of the exercise was flown at altitudes above 40,000ft as interceptors attempted to catch the high-level bombers. Fg Off Pettit confirmed, '…the Canberras were certainly high flying, in excess of 50,000ft. On one sortie, we decided to see how high we could get to have any chance of getting one. I think we made about 55,000ft, but could not do anything, because maximum Mach number and stalling speed were just about coinciding. We were lucky that the hoods stayed intact, as a pressure loss would have been a disaster, but we were young then and hadn't done the aeromed course!' On days of good weather, there was plenty of flying during the exercise period running from 06:00hrs to 18:00hrs each day.

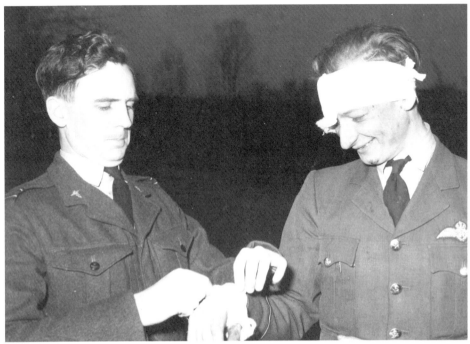

A very fortunate Fg Off S.H.R.L. D'Arcy is treated by Fassberg's station medical officer after ejecting from his Venom after it disintegrated during a high-angle bombing pass on 23 March 1954. (Sam D'Arcy)

It was during this exercise that the squadron suffered its first Venom accident when Fg Off T.J. Bolger suffered an engine failure while patrolling at 41,000ft to the southeast of Newcastle. 'Pat's Number 2 was Ron Williams,' remembered Fg Off Pettit. 'He said that Pat suddenly shot away from him (engine overspeed, and loss of main turbine, I believe). He saw bits coming out of the jet pipe, realized that Pat was in trouble and immediately closed with him to lead him down. He managed to get into a position where Pat could formate on him, not easy with a dead engine, and made appropriate calls for guidance, and descent through cloud. I think Pat may have had emergency radio for a short time, but he was completely iced up, and Ron did a super job to stay with him. When they eventually broke cloud base, which was quite high, Pat had managed to scrape off enough ice to see where he was going, and appeared to be lined up with the Boulmer runway. What he could not see were the sheep pens along the whole width and length of where he was aiming. When he eventually saw them he was too low to bale out and had to land, so he landed instead in a ploughed field at the side of the runway and put the aircraft down and miraculously it stayed the right way up. He said at the time that he just undid his straps and walked out of the front of the aircraft.'

In fact Bolger's forced landing due to engine failure was one of three similar events in the summer of 1953. On 18 June, Fg Off P. J. Fitzgerald had managed a successful belly landing at Fassberg when the engine in his Vampire failed at 2,000ft and just 11

The wreckage of Fg Off D'Arcy's Venom WE368 laid out on the floor of the squadron hangar. Nothing is left of the cockpit: the forward fuselage was manufactured from plywood. (Sam D'Arcy)

days after Bolger's landing at Boulmer, Fg Off D'Arcy landed another Venom in a field near Visselholvede after a broken quill drive caused his engine to fail. Problems with the Venoms continued into September with a 5 day grounding in the middle of the APC detachment to Sylt. However, normal flying resumed at Fassberg in October with the squadron's participation in two weapons demonstrations at Sennelager on 14 and 26 October.

In November 1953, 14 Squadron's Venoms were tasked with carrying out a trial of dive-bombing techniques. The range at Fassberg, just a few miles to the east of the airfield proved an ideal test area: aircraft could be loaded with bombs and go straight to the range and return to be re-armed for another sortie in quick succession. According to Fg Off Pettit, '...a left-hand pattern in the range usually took us over the edge of the airfield....We used to get up to four sorties with four rockets each out of one fuel load, and an engine-running re-arm was normal.' However, what no-one realized at the time was that the swiftly repeated dive-bombing profile was exposing the aircraft to metal-fatigue cycles much more quickly than the aircraft designers had envisaged. Despite interruptions of poor winter weather and Battle Flight commitments over the winter months, the first phase of the trial, which had concentrated on low-level delivery, was completed in February 1954. Phase two of the trial looked at higher-level delivery profiles, designed to keep aircraft out of the reach of small-arms fire. This new profile involved tipping in from 18,000ft into a 60° dive and releasing the bomb at 13,000ft so that the aircraft remained above 10,000ft during the recovery. This phase was well underway on the evening of 23 March when Fg Off D'Arcy tipped in for another diving attack at the start of his fifth range detail of the day. On the airfield Flt Lt Broad was talking to one of the ground crew, '…I was standing on the flight line outside 14 Squadron's hangar when I heard from the direction of the range what sounded like a sonic boom. I looked in that direction and saw high up a point of light descending. One of the airmen asked "What's that, Sir?" and I had time to say it was a Venom crashing as I rushed indoors up to my office to get my binoculars. I was in time to get a view of the wreckage hurtling earthwards but no more and no sign of a parachute. However, our anxiety was very shortly dispelled when a call came through from the range to say that Sam D'Arcy had ejected through the canopy at a very low-level and was safe.'

Meanwhile, Fg Off Headley, who was on duty as the Range Safety Officer (RSO) for the day, saw '…a 25lb practice bomb explode on the range followed by three more in a stick going up the range and almost at the same time there was a very big bang which sounded a bit like a supersonic bang. Looking up there were bits coming down, one burning bit crashed into the ground and others floated down…' After D'Arcy had been picked up by the crashwagon, Headley found him 'standing on at the top of the steps with a patch above his right eye. I said, 'Thank Christ you're OK, Sam' – I was fairly shaken up by the whole thing. Sam just looked at me and said 'Hello, Don, where did my bomb drop' which has to be the coolest thing I ever heard!'

All Venoms were grounded while the accident was investigated and it was later found that all but two aircraft had cracks in the wing structure. The problems with the serviceability of the Venoms continued throughout April and May, but luckily there were still enough Vampires, some collected from 98 Squadron, to keep pilots in some sort of flying practice and to meet the squadron's commitments for Battle Flight. Unfortunately, even the Vampires suffered problems: on 22 April, Fg Off M.S.E. Stilwell suffered an engine failure on take-off and forced landed in heathland to the east of Fassberg. Stilwell was unhurt, but the aircraft was written off. Over the next few months more Venoms emerged from the contractor's working party in the adjacent hangar and were released for flying. Eight Venoms deployed to Wildenrath on 8 June to take part in the Queen's birthday flypast 2 days later. By the middle of June matters were still improving and eleven Venoms were available to fly to Sylt for the six monthly air-to-air firing camp. The APC started on 21 June, but the weather was atrocious. 'Flying had stopped on the Saturday,' recalled Flt Lt Broad, 'and the general game plan was that on Saturday night we would head into Westerland to celebrate. This would be followed by a leisurely Sunday morning, followed by a few lunch-time drinks, a bracing walk in the afternoon and by Monday morning we would all be fit and well for the flight home.

'The first part of this plan went well and most people went into Westerland; however, as our Wing Commander Flying rolled back to Sylt around dawn on the Sunday morning the weather was bloody, heavy rain and cloud on the hangar roofs. 'This looks like a bloody awful day,' he said, 'let's go home!' So at an unearthly hour of about 08:30hrs, I was roused from a deep alcohol-induced sleep to be given this news. Eventually I collected my four and we started up taxied out and then my R/T failed; I handed over the lead to Dickie Adams (Fg Off R.J. Adams) who was newly married

A Venom FB1 starting up in the summer of 1954. The smoke comes from the cartridge used to start the engine; the trolley provides electric current until the engine-driven generator comes on line. (Frank Solomon)

and buying a camera, activities which had reduced both his desire and financial ability to wallow in the fleshpots of Westerland and hence he was in better shape than most of us. I went back into dispersals, leapt out, banged the R/T set which fixed it and taxied back out again to catch up with Dickie only too happy to let him lead. We took off straight into the murk,, but the weather cleared completely by Schleswig so we had an uneventful trip home, somewhat, enlivened by the R/T chat; the indomitable Sam D'Arcy had rounded up seven aircraft which he was leading back to base. Number 7, thought to be Sergeant Pilot 'Ginger' Stone (Sgt P. M. Stone), was effectively unable to speak and only incoherent honks came from him.

'Anyway, thankfully we made Fassberg without accident and all landed successfully. However, the confusion at Sylt on take-off with R/T failures, pilots forgetting to check in etc., resulted in ATC records showing only forty-nine take-offs - however fifty-three aircraft landed!'

Like most RAF stations of its day, Fassberg was largely a community of single young men bound together in a culture of 'work hard, play hard.' The healthy competition between the squadrons frequently led to high-jinks bred of an entertaining mixture of ingenuity and puerile humour. One example was a large wooden cannon, originally a stage prop, which was routinely stolen and re-stolen between the squadrons at Fassberg and Celle. Another cannon-themed episode resulted when a collection of interesting-looking scaffolding poles arrived at Fassberg. These were intended as frames to support camouflage netting over dispersed aircraft, but unfortunately they arrived without any instructions on how to assemble them. Seeing a wonderful opportunity, the great minds

Fg Off P.G. Peacock with the newly-presented Sovereign's Standard at the parade on 21 August 1954. Completing the standard party are Sgt P. Kavanagh (Standard Warrant Officer) and Sgts D.E. Smith and R. Woodyatt (Escorts). Heavy rain on the day meant that the presentation had to be held inside the squadron hangar. (© Crown Copyright 1954)

were diverted from the usual thoughts of stealing from other units and concentrated instead on finding the most original way of using the poles. The 14 Squadron solution used a pole as the barrel of a cannon, which when loaded with a thunderflash and a box of maltesers could be used to fire chocolate 'grapeshot' into social gatherings, causing much hilarity amongst the firers. Thereafter, the cannon became part of squadron life and was used to fire salutes at occasions such as the AOC's inspection. Another original use for the thunderflash was devised Fg Off Crook, whose enthusiasm for pyrotechnics led to his demise as the squadron adjutant. Sqn Ldr Lawrence was accustomed to summoning his adjutant by pressing a button in his office which rang an electric bell in Crook's. Unfortunately, this arrangement proved too much of a temptation for the mischievous Crook: one day he diverted the electrical wiring so that Lawrence's press on the button, the following morning, was followed a loud explosion in the grass outside his office!

The Squadron Standard

In 1943, King George VI had granted his Sovereign's Standard to certain RAF squadrons, in recognition of 25 years or more of distinguished service. Among the chosen units was 14 Squadron, but war and national emergency had meant that ceremonial niceties were relegated to the 'back burner' at the time. In the early 1950s, the first few Standards were presented and as one of the RAF's most senior units, 14 Squadron was among the first to receive the Sovereign's Standard. Preparations started in July with drill practice for the entire squadron and rehearsals were held every morning.

When the news that the squadron was to be presented with a Sovereign's Standard, Flt Lt Broad realized, 'that there would need to be an appropriate amount of ceremony; however when the CO decreed that for a month before the airmen would have an hour's drill early each morning before work started, I thought this was going to break the squadron's morale. At that time everyone was working like beavers to try and get some serviceability and I thought this would be the last straw. Here I have to admit that I was quite wrong.

'We had some advice from the 2TAF protocol department which was to the effect that two flights of forty-five airmen should escort the standard, as we had an airman strength of sixty-two, one of whom was excused boots and one sick, we compromised on two flights of thirty. Anyway, the airmen started their drill under the tuition of an RAF Regiment NCO, the officers learned sword drill, and the standard party (Fg Off P.G. Peacock and three SNCOs[15]) organized itself.

'Morale, in fact, did not suffer appreciably once the airmen got into the spirit of the thing, far from it and I became aware during rehearsals that actually I had a very smart and keen outfit behind me. We had our final dress rehearsal on the station parade ground lined with station personnel for the occasion. We marched on splendidly but came to a halt in front of the station commander a little too close. From where I stood the resultant saluting with swords was reminiscent of the *Prisoner of Zenda*; then one of the station personnel lining the parade ground fainted and skewered himself with his bayonet, but apart from that all went well.

'Came the great day on 21 August 1954 and the weather was awful. We had to switch to an indoor parade in our hangar, which was in some ways easier, as chalk marks had been surveyed into appropriate spots. However two problems arose, the first problem was

the flaming row that developed among the airmen, as on the day we had no one sick and hence sixty-one candidates for sixty slots – almost unbelievably no one wanted to miss the parade. I cannot remember how we sorted that one out, but the CO did. The second problem was that unlike the open-air parade where we marched on smartly, now we had to debouch [enter] through a quite narrow door and march off immediately on the far side without looking like a football crowd: this our airmen managed to do. However, the parade itself went off very well and subsequently we were delighted to hear that two Guards officers had expressed the wish that their lot would do as well!

'For the rest of my time on the squadron it guarded its reputation for drill fiercely: new airmen posted in were taken to the back of their barrack block to be instructed by old hands in how 14 Squadron did it.'

Appropriately, the standard was presented by AVM Traill, the former squadron commander who had visited the unit exactly 2 years earlier. After the presentation ceremony the whole squadron was able to celebrate in a more informal style.

Enough Venoms remained serviceable through September and October for the squadron to take part in 'Exercise Lucifer', a fire-power demonstration for the Imperial Defence College, on 2 September and 'Exercise Battle Royal', an army exercise which ran from 23 to 27 September. The squadron was tasked with ground-attack sorties from dawn to dusk during this latter exercise, which also involved trying to locate a number

A four-ship formation of 14 Squadron Venom FB1s over northern Germany on 6 August 1954. Flt Lt J.A. Macpherson (WE410) leads Fg Off D.G. Headley (WE349), Flt Lt R.N. Broad (WE363) and Fg Off R.J. Adams (WK413). (Don Headley)

of 280mm nuclear artillery guns. Flt Lt Broad remembered the flying as being, '… almost entirely armed recces [reconnaissance] in the exercise area, involving an enjoyable combination of low flying and tank hunting.'

However, by autumn 1954 the days of carefree low flying were almost at an end. As the British military presence in Germany had evolved from that of an occupying force into that of a supportive ally, so the rules, particularly those about activities which might impinge on the German population, were tightened. One of those activities was low flying. In the immediate post-war years, pilots had been free to fly over Germany as low as they wished wherever they wished; however, by the mid-1950s a formal low-level flying system comprising six large Low Flying Areas (LFA) linked by a transit route had been established in northern Germany. Flight to and from the LFAs was supposed to be conducted at 2,000ft, although pilots were permitted to fly lower if forced to do so by the weather. Once inside the LFA, low flying was permitted down to 250ft, but with no radar altimeter fitted to any fighter aircraft of the day, there was no way of measuring this accurately in the cockpit. It was also accepted that in order to find military vehicles hidden along the edges of woods, pilots would have to fly below the height of the tree line in order to see them. Furthermore, pilots would have to fly at tree-top height if they were going to find any sort of cover from the flat land of the North German plain. Thus in practice pilots still enjoyed almost total freedom in the LFAs and no one worried much if, for example, Flt Lt Timilty inadvertently knocked the radio aerial off an army jeep with his wing, or Flt Lt Broad left a wake across the Steinhuder Meer from his own lower-radio aerial. In the early 1950s, constant practice gave pilots great confidence at operating at low-level: on one of his early formation sorties with 14 Squadron Sgt R.R. Smith found himself following three other Venoms under a large bridge on the Kiel Canal. Unfortunately, it was difficult to find a tactical justification for the practice and when a café on the canal reputedly advertised good views of Venoms routinely flying under the nearby bridge, the low-flying rules in Germany began to be enforced more seriously.

On 25 October, the squadron deployed 'into the field' for 'Exercise Cornwall'. However, that autumn things started to go wrong with the Venoms again. Three aircraft were lost: one when Fg Off E.J. Cross lost control during a night go-around after a GCA (he sustained serious injuries when his ejection seat fired as the aircraft broke up on the runway), a second in a forced landing by Fg Off D.F. Madgwick after an engine failure and the third when Fg Off G. Steggall ran off the runway after a brake failure. The Venoms were grounded from 1 to 8 November because of a spate of fires in the air and were only allowed to fly without tip tanks for the rest of the month. The mystery of the airborne fires was eventually solved by Flt Lt J.deM. Severne, a flight commander on 98 Squadron whose aircraft caught fire during an aerobatic sortie. He ignored the standing instruction to eject from the aircraft and brought it back to a forced landing at Fassberg.

In fact, the inherent unserviceability of the Venom caused headaches for the squadron throughout the winter of 1954. The problems were caused by the build standard of aircraft, a degree of mismanagement of the servicing schedules and a shortage of qualified engineers on the squadron. The roots of this manpower shortage lay in the previous year when engineers were detached from the frontline squadrons to help clear a backlog of modifications at the MUs. Soon after arriving at Fassberg in January 1953, Corporal M. de Torre, an instrument fitter, was, '…sent on detachment to Colerne…my job was to carry out servicing on the many Venoms that were being modified at the Maintenance Unit there. Apparently, the Venoms were suffering from all sorts of problems which held up their return to units and instrumentation was one of them. I returned to Fassberg, and was soon joined by another instrument fitter, Corporal John Talbutt… [we had] quite a few problems with jet-pipe temperature (JPT) gauges and the associated wiring, also flap-indicator wiring. On one aircraft, a multi-way plug located between the cockpit and rear bulkhead was found to have badly-corroded pins and sockets, which resulted in an STI (Special Technical Instruction) to be carried out on all Venoms.

'Another problem that required lengthy 'down time' was rectifying fuel content gauge faults. After laying on ones back to change a sensor unit, the system had to be calibrated with tanks empty, then full, this involved a fuel bowser doing the necessary work, not once but sometimes twice, this was necessary after adjustment to the sensor unit at empty and full tank levels.' Added to all this inconvenience, throughout the year contractor's working parties had been busy, firstly checking the wing spars and then modifying the fuel systems on all Fassberg's Venoms. All this took time and none of it was helped by what HQ 2 Group staff described as an 'erratic and inadequate supply of modification sets.' In an attempt to alleviate the crisis, the squadron's two flights pooled their resources so that, from December onwards, 14 Squadron's engineering was run effectively as a single flight. But even despite this drastic arrangement the pilots struggled to keep current.

Although the unit claimed to have met its flying task for December 1954, this was only achieved by 'double counting' the hours flown in the two-seat Vampire T11 trainer as separate flights for each pilot. As the winter progressed most pilots were down to only 5 hours of Venom flying each month.

The lack of flying was not helped by the squadron's six-monthly detachment to Sylt which was due in January 1954. The ground crew arrived there on 11 January, but poor weather and snow, which closed the runway at Sylt, ensured that the aircraft never left Fassberg. In the end, the ground crew returned to Fassberg on 29 January. Foggy mornings through the next month limited flying, but Flt Lt J.A. Macpherson led eight aircraft to the range on 24 February for a fire-power demonstration to the Royal West Kent Regiment. Heavy snow then fell, bringing flying to a halt for much of March. In fact, this breathing space provided an opportunity for pilots to prepare themselves for their imminent conversion to the Hawker Hunter. The shortcomings of the Venom had already been clear and the RAF's Venom units started to trade their aircraft for the superior Hunter. To ease the way for this conversion, the two flight commanders, Flt Lts Broad and Macpherson had both been sent to West Raynham to fly the Hunter and learn about its systems: when they got back to Fassberg they in turn were able to give lectures to the squadron pilots.

When the weather improved sufficiently at the end of March; Venom flying continued. There was an intense programme of rocket firing, napalm dropping and strafing on the Fassberg range to try and make up for the lost opportunities at Sylt in January. The squadron also took part in a number of Wing formations. The first of these, which included eight aircraft from 14 Squadron and took place on 29 March, was a low-level attack on Diepholz airfield. On 6 April, twenty-four aircraft from the Wing flew against Royal Artillery units deployed on Hohne Range and 2 weeks later there was another Wing attack against the RAF Regiment at Wesendorf. Apart from these formalized attacks on ground troops, any army units were considered 'fair game' during routine training sorties. On 3 May, Fg Off C. Crook led a four-ship made up of Fg Off J.R. McEntegart and two pilots from 98 Squadron to practice low-level battle formation. Soon after take-off, they came across a troop of Centurion tanks on the Munsterlager training area just to the north of Fassberg. Although they were still outside the designated low flying area, they were within a military range, so Crook manoeuvred to overfly the tanks at a low height. McEntegart followed him, but hit trees some 400yd beyond the tanks. After flying on for some 450yd the Venom hit the ground and exploded. Unfortunately for Crook, MacEntegart was the godson of ACM Sir Harry Broadhurst, who held him to be responsible for the accident. Although Crook was exonerated at the subsequent Court Martial, his next posting was to the career-limiting target towing flight at Sylt. MacEntegart's funeral was held on 6 May, just 10 days before the squadron's last flying day at Fassberg. The experience of 14 Squadron's operations from Fassberg put the risks of fast-jet flying, even in a 'cold' war, into perspective: four years of Vampire and Venom flying had cost the lives of four pilots and sixteen aircraft had been destroyed.

The squadron officers held a Farewell Ball in the officers' mess on 10 May and the next week was spent preparing for the squadron's move to Oldenburg. The road party with all of the squadron's heavy equipment left Fassberg on 22 May. The following day 14 Squadron arrived at its new home: eight factory-new Hawker Hunter F4s awaited them.

NOTES

9   An ex-*Wehrmacht* PzKpfw VI Tiger which served as a rocket and napalm target for many years with surprisingly little damage to show for the attentions of the RAF.

10   Vampire VV538.

11   General Sir Charles 'Splosh' Jones, GCB, CBE, MC (1906–1988), was taught to fly in a De Havilland Tiger Moth at Fassberg the following year.

12   Sgt Sinclair who landed Vampire WA109 back at Fassberg.

13   Wunstorf.

14   Operational Readiness Platform (ORP), an area of hard standing next to the runway which was specifically designed for aircraft at readiness.

15   Sgt P. Kavanagh (Standard Warrant Officer) and Sgts D.E. Smith and R. Woodyatt (Escorts).

3

1955-1962

THE HUNTER

At Oldenburg, 14 Squadron joined 124 Wing, comprising 20 and 26 Squadrons, both of which still flew the Canadair-built Sabre F4. The squadron was also reunited with an old friend in the station commander, Gp Capt D. C. Stapleton, DFC, AFC, who had joined 14 Squadron as a junior Plt Off in 1937 and left the unit 4 years later after commanding it through the darkest days of the Western Desert campaign. Stapleton wasted little time in getting to renew his acquaintance with his old squadron and flew a 14 Squadron aircraft on 28 June. However, any hopes that Stapleton's previous allegiances might lead to preferential treatment were quickly dashed: '…far from that being an advantage…,' recorded Fg Off J. Marriott, '…he tended to give us a hard time. He was a fair man at heart, but I think he hoped that by giving us a hard time we might perform better.'

The first Hunter had been air tested by Flt Lt MacPherson on 1 June 1955 and the following day Sqn Ldr C.W. Beasley and Flt Lt I.G. Stanley flew the squadron's first flying exercise on the type. In the following months the whole squadron, which was for now declared as being 'non-operational,' would be involved in converting onto the new type. With no two-seat version of the aircraft, Flt Lt Pettit's conversion was typical: '…we had a sort of ground school, and questions, and one of the flight commanders would sit you in an aircraft then go through the various systems with you, while standing on the steps. After a pre-flight briefing, he would them accompany you to the aircraft and go through the start-up procedure as far as pressing the start button, make sure you knew how to shut the hood and leave you to it. He would then go either to air-traffic control (ATC) or the runway-controller caravan to watch progress and wait for your safe return. There were weather restrictions, basically…no need for an instrument let down! In my case, poor old Bob [Broad] had a few kittens as the weather worsened markedly after I got airborne and disappeared into the murk at about 1,000ft. I eventually got to

Pilots from 14 Squadron pose with a newly-delivered Hawker Hunter F4, painted with the new blue-and-white diamond squadron markings, outside the squadron hangar at Oldenburg, summer 1955. The squadron dog 'Raq' is on the right. (Bob Broad)

about 40,000ft, still in cloud and decided it would be a good idea to go home. I called for a QGH, which was excellent, and I broke out of cloud at about 800ft, lined up with the runway for a straight in approach and landing, and Bob was there to meet me when I got back to dispersal.'

In fact the conversion of pilots was not the only reason for the squadron to be considered non-operational: for while in pure flying terms the Hunter's blend of speed and manoeuvrability surpassed that of any other RAF aircraft (and most others in Europe, too), it was at that stage quite useless as a weapons platform. Flight trials in the UK had shown that firing the aircraft's 30mm Aden cannon disrupted the airflow into the engine intakes, particularly at high altitude, causing the engine to surge, and until that serious fault could be remedied the guns could not be fired.

At Fassberg the squadron had been a 'fighter-bomber' unit and although pilots had experience of the air-to-air day fighter role, they had tended to regard their main role in both Vampire and Venom as that of low-level ground attack. At Oldenburg they would become a pure day-fighter unit and the squadron would have to work hard to become combat ready in this new role. In fact the conversion to the Hunter was reasonably straightforward, but it was not without some mishaps. The first of these occurred on 17 June when Flt Lt Broad was, '...suddenly called by ATC that one of our Hunters was in some trouble. We hurried out to see it land and it looked rather like one of those elderly pigeons one saw in London who has obviously passed its sell-by date; it drooped all over. The pilot, Colin Field [Fg Off C.P. Field], was helped out with a nose bleed and the g-meter stuck firmly at twelve. His story was that he had gone into a tight turn at speed (as indeed he was meant to) and it had then pitched up, which was a known fault of early Hunters. So the incident was attributed to pitch-up and no more was said. Anyway the aircraft was straightened up somewhat, the pitot tube re-aligned and after a phone call to Neville Duke [chief test pilot] at Dunsfold (who recommended less than 250 knots and no airbrake) I limped it [flew it carefully] back to Dunsfold. Hawker's final estimate was that it had pulled 14g.'

The second accident, which was altogether more serious, happened almost exactly two months later as a formation of four Hunters practiced battle formation at high altitude. When flying in battle formation, four aircraft were divided into two elements comprising an element leader (Number 1 or 3 in the formation) and a wingman (Numbers 2 and 4). Each wingman flew in a loosely staggered position around 300 to 400yd behind his element leader, while the Number 3 maintained position 2,000yd abreast of the formation leader, enabling each element to look behind and beneath the other element, thus securing the blind spots directly astern and underneath the aircraft. In order to maintain this formation when a 90° turn was required the 'outside' element would turn first and cross behind the 'inside' element, who would delay their turn so that when they rolled out they would once again be exactly abreast of the other element. Practice and judgement were needed to make the geometry of such turns work properly, particularly at high altitude where the aircraft's turning performance and the engine response could both be more sluggish than at lower altitude. On 18 August, Fg Off Carder was leading Fg Offs W. Deluce, Steggall and Field at high altitude to the northeast of Bremen. As Number 3, Steggall was leading the second element in, '…classic battle formation at 40,000ft on a perfect day, no cloud, no haze and little high-altitude wind. I think I was leading the turn after a 90° port was called. About half way round the turn, after I had checked that the leader was turning as expected, I looked left behind me to see whether Number 4 had crossed over. It was at this point I saw a Hunter with fuel spraying from a wing. As I expected the Number 2 to be on my right and close to the leader in order to cross to the leader's right I called to report that I thought that Number 4 was in trouble. Colin Field was quick to point out that he was OK. I could see the leader so that meant that Number 2 must be in trouble. I turned towards the damaged aircraft and I soon spotted the second aircraft. Both of them were a lot lower by now so I could not tell which was which, but I saw that they were both Hunters. We were not briefed that there would be a 'bounce'[16], (we all had less than 20 hours on type) and we were concentrating hard on the geometry and engine response of high-level formation.' During the formation turn, a fifth Hunter, flown by Sgt Stone, had blundered into the middle of the group in an attempt to bounce it. Unfortunately, Stone had not seen Deluce who was straggling slightly out of position and he hit Deluce's aircraft with catastrophic results. Deluce managed to eject from his aircraft but his seat had been damaged in the collision. His parachute became entangled and he was killed when he hit the ground; Stone, whose seat was also damaged when he ejected through the canopy, managed to manually separate from his seat successfully and sustained only heavy bruising to his shoulder.'

The remainder of the year was taken up by the Hunter conversion, a task which expanded with the arrival of another eight new pilots (Flt Lts J. Hodgson, P.C. Mellett,

Fg Offs R.F. Hoyle, B.B. Batt, Plt Offs S.A. Baugh, D.L. Parsons, D.C.D. Potter and R. Rankin) during the latter half of the year. Unfortunately, the increased number of pilots was not reflected in the number of ground crew and shortage of manpower proved a problem in the autumn. On the positive side, however, the gun-firing problem had been resolved sufficiently to allow some air-to-sea firing during October. The month also saw the start of night flying.

Winter weather caused the usual disruption to flying, which in turn gave the pilots the opportunity to practice their escape and evasion techniques during an exercise on 18 November. This was not necessarily a popular experience! Some of them also attended the Winter Survival Course at the newly opened RAF winter survival school at Bad Kohlgrub over the winter months. Despite these hardships, though, the squadron was declared sufficiently operational to start taking its turn with Battle Flight duties from 28 December. The flying rate steadily built up through the first three months of 1956, a reflection as much as anything else on the sterling efforts of the ground crew who regularly had to work in temperatures well below freezing, both out on the line and in the hangars. Much of the flying was spent in pairs at 20,000ft practicing ciné-weave, a gunsight handling exercise designed to get the pilots ready for air-to-air

Hunter F4s of 14 Squadron's and Canadair Sabres 5s of 410 Squadron (RCAF) line up on the runway at Marville-Montmedy for a mixed close-formation flypast on 17 July 1956. (Smudge Smith)

firing on the 'flag'. The squadron also managed to borrow a Gloster Meteor target tug, complete with 'flag', so that pilots could practice the manoeuvres (though not the gun firing) that they would be using on the range. There were also Practice Interceptions (PIs) against Canberras to give some variety.

On 3 February, the squadron celebrated its 41st birthday with an all-ranks party in the pilot's crewroom, an event that doubtless resulted in more than a few sore heads the following morning! The squadron cannon, which had also made the journey from Fassberg, was used to fire a salute during the celebrations.

The first Hunter APC at Sylt was held during April as a joint detachment with 26 Squadron who had recently re-equipped with the Hunter. The detachment was joined by Gp Capt Stapleton, who spent four days flying with his old squadron and firing on the 'flag'. With only the air-to-air role to concentrate on, the APC was devoted entirely to aerial gunnery. The number of hits on the 'flag' was measured using the simple method of dipping the cannon shells in paint and loading each aircraft with shells of its own distinctive colour. When a shell passed through the fabric of the 'flag' it left a trace of coloured paint, identifying which pilot had scored that hit. On completion of the range sortie the 'flag' was dropped by the side of the runway and then taken to the squadron dispersal; here under the critical eye of the squadron Pilot Attack Instructor (PAI) the number of holes of each colour were counted to give each pilot's score. For the squadron pilots the previous months' practice had clearly paid off, as all except one pilot was able to qualify in air-to-air firing. The unfortunate exception was Fg Off R.C. Elsby, who was taken sick at the beginning of the detachment and whose subsequent sorties were marred by a run of bad luck. On separate sorties he experienced a 'flag' becoming unserviceable when the spreader bar (to which the fabric of the flag was attached) was hit, a 'flag' falling off the tow on the way out to the range, a 'flag' being shot off the towing cable, and finally weather being below limits on the range. At the end of the detachment, all the Hunters from 14 and 26 Squadrons flew past Sylt at low level in a combined formation before splitting into fours for the transit back to Oldenburg.

At Oldenburg it was back to the routine flying and holding Battle Flight readiness. The last day of 14 squadron's Battle Flight was 18 June, a day which was enlivened by a series of scrambles, a total of twenty-nine sorties. Leading a pair, Sgt Smith was, '...scrambled first to go after a four from Jever. This was at high level and we were trailing. Of course a dogfight developed and other aircraft joined in. This turned into a real operational exercise because the pair and the four were alternated into the mêlée as the day progressed. On about the third time that I went in, I counted twenty-seven aircraft, Hunters, Venoms and Meteors and the closest I got to a mid-air collision was as I was rolling in to go down on a target, the centre-belly section of a Hunter went across my nose! During the day the circus gradually got lower until it finished at about 6,000ft over HQ 2 Group with the AOC cheering "His Boys".' Two weeks later, a section of five Hunters was vectored to intercept a 216 Squadron (Transport Command) De Havilland Comet C.2, which was carrying the Secretary of State for Air, Rt Hon E.N.C. Birch, accompanied by a number of senior air officers, returning from the Soviet Air Show at Tushino. Intercepting a high-performance airliner was an interesting diversion to both the ground controlled intercept (GCI) controllers and pilots alike and it doubtless provided some entertainment for the distinguished passengers.

The squadron's first squadron exchange with a NATO partner was held between 10 and 19 July with 410 Squadron RCAF, a Sabre 6 equipped unit based at Marville-Montmedy, some 30 miles southwest of Luxemburg. Numerous mixed formation and air-combat sorties were flown during the detachment. The Canadians were equipped with, '...Orenda-engined Sabre 6s – more powerful than the American [built] version,' recalled Sgt Smith, 'but we could out climb them; they had a turning advantage but we could stay with them using ten flap!' Other highlights of this detachment included interceptions with French Air Force Dassault MD.454 Mystère IV and a flypast over Verdun and Metz on 18 July by a large mixed formation of Hunters and Sabres.

The following month saw the introduction of 'Rat and Terrier' exercises. One Hunter, the 'Rat,' would set off and act as a low-level intruder for two others. He would broadcast his position and heading with a one minute delay to simulate reports from ground observers. The leader of the 'Terrier' pair would navigate following the reported position of the intruder at 1,500ft, while his Number 2 would fly at low level in an attempt to 'skyline' the target. It was, in Sgt Smith's words, '...great fun!'

The squadron Supermarine Spitfire Mk.IX, with the ground crew who restored the aircraft from being a wreck on the crash-dump at Eindhoven. The aircraft was presented to Gp Capt D. C. Stapleton on 23 April 1957. (Smudge Smith)

The Squadron Spitfire

On 19 September 1956, the squadron deployed to the Dutch airbase at Eindhoven for ten days to participate firstly in 'Exercises Stronghold' and 'Whipsaw'. 'Stronghold' which ran from 20 to 22 September, was designed to exercise the UK's air defences, while 'Whipsaw' was run by SACEUR between 25 and 28 September. On 'Exercise Stronghold' Sgt Smith was, '…involved in three mass raids to test the UK air defences, two on 21 September and one on 22 September. The whole Wing was involved from Eindhoven, as was almost every other outfit in Germany; there were hundreds of aircraft and we were allocated levels to fly at there and back. We had big formations above and below and it was a most impressive sight. We did not see many interceptions though!'

During the detachment to Eindhoven, the squadron personnel noticed the abandoned hulk of a Supermarine Spitfire[17] on the airfield crash dump. Feeling that this was a very ignoble end for such a magnificent aeroplane, they decided to rescue it. At the end of the detachment the remains of the Spitfire were loaded onto a lorry and taken to Oldenburg, where, for the next six months, volunteers from the ground crew worked to restore the aircraft into a presentable condition. The Spitfire was repainted in RAF colours, complete with 'invasion stripes' as a tribute to 124 Wing's operations as a Spitfire Wing during the invasion of Europe. One major challenge for the restoration team was in finding a replacement canopy, since the original had long since been lost. The solution came in the form of a canopy from a Canadair Sabre 6 which, though it did not fit exactly, was a sufficiently close fit to make the aircraft up to presentation standard.

The Spitfire was presented to Gp Capt Stapleton at his farewell parade on 23 April 1957 on a day which was so foggy that it was hard enough to see the aircraft, let alone notice the slightly strange canopy! Stapleton in turn presented the Spitfire to 124 Wing and returned it to the guardianship of 14 Squadron. The Spitfire remained with the squadron through its various moves for the next five years.

The squadron returned to Sylt on 22 October 1956 for more air-to-air firing. Over the next 4 weeks, pilots first qualified on a 'flag' towed at 10,000ft and then moved on to a 'flag' towed at 20,000ft. With average scores around the 10 percent mark, Flt Lt J.K. Maddison, AFC and Sgt Smith both did remarkably well with scores of 25 percent, which were thought at the time to be RAF records. In fact such scores would be easily surpassed with the radar-ranged gunsights fitted on later marks of Hunter. For some pilots the detachment offered the rare treat of firing on towed glider targets, which offered more satisfying targets than a mere 'flag'. According to Sgt Smith, '…glider targets were towed similarly to the flags and we attacked them in pairs so that if the leader missed, Number 2 had a go. I was flying as Number 2 to Hank [Beasley] and he hit right in the wing root so that bits of glider came hurtling towards me. I well remember a wheel passing over my head!'

The detachment to Sylt coincided with the flashpoint of the Suez Crisis when British and French troops invaded Egypt to take control of the Suez Canal. Although the crisis had little perceptible effect on units in Germany, some pilots expected that they might be sent to the Middle East. Fg Off Batt thought, '…14 Squadron was perhaps number three on the Germany list to go.' The Soviet invasion of Hungary in early November was also something of a non-event for squadron pilots.

Through the winter the squadron maintained its Battle Flight commitment, which at times and despite the winter weather, could be busy. On 18 December alone there were eleven Battle Flight scrambles: two three-ship, seven pairs and another single aircraft were launched in daylight hours and another three-ship took off for a night sortie.

The 22 March 1957 was a very sad day for 14 Squadron: the squadron dog, 'Raq', was run over by a car outside the station that evening and had to be put down. In the words of a brief epitaph in the *Flight Comment* magazine a year later, '…he tried once too often a quarter attack on a moving car and misjudged it.' 'Raq', a black Labrador, had joined the squadron as the pet of Fg Off Checketts. When Checketts left Fassberg in March 1954, he left the dog in the charge of the squadron pilots. 'Raq' probably could not believe his luck: whereas Checketts had treated him strictly as should befit a gun dog, the other pilots were much more easy-going and spoiled him. 'Raq' particularly enjoyed the detachments to Sylt where he often caused embarrassment to the duty dog walker by sniffing around nudist sunbathers on the beach. His affections were described as being, '…transferrable: they could be bought for a piece of chocolate, but after your supply was gone he would sit before someone else, beseechingly drooling saliva, begging for more!' 'Raq' was buried outside the pilot's crewroom on 24 March.

Four days of March were also spent participating in 'Exercise Hargil', a trial into the detection of, and defence, against fast low-flying aircraft by anti-aircraft guns. A defensive force of thirty-three light anti-aircraft guns was sited around the airfield perimeter at Ahlhorn and the Hunters flew against them daily between 11 and 14 March.

Hunter F6

From the beginning of April, the Hunter F4s began to be replaced by the latest version of the aircraft, the Hunter F6. The new machine was fitted with the much more powerful Rolls-Royce Avon Mk.203 engine, giving it a far superior performance over the F4. Improved flying controls also cured some minor shortcomings in the handling characteristics of the earlier marks of Hunter. However, one drawback of the more powerful engine was a higher fuel burn and therefore a shorter range – a perennial problem with British fighter aircraft of the period; this deficiency would be corrected early in 1958 by the fitting of 100-gallon drop tanks to the underwing pylons. Further improvements over the following year included 'dog tooth' extensions to the outboard leading edges of the wing and the introduction of a radar-ranged gunsight, both of which gave the aircraft a much better operational capability.

The arrival of the new aircraft coincided with the publication of the 1957 Defence White Paper, which, amongst other things, heralded a massive reduction in the size of the British armed services in general, and the RAF in particular. The brunt of the RAF cuts would be borne by the 2nd Tactical Air Force (2TAF) in Germany, which would be reduced to half its size and concentrate on the nuclear strike and reconnaissance roles. In the short term, 14 Squadron would be directly affected by this development in two

The graceful lines of a factory-new Hunter F6 XG292 flown by Fg Off R.M. Moon for a ciné practice sortie on 27 March 1957. The 'dog-tooth' modification to the leading edge of the wing has not yet been incorporated. (Smudge Smith)

ways. Firstly, the disbandment of a number of the fighter-bomber squadrons in Germany meant that those remaining units equipped with the Hunter F6 would resume the day fighter ground-attack role, at least until the Hunters were withdrawn from Germany. Secondly, the accelerated handover of flying stations to the newly-formed *Luftwaffe* meant that 124 Wing would need to be rehoused when Oldenburg reverted to German ownership later in the year. In the longer term, 14 Squadron's survival would be at stake when the day-fighter role was eventually given up in Germany.

In the shadow of these impending changes, the squadron got on with the conversion to the Hunter F6. This task took the 3 weeks to complete, during which time it was non-operational. It was during this time, too, that the squadron suffered another mid-air collision. Fg Off Field reported shortly after take-off that he had an undercarriage malfunction and Flt Lt R.E.W. Loverseed went to his aid. While Loverseed attempted to perform a visual inspection, the two aircraft collided. Both were damaged but the pilots were able to land them successfully. In Loverseed's case it was a particularly good effort, as the spine of his aircraft, which carried the control runs, had been severely damaged and the aircraft was barely controllable.

The conversion was complete by the beginning of May, a month in which the squadron managed to fly over 400hrs - a figure not seen since the heady days of Max Sutherland's Vampires 5 years earlier. This achievement was despite the almost inevitable teething problems with a new aircraft, for snags with the fuel system and elevator controls had already started to cause problems. Apart from manning Battle Flight from dawn-to-dusk on a number of days, the squadron also participated in 'Exercise Vigilant', the UK's annual air defence exercise on 25 to 27 May.

Sadly, the activities in May were paid for in June, when problems with aircraft serviceability, exacerbated by what Sqn Ldr Beasley called, '...the appalling lack of spares,' limited the flying achievement to well under half of May's figure. However, the serviceability held up for the year's APC between 8 and 31 July and the gunnery scores showed an improvement over the previous visit to Sylt. Perhaps this was due to the better gunsight on the Hunter F6, or perhaps it was just an indication of the expertise within the squadron! However, air-to-air gunnery was something of an art rather than a science and not all pilots found it easy. One pilot who had a natural flair was Sgt Smith. LAC F. Davies, an electrical mechanic remembered: 'The highest scoring pilot in the squadron during that summer was, actually, a sergeant pilot. There is a tale, whether apocryphal or not has never been established, that one of our junior pilots was consistently low scoring and, after the end of the first week, on the instruction of the CO, he only flew in a pair with the sergeant pilot and that the squadron armourers randomly mixed the coloured shells in their gun packs.'

The pilots returned to Oldenburg on 31 July and since the ground crew would still be travelling back from Sylt the next day it seemed reasonable to assume that they would not be flying on 1 August. As a result all the officers invited themselves to the house of the newly-married Fg Off T. Barrett, where they held an impromptu party which went on into the early hours. Unfortunately, the recurring NATO 'Exercise Drumfire', a no-notice readiness exercise, was called early on 1 August. 'While the single chaps were walking back to the mess from the party,' recalled Fg Off Marriott, 'the Drumfire siren went off. The station commander (Gp Capt P. H. Cribb, CBE, DSO and Bar, DFC) in his

Land Rover, intercepted 'Hank' Beasley and his merry men on their way to the mess, and escorted them to the squadron. Because of their erratic behaviour he quickly decided to send them all to bed. Then he, the wing commander flying (Wg Cdr I.B. Butler, DFC, AFC) – and 'Smudge' Smith, flew the aircraft until lunchtime, by which time everyone had sobered up. I had not left married quarters after the party – so didn't meet station commander or hear the siren. I went to work at normal time (08:30hrs) to see a notice on the F700 office door saying 'Wanted – Sober Pilots'. However, despite the handicap of having no pilots and no engineers, the squadron still managed to fly seventeen pairs sorties on the exercise by using Oldenburg's aircraft servicing flight, supervised by 14 Squadron's own Flt Sgt Winrow, to turn around the aircraft. Later in the month an exchange with 66 Squadron, another Hunter F6 unit, at Acklington, gave Flt Lts Maddison and Loverseed and Fg Offs Rankin, Batt, D.N. Cousins and R.M. Moon and Sgt Smith, the opportunity to sample fighter command's operations. Meanwhile, seven of 66 Squadron's Hunters flew to Oldenburg to experience flying in Germany.

The effects of the Defence White Paper started biting at Oldenburg in September with the disbandment of 26 Squadron and preparations for the move to Ahlhorn, which would be the Wing's temporary home while the runways at Gutersloh were resurfaced. To an extent the demise of 26 Squadron was an administrative exercise in that the pilots were simply redistributed between 14 and 20 Squadrons, so the latter two units benefitted from the 'migration' of experienced pilots. The flying during the month was also influenced by the White Paper with a start made to air-to-ground strafing. The range at Strohen to the east of the Dümmersee was used for this event, but the weather was too poor to achieve much. September also contained 'Exercise Counter Punch', an Air Forces Central Europe (AFCENT) led exercise of the integrated air-defence system in continental Europe. Unfortunately for 14 Squadron, most of the targets for interception were at the limits of the Hunter F6's range, which at least brought home to 2 Group's staff officers the need for Hunters to carry drop-tanks as a matter of routine.

The squadron's final days at Oldenburg provided Sgt Smith with his, '…only "real" scramble.' On 17 September, he was, '…at crewroom readiness at 16:45hrs when the nightfighters were due to take over at 17:00hrs. The red telephone went for "Scramble Red Section." I said "Don't be so bloody silly it's nearly five o'clock!" "No Smudge this is for real." So Brian Batt[18] and I hared out and were airborne within about four minutes. We roared into the climb checking gunsights on. The target was identified a few thousand feet below, a lumbering twin-engined aircraft coming from the east. Brian fortunately was our aircraft recognition ace and he said "it's an Elizabethan." The GCI controller asked if we could get the registration, so we flashed across the top to try to read off the wings but there was too much glare off the silver finish so I decided to go alongside and read from the fuselage. The Elizabethan cruised at about 180, so I hung the gear and some flap in order to slow down. First of all a passenger saw me, then a stewardess and she told the captain. I was not able to perform the correct interception break off upwards and away so I rolled downwards, passed the registration to the controller and asked him to make sure that the tape was preserved. I learned that the Elizabethan had come through from Berlin without a flight plan and, sure enough, about two weeks later the wing commander had me in to say that BEA had filed a complaint about me bouncing their aeroplane. I explained that Brockzeital had it all on tape and no more was said.'

Four Hunter F6s on the break into the circuit at Ahlhorn on 21 April 1958. (© Crown Copyright 1958)

Ahlhorn

On 1 October, all fourteen of the squadron's Hunters flew to Ahlhorn. The following week was spent unpacking and settling into the new accommodation and on 5 October 1957, Sqn Ldr K.E. Richardson took command of 14 Squadron. Flying operations started again on 7 October, but a week of fog precluded much flying, and the squadron started Battle Flight duties on 15 October. Although the squadron's new home was known as 'Appy Ahlhorn' the 12 months spent there were not the squadron's happiest days: the large influx of pilots from other units brought with it a number of personality clashes which upset the harmony which the unit had enjoyed at Oldenburg.

The winter of 1957/58 was a harsh one and snow and ice severely limited the flying programme. However, the introduction of drop tanks in January did at least represent a major step forward in getting the best out of the Hunter F6. On 4 February, the squadron deployed to Sylt for a 6 week APC, during which the armourers performed particularly well, especially considering that of fifteen armourers, all but three had only joined the unit within the previous 2 months and none of them had prior experience of the Aden cannon. The APC was also remarkable for Flt Lt M.I. Stanway's score of 78 percent on the 'flag' and for Fg Off J. McVie's canopy which, on 17 February, shattered on take-off. McVie was flying Number 2 in a two-ship sortie, '…shortly after take-off the left rail on which the canopy runs lifted off from its seating and the canopy shattered. My bonedome saved me from head injury and on landing I found that my seat harness had been undone by part of the canopy hitting the [ejection] seat barostat.' The aircraft was so badly damaged by fragments of canopy that it had to be returned to the MU for repair.

During late April, four aircraft detached to the Danish Air Base at Aalborg for a 14 day squadron exchange with 724 Squadron RDAF. The latter unit flew the Hunter Mk.51, which was the export version of the Hunter F4. During the exchange, which lasted until 6 May, 14 Squadron pilots rotated through Aalborg to give as many as possible the chance to enjoy the pleasures of Denmark. The flying during the detachment consisted of PIs and high-level battle formation practice. Another exchange followed later in May, when six aircraft and eight pilots carried out a reciprocal exchange with 263 Squadron at Stradishall. For their part, the 263 Squadron pilots were able to bolster 14 Squadron's Battle Flight, but the main benefit of this detachment for the 14 Squadron pilots was being shown the 'naval method' of flame-out landing. This was considered to be rather better than the spiral technique they were used to. For flame-out approaches the squadrons in Germany still used a method perfected for the Vampire which involved homing to overhead of the airfield and then spiralling down in a continuous turn. When the pilot was clear of cloud he could then manoeuvre to pick up the normal forced landing pattern. Although this technique worked reasonable well it was not entirely practical on a day of low cloud base, whereas the naval method was. The new technique needed more input from the radar controller, who vectored the pilot to a position on the extended centreline of the runway in use, where the range to touchdown in miles was the same as the height above the runway in thousands of feet – for example 10 miles at 10,000ft. At this point the Hunter pilot lowered the undercarriage and lowered the nose of the aircraft to follow a 'one-in-one' vertical profile, from which in virtually any weather conditions the aircraft could land straight ahead on the runway.

The NATO 'Exercise Full Play' in early June was the last outside tasking for the squadron for the summer months. During the month the squadron establishment was reduced to twelve aircraft and sixteen pilots – which coincided with the re-formation of 26 Squadron. The reduction was easily achieved by returning four of the ex-26 Squadron pilots to their old unit. The rest of the summer was spent in routine training, mainly high-level PIs, and preparing for the move to Gutersloh. One such preparation was recalled by Fg Off R.J. Honey, '...various members of the squadron decided to leave a mark for the future, and we painted the squadron's fuselage markings on the roof of our hangar just before leaving. The stores people were, I think, pleased that we used up their whole stock of blue and white paint so they were not bothered with accounting for it on the move to Gutersloh.'

Gutersloh

On 15 September 1958, the squadron moved to Gutersloh, which would be its home for the next four years. The three Hunter squadrons from Ahlhorn (14, 20 and 26 Squadrons) joined 79 Squadron, which was equipped with the Supermarine Swift FR5 reconnaissance aircraft. The new accommodation was very comfortable and with 26 Squadron back in business the old rivalries – and puerile humour – resurfaced. According to Fg Off Honey, '14 Squadron had a hangar where the aircrew offices, including the operations room, were on the first floor with windows looking out to 26 Squadron's similar accommodation, except that it was a mirror image of ours. It was therefore possible to see all the activity in 26 Squadron's aircrew accommodation from ours. On days when there was little activity, and perhaps only one 26 Squadron pilot was in view in their accommodation, it was possible to ring 26 Squadron's crewroom, watch the pilot race to it and just as he arrived at the phone, cancel the call and ring the planning room instead. Off would go the pilot to the planning room, again only to find the phone stop ringing as he approached. It was possible to lead him a merry dance, until suddenly the penny dropped and he looked across to our hangar to see half a dozen grinning 14 Squadron pilots who had been watching his antics. This joke could of course be reciprocated.'

The squadron settled quickly into its new home and Fg Off Honey noted, '...flying from Gutersloh was more varied than at Alhorn.' The squadron's role now included some ground-attack work: low-level simulated attack sorties provided some added variety to the staple of medium-level flying. Pilots were also able to practice strafing attacks regularly at Strohen range. 'We also practiced air combat,' recalled Fg Of J.M. Preece, '...these were the days before too many airliners could make it into the upper-air space, so we had tremendous freedom to operate all over Western Germany and the Low Countries without worrying too much where we were. A normal practice interception sortie would start with the radar controller splitting the pair of Hunters to intercept each other, but if any other fighters were seen on radar, the controller would ask the leader if he was interested in intercepting

A pair of Hunter F6 aircraft (XJ691 and XG274) airborne over northern Germany, late 1959 or early1960. Typically, the Hunters would fly in pairs.

some trade, which one never refused, and soon you were in the thick of a dogfight with Dutch or Belgian Hunters, German or Canadian Sabres or USAF F-100 Super Sabres. It was always more fun to pit your aircraft against a different machine. We were faster than the Sabre but they turned well and you had to be skilful to get one in your sights. If they had iron crosses on the wings it was particularly satisfying!'

The squadron began preparing in earnest for the APC in December by borrowing two target tugs and 'flags' from Sylt so that pilots could practice the range pattern. Unfortunately, poor weather meant that there was only a limited benefit from this opportunity. On 1 January 1959, eleven aircraft flew to Sylt for a detachment which proved to be very successful, despite the continuing efforts of the weather to disrupt events. Although ice and fog did curtail the flying and compromise the pilots' continuity, the results on the 'flag' were much better than at previous APCs. This was undoubtedly due to the recent introduction of the radar-ranged gunsight.

On 3 February, the squadron returned from Sylt and settled into a routine of training at both high and low-levels, a series of one-day exercises (such as 'Exercise Battle Call' on 24 February and 'Exercise Amled' on 27 February) and covering Battle Flight duties. The latter had become a rather more serious role than hitherto: the Gutersloh Wing was responsible for policing the Air Defence Identification Zone (ADIZ) a 30-mile wide strip which ran just inside the Inner German Border (IGB). According to Fg Off Preece, '…there was always a Battle Flight pair of aircraft on standby from dawn to dusk. This could be a five minute relaxed state in the crewroom or two minute readiness in the cockpit. A [Gloster] Javelin night-fighter squadron covered the hours of darkness. The 'enemy' aircraft were heavily armed and we learnt various attack techniques to get within gun range (less then 800yd) before we were too much of a sitting target for the bombers' rear and ventral gunners. Quarter and snap up attacks were most likely to succeed. Battle Flight scrambles were no longer mainly a training exercise – they were all "for real" and the fully-armed Hunters were launched to intercept any aircraft which penetrated the ADIZ.'

During March, Battle Flight was scrambled five times. One scramble found a *Luftwaffe* Republic F-84F Thunderstreak, lost and suffering from a radio failure: on three other occasions the target was an English Electric Canberra which was carrying out covert reconnaissance along the IGB. On 19 March, Fg Off McVie and Plt Off H. G. Cracroft were scrambled[19] to intercept a Canberra B(I)8 which had strayed across the border during an exercise sortie. The Hunters were hastily called off when the GCI controller identified two Soviet fighters climbing to intercept them. Meanwhile, the Canberra continued its flight and returned to base with the crew completely oblivious to the drama they had caused! Battle Flight scrambles continued at a rate of about four or five a month, usually for F-84s, F-86s or a Lockheed T-33 Shooting Star which had become lost and flown into the ADIZ. The occasional practice scramble was ordered if things were quiet, just to keep everyone on their toes. Aircraft could also be diverted from routine-training flights for operational use: on 8 May, one pair was taken off task to investigate a radar contact at 8,000ft over the border, but they became short of fuel before they could complete the interception and had to recover to Gutersloh; a second pair launched from Battle Flight managed to identify the contact as a German civilian Cessna T-50 light-transport aircraft, which was flying along the border. Another scramble later in the year involved a USAF aircraft which had violated the IGB on 19 September. Unfortunately, the Russian fighters which launched to investigate, violated the border in the other direction and the Gutersloh Battle Flight was scrambled in response. To the disappointment of the Hunter pilots, no contact was made with the Russians!

One perennial problem for the command and control of fighters was secure communication with aircraft being held at readiness. Previous methods of scrambling fighters had been rather hit and miss. Fg Off Honey took part in one exercise at Ahlhorn where, '…aircraft were scrambled by ATC firing an appropriate colour Very flare. Red for the 20 Squadron pair, white for the 26 Squadron pair and green for 14 Squadron, for example. We would sit at cockpit readiness, and as the sun made us sleepy and our attention wandered after say half an hour, we were jerked into life by the sound of a Very being fired. Unfortunately, by the time we heard the sound, the Very had almost always fallen to ground and we could not tell the colour. Then the pantomime began. Wait to see if another pair started, if no one did then it must have been for us, start up immediately, only to find that the same logic was going on with the other two pairs; final result, six aircraft starting up to launch to the great annoyance of the SATCO and Wingco Flying.' The air-defence 'Exercise Topweight', which started with a no-notice callout at 01:30hrs on 13 April, was the first in which 'telebrief' was used to communicate with pilots at readiness on the ORP. Over the three days of the exercise this method proved to

A Hunter is framed in the gunsight during a ciné-weave exercise. The ciné-weave pattern involved tracking an aircraft as it followed a prescribed set of manoeuvres, ending with a half-barrel roll to finish inverted. The target in this photograph has another 40° to go as it rolls left towards the horizon.

be very effective and reliable. Quite apart from the command and control aspects, 'Exercise Topweight' generated a busy flying programme and each squadron pilot had some six scrambles over its course. The GCI controlling was of a high standard too, vectoring the squadron on to fifty-four successful interceptions, mainly against Canberras and Republic F-84F Thundersteaks.

During the following week a *Luftwaffe* Nord Noratlas transport aircraft called in at Gutersloh. Its pilot, an RAF officer serving on an exchange posting, strolled across to the 14 Squadron offices where a diarist recorded that a little later, '...half a dozen pilots could be seen talking to a youthful Flt Lt and it would have been deduced that he "had got some in" if only by his AFC [sic] and the respectful gaze of the mob.' The youthful officer was Flt Lt J.A. Kennedy, DFM who had flown the Martin Marauder with 14 Squadron during 1943. Now based at Wuntstorf, Kennedy invited some of the members of his old squadron to join him on a short trip in the Noratlas while his German student flew some instrument approaches.

Four Hunters practicing close formation, on 25 May 1960. Flt Lt I.P. Rothwell (XJ690) leads Fg Off J.M. Preece (XJ691) Flt Lt F.D.G. Clarke (XJ646) and Flt Lt J.L. Norman (XJ644). (John Preece)

After the disruption caused by the wintery conditions at Sylt in January, a second APC during June enjoyed much better weather. The summer months also heralded the flying display season. For 14 Squadron this was of particular interest because their own Flt Lt R. Chick had been selected to be RAF Germany's Hunter display pilot. One of his first displays was at the squadron's former home at Oldenburg, now a *Luftwaffe* base. On 4 and 5 July, Chick displayed to a crowd of around 100,000.

The end of the summer was marked by another squadron exchange with 724 Squadron RDAF, which was now based at Skrydstrup. Four aircraft (flown by Sqn Ldr Richardson, Flt Lt Chick, Fg Offs D. Keys and Preece) flew to Denmark on 24 August. Two more pilots, Fg Offs A.C. McLauchlan and A.C. Edmunds, accompanied by the ground crew joined them there, courtesy of a RDAF Douglas C-47 Skytrain, and on 30 August Flt Lt F.D.G. Clark and Fg Of K.G. Cooper swapped places with Sqn Ldr Richardson and Fg Off Preece for the last 4 days of the detachment. Four RDAF Hunters deployed to Gutersloh for the duration of the exchange for a reciprocal visit.

Popular though the Hunter was amongst its pilots, it still suffered from a chronic lack of serviceability, which frequently limited the squadron's flying hours. The squadron's 'First Line' servicing crews, run by Sgt A. Bourne, worked wonders on the aircraft wherever they could, but many faults remained unfixable because of delays in the supply chain or man-power shortages in Gutersloh's aircraft servicing flight. This problem was compounded by a backlog of aircraft waiting for 'Minor' servicing. A short-term fix arrived in July 1959 in the shape of the Hawker Hunter T7 at Gutersloh. This training aircraft was intended for carrying out dual-check rides and instrument ratings, but in practice it simply became an extra aeroplane to help fill the holes in the flying programme. A more permanent solution to the serviceability issue arrived in October: all 6ft 5in of Fg Off F. Sayer, the new Squadron Engineering Officer. Fg Off Sayer was the first professional engineer officer to have served with the squadron since wartime and his expertise and experience were sorely needed. On 23 October, he certainly got off to a good start when eleven Hunters were all serviceable: indeed serviceability improved noticeably from then onwards.

The autumn of 1959 presented an opportunity to concentrate on air-to-ground strafing using the range at Strohen. By December, practice was beginning to show with some amazing scores. On 7 December, Fg Of I.P. Rothwell must have thought that he would easily hold the squadron record with a very respectable 83 percent score, but he was beaten the following day by Flt Lt J. Bredenkamp with an incredible 98 percent. Much to everyone's disbelief, even this score was not enough to beat Fg Off D. Keys' subsequent 100 percent! December also saw the first of the NATO 'Exercise Quicktrain' a no-notice 'generation exercise' which required units to come to full-operational readiness as quickly as possible after the exercise was called. On 11 December, everyone at Gutersloh was summoned to work by the sirens sounding at 05:45hrs. Just 40 minutes later, 14 Squadron had six aircraft ready to launch, with another two declared combat ready shortly after. Four aircraft were scrambled at first light. 'Exercise Quicktrain' and similar 'no-notice' callouts would become part of life in RAF Germany for the next 30 years.

Christmas 1959 was celebrated in the usual RAF Germany style with numerous parties. The airmen's block, which was decorated as a pre-historic cave, won first prize in the 'Barrack Block' competition; throughout the festive season it provided a warm welcome for all squadron, members regardless of rank, in an atmosphere worthy of any nightclub!

1960

For 14 Squadron, January meant another detachment to Sylt. On 5 January, most of the ground crew flew to Sylt in a Blackburn Beverley C1 of RAF Transport Command and they were followed by ten Hunters the next day. The first week of the detachment was used for training in ciné-weave at 40,000ft in preparation for the Duncan Trophy. Throughout the 1950s, the trophy had been awarded annually to the fighter squadron in Germany which had gained the highest score in air-to-air firing. However in 1960, it was decided that air-to-air firing against the 'flag' was too much of an academic exercise and that a more tactical profile would give a better representation of a unit's proficiency: thus the Duncan Trophy had become a ciné-weave competition. The squadron's top-scoring pilot in this event was Fg Off Preece, who described how, '...the exercise involved filming another Hunter doing a set weave pattern whilst the attacker closed from 700 to 200yd, keeping the 'pipper' on the rear of the target's canopy. We were sometimes able to get 100 percent accuracy on this.' On 12 January, air-to-air firing began and continued until the detachment ended on 9 February with a squadron average score of 25 percent. On the same day Sqn Ldr A.S. Foulkes assumed command of 14 Squadron.

As in the previous year, the month or so after APC was spent settling into 'routine' flying, including one-day exercises. In particular, 'Exercise Amled' punctuated almost every month with scrambles to intercept Canberras or F-84s, however unlike many similar exercises at least 'Amled' did offer some good flying. For example, 'Exercises Gateman' on 19 May and 'Yeoman' the following day provided respectively just two sorties and six sorties, but no targets. In contrast the 'Exercise Amled' on 27 May, provided seven scrambles leading to twelve interceptions. Another squadron-level exercise, which was run for the first time in April, was an Operational Turn Round (OTR) in which a pair of aircraft took off with fully-loaded guns, which they fired out into the sea. They then returned to Gutersloh where they were refuelled and re-armed as quickly as possible before setting off again. A good OTR could be completed inside 10 minutes, but much like a Grand Prix pitstop, it needed practice by the ground crews.

Traditionally, the end of each course at the Day Fighter Combat School (DFCS) at West Raynham was marked by a mass fighter sweep across the Netherlands and northern Germany. In the knowledge that the course attended by Flt Lt Chick was due to finish in late May, Sqn Ldr Foulkes held back 15 hours of its flying task to allow 14 Squadron pilots to get the most out of the DFCS sweep. The squadron diarist recorded, '...on Friday morning [27 May] five aircraft were scrambled to help the Wing sort out the assorted fighter genii from Raynham. Elaborate plans had been laid as to how this was to be accomplished and 14's task was to engage the top cover Hunters whilst 26 [Squadron] smashed through and tracked the

Jav[elin]s. Very Good. There we were sat at 48 thou[sand feet] looking for the top cover and all we could see was a whirling, rolling, diving mass of aircraft about 10 thou[sand feet] below. The Dutch had got there first and had succeeded in disrupting the ranks of the mighty and confusion was now reigning. Uncle Fil [Flt Lt Champniss] threw caution to the winds and in we went. After that things became a trifle confusing. This was summed up by an odd looking section which finally broke into the Gutersloh circuit from close formation. Leading it was R. Chick in horrid honking-green Hunter of DFCS, Number 2 was Pring [Fg Off Preece] in 14 colours, Nosher Browne [Fg Off J.A. Browne] was Number 3 (26 Squadron) and a red DFCS Hunter Number 4. Anyway, a rather splendid time was had by all and the members who went along to the debrief learnt a lot from it.' For Plt Off Cracroft, '…it was one of the most memorable flights I had in the RAF, it was a wonderful sunny day with very good visibility and at one time I counted some fifty aircraft in various dogfights! When I recovered to Gutersloh, I had one of the DFCS Hunters on my wing who was very short on fuel!'

The year's squadron exchange was with 326 Squadron RNLAF, a Hunter F4 unit based at Woensdrecht, some 15 miles to the north of Antwerp. The reciprocal exchange started on 8 June with eight aircraft from each unit flying to the other's base. In each case, another four pilots travelled with the ground crew in the two C-47s provided by the RNLAF at the beginning of the exercise (the RAF provided two Handley Page Hastings C 2 aircraft for the return phase at the end of the week). The Dutch pilots caused something of a stir when they arrived at Gutersloh: each one climbed out of his Hunter dressed in identical traditional Dutch costume of blue smock, red scarf, black cap and clogs! For the away team at Woensdrecht it was a case of 'work hard – play hard' for the week. An intensive daytime flying programme, including PIs and low-level route flying was followed by an equally intensive party programme hosted by the Dutch 'home team.' At the weekend, the 14 Squadron personnel were treated to a visit to Amsterdam and there was another visit to the city at the end of the detachment for a mass visit to the Amstel brewery. According to the squadron diarist, '…a very haggard bunch of drivers airframe staggered home to Gutersloh.'

Although the serviceability rate of the Hunter seemed to be improving, there were still problems with the supply of spares. The decision was taken to limit the squadron flying programme to twenty sorties each day, using waves of just four aircraft. This at least provided a mechanizm to hold a reserve of useable aircraft in case one of the four fliers became unserviceable. Gun firing continued through the summer both on the air-to-ground range and the air-to-air range at Trimingham, just off the Norfolk coast, where the guns could be fired at 40,000ft. The Trimingham range slots were used in conjunction with OTRs at Gutersloh. The squadron also began high to low level ground-attack sorties; a high-level transit to the low-level area enabled the pilots to range further afield than had been the case previously. The driver behind this change was Flt Lt Chick, who was keen to introduce a more realistic approach to low-level flying after his experiences on the DFCS course. Over the next few months the 'low-level strikes' became more ambitious and by November pilots were taking part in high-low-high sorties simulating cannon attacks against targets in East Anglia or southern Germany. Although it seems unlikely that the RAF would have actually used the Hunter in such a way in the event of war, the exercise did provide some challenging and enjoyable flying for the pilots.

On 15 August, the squadron was hit by tragedy when Sgt A.C. Priestley was killed in a road accident while he was off duty. The loss of this very capable young radio and radar technician hit the unit hard and most of the squadron was present at his funeral on 19 August. Unfortunately, this was on the same day as the DFCS end of course sweep led by another 14 Squadron member, Flt Lt D.C.G. Brook. In fact, the squadron managed to launch four aircraft in the afternoon led by Fg Off Preece. The DFCS sweep was a formidable force, comprising ten Hunters and six Javelins, but it did not intimidate the RNLAF who intercepted the sweep and spilt them up completely so that by the time the RAF Germany fighters arrived there was not much left to fight! Preece's formation had to make do with intercepting a mere four Javelins.

The squadron was given a good workout during 'Exercise Flashback' on 22 and 23 September. The exercise was called at 20:03hrs on 20 September and 20 minutes later 14 Squadron had nine aircraft at five minutes' readiness. The following day, the first of thirty-six scrambles was called at 07:00hrs and on 22 September all nine aircraft were scrambled at 05:50hrs and redeployed to Geilenkirchen. Here, they operated from the 11 Squadron dispersal. Fg Off Sayer was flown there in the Hunter T7 while a RAF Germany communications flight Hunting-Percival Prembroke C.2 delivered an NCO and six airmen to Geilenkirchen 3 hours later. Over the next two days, the aircraft maintained 5 minutes' readiness from 05:30hrs until 19:00hrs and between those times they were continuously scrambled via 'telebrief'. A total of sixty-nine air-defence sorties were flown and most pilots flew four times each day. By the end of the exercise everyone was feeling the fatigue. Geilenkirchen was also used as a temporary base for flying during the following month while holes in the runway at Gutersloh were repaired. The four Hunters and eight pilots who deployed there on 9 October were joined by another pair which had been at West Raynham. With the Canadian sector fairly close to Geilenkirchen it was natural that most of the activity was flying air combat sorties against the RCAF Sabre units in the area.

The Last Hunter Squadron

A busy and varied flying programme throughout the autumn brought the year to a close. The end of the year also brought the disbandment of 20 and 26 Squadrons, leaving 14 Squadron as the only day-fighter unit in RAF Germany. From 1961, responsibility for the daytime security of the ADIZ in northern Germany would rest solely with 14 Squadron. The unit was expanded slightly with the addition of five extra aircraft, bringing the unit establishment to sixteen Hunters; the squadron also absorbed some more pilots from the recently disbanded units. In fact, after the turnover of personnel at the end of 1960 only eight of the 'original' 14 Squadron pilots remained with the unit. The number of ground crew also increased to reflect the squadron's increased engineering workload. During winter months, Battle Flight was mounted every day from 07:00hrs to 15:00hrs GMT and in the summer it started 2 hours earlier and finished 2 hours later; as previously, the hours of darkness were

Fg Off B. J. Tonkinson looks over Battle Flight at Jever, 1961. The wingtips on the nearest Hunter (XG251) have been painted white to make it easier to see them clearly when debriefing gun-sight films – the films were processed in 'negative' so the white wingtips would show up as black on the film.

covered by the Javelins. Sqn Ldr Foulkes noted that 'permanent Battle Flight is an onerous and boring task' which impinged on the squadron's routine flying.

In fact the squadron was able to maintain an intensive flying programme through the early months of 1961, with 'low-level strikes' (increasingly flown as four-ship instead of just pairs) as well as four versus two air-combat sorties, strafing at Strohen range and air-to-air firing at Trimingham range. 'Exercise Round Robin', a routine cross-servicing exercise, also involved a pair of aircraft each month deploying to another NATO base for a turn around between sorties. Some of the stations visited during the year included Luxeil, Leeuwarden, Ramstein and Ahlhorn. 'Exercise Quicktrain' also periodically checked the squadron's ability to prepare for war.

The runway at Gutersloh was closed again over the spring and summer 1961, so 14 Squadron deployed to Jever in March. The move coincided with the start of concentrated practice of ciné-weave in preparation for what was to be the final Duncan Trophy. However, despite all the practice and 14 Squadron's creditable average in the sorties flown from Jever, the Duncan Trophy for 1961 was won by the Javelins of 5 Squadron. The APC at Sylt, in May, provided the usual opportunity to fire against the 'flag' and to enjoy the 'scenery' on the beaches between flights! During the detachment to Sylt daylight Battle Flight was covered by the Javelins of 85 Squadron's from Geilenkirchen.

The hard work of the squadron's ground crew was recognized by various awards during early 1961: in January, Sgt J. Walker was awarded a C-in-C's commendation for his work the previous year and SAC N.S. Cooper was similarly awarded an AOC's commendation. Four months later, Cpl Tech Johnstone was recommended for a 'Good Show' award for finding a loose mass-balance weight on an aircraft rudder, a fault which was difficult to see and could have caused a serious problem if the aircraft had flown.

Perhaps unsurprisingly after the busy months of April and May, aircraft serviceability suffered somewhat during June, but even so the squadron participated in an army co-operation excercise and, on 29 June, 'Exercise Bombex'. This involved four Hunter F6 sorties and four Hunter T7 sorties intercepting V-bombers leading to claims against four Handley Page Victors and two Vickers Valiants. A Victor was also amongst the aircraft intercepted in the ADIZ during the numerous Battle Flight scrambles during the summer. One scramble in July was to rescue a *Luftwaffe* T-33, which was observed by the radar controller flying triangular patterns, indicating that it was suffering a complete radio failure; the aircraft was located and shepherded back to Oldenburg.

Low-level strikes continued to feature throughout the summer months. An army co-operation exercise in June, arranged by Maj Williams, Ground Liaison Officer (GLO) at Gutersloh, was particularly valuable in this respect because it provided pilots with realistic targets. Previously buildings and bridges had been used as targets, but while there was some challenge in locating such structures while flying at high speed and low altitude, they would probably have been immune to the weaponry carried by the Hunter. Attacks against 'softer' targets such as troops and soft skinned vehicles were a much more appropriate target for rockets or Aden cannon and finding them presented a further challenge to the Hunter pilot. Thanks to Maj Williams, 14 Squadron aircraft were able to practice simulated attacks on various army units deployed on exercise in Germany and against radar-controlled anti-aircraft guns on the disused airfield at Varrelbusch (to the southwest of Oldenburg). They were also able to try their hand at tactical reconnaissance against units 'in the field' at Zwolle in the north-east Netherlands. In July, low-level strikes were also flown to support an exercise at Ahlhorn in which over seventy radar-controlled guns had been deployed around the airfield. The summer also saw wider ranging ground-attack sorties with high-low-high profiles flown against targets in East Anglia and in LFA3 to the southeast of Gutersloh.

Despite the low-level work, the squadron's primary air-to-air role was not forgotten. 'Exercise Amled' on 27 July involved twenty-five scrambles resulting in eighteen kill claims and 'Exercise Cat & Mouse', on 15 August, involved the interception of four Belgian Air Force F-84s over Hamburg with claims against all four of them. Four days previously six aircraft intercepted the DFCS Sweep. A break from Battle Flight in the latter half of the month also provided an opportunity to practise six-ship tactical formations at high level.

The summer of 1961 also marked the permanent closure of the range at Strohen and strafing was carried out instead at Nordhorn. The squadron's strafing there got off to an exciting start when one pilot fired 130 rounds of high-explosive (HE) shells instead of the permitted ball ammunition. This brought a temporary halt to strafing while the range was closed and made safe.

Flt Lt J.M. Preece at high-level during a Practice Interception (PI) sortie on 14 March 1962. The aircraft has two extra drop tanks fitted to extend the range: in this fit a Hunter could manage a 90-minute sortie duration. (John Preece)

The Berlin Wall

Meanwhile, during the summer of 1961 the political situation between East and West deteriorated further. Amid growing tension, the East German government closed the border between East and West Berlin on 13 August. Construction of the infamous 'Berlin Wall' started on the same day and Berlin became a divided city. Increased Soviet military activity in East Germany focussed NATO's interest on Berlin and the air corridors which linked it to the west. At Gutersloh, Battle Flight was increased to six aircraft, comprising a pair at two-minute readiness on the ORP, another pair at 5 minutes and a further pair at 30 minutes. Having moved back to its home base on 5 September, 14 Squadron now mounted Battle Flight from dawn-to-dusk each day. The force was further augmented by Javelins from 41 Squadron, which deployed to Gutersloh from 8 September. The heightened tension was reflected in the twenty-six operational scrambles during the month, approximately three times the normal launch rate, as activity in the ADIZ and the Berlin corridors increased. Of course the increased number of aircraft required by Battle Flight correspondingly reduced the number available for routine training flying and a planned squadron exchange was cancelled because of the operational commitment. Amongst other things the crisis served to show that although the Hunter F6 was much loved by its pilots, it was fast becoming obsolete when compared to the aircraft such as the MiG-21 ('Fishbed') which faced it on the other side of the 'Iron Curtain'.

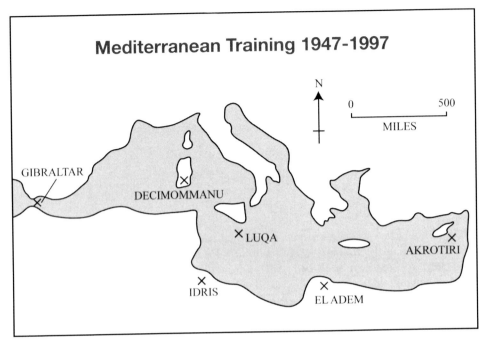

Tension eased slightly in September, allowing the squadron to resume its normal flying programme. The army 'Exercise Spearpoint', which was held from 9 to 13 October, provided an abundance of armour, soft-skinned vehicles, pontoon bridges and helicopters, all of which provided ideal targets for simulated strikes. A total of 109 low-level sorties were flown on this exercise. The year wound down as decreasing daylight and increasingly poor weather, as well as the usual unserviceabilities, limited flying hours. Only four Hunters were available to intercept seven DFCS Javelins which flew into Gutersloh on 2 December, but all four claimed 'kills' against the Javelins. Flying stopped just before Christmas, although the Battle Flight commitment continued through the festive season. The Christmas and New Year were celebrated in the typically boisterous fashion with many parties thrown over the period. Amongst these, special note was made in the squadron's Operations Record Book of the 'Roman Orgy' thrown by the squadron's bachelors on 15 December, an event which was described as one, '...which may well receive the Party of the Year Award!'

From the flying perspective the New Year got off to a slow start, but this was not true of Fg Off I.D.C. Tite who won the RAF Skiing Championship at Zermatt. The New Year also brought a number of visitors to Gutersloh in response to developments in East Germany. A detachment of six, and later eight, Javelins from 33 Squadron was established throughout February and March and four English Electric Lightnings from 56 and 111 Squadrons, deployed daily to Gutersloh; additionally, four pilots were detached from 92 Squadron to help bolster 14 Squadron's aircrew manpower. Station alerts in March also ensured that all of Gutersloh's units could get ready for war quickly.

Despite the emphasis on the operational situation, the squadron managed to run a programme of four-versus-two air-combat training and during 'Exercise Roulette', the four pairs which were scrambled on 5, 13 and 27 April intercepted four F-86s, two T-33s and an F-84, also two details of Hunters from 54 Squadron who were in transit to use the range at Nordhorn. The squadron exchange was resurrected in 1962 and six aircraft and nine pilots deployed to the RDAF base at Skrydstrup on 1 May for a 10 day exchange with 724 Squadron RDAF. An equal number of Danes arrived at Gutersloh. Halfway through the exchange, five of the RAF pilots were changed over to give the maximum number of people a chance to visit Denmark. Apart from the busy flying, the highlight of the exchange was undoubtedly a trip by RDAF C-47 to Copenhagen in the middle weekend; the 'away team' arrived back at Gutersloh suffering from 'professional and social exhaustion!' The end of the exchange coincided with the beginning of an exercise regime which would dominate the life of RAF Germany squadrons for the following three decades: Tactical Evaluation (Taceval). The Taceval was a formal no-notice test carried out under the auspices of Commander Allied Air Forces Central Europe (COMAAFCE) to verify the ability of NATO units to come to full war readiness in their allotted time and then to carry out their war role effectively in spite of any enemy actions. Gutersloh's first Taceval was called in the early hours of 9 May and despite six aircraft being in Denmark, 14 Squadron was able to generate sufficient Hunters to readiness. The aircraft were launched for low-level strike sorties that afternoon and the following day were sent for a single 'operational profile' strafing pass at Nordhorn. As if Taceval was not enough, the squadron's readiness was tested again with 'Exercise Quicktrain' 11 days later.

The summer brought with it more opportunities to work with the army. During an army co-operation exercise on 26 and 27 June, fourteen sorties were flown against targets at the extreme range of the Hunter. Four further pairs sorties were flown against army targets on 12 July. On 2 August, a ground-attack demonstration by four aircraft on Hohne range, left three trucks burning an hour after two passes' worth of HE shells had set them ablaze. Meanwhile, the display season had started again: Flt Lt Preece led a section of three Hunters in the flypast by NATO aircraft over the Joint Headquarters at Rheindahlen on 15 June to mark the 10th anniversary of NATO. On 11 July, Flt Lt Brook gave a solo-aerobatic display when the Secretary of State for Air visited Gutersloh. A ten-aircraft formation flypast was also mounted for this latter visit.

The armament practice station at Sylt had closed in 1961 as part of the contraction of RAF Germany, leaving a question mark over where the last Hunter day-fighter squadron might hold its overdue armament practice camp. The solution was to use the facilities in Cyprus, where both weather conditions and airspace were ideal for air-to-air gunnery. Flt Lt D. Morter and the squadron engineering officer Flt Lt P. O'Connor in the Hunter T7, accompanied by Flt Lt L.E. Wagstaff in a Hunter F6, flew to Cyprus for a preliminary visit in July. Another preparation for the APC was the handover of the Gutersloh Battle Flight commitment to a detachment from 43 Squadron, which arrived from Cyprus in early August; in return, 14 Squadron's Hunters would cover the Cyprus Battle Flight from Nicosia during their stay on the island.

The squadron, under the new CO, Sqn Ldr E.H.C. Williams, deployed to Cyprus the following month. Fourteen Hunter F6s and one T7 left Gutersloh on 9 August routing via Orange to Luqa to night-stop and then on via El Adem to Cyprus the next day. On 10 August, 'Crusader Formation' arrived at Nicosia in great style as a huge diamond formation. The ground crew followed in a Bristol Britannia C.2 and a Hastings supplied by RAF Transport Command. Over the next 4 weeks, the squadron personnel spent the mornings working hard at the routine of APC: armourers loading the guns, line mechanics servicing the aircraft and pilots firing against the 'flag'. In the afternoons it was too hot for work and everyone was free to amuse themselves on the beaches. There were numerous parties, too, including an all-ranks party in the NAAFI at Nicosia on 6 September.

One of the many high points of the detachment was a gunnery competition against the resident 43 Squadron. A challenge issued to OC 43 Squadron (Sqn Ldr P.G. Peacock, an ex-14 Squadron man!) on 29 August drew his attention to the fact that his, 'Junior Squadron [was] not yet aware of' the fact that 14 Squadron was 'the Only Best Squadron', and suggested that this shortcoming should be remedied by a gunnery competition in which 'each squadron [was] to supply four of its most Stalwart Men' each firing fifty rounds. Two days later, a note accepting the challenge was nailed to OC 14 Squadron's door! The competition took place on Saturday 1 September and started with a theatrical attempt to intimidate the opposition by 14 Squadron's four aircraft all taking off in close-echelon formation. Twenty minutes later the 'flag' was dropped on the airfield and the personnel of both squadrons waited with bated breath while neutral umpires from 70 Squadron hurried to count the holes. The four pilots[20] from 14 Squadron did well, scoring seventy-five hits, despite Flt Lt Preece's radar not working; 43 Squadron scored only sixty-two hits, but the sense of victory was slightly dampened by the knowledge that Sqn Ldr Peacock had suffered a double gun-stoppage and had been unable to fire at all. Flt Lt O'Connor reported, '...he was last seen angrily stalking his engineer!' A boisterous party followed in the mess.

The Hunters returned to Gutersloh, retracing their steps through El Adem, Luqa and Orange on 11 and 12 September. Luckily, Flt Lt O'Connor accompanied them in the T7 because at El Adem, there was, '...a problem with the undercarriage of the CO's Hunter. On landing he told me that he'd had trouble retracting it after take-off, so I had a look around but couldn't see anything wrong. We decided that for the next leg he would take off first, and the rest of us would follow if he was OK. He roared off down the runway, then flew over a minute later, undercarriage firmly down. We had to sit and wait while he flew around for nearly an hour burning off fuel to get down to landing weight. When he taxied in, furious, I looked into the undercarriage bay and there was a wire hanging loose. I fixed it; he took off again, and up went his wheels. We all quickly strapped into our aircraft and got airborne and in formation for the overwater leg to Malta. At last we arrived back at Gutersloh, breaking through low cloud to see our home runway, welcomingly wet and cool after our long hot absence.'

Back at Gutersloh, 'Exercise Nightjar' from 24 to 28 September, provided a welcome variety from air-to-air firing in the form of fifty-nine low-level sorties against army units deployed in the field. Some pilots were also drafted in as Forward Air Controllers (FACs) to help the Hunters locate the targets. September brought with it the news that everyone had been dreading – that 14 Squadron would be disbanded at the end of the year. The news was softened by the knowledge that the squadron would continue, albeit in a different role, because its number plate would be transferred to 88 Squadron, a Canberra B(I)8 unit at Wildenrath.

Rather than winding down slowly, 14 Squadron spent its last three months as a day-fighter squadron working hard. The 'Cuban Missile Crisis' which was played out over October no doubt gave some edge to the training. Four Royal Norwegian Air Force (RNoAF) F-86K Sabres were hosted at Gutersloh between 3 and 9 October, flying PIs with 14 Squadron's Hunters. Despite a shortage of technical manpower as technicians were posted away from the unit, the squadron's engineers managed to provide twelve aircraft for a formation flypast led by Sqn Ldr Williams. On 30 November, the squadron flew fifty-six sorties which was thought to be a record for a peacetime squadron on a normal operating day. Between 3 and 6 December, the squadron flew twenty sorties with a detachment from DFCS, which was visiting Gutersloh. Meanwhile, the unit's ability to come to war readiness was tested and practiced with a station exercise in November, followed by 'Exercise Quicktrain' on 13 December.

The last Battle Flight scramble by 14 Squadron Hunters was on 15 December when Fg Offs T. Nattrass and P. Jevons launched[21] in the early afternoon to intercept a USAF North American B-66 Destroyer in the ADIZ. At midnight on 16 December, the squadron ceased operations, marking 'the end of the last traditional Day-Fighter squadron in the RAF.'

One honorary member of the squadron, Lt H. Uhr, a *Luftwaffe* GCI controller, '...spent sometimes up to seventy-four hours a week in our concrete castle watching the radar sweeping clockwise on the large horizontal 21in console for hours on end. The only joy and an adrenalin kick comparable only to the best excitement nature can offer was to get to control a mission of Hunters. Either doing some PIs, chasing some intruders (most of them innocent light planes who got lost in the ADIZ) or patrolling in view of contrails of a pair of MiG-17 on the other side of the "curtain" only some 15 to 20 miles apart. Controlling Hunters at high altitude was the uppermost challenge. You had to be precise or you failed...So finally, on 3 December 1962 I controlled my last pair of Hunters, Mission 24 intercepted two other Gutersloh pairs, Missions 23 and 25. On 17 December I and my girlfriend were invited to join the gloomy saturnalia honouring the disbanding of the last RAF day-fighter squadron.'

On 18 December, the Squadron Standard, carried by Flt Lt Tite, with Sgts Taylor, Sawyer and Lawson as the escorts, was marched onto the parade ground at Wildenrath. Under the eye of AVM E. Gordon-Jones, CB, CBE, DSO, DFC and Bar, AOC RAF Germany, it was handed over to Fg Off R.M. Bayne of the new 14 (Canberra) Squadron.

NOTES

16   An aircraft carrying out simulated attacks on the formation.

17   Spitfire Mk.IX MK732 eventually found its way back to Holland in the 1990s and was restored to flying condition.

18   Sgt Smith in XJ960, Fg Off Batt in XJ673.

19   Cracroft in XJ642.

20   Sqn Ldr Williams, Fg Off Tite, Flt Lt Preece and Fg Off D. M. Barr.

21   Nattrass in XG131 and Jevons in XJ717.

4

1963–1970

THE CANBERRA

Strike Squadron

Under the 'nuclear tripwire' strategy of the early 1960s, the primary role of NATO air forces in Europe was that of tactical-nuclear strike. To meet its commitment to the Second Allied Tactical Air Force (2 ATAF), RAF Germany provided four English Electric Canberra squadrons, each comprising twelve aircraft, which were based at the four 'Clutch' airfields grouped along the Dutch border. The new 14 Squadron, commanded by Wg Cdr G. Strange was based at Wildenrath, immediately to the west of Mönchengladbach. The other units were based at Geilenkirchen to the south, and Brüggen and Laarbruch to the north. Wg Cdr Strange's unit was as different from its previous incarnation as a Hunter squadron as the preceeding Vampire squadron had been from its Mosquito predecessor. With thirty-four aircrew (including two NCO aircrew), the unit was twice the size of the Hunter squadron and its role as a bomber squadron contrasted with that of the Hunter day fighters.

In the event of war during the late 1940s or early 1950s, NATO bombers might have flown at medium or high-level to attack targets in Eastern Europe, but by the late 1950s surface-to-air missiles (SAMs) and supersonic fighter aircraft had effectively closed off that airspace. Instead, NATO aircraft would have to fly at low-level to penetrate the Warsaw Pact defences, keeping below the engagement height of radar-guided missiles. To meet this new requirement, the Canberra, which had originally been designed as a high-level bomber, was redesigned specifically to fulfil the low-level tactical nuclear strike and interdictor roles. This variant, the Canberra B(I)8, was identifiable by an offset fighter-style 'bubble canopy' which gave the pilot the all-round view needed for low-level operations. A glazed nose cone also gave the navigator, lying prone in the nose of the aircraft, a good forward view. As a strike aircraft the Canberra was armed with the US-supplied 1,650lb Mk.7 nuclear bomb and as an interdictor, a gun pack housing four

20mm Hispano cannon was fitted in the bomb bay. For most of the time the squadron was declared to SACEUR as a strike unit and the routine flying reflected that role, but for one month each year the crews would practice the interdiction role.

Although flying at low-level provided a means for a strike aircraft to penetrate the Warsaw Pact air defences, it presented another problem on reaching the target: how to ensure that the aircraft was far enough from the nuclear explosion to ensure that it was not destroyed by its own weapon. The method used in the Canberra for the Mk.7 bomb was the Honeywell Low Altitude Bombing System (LABS) which provided the aircraft with a stand-off range of some 7 miles by means of throwing (tossing) the bomb forwards towards the target, while the bomber escaped in the opposite direction. The LABS comprised an artificial horizon, which could cope with extreme attitudes (most instruments of the day could not) and a flight-director system, which gave pitch and roll commands to the pilot by means of two needles on the artificial horizon. 'In the Canberra LABS System,' recalled Flt Lt J.H. Hanson, 'the distance to the target from the pull up point was based on 435kt IAS. It was then necessary to find an Initial Point (IP) and measure the distance to determine the time from IP to pull up. This time was set on the LABS instrument timer. Navigation to the IP was done visually by navigator and pilot. When the navigator called 'IP IP Now' the pilot triggered the LABS instrument, which ran down the time to pull up, at which point the horizontal needle dropped and was brought back to the horizontal by pulling back and applying 3.4g. The vertical needle aided wings level during pull up. At approximately 60° pitch a red light illuminated indicating 'Bomb Gone'. Passing the vertical, the artificial horizon would topple and swiftly re-erect to show the aircraft coming down, inverted at the top of the loop. The navigator would start timing from pull up and at 21 seconds would yell "ROLL!" At this point the aircraft was going down at approximately 20° and was recovered by a half-barrel roll to get down to low-level. The alternate release was straight up, red light on at 90°. It was there to be used if the IP was missed. I liked to use it on exercise against airfields, as I could fly a no notice arrival down the runway before pull up.'

The LABS delivery could place a bomb within a few hundred yards of the target, which was deemed close enough for a nuclear weapon, but clearly even this degree of accuracy depended very much on the ability of the pilot to follow the LABS profile accurately; the survival of both aircraft and crew also depended on the pilot's ability to fly the recovery manoeuvre safely and consistently. Practice was the secret to success in both of these cases. The bombing range at Nordhorn offered some opportunity to carry out LABS deliveries, but crews often took advantage of the long range of the Canberra and the much better weather factor in Libya to use the ranges at Tarhuna and El Adem. During most months a small detachment of one or two aircraft spent a week at Idris, near Tripoli, for intense LABS practice. A measure of the intensity of that practice can be gauged from Flt Lt Hanson's forty-one LABS runs in 8 days during a detachment to Idris in November 1962. When new crews arrived on the squadron they were quickly checked out to ensure that they were competent to fly the LABS manoeuvre and then they were dispatched at an early opportunity to do come consolidated practice on the Libyan ranges. Once they were judged to be competent they became qualified to take their place on the QRA roster.

An English Electric Canberra B(I)8 on nuclear Quick Reaction Alert (QRA) at Wildenrath in the late 1960s. Almost continuously, from January 1963 until October 1986, 14 Squadron mounted QRA, with nuclear-armed aircraft ready to launch within 15 minutes. (John Galyer)

Each strike squadron held two nuclear-loaded aircraft at 10 minute readiness 'Quick Reaction Alert' (QRA) for immediate response in case of surprise attack by the Soviets. In terms of the tedious duty of manning QRA, this aspect was much like the Battle Flight commitment for the fighter squadron. Twice or three times a month, each crew took their turn of a 24 hour duty in the QRA 'cage' – a wired-off area near the runway threshold containing a very basic weather shelter for the aircraft and a hut which provided equally basic accommodation for the crews and the USAF Alert Duty Officer (ADO). The nuclear weapon remained under the custody of the ADO until the aircraft was formally released by SACEUR. Every procedure involving a nuclear weapon or strike-loaded aircraft was subject to the 'two man principle' in which no one person ever had sole access to the system: around the loaded aircraft a 'No Lone Zone' (which could only be entered by a minimum of two authorized personnel) was strictly enforced by an armed team of RAF and USAF police. Although the Canberra would only launch in the event of real war, exercise alerts were called frequently to ensure that every aspect of the pre-release sequence worked as it should. When the alert klaxon sounded, '...all Hell broke loose,' recorded Flt Lt P. J. Wilkinson. 'While the ADO hustled back to his cubicle, the crews would run towards their aircraft, careful to stop well clear of the No-Lone line, given the proven trigger-happiness of the USAF police. Once the ADO arrived at the shelter, he and the navigator would go beneath the aircraft, agree the contents of the message and make the appropriate authentications on the coding machine. Pilot strapped in and poised his fingertips over twin starter buttons, with his other hand prepared to throw the battery master switch. The aircraft was set and remained on alert with all starter systems selected, only requiring battery power to be connected to make it ready for start and scramble.'

Although the role of a Canberra squadron in Germany differed fundamentally from that of a Hunter squadron, there were many similarities in lifestyle for squadron personnel. The QRA roster was much like the Battle Flight equivalent and the many no-notice readiness exercises such as 'Exercise Quicktrain' were exactly the same. The other routine exercises, too, were the same ones, except that aircrew saw them from the opposite perspective. While the Hunter pilot saw 'Exercises Amled', 'Co-op' or 'Cat & Mouse' as opportunities to intercept other aircraft, the Canberra crew looked upon the same exercises as being the target for fighter aircraft. Like the Hunters, the Canberras took part each month in exercises like the cross-servicing 'Exercise Round Robin', but they also ventured further afield. 'Exercise Southern Ranger' involved two or three aircraft each month flying to Luqa, Akrotiri or Gibraltar, while an 'Exercise Extended Southern Ranger' featured even more distant destinations. For example, in January 1963, Fg Offs R.G. Valentine and M.D. Rossie flew to Khormaksar (Aden) via Akrotiri and Bahrain, returning via Khartoum, El Adem and Luqa; the following month Fg Offs R.T.V. Kyrke and M. Wright flew to Nairobi.

Taceval 1963

January 1963 saw arctic conditions throughout Europe, and layers of snow and black ice left the runway at Wildenrath unusable for the first week of the month. 'My first Christmas in Germany was the very cold winter of 1962/3,' recalled SAC J. Newland, 'youth was still on my side, so the enormous areas of snow cleared from taxiways was not a problem. My security clearance took forever, but somehow I was locally cleared to break ice off the QRA aircraft with the most-used of ground crew tools, the broom handle. This was the last of the days when QRA aircraft where still parked without a shelter, and the barbed wire seemed to mock us in that cold. Stand-by ground crew had to carry a pistol, on the other side of your belt was the pouch for the six rounds, to be kept in the plastic bag. A chargeable offence if taken out of their wrapping!' Thanks to hard working snow-clearance parties the runway was eventually cleared on 8 January. This proved fortuitous as 'Exercise Taceval' was called at 06:00hrs on that day. The exercise got off to a very slow start: personnel, some of whom had to travel in from the outskirts of Köln (Cologne), found it difficult to get to the squadron site in the wintry conditions and the low temperatures made it difficult to load the aircraft. Even in good conditions loading the Mk.7 bomb into the Canberra was a complex operation: '...the American nuclear weapon the aircraft carried fitted snugly into the bomb bay of the aircraft, but,' explained SAC Newland, 'was too big to load as the fuselage clearance was too low. So all trades mucked in, as we had to manually jack the aircraft up so the weapon could be slid in from rear into the aircraft's bomb bay.' However, eventually all the aircraft were readied and twelve sorties were flown with practice bombs. All the crews were in early the following morning in readiness for a mass launch, a practice of the release procedures for the final stage of nuclear war – the Composite Launch Sequence Plan (CLSP) in which all of NATO's nuclear assets would be launched against pre-planned targets. Once airborne the aircraft routed through Nordhorn range where they carried out a First Run Attack (FRA) LABS profile, releasing a 25lb practice bomb. On such occasions crews felt that their reputation and honour were on the line. The morning of 9 January was very foggy and Flt Lt Hanson, flying with Fg Off E.B. Gorman recalls, '…heard the crew in front of us abort their run, unable to see the initial timing point. They were at 250ft, as I should have been, but I had eased up to 400ft and got a better slant range [visibility]. Ted saw the IP and up we went. The winds aloft cancelled out any errors and we heard the range safety officer's magic words 'DH'[22] We had won the Sweep! In 5 years of LABS bombing I never had a DH before or after this one.'

Another Taceval followed on 28 March, this time an afternoon alert on a much warmer day. The QRA aircraft were ready to launch within 15 seconds and the rest of the aircraft were loaded within 2½ hours. Once the aircraft were declared ready, the nuclear weapons were downloaded and replaced by practice bombs in preparation for the CLSP launch the following morning, which followed the same pattern as the previous Tavecal, 2 months previously.

Meanwhile, routine flying continued. Because of the poor weather in Germany at the beginning of the year, Sqn Ldr Smith ran a small detachment in Malta for the first 14 days of February to give new crews an opportunity to continue with their conversion to the Canberra B(I)8. From Luqa they could fly high and low-level sorties and use the range facilities at Tarhuna. Back at Wildenrath, the weather improved sufficiently in the latter half of the month for low flying in both north and south Germany, and also for night flying.

A last salute to 88 Squadron was held in the officers' mess on 11 April. Amid much shouting and free-flowing beer, all the officers who had served with 88 Squadron were presented with a squadron tankard. The final link with 88 Squadron was broken 6 months later, on 30 October, with the death of 'Sqn Ldr Fred Aldrovandi', who had been 88 Squadron's mascot. 'Fred' was a rock python (reflecting the snake in 88 Squadron's badge) who enjoyed a pampered existence, which included receiving the lunchtime treat of a white mouse purchased from Harrods once a month! Over his career 'Fred' had accumulated a large number of flying hours, most of them fast asleep thanks to the low temperatures in a Canberra at high-level.

The first round of the RAF Germany LABS bombing competition, which was contested by the four strike squadrons, began in April 1963. In each round, a team of three aircraft from each unit flew a low-level route and carried out a timed first-run LABS attack at Nordhorn. Points were awarded for time to get airborne, navigational accuracy (judged from photographs taken by the crew of their pre-determined turning points) and the results of the LABS attack. On 8 April, Wg Cdr Strange and Fg Off Kyrke both scored maximum points for their navigation and were pleased with their bomb scores of 800yd and 200yd respectively. Unfortunately, the squadron's third aircraft became unserviceable before take off, so it scored no points and at the end of the round the squadron was lying in third place. Subsequent rounds followed in June (which 14 Squadron won with three bombs within 250yd) and August, when the squadron was represented by Fg Offs D. Gillanders and R. Wheeler and Flt Lt R.

Hornsey. The competition was formalized the following year into the Salmond Trophy, an annual navigation and bombing competition between all RAF Germany ground-attack squadrons.

Exercise Orange Grove

On 11 April, the squadron started its month-long annual refresher in the interdictor role; LABS equipment was removed from the aircraft and gun packs and underwing pylons were fitted. Flying in pairs the crews re-familiarized themselves with close and battle formation. However, the main part of the interdictor training was 'Exercise Orange Grove', an armament practice camp (APC) using the ranges in Cyprus and Libya. The advance party, comprising Flt Lt Hanson and Fg Off Gorman set off for Cyprus in a Canberra T4 on 18 April and they were followed 4 days later by six Canberra B(I)8s and a Bristol Britannia carrying the remaining squadron personnel. The squadron set up in Number 4 dispersal at Akrotiri, where two wooden huts provided accommodation for ground and aircrew. By 24 April, they were ready to start flying. The first wave were airborne at 07:00hrs to carry out shallow dive-bombing attacks on the raft targets in the sea on the Episkopi range; later in the morning strafing was carried out at Larnaca. By the afternoon the temperature had risen and the air was considered to be too bumpy for weaponry, so this time was reserved for sunbathing and recreation! This pattern of flying in the morning and free time in the afternoon was continued through the detachment. The ground crew enjoyed the detachment, memorable for SAC Newland for, '...its Mediterranean warmth, local interest and diversions. The aircraft had gun packs now so when marshalling you stood on the inside of the turn. Going with a crew onto the range was exciting as the aircraft dropped toward the target; the fact the pilot was the only one with an ejector seat did not really hit home for many years, but it was fun!' Four night-bombing sorties were also flown at El Adem range on 30 and 31 April by Flt Lt Valentine and Fg Off Kyrke. Operating as a pair, the lead aircraft dropped a 4.5-inch flare to illuminate the target and the other aircraft then made four bombing passes under its light. Seven more pairs visited El Adem at night during early May and once again the leader illuminated the target by dropping a flare from 8,500ft to allow the Number 2 to attack. On 16 May, live 1,000lb HE bombs were used instead of the usual 25lb practice bombs; the live weapons were dropped in a shallow dive from 3,000ft, releasing at 1,500ft. By this stage of the APC the crews were proficient enough at strafe to use an 'operational pattern', pulling up from low-level rather than flying in an academic circuit. Strafing was not without its risks, though, and Sqn Ldr W.G. Holmes was hit by a ricochet which damaged the leading edge of a wing. Three crews had to return to Wildenrath on 1 May when 14 Squadron took responsibility for a second QRA aircraft, but the rest of the squadron remained in Cyprus until 21 May.

On their return to Wildenrath the Canberras were converted back into the strike role and the squadron soon settled back into the routine of LABS training. Over the summer, a number of less familiar ranges were visited to see if they might be used to provide some variety for LABS work. These included the Dutch range at Vliehors, on the westerly tip of Vlieland island, the French range at Suippes, near Châlons-en-Champagne and Wainfleet in the Wash (Essex). Unfortunately, Vliehors was found to be unsuitable because of its lack of lead-in features and a target that was almost invisible from low-level, but Suippes and Wainfleet were both eminently suitable. In fact the reconnaissance at Suippes proved prescient, as the range would be used later in the year for the Air Forces Central Europe (AFCENT) tactical weapons meet; and Wainfleet was used for LABS practice throughout the summer. Exercises punctuated the routine at Wildenrath, with a station exercise on 10 June and 'Exercise Backlash', which ran between 26 and 28 June. The latter was designed to test the radar defences at Laarbruch, Jever, Brockzetal and Uedem, but it also offered some useful and challenging flying for the Canberra crews, who had to adhere to strict Time Over Target (TOT) specified for each attack in the exercise plan. All the flying was at low-level, flown at 250ft and 300kt, accelerating to 430kt for the attack runs. The exercise also included a night sortie, which was also flown at low-level, although the minimum altitude for this was 500ft. In fact, Canberras routinely practiced night low-level flying, with the only restrictions being to remain in the Low Flying Areas (LFA) and to fly at 500ft above the highest obstacle.

Although crews could fly around Germany at low level in darkness with reasonable accuracy, visual navigation at night could never be precise enough to make a successful LABS attack. Night low flying was, therefore, essentially an interdiction procedure and even then it depended on some form of illumination over the target; this was provided by dropping flares, just as crews had practiced at El Adem during 'Exercise Orange Grove'. However, those flares were old wartime stock and they were coming to the end of their shelf life. A possible replacement for these ageing pyrotechnics was the more modern Swedish-manufactured 8-inch Lepus flare, which produced a dazzling 2.8 million candle power light. Flt Lt Hanson was sent to Boscombe Down[23] on 15 July, along with a crew from 16 Squadron, to take part in an evaluation of the Lepus flare. Over the next fortnight, followed by another 10 days in August, the two aircraft practised night attacks, with the 16 Squadron aircraft leading and dropping the flare from a toss delivery and the 14 Squadron aircraft making shallow dive attacks under its light. Flt Lt Hanson 'ran to the target at 350kt and 3,000ft. I watched the lead aircraft pull up and when the flare ignited, I pulled up and rolled left, identified, and in a shallow dive, dropped a 25lb [practice bomb] on the target. Recovered, reversed and completed a second attack before the flare reached the ground. I remember night being turned into day with three million candle power floating down whilst I dived below it and managed two attacks before the flare hit the ground and the light went out. And how! Back into a black night with night vision completely destroyed. I just made sure that my aircraft was going up! On the first attempt at dropping, the parachute did not open and the flare did not ignite but just fell to the ground. On the next night, the flare ignited but, just as I got close to flying under it, the parachute failed and it all fell to the ground. The nights of the 25 and 26 July were successful when I managed two attacks and dropped two 25lb [bombs] each night.'

Various exercises followed through the autumn, including routine ones such as 'Round Robin', 'Quicktrain', 'Actfast' and 'Exercise Cat & Mouse'. On the latter, which was held on one day nearly every month, the squadron provided high-level targets for fighter aircraft, including being intercepted by Javelins over Köln on 3 September. The strike exercise 'Exercise Leon Vert', which started on 10 September, initially followed the familiar pattern of any other strike exercise: the squadron personnel reported to the squadron hangar and the aircraft were strike-loaded and brought to readiness during the day. However, there was a new twist when four aircraft were dispersed to the RNLAF base at Gilze-Rijn. Simulated strike sorties were launched from Wildenrath and Gilze-Rijn at 05:30hrs the following morning against targets in southern Germany. During the morning, Gilze-Rijn was 'exercise destroyed', forcing the aircraft that had started the day there to divert elsewhere and make arrangements to continue operations. Meanwhile, back at Wildenrath the flying continued until after midnight.

Routine LABS training continued through the autumn and winter, both in northern Europe and through a rolling detachment of two aircraft at Idris. One newly-arrived crew was Flt Lt Wilkinson and Flt Lt N. O'Shea for whom, '…the need to be LABS-qualified was overriding, and we had a hectic Sunday, December 15, when the weather cleared for long enough for our flight commander, Sqn Ldr Bill Holmes, to join us in a [Canberra]T4 and check me out on the LABS manoeuvre overhead base. Paddy [O'Shea]sat in the back and kept a watchful eye on it all, paying very careful attention to the progress of each recovery and descent to low level. A 35 minute sortie gave time for six manoeuvres, and that earned the necessary tick in the box. Quick cup of coffee and then into a B(I)8 for a run to the sun – in this case the sun of Libya and the RAF base at Idris, south of Tripoli. There, the temperature was a pleasant 24°C and the skies were clear with unlimited visibility. Just the job for the next three days when we flew thirteen sorties to, from, and through Tarhuna Range. Each sortie comprised the brief transit to the range area, a first run through to check conditions on the range and in the aircraft's systems, then four LABS attacks and back to base for a very quick reload. Sometimes this was done with engines running but, however it was done, it gave the crew just time for a quick can of orange juice and off again for the next batch of four bombs. The range was just a few miles away from Idris, and the terrain was typically desert with very few features to orientate on. There was one exception or, rather, two. As the aircraft rolled right way up in the descent from the top of the loop, you looked ahead for two distinctively conical hills about 15 miles back toward the range entry point. Steering to pass between those meant that a 180° turn once clear of them would bring us back on to the correct approach line for the run to the target. Inevitably, I suppose, given their shape, those hills were known to all range users as 'the tits'.

'Three crews had flown down to Idris in two aircraft. The regular navigator maintained his prone position on his couch for the sortie, and the spare man sat on a miniature seat (a sort of metal-encased cushion on the floor against the aft cockpit bulkhead, optimistically named the 'crash seat', but with very little chance of surviving such an event) positioned just below and to the right of the operating pilot's right buttock. In the event of dire emergency there was going to be a little congestion at the doorway! Whatever the discomfort, it did mean that there was always a spare crew on the ground while flying was in progress. A tossed coin would decide which one of the pair would assist out at the range, adding manpower to the range safety team in the control tower out in the desert. There was always a chance to visit and cheer him up during the customary 'height check' pass over the tower when joining the range.'

When the weather was not good enough for low-flying in Germany, the squadron flew medium-level transits to and from the Low Flying Areas in the UK in order to low fly in Scotland or Northern Ireland. These sorties, known as 'high-low-highs,' included interdictor sorties which were flown through the winter months. On 7 November, two aircraft participated in 'Exercise Roulette' which involved flying against army units deployed in the hills near Holzminden to the east of Paderborn. In the following month, formation sorties were flown to Scotland against targets near Perth. The last of these was flown as a three-ship on 31 December, for there was only the briefest break during the festive season. In early 1964, various air defence exercises gave crews an opportunity for fighter affiliation against types such as RDAF F-86s, RAF Javelins and Lightnings ('Exercise Kingpin' in January), or RCAF Sabres and USAF North American F-100 Super Sabres ('Exercise Co-op' in February), but most of the flying was spent at low level in Germany or visiting the range at Tarhuna. In the newly-instigated Salmond Trophy, 14 Squadron came a close second to the eventual winners, 213 Squadron, after unexploded practice bombs reduced the team's score. A month of interdictor training culminated in a firepower demonstration for the C-in-C RAF Germany at Nordhorn on 19 March. All of the RAF Germany ground-attack squadrons took part and 14 Squadron noted with some satisfaction that their strafing scores were better than both Hunter squadrons!

Tactical Weapons Meet 1964

On 13 April, Wg Cdr K.B. Rogers, DFC, AFC took command of 14 Squadron. The routine of early summer was punctuated by Taceval, which was called late in the evening of 2 July. The aircraft loading continued through the night and a wave of eight aircraft accompanied by an evaluation team member, was flown on the Friday. After a weekend break, the exercise continued on 6 July with another wave of eight aircraft carrying out a first run LABS attack at Nordhorn.

At the end of the following week, two aircraft and crews joined two more Canberras from 3 Squadron to make up the RAF team for the AIRCENT tactical weapons meet. This annual event, which had been started in 1962, was a weaponry competition between 2 ATAF and 4 ATAF. The airfield at Chaumont, to the east of Troyes in France, was re-opened for the 14 days of the competition. Apart from the RAF's Canberras, the 2 ATAF team comprised F-84Fs of the Dutch and Belgian Air Forces, while the 4 ATAF team consisted of Canadian CF-104s, F-84s from the *Luftwaffe* and F-100Ds from the USAF and French Air Force. *Flight* magazine reported, '...the American half of the Suippes range, between Metz and Rheims, was used for weapons firing. Although only a few minutes' flying time from Chaumont, aircraft took circuitous routes to the range, passing over navigation check-points on the way. These points were manned by NATO judges, who awarded marks for accurate arrival times.' Fortunately, the 14 Squadron crews had visited Suippes periodically during the year and their familiarity paid dividends: although 4 ATAF were the overall winners of the weapons meet, the 14 Squadron Canberra crews distinguished themselves by scoring a high proportion of the total points achieved by the 2 ATAF team. It is interesting to note that even in 1964 *Flight* took the view, '...despite [their] accuracy it became quite apparent that the time for a Canberra replacement is near.' In fact, it would be another 6 years before the Canberra was replaced.

August was time for the annual APC, but with political difficulties in Cyprus, the detachment was held instead in Malta. Six aircraft and fifteen crews deployed to Luqa on 10 August and over the next two weeks bombing sorties were flown at Tarhuna and

A 14 Squadron Canberra B(I)8 arrives at Chaumont for the AIRCENT tactical weapons meet, July 1964. (14 Squadron Association)

El Adem. Flt Lt Wilkinson recalled, '…the sortie pattern was regular: leave Luqa with four practice bombs, fly direct to the range, carry out shallow dive attacks and land at Idris for a refuelling and rearming turnround. Much hotter than on my first trip there in December 1963, so it was essential to employ sun shelters over the cockpit during the turnround, which was carried out quickly but not quickly, enough to stop temperatures in the cockpit from rising to alarming levels. Getting back in for the second sortie was uncomfortable and it was essential not to delay too long between engine start and getting airborne. Once up, the cooling system of the B(I)8 was efficient, although occasionally disconcerting, as large hailstone-sized chunks of ice blasted out of the louvres all round the cockpit. Four more attacks on the dive targets and then climb out for the return to Luqa, taking on average around an hour for the whole sortie. The last day's flying of the week's deployment saw us dropping, not the standard small practice bombs, but the 'operational' weapon – the 1,000lb bomb. These were dropped from the wing pylons, so just two attacks. There was a noticeable lurch as each bomb left the pylon, and the resulting tower of sand from the desert floor was sobering. There were few volunteers to man the range safety tower for those passes.' The range details on El Adem range also included night bombing under flares which Flt Lt Wilkinson described as, '…what I still recall as the most hairy attack profile ever…we had to drop our own flares with sufficient accuracy to be able to see the target in their glare, then whip round into a 30° dive towards the target ready for bomb release and climb away. I was only too aware that the flares I had dropped were somewhere just above me and falling fast. So, right eye swivelled upwards and left eye downwards at a speck of white in the sand, and go for it.'

On return from Malta, five crews led by Sqn Ldr Holmes detached to Wyton to work up for a tactical display at the SBAC Air Show at Farnborough. After three practices flown in the first days of the month, the 'Airborne Assault Demonstration' involving all three services was performed daily at the show from 7 to 13 September. SAC Newland remembers, '…was lucky enough to be on the squadron detachment to RAF Wyton for the Farnborough Air Show, managing to get onto an aircraft for the mock-attack demonstration. Somewhere in the press photos I am shown waving at the crowds during the flypast.' The demonstration starting with a 'softening up' attack by a flight of Hunters, followed by 14 Squadron's four Canberras, and then eight Supermarine Scimitars and eight De Havilland Sea Vixens from the Fleet Air Arm (RN). An 'armada' of Westland Wessex helicopters then brought in troops to secure the landing zone and in the grand finale, six Armstrong Whitworth Argosy transports delivered the main force of troops and their equipment. The correspondent of *Flight* magazine enthused that it had been, '…undoubtedly the biggest display of its kind yet staged in Britain' and that it had filled, '…ten crowded, fast flying minutes.'

The Indonesian Confrontation

By mid-1964, the western hemisphere was locked into political and military stalemate by the 'Cold War', but on the other side of the world, the status quo in the post-colonial Far East was fast unravelling. The Gulf of Tonkin incident in August heralded the beginning of US involvement in Vietnam and, further south, an armed revolt in Brunei was threatening British interests in the region. Indonesian-backed rebels, opposed to the amalgamation of the northern provinces of the island of Borneo into the newly-established state of Malaysia, had started an insurrection against the Sultan earlier in the year. The British were quick to reinforce Brunei, but the situation swiftly degenerated into a covert war between British and Commonwealth forces and those of Indonesia. Although hostilities were largely restricted to Borneo itself, the Indonesians attempted to escalate the situation in September 1964 by landing paratroops on mainland Malaya. All of these events must have seemed a long way from Wildenrath where, as Sqn Ldr P.F. Rogers said, '…cocooned in Germany without TV or regular access to English newspapers, we were little more than vaguely aware of Sukarno's sabre rattling.' Even if members of the squadron knew of RAF Germany's commitment to the Tactical Air Reserve (TAR) they would not have guessed that it might be called upon that autumn to reinforce the Far East. However, the developments in Malaya triggered contingency plans at HQ RAF Germany and in turn, on 16 September, 14 Squadron was tasked to convert five Canberras to the interdictor role. On this occasion no further instructions were received, so the aircraft were stood down 6 days later and returned to the LABS role; routine flying continued through into October.

On the afternoon of Friday, 23 October, Sqn Ldr Rogers was the only senior officer left on the squadron: Wg Cdr Rogers was attending a meeting in London and Sqn Ldrs Holmes and R.A. Stubings were away from Wildenrath on an 'Extended Southern Ranger' exercise to Rhodesia. After locking up the squadron office, Sqn Ldr Rogers was in the mess bar enjoying 'Happy Hour' when, '…halfway through my first Heineken I was called to the telephone. OC Operations Wing (Wg Cdr Bill Hedley) asked me to come down to his office where there was a signal I should see. His tone of voice suggested now, not when I had finished my beer. The signal, from HQ RAFG, was short and to the point. The squadron was relieved of its nuclear commitment forthwith; four aircraft fitted with gun packs and tip tanks were to take off at 08:30hrs on Monday for an unspecified

Indonesian Confrontation 1964

location in the Far East; a route-support Britannia would be provided for an unspecified number of ground crew. The operation would be known as 'Operation Accordion'. After a hectic weekend preparing the aircraft and personnel, the last airtest was completed at 03:00hrs on the Monday morning. At 07:30hrs on 26 October, four Canberra B(I)8s from 3 Squadron left Geilenkirchen, led by their squadron commander Wg Cdr J. Field, bound for Akrotiri. An hour later 14 Squadron's four-ship departed from Wildenrath to follow the same route. Unfortunately, things soon started to go wrong and Flt Lt Hanson had to return to Wildenrath with a fuel pump problem. The three remaining aircraft safely reached Cyprus where they met up with the 3 Squadron crews and Wg Cdr Field, who would command the Canberra detachment in the Far East.

Flt Lt Hanson rejoined the others at Akrotiri the next day and all four 14 Squadron aircraft continued eastwards for what was, for Sqn Ldr Rogers, '…one of my favourite legs (when the weather is good that is): along the length of Turkey, right-hand down over Lake Urmia and south through Iran into the Gulf and then to Muharraq (3 hours, 45 minutes). A quick turn-around and a short flight (1 hour, 25 minutes) over the Empty Quarter brought us to Masirah for a night stop. This was before the runway was lengthened at Masirah and since we were operating close to our maximum all up weight, it was imperative to get airborne when the ambient temperature was at its lowest, ie about dawn. This we did, but on the climb out Tony Salter reported a No 3 tank pump failure. So, bearing in mind our instructions to stick together, the sortie was abandoned and we returned to Masirah. The Canberra B(I)8 had no fuel dump facility and we had to burn-off for about 90 minutes before getting down to a safe landing weight. We set up a 'racetrack' down the length of the island, at the western end of which were the interesting ruins of a fort, and out to sea to visit a 'supertanker' heading west. We tried, unsuccessfully, to raise it on 121.5 [kilohertz, the international distress frequency] to explain why it was being beaten up every 10 minutes by a long line of Canberras.'

The Salter's aircraft was repaired by the squadron's ground crew, who diverted to Masirah while en-route to Tengah, and it was ready for another attempt the following morning. On Wednesday, 28 October, the Canberras set off again and after a 4 hour flight across the Indian Ocean they reached Gan in the Maldives.

'Next morning,' continued Sqn Ldr Rogers, 'the weather forecast en-route and the terminal forecast for Butterworth were thoroughly unpleasant to say the least... cumulonimbus [cloud] tops up to 50,000ft lay across our track and the Butterworth forecast was 600ft [cloud base] in heavy rain. With the extra ironmongery we were carrying I do not think we got much above 41 to 42,000ft: right in the cumulonimbus tops. The turbulence was bearable but the fish bowl effect, a complete white-out, was not amusing. I logged 1 hour and 50 minutes of actual instrument flying. The weather forecast from Gan was spot on: 600ft in rain, but Butterworth approach radar had packed it in for the day and dusk was upon us. As usual, the leader's fuel state was the highest and so I was the last to land. We kissed the concrete after the least enjoyable 5 hours flying that I can remember. We were met in dispersal by a 3 Squadron crew, who had flown over from Kuantan bearing Wg Cdr Field's compliments. "Would we do a quick turn round and join him at Kuantan asap?" The lack of enthusiasm evident on the grey faces around me, and my own fatigue, led me to decline the offer.'

On the following day, Sqn Ldr Rogers led his formation on the short flight to Kuantan where they joined the rest of the RAFG detachment. The five crews from 14 Squadron[24] formed 'B' flight of the Canberra detachment with the five crews from 3 Squadron[25] making up 'A' flight. Kuantan, on the east coast of Malaya, some 200 miles north of Singapore, boasted only very basic facilities – the relatively short north/south runway was surrounded by jungle and the accommodation was all under tents. It had been activated 12 months previously for use by a detachment of Canberras from 45 Squadron when the confrontation had intensified. The airfield was defended by 40mm Bofors anti-aircraft guns and slit trenches were dug near the tents to provide some protection in case of air attack. 'Living conditions at Kuantan were pleasant – even enjoyable,' recalled Sqn Ldr Rogers. 'We slept two to a tent; mine was shared with the civilian 'met' officer seconded from HQ FEAF. The field kitchen fed us well, although the evening meal, high tea, was a little earlier than most of us were used to. There were

The western dispersal at Kuantan airfield, taken by Flt Lts J.H. Hanson and N. O'Shea on 1 November 1964. Five of the detachment's Canberras can be seen on the circular pans and another is on the taxiway. (Peter Rogers)

open-air showers a short stroll south of the tents and chemical toilet latrines a little further south. As an aside, the stores-issue toilet paper was a little too fragile for the high-humidity circumstances, but copies of *The Straits Times*, purloined from Tengah, proved to have excellent wet strength. The officers' mess tent was well-equipped, although it blew down during one of the regular evening thunderstorms.' Rogers also noted that, 'Beer re-supplies (the local Tiger Beer) were regular and we had no cause to broach our emergency liquor/stock.'

After a day to settle into their new home the Canberra crews started flying on 3 November. All sorties from Kuantan were flown in pairs at low level. Sqn Ldr Rogers soon found, '…one significant hazard in operating the Canberra B(I)8 in the hot parts was the risk of heat exhaustion or dehydration while preparing to fly. The 'bubble' canopy had no form of ventilation and the pilot broiled until the aircraft became airborne and the air conditioning cut in. We established a Standard Operating Procedure (SOP) which put a 5 minute limit on the time spent in the cockpit on the ground; if you were not airborne (or could not get airborne) within 5 minutes of getting into the cockpit, you had to abandon the attempt.' Flt Lt Hanson remembered, '…it was north-east Monsoon time so the morning flights were flown in good visibility, below solid stratus. It was interesting operating over the

Members of 14 Squadron (RAF) greet crews from 14 Squadron (RNZAF) at Kuantan on 9 November 1964 in front of one of the latter's Canberra B(I)12 aircraft. The New Zealanders were based at Kuching during the 'Indonesian Confrontation'. Third from left is Flt Lt C.P. Manville, then Flt Lt E.G. Coppard, then Sqn Ldr P.F. Rogers. (Peter Rogers)

jungle, just above treetop height with the radar altimeter showing at least 100ft. I crossed one or two dark brown rivers with a 'V' wake from some aquatic resident clearly visible.' Most low-level routes included a bombing or strafe pass at China Rock, a small island some 25 miles east of Singapore, and a refuelling stop at Tengah. Here, according to Sqn Ldr Rogers, '…with half the V-Force at Tengah in addition to its normal complement of Canberras (45 Squadron), Javelins and Hunters, parking space was at a premium. However, we negotiated space for two of our aircraft every night on the grounds that it would give crews a break from the rigours of tent life and field kitchen food. In practice, of course, it gave crews the opportunity to grab a cab and head for downtown Singapore and the delights of Bougis Street.' Despite the practical difficulties of operating in tropical conditions a long way from home, the only safety incident occurred on 10 November when the port main wheel of a 3 Squadron aircraft[26] collapsed at Kuantan after landing, just as the 14 Squadron crew, Flt Lt P. Marsh and Flt Lt M. Grange, taxied clear of the runway. Happily the crew was unhurt and found to be blame free, although the aircraft was badly damaged.

Apart from the 'flag waving' exercise of deploying Canberras to Kuantan and being seen to carry out an intensive-flying programme over Malaysia, there was also a requirement to make contingency plans in case of open hostilities with the Indonesians.

The Canberra detachment at Kuantan was tasked with planning an attack by six aircraft on a remote airfield in Java. However, when Sqn Ldr Rogers, who would lead the operation, started looking at the details he found that there were practical difficulties: '…the only target intelligence that could be provided was a vertical view, taken in 1945 from 30,000ft, which merely showed an anonymous jungle clearance. We were asked to imagine a single concrete runway and an ASP loaded with an assortment of Soviet aircraft.' On the other hand there were some unorthodox intelligence sources for other possible targets. Flt Lt Hanson recalled, '…some Decca engineers [were] called in to brief us on the siting of some radar dishes that they had just finished installing near Medan'.

Part of the SEATO response to the 'Indonesian Confrontation' was the deployment of 14 Squadron (RNZAF) to Labuan, just off Borneo, in October 1964. Coincidentally, the New Zealand squadron also flew the Canberra interdictor, although their B(I)12 version had further refinements over the B(I)8, including an autopilot, a radio compass and a fan in the cockpit! Both detachments tried to arrange a meet-up and the OC of 14 Squadron (RNZAF) was able to fly across to Kuantan to meet with the representatives of 14 Squadron (RAF). After 14 days at Kuantan the RAF Canberras were recalled to Germany and left Malaya on 17 November. A week later all the aircraft had been returned to the LABS role.

Little had happened at Wildenrath during the absence of the 'Operation Accordion' crews: migrating birds had stopped low flying in Germany and in any case flying was severely restricted because of the depleted manpower and poor weather. Nevertheless, some 'high-low-high' sorties were flown to the UK. This pattern continued into December. Although the manning and bird-induced problems were largely solved by the end of the year the winter weather remained unkind. A further restriction was caused by political problems in the Middle East which precluded any 'Extended Rangers' through Persia, Turkey and the Sudan, so rangers were limited to the Mediterranean area.

On 21 December, Flt Lt A. Salter and Flt Lt G.A. Taylor were faced with an interesting problem when Air Traffic Control (ATC) reported that something had fallen from their aircraft shortly after take-off. They flew past the tower for a visual inspection and the observers on the ground could see that one of the nosewheels was missing and the remainder of the nose-wheel assembly had been bent backwards at an angle of some 70°. After burning-off fuel they returned to Wildenrath where a foam strip had been laid along the runway. Flt Lt Salter landed the aircraft and held the nose off the runway until 65kt, at which point the remains of the nosegear collapsed. After the aircraft ground to a halt, the crew was able to clamber out unharmed.

APC Akrotiri 1965

Eight days later a round of the inter-squadron bombing competition brought frustration when snow obscured many of the targets; one such was a duck pond, which was invisible under snow and ice. To make matters worse, two aircraft were unable to drop on the range because of the weather. The poor weather continued into January 1965, but at least the routes for 'Extended Rangers' had been re-opened, so a lucky few were able to fly off for some sunshine! The rest of the squadron did not have to wait long for their turn, when they deployed to Akrotiri on 5 February for the year's APC. As in

Two Canberra B(I)8s on the pan at Idris in 1965 – note the mobile sun shelters which gave some relief from the heat of the sun . (Phil Wilkinson)

previous years, the pattern was for waves of four aircraft operating in pairs carrying out shallow dive-bombing at Episkopi, strafing at Larnaca and night bombing at El Adem. 'Every sortie would start and finish in close formation,' recalled Flt Lt Wilkinson. 'The Episkopi targets were so close to the end of the Akrotiri runway that it was almost possible to be in the pattern before the undercarriage was fully locked up. Larnaca range was unique for one feature – the Cypriot scrap merchants who collected up the 20mm shell cases ejected from the gun pack. Given that each of the four Hispano cannons had 550 rounds to fire, a long-range detail could eject a fair weight of brass. The only problem was that these fellows on the ground could not wait until we had finished. As two aircraft joined the range and were allocated their targets from the row of eight that ran along the beach, it was quickly clear to the scrapmen which targets were to be used. Down the track we would fly on the first dummy pass, and by the time we rolled in for the first live shoot, the team were poised underneath, running forward as we opened fire, holding out their wicker baskets. There was a reasonable rate of cash for the scrap per 'oke' (the volume measure that the basket contained). This did occasionally lead to friction down below, as scrap man 'A' accused scrap man 'B' of poaching. Scuffles and knife wielding kept them busy as we pulled out of the dive, received our (invariably excellent) scores from the Range Safety Officer (RSO), and turned downwind for the next pass. All fighting stopped as we came down again, and so it went on. Occasionally, the RSO would feel these chaps were getting too close for comfort to the target array, so one or other of the pair would be called in for a 'discouraging' low pass across the range. Great sport.' A remarkable fact of the detachment, which lasted until the end of the month, was that only one sortie was lost due to unserviceability.

The brisk pace of flying operations continued through the spring and early summer with routine training and the usual minor exercises. Longer-range sorties included LABS training on the range at Tain in north-east Scotland (refuelling at Lossiemouth), and 'Extended Rangers' to Nairobi and Salisbury [Harare]. In April, six crews started working up for a flypast for HM the Queen, who would be visiting RAF Gutersloh the following month. 'The cunning plan,' explained Flt Lt Wilkinson, 'was devised to fly a formation, drawn from every RAFG squadron, over the saluting base at RAF Gutersloh on May 26. The formation would thus range from helicopters and slow movers like the communications squadron's Pembrokes, up to and including the Javelins of 5 and 11 Squadrons. Sandwiched in between were the Canberras of the four strike and three reconnaissance squadrons. Each squadron was to provide a formation of six. Thus something around sixty-five aircraft would be aiming to get to Gutersloh at about the same time.' The work up was not without its moments of excitement and Flt Lt Wilkinson, flying as Number 6, will, '…never forget looking out to starboard and seeing Ken Allan (Number 4) picking up slipstream from Number 2 ahead of him and finding he could not control a roll to port. Fortunately, he could push the stick forward, and as the roll developed he passed under Tony Salter to his immediate left and under me before rising gracefully up alongside on my left!' On the day of the flypast the weather was challenging, but despite the low-cloud base, all went well and the Queen was said to have been pleased with the results.

Summer Exercises

Life on a Canberra squadron in Germany the mid-1960s was certainly both busy and varied: the exercise flying in the second half of the year would be achieved while maintaining the two QRA aircraft as well as mounting regular LABS detachments to Libya and typically two or three 'Extended Rangers' to Aden, Nairobi or Salisbury each month. Other monthly commitments would include 'Exercise Round Robin', cross-servicing sorties and the reaction and generation 'Exercises Quicktrain' and 'Actfast'. The LFAs in Germany were available for daily flying, although the majority of the routine training was flown as 'high-low-high' sorties to the UK.

The summer's undoubted highlight was a squadron exchange with the USAF (Europe)'s 10th Tactical Fighter Squadron based at Hahn. Four Canberras and five aircrews, led by Wg Cdr Rogers, detached to Hahn for 9 days on 16 June. At the same time six F-100D and one two-seat F-100F deployed to Wildenrath. While the social scene was a bit restrained at Hahn, at both bases the flying included back-seat trips for RAF personnel in the F-100F. Fg Off D. Jordan thought it was, '…a good detachment, they allocated several of their pilots to eat/drink with us till all hours, then after we had landed in the morning, they were just going off on their first sortie! I twice flew two flights in a day, a total of ten in 10 days, so quite busy.'

Throughout the rest of the summer the 'exercise season' was in full swing, including 'Exercises Spread Eagle', 'Black Eagle', 'Sky Blue' and a first attempt at working with a Forward Air Controller (FAC). The former exercise, on 1 July, involved three aircraft carrying out 'search and attack' sorties against army units – mostly single missile sites – deployed in the field. The results were encouraging, given the small size of the targets, and the crews enjoyed the variation from more traditional static targets. In fact, army targets provided something of a temptation for those like Fg Off Jordan who enjoyed flying low: on one sortie he flew, '…with Dick Wright when we were given an area to find an army convoy. After a short time within this area we found them, as they stood out so easily, driving along these dirt tracks. Gave them a low buzz and they scattered into the trees. Being army and following rules, they kept their lights on so it was quite easy to track them. I gave their position to the controller and carried on buzzing them. On one pass I mushed a bit and on return the ground crew found some bush particles around the fuel vent which protruded about 6in from the underside of the fuselage – lucky.' The FACs, too, found working with the Canberras a bit of a novelty. On one sortie flown by Fg Off J.T. Galyer, '…the FAC was a Belgian pilot who picked me up early and was directing me to the army when I was bounced by a Dutch F-84: the Belgian then proceeded to help with the evasion 'Reverse now! Go high etc' – it was great stuff, then I took a couple of pictures of tanks and went home.'

'Exercise Black Eagle', starting on 6 July, was a Danish air-defence exercise which comprised low-level sorties in Denmark. Some of these sorties were quite complex, involving attacks against two or three targets in North Denmark and, in two cases, lasting for 3 hours. 'Exercise Sky Blue', which took place a month later was the major NATO air exercise in the central region. It coincided with 3 weeks of interdictor training during which the squadron carried out dive-bombing and strafing at Nordhorn and Helchteren. The latter range in Belgium was only a short distance to the southwest of Wildenrath, but unfortunately the strafing target was considered to be too large (easy to hit) for qualification scores!

The annual Taceval commenced at 05:00hrs on 8 September. After a successful loading phase, six aircraft were sent to drop at Vliehors using the 'alternate' LABS delivery. This profile involved overflying the target and releasing the weapon almost vertically upwards during the LABS manoeuvre and some very good results were obtained during these sorties.

The final exercise of the summer and autumn was 'Exercize Dazzle'. Ten crews and eight aircraft deployed to Akrotiri on 5 October to participate in NATO's major exercise in the eastern Mediterranean. Over the next few days the crews settled in with some trips to Episkopi range, before the exercise proper started on 8 October. Most sorties were flown as a high-level leg outbound before returning at high- or low-level towards Akrotiri for an airfield attack. Akrotiri's defenders included Hunters, Javelins and Lightnings, although on 9 October when Flt Lt Galyer, '…approached[27] Akrotiri ATC was in turmoil as a series of transport command aircraft, at 20 minute intervals, were also arriving on this exercise! A case of left and right hand, as they were not due to arrive until long after we had done our thing. I have no intercept actions recorded so whether the 'trucky' chaps put paid to the defenders getting airborne I cannot recall.'

In contrast to the active summer and autumn, the seasonal weather kept the winter months relatively quiet. The loss of several tour-expired crews at the end of the year and the subsequent influx of inexperienced crews also served to limit the flying

The wreckage of the USAF Consolidated B-24 Liberator Lady be Good *in the southern desert of Libya in February 1966. Locating the B-24 became something of a tradition – as well as a test of navigational skills – for aircraft flying out of El Adem.* (John Galyer)

programme. However, the first major detachment of 1966 was the annual 'Exercise Citrus Grove' APC detachment to Cyprus. Five Canberras, plus a Britannia carrying fifty-eight ground crew and another nineteen aircrew, left Wildenrath for Akrotiri on 8 February. Over the next 4 weeks the Canberras flew twelve sorties a day practicing bombing and gunnery at Larnaca and bombing with 1,000lb bombs under night flares at El Adem. Apart from hosting APCs, Akrotiri was home to four resident Canberra squadrons and rivalry with the visiting RAF Germany squadrons was inevitable. 'The Cyprus-based Canberra crews,' recalled Flt Lt Wilkinson, 'were quick to suggest that the RAF Germany team was unlikely ever to match their skill in locating the wreck of the *Lady be Good*, a USAF Consolidated B-24 Liberator which had crashed in the desert in 1943.' The wreckage of the aircraft was some 350 miles south of El Adem and finding such a small target in the midst of a featureless desert with only a compass and a stopwatch was indeed a challenging test of navigation. On 22 February, Flt Lt B. A. Whitley and Sqn Ldr Stubings took up the challenge on the return leg of their sortie. After refuelling, Whitley and Stubings set off southwards and landed at Akrotiri a few hours later with suitable photographic evidence that they had overflown the *Lady be Good*. After their success, it became routine for crews to return from El Adem on a 'high-low-high' profile via the *Lady be Good* and 100 percent success rate in finding the

Two Canberra B(I)8s at low-level over northern Germany on 10 Jun 1966. Flt Lts P.J. Wilkinson and E.G. Coppard (XM278) lead with Flt Lt J. Parker and Fg Off R.A. Forrester (XM264) and Number 2. (Phil Wilkinson)

B-24 on subsequent sorties said much for the skill of 14 Squadron's crews. In the last week some variation to the range work at El Adem was introduced with control by a FAC. After transiting from Akrotiri, crews started off by flying a 30 minute low-level sortie over Libya before being called in by the FAC to strafe truck targets on the range.

The successful APC finished on 3 March and the squadron returned to the routine of life at Wildenrath. One Canberra[28] was kept in the interdictor fit so that the new crews could continue their work-up. Squadron members also celebrated the unit's 50th Anniversary in April with a boat trip on the Rhine, followed the next evening by a dinner dance at the Bruggen Burg Hotel.

A New Weapon

The summer of 1966 brought a new squadron commander in the person of Wg Cdr R. McA. Furze, AFC and a new strike weapon in the form of the US-supplied 2,100lb Mk.43 nuclear bomb. The conversion to the new weapon took 3 months during which time the squadron was non-operational in the strike role. While ground crews familiarized themselves with the loading procedure for the new weapon, the aircrew had to learn the associated operational techniques. This included a new laydown attack, which was a much more accurate – and less dangerous – profile than the LABS method.

Canberra B(I)8 XM264 over Limassol, Cyprus, on 6 January 1967, flown by Flt Lts J. Sewell and I.R. Brock, en-route to Larnaca range during the annual Armament Practice Camp (APC). The bulge under the belly of the aircraft is the gun pack, mounting four 20mm Hispano cannon; the under-wing pylon for practice bombs is also visible. (Jim Sewell)

The aircraft were fitted with a new Belgian-built SFOM gunsight, which allowed the pilot to select the depression angle for the sighting 'pipper' (previously it had been a fixed sight) which made weapon aiming much easier. As a result of this modification, laydown bombing errors were reduced to 100ft, or ten times more accurate than a LABS delivery. One bonus of the lack of QRA commitment for three months was that all the squadron officers were able to attend a 'dining-in night' on 9 September to which the pilots from the *Luftwaffe* F-104 Starfighter Wing at Buchel had been invited. This was the 'return match' following a visit by 14 Squadron to Buchel in May and a good night was had by all!

The joint RAF/USAF Nuclear Safety Team (NST) which inspected the squadron at the end of October declared the unit operational again and the squadron resumed QRA duties on 4 November. Two station exercises followed in the next 7 days, before the Taceval Team called at Wildenrath at 16:00hrs on 14 November. That evening was spent by the ground crew loading strike weapons on the aircraft in appalling weather while the evaluators examined the aircrews' knowledge of operational procedures.

Poor weather continued through the next day, preventing any range work for the nine aircraft, which were scrambled at first light for a low-level sortie in North Germany. The afternoon wave was completely cancelled, too. On the last day of the exercise, eight aircraft were launched to Wainfleet range. Three of these were recalled by ATC because of the weather conditions over Holland, but five aircraft managed to press on to the range where, despite strong crosswinds and fierce turbulence, they achieved satisfactory scores. The Taceval Team was obviously impressed by what they saw because 14 Squadron was awarded the first '1' or 'Excellent,' assessment of an RAF strike unit.

After concentrating on the strike role for much of the summer and autumn, five aircraft were converted into the interdictor role during December in readiness for the following month's APC. Flying continued throughout December, but the squadron suffered a spate of engine surges and flameouts caused by icing. Although the year ended with the disappointment of losing the finals of the Aircrew Football cup to 213 Squadron by three goals to four, the New Year heralded more cheerful times: everyone had a share of sunshine during January when five aircraft, eighteen aircrew and fifty-eight ground crew deployed to Cyprus for the 'Exercise Citrus Gove' detachment.

Back at Wildenrath, 1967 got off to a fine start, too. Good weather in the first few months meant a busy flying programme, which also included night low flying. A new night low-level route through Benelux was introduced in March, but although the route ran through Vliehors range, night bombing there was not yet approved. On the few days that low flying was not possible, the squadron also started making use of Radar Bombing Scoring Units (RBSU) at Lindholme (South Yorkshire) and Tunby (Lincolnshire). A new site, RAF Dunkeswell in south-west England was established in April, with the callsign 'Cider', and offered another option if the east coast was affected by weather. The usual 'lone ranger' flights were also carried out and during one of these to Gibraltar, Flt Lts Smith and Collins were tasked to find and photograph a Russian trawler.

Among the new crews who started their tour with 14 Squadron over the winter were Flt Lt R.J. Adams, who had previously flown Vampires and Venoms with the squadron at Fassburg in the 1950s, and a 'first-tourist' crew comprising Fg Offs R. N. Swann and M.D. Anderton. The latter crew had something of a baptism of fire on 28 April when they returned from a LABs bombing sortie on Vliehors range: as they set up for an ILS approach at Wildenrath, in thick cloud some 8 miles from runway, the aircraft[29] was struck by lightning. There was a vivid blue flash in the cockpit which temporarily blinded Fg Off Swann, who also received a severe electric shock. Although Swann was able to ask for a radar talkdown, it was Anderton's instructions to his almost incapacitated pilot all the way down to touchdown that enabled them to land safely. Only after landing did the crew discover that the force of the electrical surge had been enough to blow both wing-tip tanks off the aircraft!

Tactical Weapons Meet 1967

The great excitement of the year was the announcement that RAF Wildenrath would host the 6th AFCENT Tactical Weapons Meet (TWM) in June. Furthermore, 14 Squadron would provide all the crews to represent RAF Germany in the 2ATAF team. The six crews[30] were selected at the end of April. Flt Lt Skinner pointed out, '…this gave us about four weeks to choose our aircraft and calibrate the navigation and bombing gear. Each crew was given an aircraft which they flew constantly, logging every slight variation in the equipment under all conditions of flight... Our altimeters were calibrated by photographing all our releases with an aircraft-fitted camera, which gave us very accurate height and bomb trajectory information. Aircraft gunsights were checked daily and every bombing result listed against aircrew and aircraft to detect any idiosyncrasies. Even the plotting of bomb strikes at the range was checked by digging up the numbered bombs and relating the positions to the scores given. Wind corrections were meticulously calculated and re-checked on subsequent flights, until we were satisfied that we had eliminated every possible source of error.'

The visiting teams arrived on 16 June. For the next 14 days, Wildenrath was home to F-84F Thunderstreaks and F-104G Starfighters of the Belgian and Netherlands Air Forces, and F-104G Starfighters of the *Luftwaffe's* North Group (representing 2 ATAF) and Fiat G-91s and Lockheed F-104Gs of the *Luftwaffe* South Group, Lockheed CF-104 Starfighters of the RCAF's 1st Air Division, and USAF McDonnell F-4C Phantoms from UK bases (representing 4 ATAF). A guest team of five French Air Force Dassault Mirage IIIEs added to the diversity.

The competition itself started in earnest on 19 July and Flt Lt Skinner recorded, 'The first two days of the meet were given up mainly to day and night familiarization trips for the visitors... it soon became very apparent that the competition would be very keen...the points gained for conventional missions were continually neck-and-neck between the teams, but 2 ATAF soon established a good lead in the nuclear attack missions, which they successfully held for the remainder of the meet.' In the unofficial competition between the national strike teams, 14 Squadron's crews took an early lead, but the Canadian and USAF crews were close behind. In competing with much the more sophisticated Phantoms and Starfighters, the Canberra crews had to work hard. 'Each crew,' continued Flt Lt Skinner, 'was required to fly eight sorties, four of which were trips to the bombing range for weapon delivery, two were full day sorties where a simulated target had to be overflown exactly and on time before the subsequent weapon delivery at the range would count, and two night navigation sorties, finishing at the range with night bombing. The scoring for these sorties was exceedingly rigid and, to gain full marks from a day sortie, entailed overflight of the simulated target within 6 seconds and a bomb score of less than 3yd [9ft]. Scoring of other sorties was equally rigid, and being as much as one minute out on a target meant disqualification.' For the night bombing the Canberra crews used the Decca navigation system and by following an attack track that coincided with a Decca gridline they were able to get quite accurate bombing results. However, Fg Offs Morris and Wilson used an unofficial improvement to this method: they had noticed a factory with an illuminated roof window along the attack track and knew that if they released at a certain time after they had overflown it they would be guaranteed a good bomb! By fair means or foul, the Canberras held on to their lead until the last round when the Canadian pilot Flt Lt A.E. Mackay put the RCAF five points ahead. The Canberras still had one sortie in hand and although the crew dropped good bombs, an error in the Decca equipment meant that they did not score well enough to wrest the lead back from the Canadians. Nevertheless, the 14 Squadron team did

Winners of the Night Laydown Trophy at the 6th AFCENT tactical weapons meet in June 1967 – Flt Lt J.C. Vernon, Wg Cdr E.M. Higson (2 ATAF Team Leader) and Flt Lt W.H. Yates. (Bill Yates)

extremely well and finished 130 points ahead of the USAF Phantom crews. In the overall competition, the 2 ATAF team won the Broadhurst Trophy and individually four 14 Squadron crews came in the top six places. Of these, Flt Lts Vernon and Yates came second overall and also won the competition for the night-laydown bombing, with Fg Offs Morris and Wilson hot on their heels.

Meanwhile, the rest of the squadron had been kept busy. Four aircraft were required to cover the QRA commitment and the remaining combat-ready crews spent much of the 2 weeks of the TWM covering QRA. The remaining three B(I)8s and a T4 detached to Bruggen under Sqn Ldr D. J. Ward on 12 June to provide some flying for the rest of the crews. Although the working hours at Bruggen were limited because of the lack of ground crew, the bulk of whom were fully committed to the TWM and of course QRA, the detachment managed a respectable amount of flying.

The annual NATO air exercise in the central region, 'Exercise Sky Blue', kept the squadron busy in the first week of July. In the middle of 'Sky Blue', during one day three high-level sorties were flown against the UK as part of the UK air defence

'Exercise Kingpin'. The remainder of the month was an interdictor camp, which gave the combat-ready crews a chance to refresh their skills in tactical formation flying and conventional weaponry. Apart from practicing co-ordinated attacks on the range at Nordhorn, crews also made the most of the summer weather to carry out low flying throughout Germany. 'Exercise Actfast' was called at 09:00hrs on 18 July and in the afternoon four aircraft were launched to the 4 ATAF area of southern Germany. One of these aircraft[31] was flown by Fg Offs Morris and Wilson. They were flying along the centreline of the low-flying link route to the north of Frankfurt at the authorized height of 250ft above ground level and Fg Off Wilson was map reading on the navigator's couch in the nose of the aircraft. As they crossed a low valley he was suddenly aware of wires ahead and a moment later the aircraft lurched violently to the right. Wilson was briefly aware of a loud scraping noise and of a shower of sparks inside the fuselage. The aircraft had hit two of six high-tension electricity cables which spanned the valley. The starboard tip tank had been wrenched off the wing and a length of cable, which was embedded into the leading edge, had cut into the wing fuel tank. The other cable had smashed into Morris' cockpit, distorting the canopy arch and crazing the armoured windscreen so that he could not see through it. Wilson later estimated that the impact had cost the Canberra 100kt of airspeed. Morris managed to retain control of the aircraft and climbed away. After burning off the fuel in the left tanks to get the aircraft to a safe weight for landing the crew flew a GCA into Wildenrath. In the last few feet Wilson, looking through the glazed nose, had to talk Morris down onto the runway. The next day Wilson visited the sight in a Westland Wessex helicopter and even at low speed and with prior knowledge it was almost impossible to see the wires; the pylons, set amongst 60ft high trees, had also been painted green so that they merged into the background! As a result of this accident, the RAF's rules for low flying were amended. The crew had been authorized to fly at 250ft above ground level and had hit an obstacle some 279ft above the surface – thus they had not broken any rules! The amended instructions, which came into force shortly afterwards, for low-flying introduced a 250ft 'Minimum Separation Distance' from all obstacles. Another change to the low-flying regulations in Germany, though not due to this accident, was the restriction of night flying to a small number of pre-planned 'standard' routes, rather than the free range within the LFAs which crews had previously enjoyed.

During the autumn, the runway at Wildenrath was closed for repairs, so aircraft were detached to Bruggen to continue flying. The first squadron exchange for over 2 years took place at the beginning of November as a 'one-way' detachment to the RNoAF airbase at Rygge. The airfield, situated some 70 miles south of Oslo, was home of the RF-84Fs of 717 Squadron RNoAF. Flt Lt J. Sewell noted in the Squadron Operations Record Book, '…whilst the social life was a little lacking most members seemed to have an enjoyable time.' There was some interesting flying to be had too: Norwegian mountains made a welcome change from the flat plain of northern Germany and the fact that most of the area was outside the coverage of the Decca navigation system provided additional challenges for high-level navigation. Soon after their return from Norway, the squadron deployed for the 'Exercise Citrus Grove' APC. This time, instead of the more usual Cyprus, it was held at El Adem. Perhaps this change of venue was chosen to project UK airpower into the region after the 'Six Days War' in June between Egypt and Israel. Unfortunately, the weather in Libya was not particularly kind, which limited the flying at El Adem; but worse was in store at Wildenrath where poor weather prevented any local flying until 28 December! Fortunately, January 1968 brought an improvement. Three four-ship attacks[32] against Gutersloh, which were carried out as part of 'Exercise Gennett' on 26 January, provided excellent training in the interdictor role and enabled the crews to consolidate some of the skills they had been practicing in Libya. More opportunity came in March: a busy month in which the squadron managed to fly nearly 500hrs in the low-level airspace of northern and southern Germany, the UK and France. Fighter-affiliation sorties were flown as pairs[33] on 27 and 28 March. Strike training was not forgotten and March also saw the third round of the Salmond Trophy in which 14 Squadron were lying in second place. There was some more fighter-affiliation training on 25 April when Flt Lt R. Moore, who, with his navigator Flt Lt G.A. Pearce, was, '…acting as a target for a NATO air-defence competition over Holland. The area for the competition was a box orientated southwest/northeast about 40 miles long and 10 miles wide over the Dutch polders. We were given an entry point on the southern boundary and an exit point on the northern boundary. Whilst in the area we were required to be radio silent, yet monitor the controllers (safety) frequency with the authority to go 'no-duff' if at any time the intercepts became dangerous. We were cleared to operate not below 500ft along a timed track of our choosing. On our sortie the USAFE had a four-ship defending the box, split into two pairs: one high, one low. In the event they had some trouble finding us, even though we flew underneath the lower pair! Eventually, they spotted us as we left the area and attacked outside the box – naughty.'

In late spring, a number of 'Southern Rangers' and 'Extended Southern Rangers' included one by Fg Offs Morton and Tebb to Masirah. During their detachment they flew a low-low sortie in Iran on 8 May and returned from Masirah via Tehran on 10 May. Five days later Fg Offs M.F.E.W. Pluck and R.W.D. Trotter made an unscheduled landing at Ramstein after an engine seized, giving Fg Off Pluck his first real asymmetric landing. 'We were well south of the Rhine,' explained Pluck, 'when there was a large "BANG". My immediate thoughts were "What have I done – Birds?" (Birds were an ever-present danger, even at night). I climbed up and checked the engines: one was sounding and looking very unhealthy. It was at this point I departed from command SOPs, which said to shut the engine down to save it from damage. Asymmetric operations were much discussed by the pilots with significant input from the navigators, who did not have an ejection seat in the B(I)8s, as the Avon engine would more than likely seize solid if shut down after damage. The squadron pilots agreed to keep the engine running at idle, as we practiced in that configuration, rather than have a 'Flat Plate' on one side. We squawked 'Emergency', but this was ignored and we headed towards USAFB Ramstein and its 12,000-foot runway. Then the engine stopped – 'Flat Plate' – emergency drill again! I set up for the one engine approach to Ramstein. The 'decision height' was 600ft as you would need to dive the B(I)8 to increase speed so that you could apply power to overshoot (crawl). Many pilots had and would continue to get this wrong and make a hole about 1½ miles short of the runway upside down and to one side – Dead Ants! The major reason for this was the OCU, in the lighter T4, [which]taught pilots to fly line A and B speeds and land right on the threshold at the precise speed. So there were different techniques operated by squadron pilots for the T4 and the B(I)8s. The major problem was that the flaps were either up or down and took 13 seconds to travel and, as they did so, the attitude of the aircraft would change, making you appear to go high on the glide path. The danger was to reduce power at this point and as the flaps continued to travel to the max drag position, power up – Dead Ants. Back to Ramstein. We continued on the GCA, where at some point the controller told me I was 'dangerously high' on the glide path (he was used to talking down F-104s, Martin RB-57E Canberras etc.). At 600ft Roy and I agreed we would continue and the flaps went down some time later with a little nudge of power. We landed safely, a little in and a little fast. I explained to ATC that I needed clearance instructions whilst I was still moving. I was told to stop on the runway, which I did. Another controller told me to clear the runway to the right. I explained that I could only move in a circle, as we used engine and brakes for steering on the ground. After a demonstration he understood. Result: Ramstein's runway blocked with a Canberra stuck on it!'

Fg Off Pluck had another exciting experience 14 days later during his dual check with the newly-qualified QFI, Flt Lt A. Gregory. 'We had done the upper air work and I was doing the approach. Tony [Gregory] decided he would talk me through doing a roller landing. You had to be specifically cleared to do rollers because of the tendency for the Avon engine to surge. I landed and Tony took over. We lifted off well down the runway and as Tony called for the gear and flaps to be raised a large cloud of birds rose in front of us. We suffered a number of strikes, particularly in the port engine and immediately had around 30° of bank, very near the ground. Everything appeared to be happening very slowly, Tony and I had a conversation that went something like this; Tony: 'I don't think we are going very far like this;' Malcolm [Pluck]: "Agreed," the gear and flaps are still down;' Tony: "Better put her back on the ground!"'…We hit the barrier at a fair speed and the barrier caught us behind the canopy. We thought we had pulled the barrier out. Fortunately only one side had come away. I recall seeing a little blue Volkswagen travelling along the 221 road and thinking we were just about to spoil his day when the barrier pulled us to a stop. The bomb doors were open. The airbrakes were out. This action by myself [damaged] the aircraft,[34] [but] I would have put my hand out of the window if I thought it would slow us down!'

The squadron retained its '1' rating after the Taceval which started on the afternoon of 27 May. By coincidence 'Exercise Actfast' had already been called that morning and seven aircraft were being turned around as the Taceval Team arrived. Despite the fact that some aircraft were already strike loaded and some had no tip tanks fitted, it is a tribute to the ground crew that all eleven available aircraft were at QRA status just 7 hours 15 minutes later. The following day there was both a day and night-flying programme, which were carried out despite the hindrance of simulated Nuclear, Biological, Chemical (NBC) conditions. The exercise finally ended in the early hours of 29 May.

Flypasts & Displays

Amongst the celebrations held across the RAF to mark the service's 50th Anniversary in 1968, was an open day at Wildenrath in the summer. However, the priority in the month before that particular event was a flypast to mark the Queen's birthday. The squadron had started working-up four aircraft in close formation in May and intensive practice followed in early June. On the morning of 11 June, Flt Lt Morris was in the mess on the first day of his annual leave contemplating a sailing holiday in the Baltic, when he was called back to the squadron to be told that they were short of a pilot for the Number 3 slot in the fly-past practice. The plan was for a close-formation practice after which the aircraft would split into pairs to finish the sortie with a routine low-level return. After successfully completing the close formation part of the sortie the 'box' began to divide. During this manoeuvre, Flt Lt Morris drifted backwards and his tailplane struck the left wing of Flt Lt P. Smith and Sqn Ldr R.J. Wells' aircraft in the Number 4 position of the 'box.' Morris heard a loud bang, but at first the aircraft seemed to be controllable. Meanwhile, in the Number 2 aircraft Flt Lt Skinner, '...saw large pieces of Canberra passing close to my left-hand side. I sent out a distress call while quickly moving clear of the formation.' His navigator Fg Off Hedges could see, '...George's aircraft had the whole of the starboard tailplane sliced off. So from the back, the tailplane was L-shaped and not an inverted T-shaped.' Morris' aircraft[35] soon became very difficult to control and Flt Lt Adams, the formation leader, advised him to abandon the aircraft. The navigator, Flt Lt Stringer, was able to bale out at 1,800ft while Morris steered the aircraft as best he could towards a clear area near Roermond before ejecting at 200ft. Luckily, Flt Lt Smith's Canberra[36] only suffered slight damage to the port wingtip and he was able to land safely at Wildenrath. It was not the best welcome for the new CO, Wg Cdr T.J. McElhaw, who had taken command of the squadron the previous week!

The 50th Anniversary Air Show was held on 6 July. A large crowd of German and Dutch civilians, as well as British servicemen and their families enjoyed the festivities. The extensive static display of aircraft from the RAF and other NATO air forces was complimented by an impressive flying display. The proceedings were opened by the 'Red Arrows', who were followed by a scramble take off by six of 14 Squadron's Canberra B(I)8s[37] and four PR7s from 17 Squadron. As they cleared the airfield, Flt Lt Galyer and Flt Lt J. J. Harreld broke off to put their Canberra[38] through its paces with a performance display. Galyer had been told that he, '...was not allowed any aerobatics, but after 'discussions' managed to include a modified LABS manoeuvre (we had stopped LABS by then)...I did my 8 minutes, arriving as fast as we could...Bomb doors/airbrake wound open for a gear and flap slow fly by – 100kt into the wind took up most of the time allowed going down the runway! Then exit to Bruggen after the modified LABS manoeuvre.' Four B(I)8s led by Flt Lt Adams and the PR7s then returned for a flypast in two boxes in close formation before landing at Bruggen. The four-ship took off again, this time in company with four Hunter FR10s for a joint-service assault demonstration, which included transport aircraft, Hawker-Siddeley Harriers and army units.

Unfortunately, the success of the air day was followed by a disastrous performance in the Salmond Trophy the next month. Despite having run a conventional weapons camp in the last half of July, the squadron trailed the others all the way through the day and night phases and finished as they had started, in fourth place. This was perhaps a reflection on a squadron that knew that the days of the Canberra were numbered. As one squadron member noted, '…to be honest there was not the level of professionalism across the board…the end of the Canberra era was approaching, and although there were a lot of 'first tourists', the more-experienced people were not very inspiring and rather set in their ways. And there were cases of straight indiscipline…overall something of a cavalier approach, we did not take things that seriously.'

The routine of early autumn was broken by the squadron's deployment to Norway to participate in the large NATO naval 'Exercise Silver Tower', which was held in the waters of the North Atlantic and Norwegian Sea in the second half of September. The largest such exercise since the Second World War saw some 100 ships from nine countries taking part. Seven Canberras deployed to the RNoAF base at Orland near Trondheim. From here they joined *Luftwaffe* F-104Gs in simulating the tactics of Soviet naval aircraft such as Ilyushin Il-18 (NATO reporting name Beagle) or Tupolev Tu-16 (NATO reporting name Badger). This involved flying in unfamiliar Russian-style formations of three aircraft, delivering attacks from low-level against naval task forces in the waters to the north of Scotland. 'Our problem,' explained Flt Lt R. Moore, 'was finding the assigned target fleet – difficult without radar. So we hatched a plan to launch the German F-104s on the first raid (they had radar). We then launched when we knew they were recovering and met halfway to obtain the location of the target from them. I think the joint maritime course staff were bemused at our success rate. All sorties were very low-level over the sea, both outbound and inbound, to the extent that our aircraft were at times salt encrusted.' Two waves of three aircraft were flown each day from 21 to 25 September.

On the evening of 17 December, Flt Lts Skinner and R.W.H. Hedges were over the English Channel descending to low level on a night 'high-low-high' sortie to south-west England. 'Shortly after going IMC [Instrument Meteorological Conditions],' recalls Flt Lt Skinner, the aircraft was, '…hit by severe turbulence and a deluge of hail[stones]. A thick layer of 'St Elmo's Fire' enveloped the aircraft[39] and could be seen corkscrewing forward of the pitot tube. There was then a sudden blinding flash of lightning and a loud explosion…[I] could not properly see the instruments and had therefore no means of ascertaining the aircraft's attitude following a severe tossing around.

'Following the lightning flash,' Skinner, 'was unable to see the instruments due to flash blindness and it seemed an eternity before sight was restored, although it was probably only a matter of seconds. The primary flight instruments were unreliable so [I] reverted to 'limited panel' recovery from unusual positions as the aircraft cleared the bank of cloud (thankful for the thoroughness of this aspect of pilot training)!' The starboard tip tank had exploded, damaging the wing tip and aileron, but thankfully Skinner was able to keep the aircraft under control. They were given a steer towards RNAS Yeovilton, but unfortunately this took them back through the line of thunderstorms and yet more severe turbulence. Once clear and having lost the main instruments, Skinner was able to fly a limited panel GCA into Yeovilton where he found, '…that hard braking was needed to stop before the far end of the runway. The aircraft was halted on the runway and the ground crew earthed the aircraft by throwing cables over the wings.' It later transpired that the pitot-static system had been damaged and airspeed had been under-reading – hence the need for hard braking after a high-speed landing!

The APC in January 1969 would be one of the last RAF detachments at El Adem before Colonel Gadaffi's *coup d'etat* in the autumn of that year put an end to the RAF's use of Libya. The deployment lasted until 29 January. During the last week, on 23 January, the squadron was asked to carry out a search for an RAF exploration party with whom communication had been lost in the desert some 450 miles south of El Adem. Wg Cdr McElhaw commandeered an 'extra' aircraft, which had been flown down from Wildenrath that morning by Flt Lt T.P. Stockley and Fg Off R.L. Hawkins as part of a 'Southern Ranger' flight. This at least meant that the APC detachment could continue without losing one of the APC aircraft.

Poor weather in February severely curtailed the flying in Germany, but Fg Off J.A. Wilson and M. Smith were able to make their way southwards on 6 February. Their aim was to visit their colleagues on the RAF winter survival course at Bad Kohlgrub. RAF crews were not permitted to fly in the 'buffer zone' within 20 miles of the Austrian border, but this detail did not deter Wilson and Smith who carried out a low-level flypast. Unfortunately, they had chosen the day that the C-in-C was visiting! As a result both crewmembers were court martialled the next month, and although Fg Off Smith was found not guilty, Fg Off Wilson was severely reprimanded.

Routine operations over the next few months included low flying in Germany, France and the UK, using the weaponry ranges in all three countries. UK flights might follow a 'high-low-high' profile returning to Wildenrath or a 'high-low' profile with a refuelling stop in the UK at, for example, Waddington or Wittering. Typically three or four 'Southern Ranger' or 'Extended Southern Ranger' sorties would also be flown each month, as well as land-aways for cross-servicing exercises. On top of this the usual run of 'routine', NATO daily exercise commitments filled the flying programme. One routine trip to the range provided excitement for the newly-arrived Fg Off J. F. Lane: 'I and my nav Bob Commander, were on a range sortie at Nordhorn as a very new green crew with less than two months in theatre as I recall, when the B(I)8 ahead of me on the run in pulled up sharply. The pilot screamed down the R/T that he had suffered a bird strike and his nav was slumped in the 'Rumbold' seat at his side. There was a lot of blood and guts all over his head and he was clearly in a bad way. The pilot sounded very distressed and I pulled up beside him and told him to formate loosely on my port side while I arrange a diversion to the nearest airfield. I transmitted a PAN call and we were vectored onto a Dutch military airfield called Twente – a short transit of less than 10 minutes. We were given a straight-in approach on the westerly runway and I broke off at 200ft with the damaged Canberra from 3 Squadron on the centreline. He landed off the first approach and his crewman was met on the runway by an ambulance.

Canberra B(I)8 WT368 at low-level during a launch for 'Exercise Taceval' on 29 October 1969. The crew are Flt Lts M.F.E.W. Pluck and G.A. Pearce. (Malcolm Pluck)

I heard later that the nav unfortunately lost his eye in this incident but subsequently returned to flying duties.' For his quick-thinking Fg Off Lane was awarded a 'Good Show' certificate by the C–in–C.

The summer of 1969 followed a very similar pattern to that of the previous year. The Wildenrath Air Show, held on 15 June, was billed this time as a celebration of NATO's first 20 years. Wg Cdr McElhaw, at the head of the squadron four-ship[40] led the flypast comprising four-ships from five RAFG Canberra units (14, 17, 213, 16 and 31 Squadrons) and later led the Canberras into the tactical-assault display. This time Flt Lt Adams with Fg Off A.J. Collins provided the Canberra B(I)8 solo-role demonstration. Once again, a conventional weapons camp at Nordhorn in the summer months did little for the unit's performance in the Salmond Trophy, where once again they took last place. However, at the presentation ceremony later in the month, SASO commented that the scores of all three squadrons had been extremely close. The year was also remarkable for having two Tacevals, one in May and another in October. The squadron passed both, but did not achieve the '1' rating that had been awarded on previous occasions. Perhaps at least some of the squadron's mediocre performance was due to a very high turnover of personnel during the year and the influx of a number of new faces. Many of these came from the Canberra units that had disbanded in Cyprus, or like Fg Offs R.M. Joy and R.A. Newman later in the year, from 213 Squadron, which had disbanded at Bruggen.

In December's 'Exercise Citrus Grove', the squadron deployed to Akrotiri, where apart from the usual weaponry practice, the Canberras were incorporated into an exercise for Sandhurst cadets. On 4 December six aircraft, operating in pairs, simulated air attacks against the cadets, much to the mutual enjoyment of crews and cadets. Another variation to the APC was the rotation of crews through Cyprus so that fourteen, rather than the usual ten, crews could participate. Four 'Southern Ranger' flights were used to fly fresh crews into Akrotiri, and crews who had completed their training flew the 'ranger' aircraft back to Wildenrath.

The final squadron exchange of the Canberra-era took place from 27 April to 5 May 1970. Four aircraft and six crews flew to Villafranca where they were hosted by the Italian Air Force' 28° Gruppo 3 Aerobrigata. The 14 Squadron crews had an 'enjoyable and instructive' detachment, which included a number of pairs on low-flying sorties in Italy. Later in the month, six aircraft deployed to the RNoAF airfield at Lista in southern Norway for 'Exercise Co-op'. However, the weather was poor and the flying was limited. Nine sorties were also flown during the French air-defence 'Exercise Datex' from 26 to 28 May, comprising simulated strikes against radar sites and airfields in northern France. However, the formation of 14 Squadron (Phantom) at Bruggen during the month made it clear that the Canberra unit was enjoying its last days.

The squadron's last Canberra sortie was flown by Wg Cdr McElhaw and Fg Off Trotter on 29 May, and included a FRA (First Run Attack) at Nordhorn before the recovery to Wildenrath. Although the aircraft landed in a thunderstorm, the rain had abated by the time it taxied to the squadron line, where the station commander Gp Capt D.G. Bailey was waiting with champagne. The crew emerged from the aircraft dressed appropriately in full mess kit! Another champagne reception awaited the last QRA crews[41] when they were declared 'off state' at 23:59hrs on 31 May. This was followed by a party in the QRA site on 1 June at which the officers were presented with squadron tankards. More formally, a parade reviewed by deputy commander RAF Germany, AVM J.A.C. Aitken, CB was held at Wildenrath 4 days later to mark the stand down of 14 Canberra squadron. The Squadron Standard was carried by Fg Off R.J. Commande, under the watchful eye of Sgt A.A. Hunter, and the escorts Sgts M. Palmer and C. Gammage.

Over the next 14 days the squadron's aircraft were distributed between 3 and 16 Squadrons at Laarbruch. Most of the remaining aircrew were also divided between the two remaining Canberra strike squadrons, although some pilots headed towards Central Flying School (CFS), while a handful of navigators were destined for the Phantom. Around half of the ground crew remained at Wildenrath to join the newly-forming Harrier squadrons. Although the Canberra squadron had largely ceased to exist by the end of June, the final act was to transfer the Squadron Standard to 14 Squadron (Phantom).

NOTES

22   Direct Hit.
23   In Canberra XM272.
24   Sqn Ldr P. F. Rogers/Flt Lt E.G. Coppard, Flt Lt A. Salter/Flt Lt G.J. Taylor, Flt Lt J.H. Hanson/ Flt Lt N. O'Shea, Flt Lt P. Marsh/Flt Lt M.J. Grange, Flt Lt D. Christie/Flt Lt C.P. Manville.
25   Wg Cdr J. Field (OC 3 Sqn)/Flt Lt M. Fortune, Sqn Ldr P. Little/Sqn Ldr M. Richards, Flt Lt G. Marsh/Flt Lt Beadnell, Flt Lt E. Denson/Flt Lt P. Broadhurst, Flt Lt N. Allen/ Flt Lt P. Nagle, Flt Lt L. Tanner/Flt Lt J. Laurenson.
26   Canberra XM244.
27   in Canberra B(I)8 WT346 with Fg Off Barnett.
28   Canberra B(I)8 WT368.
29   Canberra B(I)8 XK951.
30   Fg Off J. R. Parker/Sqn Ldr E.A. Taylor, Flt Lts J.C. Vernon/W.H. Yates, Flt Lt C.M. Labouchere/ Fg Off R.A. Forrester, Flt Lt A.H. Skinner/Fg Off R.W. Hedges, Fg Offs S. J. Morton/B. A. Tebb, and Flt Lt G. W. Morris /Fg Off D. S. Wilson.
31   Canberra B(I)8 XM278.
32   Crews: Flt Lt Adams/Fg Off A. J. Collins WT336, Flt Lt E. A. Jones/Lt J. R. Bigland, RN WT347, Fg Off Glayer/Fg Off M.J.R. Barnett WT368, Flt Lt P. Smith/Fg Off Forrester XM278.
33   27 March: Fg Off I.F. Clark/Plt Off I.A. Cameron, Fg Off Glayer/Plt Off S. Stringer. 28 March: Flt Lts Vernon/J.P. Shiels, Fg Offs Morton/Tebb.
34   Canberra T4 WH850.
35   Canberra B(I)8 WT363.
36   Canberra B(I)8 XM278.
37   Flt Lt Adams/Fg Off A.J. Collins XM264, Flt Lt I.S. Airey/Fg Off K.G. Toal WT346, Flt Lts A.H. Skinner/R.W.H. Hedges WT337, Flt Lts P. Smith/W.H. Yates WT365.
38   Canberra B(I)8 WT336.
39   Canberra B(I)8 XM278.
40   Wg Cdr McElhaw/ Fg Off I.A. Cameron WT337, Flt Lt A. Gregory/Fg Off M. Smith WT339, Flt Lt I.S. Airey/Flt Lt R.W.H. Hedges WT365, Fg Off A.N.C.M. Hall/Flt Lt B.M. Anderson XM264.
41   Wg Cdr McElhaw, Sqn Ldrs R.G. Kerr, I. Bartley and Flt Lt M.J. Steward.

5

1970-1975

THE PHANTOM

The RAF had started to procure a replacement for the obsolescent Canberra B(I)8 in the late 1950s, but that process was a long one which was frustrated by shifting tides in both political and military circles. The original replacement aircraft designed for long-range penetration at low-level and at supersonic speeds, came into existence in 1964 as the British Aircraft Corporation (BAC) TSR2. Unfortunately for the TSR2, the general election that year was won by a government determined to make radical cuts in public spending, and this political need coincided with a massive escalation in the development cost of the aircraft. The project was therefore cancelled and replaced by the General-Dynamics F-111K, which would be a much cheaper 'off the shelf' purchase from the US. However, this aircraft also overran the budget and it, too, was cancelled 4 years later. With few options remaining as the end of the decade approached, the RAF procured a Rolls-Royce Spey Mk.202-engined version of the McDonnell Douglas F-4M Phantom FGR.2 and also the Hawker-Siddeley Buccaneer S2 to fill the ground -attack roles in RAF Germany.

The early 1970s were to be a time of modernization and consolidation of the entire fast-jet force within RAF Germany. From 1970, the air-defence role would continue to be covered by the two Lightning F2A squadrons at Gütersloh, while the ground-attack and reconnaissance roles would be concentrated at the three 'Clutch' airfields at Wildenrath, Brüggen, and Laarbruch. Wildenrath would become home to three new Harrier GR1 squadrons for close-air support of the army and Laarbruch would house two squadrons of strike/attack Buccaneers and one of reconnaissance Phantoms. At Brüggen, three Phantom squadrons (including 14 Squadron) would fulfil the strike/attack role.

The Phantom represented a quantum leap in both capability and complexity over the Canberra, combining supersonic performance with a much broader air-to-ground weapons capability. The pulsed-doppler radar in the Phantom also gave it an excellent air-to-air capability. Converting to such a highly-capable aeroplane would be a more complicated task for both pilots and navigators than had been the case for previous aircraft types, so a simple one-for-one replacement of aircraft on the squadron would not be possible. Instead, parallel 'designate' squadrons were formed at Brüggen to work up to combat readiness on the Phantom while the Canberra squadrons were gradually run down. These new Phantom units were crewed by graduates from 228 Operational Conversion Unit (OCU) at Coningsby. In the case of 14 (Designate) Squadron, the core was made up from the members of 4 Phantom Course at Coningsby, who arrived at Brüggen in May 1970 under the command of Wg Cdr J.M.D. Sutton. The unit included two former members of 14 Squadron, Sqn Ldr R.J. Honey, who had previously served as a Hunter pilot and Flt Lt R.W.H. Hedges who had previously been a Canberra navigator. These crews had been preceded by Sqn Ldr H. Coriat, who set up the working accommodation for the squadron in Number 1 Hangar on the 'waterfront' (Apron) at Brüggen.

New Home at Brüggen

The first two Phantom aircraft for 14 Squadron[42] were collected from Coningsby by Wg Cdr Sutton with Sqn Ldr R.H.D. Adams and Flt Lt J. Watson (the squadron PAI) with Sqn Ldr Coriat on 1 June. That was the same day that RAFG's two Lightning squadrons were due to deploy to Brüggen while runway resurfacing work started at Gutersloh, but Wg Cdr Sutton insisted that the new Phantoms should be the first aircraft to land on Brüggen's newly-resurfaced runway. The arrival of the Phantoms was all the more spectacular when Flt Lt Watson was instructed to engage the recently-installed Rotary Hydraulic Arrestor Gear (RHAG) cable at high speed, as a final test that it worked correctly! The first two aircraft had dual controls, which allowed Sqn Ldr G. Roberts, the squadron QFI, to check out the pilots. More Phantoms were delivered over the next month and by July the squadron had nine aircraft; the arrival of four more crews in July brought the squadron's strength to 10 crews. However, the flying was very limited for the first few months, partly due to 'teething' snags with the new aircraft and partly because the engineering staff at Brüggen had insisted on centralized, rather than squadron level, servicing for the Phantom. This latter approach meant that without guidance from the operational branch, aircraft were needlessly grounded to rectify minor faults that could have been carried. The engineering problem was further exacerbated by a lack of spares – a real problem when the Rolls-Royce Spey engines were lasting for as little as 35 hours.

When aircraft were available crews carried out familiarization sorties in Germany. These sorties also included range details at Nordhorn, but they were restricted to 'dry' weaponry passes only because no guns or bombing equipment had yet been delivered. The squadron also used the presence of the Lightning squadrons as an opportunity to conduct some Dissimilar Air Combat Training (DACT). Unfortunately, these did not go well to start with, largely due to unserviceabilities in aircraft or radars, and as a result, 14 Squadron's crews were the brunt of many a derogatory comment about being a 'bomber squadron' from their Lightning flying colleagues in the mess bar. However, a winning combination of crews, aircraft and radars came together on 6 August: honour was restored and the Lightning pilots were more circumspect from then on!

AVM J.A.C. Aiken CB, Deputy C-in-C RAF Germany greets Wg Cdr J.M.D. Sutton on the occasion of the arrival of the first two Phantoms at Bruggen on 1 June 1970. (14 Squadron Association)

By early July, the Phantom unit was deemed to be ready to assume the identity of 14 Squadron and the formal parade for the handover of the Squadron Standard from 14 Squadron (Canberra) to 14 (Phantom) Squadron took place on 7 July 1970. Fg Off R.M. Joy handed the standard to Flt Lt F.J. McDonald, and it was then paraded in front of the reviewing officer, Air Marshal Sir C.N. Foxley-Norris, KCB, DSO, OBE, MA, C-in-C RAF Germany, who had commanded 14 Squadron in 1945. A four-ship flypast, which was planned to coincide with the general salute, was led by Sqn Ldr Roberts and Flt Lt I.G. Wellings and despite the C-in-C arriving 10 minutes late, the aircraft flew overhead the parade exactly on time. After the parade, Flt Lt R.G. Turnill recorded in the squadron diary, '…the C-in-C surprised us all by producing a tape recording of himself singing the 14 Squadron

Two of 14 Squadron's Phantoms fly past Schloss Hohenzollern near Stuttgart on 5 August 1970. Sqn Ldr G. Roberts and Flt Lt I.G. Wellings in XV411 lead Flt Lts K.D. Rhodes and F.J. McDonald in XV463. (© Crown Copyright 1970)

song that was current when he was the boss in 1945. Slightly risqué, it made a very appropriate addition to a very good day!'

Over the next few months, the RAF's newest Phantom squadron was host to a number of distinguished visitors, including Air Chief Marshal Sir Frederick Rosier,[43] KCB, CBE, DSO (Deputy C-in-C Central Region), Lord Carrington (Secretary of State for Defence), Air Marshal Sir H.B. Martin,[44] KCB, DSO and 2 Bars, DFC and Bar, AFC (incoming C-in-C RAFG), Air Chief Marshal Sir J. Granby, GCB, KBE, DSO, (Chief of the Air Staff) and, separately, both the RAF and RN staff college courses. Another guest, on 16 September, was Princess Anne, who visited Brüggen on one of her very first 'solo' official duties. She was treated to a flypast of all RAFG's aircraft, which included five Canberra B(I)8s, five Canberra PR7s, five Hunters, five Phantoms and four Harriers. A short flying display followed that afternoon. The next day 14 Squadron also mounted a formation of eight aircraft to 'fly the flag' and introduce the Phantom over Gutersloh, Hopsten, Laarbruch and Wildenrath; 'Crusader' formation was led by Wg Cdr Sutton who, impressively, had left the Royal Ball at Rheindahlen at 05:00hrs that morning!

Armament for the Phantom began to arrive in September, in the shape of the pod-mounted 20mm SUU-23/A, a Gatling-type cannon, which boasted an exceptionally high rate of fire. The following month 68mm SNEB rocket pods also became available and both guns and rockets were soon being fired on the Nordhorn range. As might be expected with an intensive phase of weaponry, one or two incidents occurred, including the first ricochet, received by Flt Lt Turnill and Sqn Ldr Adams, who diverted to Hopsten after the aircraft was hit in the left engine on 29 September. 'As we pulled up off the target,' recalled Sqn Ldr Adams, 'a very loud bang occurred, followed by severe vibration and terror. I started to reach for the handle, but there were no indications of fire and the aircraft continued to fly normally. Roger shut down the port engine and the vibration died away. After pause for thought we opted for Hopsten. The guy who marshalled us in peered interestedly at that engine and when we opened the canopies announced that he could see daylight all the way through from the intake to the jet pipe.' On 19 October, Wg Cdr Sutton started his take-off roll at the head of three aircraft for a rocketry detail at Nordhorn: halfway down the runway his nose-wheel steering failed dramatically and the aircraft veered off the runway, thankfully without any casualties. A third ill-fated range detail was Air Marshal Foxley-Norris' trip to strafe at Nordhorn under the supervision of Flt Lt K.D. Rhodes on 15 October[45]. Unfortunately, they had to return to Brüggen without a shot being fired when three large pigeons flew into the starboard engine. Foxley-Norris was later presented with, '...a six-inch high plastic dolly-bird. She [was] clothed entirely in pigeon feathers which the technicians at Brüggen had later extracted from that same engine.'

The squadron was able to start bombing in November when the first Carrier Bomb Light Store (CBLS) was delivered. A container approximately the same size as a 1,000lb bomb, the CBLS could carry four practice bombs. The first attempts at dive bombing resulted in some horrendous scores. 'The wrong bomb tables were sent from the OCU,' explained Flt Lt Watson, 'which caused the errors, and the OCU sent incorrect weapons charts. Soon fixed as I changed the reaction times to two seconds instead of four seconds, got accurate bomb tables from Boscombe Down, planned for 400kt deliveries and produced new charts which worked.' Watson also later, '...produced a bombing sight mounted on the canopy adjusted for drift etc.,' which further improved the squadron's bombing accuracy.

Exercises with Forward Air Controllers (FAC) were also carried out in the LFAs, but Flt Lt Turnill complained, '...although we do some FAC almost every month, we cannot afford the time to be proficient.' With more aircraft and crews – and weapons – available, the squadron's flying programme could become more adventurous and November saw the start of tactical four-ship formations fighting their way to their target against a 'bounce' aircraft. Such complex flying takes practice and for crews long out of practice it often proved difficult to see the 'bounce' early enough to take evasive action. On this subject, though, Flt Lt Turnill was more enthusiastic: '...it was great to get back into that sort of flying!' In fact from then on the squadron adopted a policy of always flying with a 'bounce' whenever possible, which kept crews sharp. Another tool to hone the skills of the Phantom crews was the squadron 'Top Dog Trophy', a competition which was run every 2 months. The first one, in September, was run by the Ground Liason Officer (GLO), Major John Cooper, and comprised a rapid plan for a sortie on two reconnaissance targets which had to be reported by

Phantom FGR.2 XV501 flown by Flt Lt R.G. Turnill and Sqn Ldr R.H.D. Adams at low-level over northern Germany in November 1970. (14 Squadron Association)

an In-Flight Report (IFREP). This competition was won by Wg Cdr Sutton with Flt Lt Wellings. The second 'Top Dog', organized by Sqn Ldr Honey and Flt Lt R. Shepherd introduced a new twist: after their IFREP for the first target, the crews found themselves being redirected to an alternative target for which they had no detailed map! Flt Lt J. Courcoux and Flt Lt Taylor only narrowly beat Flt Lt Turnill and Sqn Ldr Adams into second place.

However, after the busy days of the autumn, flying almost ground to a halt in December when extensive freezing fog shrouded North Germany for much of the month. On some days it was possible to fly above it but, '…it was somewhat alarming,' reported Flt Lt Turnill, 'to have the impression of flying at high level yet with chimneys, pylons and TV masts sticking out of the fog.' Some good news arrived in the form of new 4kg practice bombs, which proved to be a vast improvement on the previous type and crews who were lucky enough with the weather managed to achieve some good laydown bombing scores.

The New Year of 1971, piped in by Flt Lt Watson at the squadron New Year's-Eve Party, brought little change in the weather, but it did herald some major changes to the squadron. Firstly Wg Cdr D.T. Bryant, MBE took command of 14 Squadron on his predecessor's promotion and, secondly, training for the strike role started in earnest. Like the Canberra before it, the Phantom was to be armed in the strike role with an US-supplied weapon, the 2,100lb Mk.43 nuclear bomb. The custody of the weapons also remained with US forces, who took the task very seriously, as Cpl J. Malone discovered one day: 'I was on QRA and was sent up to the gate to escort a civilian electrician who had been sent over to have a look at a problem in one of the QRA sheds (they were literally corrugated-iron sheds, open at the ends). I went with the electrician to the RAF Police who was guarding the shed (the idea was that the RAF Police guarded the aircraft and the US Air Police guarded the weapon), told him what we wanted and he said "OK, you can go in." As we walked into the shed toward the electrical distribution box, we heard a metallic click behind us. I do not know if you have ever had someone standing behind you cocking an Armalite AR-15 [rifle], but the effect is immediate and shocking. Both of us put our hands up and stopped. He told us to turn around and walk slowly towards him, which we did. I told him that we had been cleared by the RAF Police and that we were not approaching the aircraft. He said, "Are you going to leave or not?" so we left.' The poor weather and an extensive modification programme to the aircraft both served to limit the flying programme in January, and provided ample opportunity for the ground study required for the strike role. The following month, Flt Lts P. Edwards and Hedges were checked out on nuclear-delivery profiles by USAF F-104 pilots and more training and checking continued over subsequent months.

The first half of the year also saw the whole of the station at Brüggen working up to its first Taceval as a Phantom Wing. The first exercises had started tentatively the previous September with a four-day exercise, during which 14 Squadron operated from revetments on the south-western corner of the airfield, and moved on through the NATO 'Exercise Quicktrain' (which was mainly for the benefit of the engineers in generating serviceable aircraft) in October. On 20 January, the first station Minival was called at 06:00hrs. After the aircraft had been generated there was a mass launch into a Wing 'Top Dog' competition in which, thanks to a perfect score by Flt Lt A.H. Dachtler, 14 Squadron beat 17 Squadron by a close margin.

Decimomannu

The closure of El Adem range after the 1969 *coup d'etat* in Libya took away the traditional fair weather venue for RAF's ground-attack squadrons' APCs. Luckily the problem was short-lived, because in mid-1970 the Canadians decided to withdraw from the Air Weapons Training Facility (AWTI) at Decimomannu in southern Sardinia. The AWTI had originally been set up in the 1950s by the Canadians, Italians and Germans and made use of the extensive air-to-ground range at Capo Frasca at the mouth of the Gulf of Oristano on the west of the island. There were also air-to-air ranges off the west coast of Sardinia. The departure of the Canadians made space for the USAF and RAF to take move in to 'Deci', as the quadri-national base became known to generations of RAF personnel. A visit to Sardinia by Flt Lt Watson in December confirmed its suitability for the Phantom and arrangements were made for 14 Squadron to hold its first Phantom APC in March 1971.

The original plan was for all ten of the squadron's aircraft to deploy to 'Deci' on 3 March in a large formation, but ATC had different ideas. In the end nine aircraft made it in smaller sections at 30-minute intervals and the last aircraft[46], which was delayed by unserviceability, followed 2 days later. Wg Cdr Bryant was welcomed by the RAF base staff after he had landed in sunshine for the first RAF Germany APC at the range. Unfortunately, the weather turned over the next few days and the first week's flying was very limited. In fact there was no flying on 2 or 3 March because of heavy snowfall; the first time in decades! However, it brightened up sufficiently in the second week to carry out retard bombing, SNEB firing and strafing at Frasca. In the third week, the crews were able to practice dive bombing, despite the limitations of a low cloud base. The two weekends in the middle of the APC gave everyone the opportunity to explore Sardinia and various climbing and walking expeditions kept people out of the bar. On the last day of the detachment, 25 March, the weather cleared completely, bringing the blue skies that would have been useful in the previous 3 weeks!

Back at Brüggen, the work-up towards full combat readiness continued with monthly station exercises. In June, the squadron was visited by representatives of the MODCAS team and NATO training division as part of the formal inspection process required before the unit could be declared to NATO as combat ready in the strike role. Nuclear procedures were also checked later in the month by the USAFE inspector general's team. A three-day Maxeval, which started on 14 June, was followed by 'Exercise Sky Blue', which was also treated by the squadron as a Taceval, but without the nuclear work. The exercise offered an interesting variety of flying which included some work with FACs, airfield attacks, night weaponry at Nordhorn and daytime weaponry at Wainfleet and Suippes. All in all it was considered to be, 'an enjoyable and exhilarating exercise.'

The beginning of July brought high expectation and rumour, as everyone at Brüggen waited for the inevitable Taceval. The squadron continued to operate from the revetments on the south-west side of the airfield and a Minival on 7 July kept everyone on their toes. Two days later, Taceval was called at 07:00hrs. The first day was taken up with the generation of strike-loaded aircraft, but some aircrew were called forward for questioning. It was a hot day, especially for the engineers working hard in NBC kit and everyone was relieved when at the end of the day they were stood down for the weekend. For Sqn Ldr Adams, '…apart from the tension, an endemic feature of these events, the overriding memory of our first Taceval was the dirt and the heat. The squadron spent three or four days in the revetments, in NBC kit and with no water. While the aircrew had some relief with visits to ops and some sort of shift system, the ground crew had little respite. Conditions for them were poor, especially for the armourers who had to make endless load configuration changes.' The evaluation started again on the Monday morning with planning and flying a six-ship airfield attack, followed by work with Belgian FACs in LFA3, to the southeast of Gutersloh. The mass-strike launch was carried out on the next morning. Disappointingly, although the bomb scores were within limits, they were not as good as they had been earlier in the year. The afternoon was spent in academic weaponry sorties to nearby Helchteren range to meet the Taceval team's requirement to see that 75 percent of the squadron's crews could qualify to Allied Command Europe (ACE) standards in laydown, dive bombing, rocketry and strafe. The sorties were flown as a four-ship with a laydown FRA followed by two 10° dive passes, two SNEB passes and four strafing passes. Again, although adequate, the scores were not as good as the squadron crews had previously managed; however, the performance was deemed to be sufficient and the Brüggen Phantom Wing passed its first Taceval.

The 'reward' was the start of QRA from the beginning of August. 'The boredom, the mess, always left in the kitchen by previous crews, the shock when the hooter blew in the middle of a deep sleep and the totally humourless US custodians who held their weapons menacingly whenever we went near the aircraft' were the hallmarks of QRA for Sqn Ldr Adams, but he acknowledged, '…there were lighter moments: to speed things up bicycles were provided and, when two crews were on QRA, a three-ship formation would peddle up and down while the 'bounce' lurked in the bushes, attempting to hurtle out at the right time to get in their six o'clock. Breaks, inward turnabouts and chaos would ensue to the astonishment of the unsmiling custodians. This all came to an end after one night when the hooter blew and we rushed out hastily draping harnesses over shoulders and pedalling off towards the aircraft. Unfortunately, Roger's [Turnill] harness got caught in a wheel; he crashed and spent the next week being mended. Bicycles were withdrawn.'

Late summer and autumn saw the start of the rounds of the Salmond Trophy, which did not go well for 14 Squadron. A disastrous day, 12 August, saw the squadron 400 points behind the leaders but even after better days in September, the squadron was still trailing badly. Meanwhile, numerous FAC exercises with the Bundeswehr (German Army) gave crews a chance to consolidate their skills in that direction.

On 31 August, Flt Lts P. Edwards and Hedges carried out a trial to investigate the handling characteristics of the Phantom in a heavy-weight fit and to compare the actual fuel-consumption figures with the theoretical predictions. They took off with a full fuel load, including three drop-tanks and four 1,000lb bombs, giving an all-up weight of 58,500lb. Despite a relatively high speed of 169kt before the nosewheel would lift off, the aircraft[47] handled well and the fuel consumption was rather better than predicted. Edwards and Hedges were also the winners, 3 months later, with the first of the reintroduced squadron 'Top Dog' competitions.

For some years the bird migration season, which ran through October, had caused a mounting hazard to low-flying aircraft in Germany, as more high-performance aircraft attempted to operate at speed in the same airspace as thousands of migratory birds. In autumn 1971 a new 'birdspeed' system introduced a limit of 360kt for aircraft within the German low-flying system when significant bird numbers were forecast. The intention was to reduce the damage to aircraft caused by birdstrikes. Unfortunately, however, this was a major inconvenience because most fast-jet aircraft, including the Phantom, did not have sufficient performance margin to manoeuvre safely at low level at such a slow speed. As a result of this policy, useful low flying was severely curtailed in the autumn months. However, some days low flying was possible, including some FAC exercises and also December's 'Top Dog' competition, which was won by Wg Cdr Bryant with Flt Lt Wellings.

The end of the year saw a number of postings in and out, with the result that much of the early part of 1972 would be spent carrying out the conversion sorties required before the new arrivals could be declared combat ready in Germany.

Missile Practice Camp

The first major event of 1972 was the detachment of four aircraft and crews[48] to RAF Valley (Anglesey) on the morning of 25 January. Each crew was to fire an AIM-7 Sparrow missile at a radar target towed by a remotely-flown Fairey Jindivik drone. The 'sortie profiles,' recalled Flt Lt Edwards, '…were usually Primary Firer, Secondary Firer and Photo Chase, so could be a pair, three- or four-ship.' The first firing sortie, flown that afternoon, was thwarted by unserviceabilities in the primary-firing aircraft's telemetry and the secondary-firer's radar. Over the next two days strong winds, in excess of 50kt, prevented flying and the fourth day, too, was cursed, this time by the presence of intelligence-gathering Russian trawlers in the Irish Sea. It was not until the fifth day of the camp that the first missile was launched. It fired correctly and passed very close to the Jindivik target, but the missile's fuzing system appeared to have malfunctioned and it did not explode. After two more days of high winds and frustration, more missiles were fired on 3 February. The first of these was seen to clear the aircraft correctly and ignite, but then it yawed to the right and dived sharply left of the firing aircraft and disappeared seaward. The second missile, fired by Flt Lts Rhodes and Smith[49], performed perfectly, but in the murky conditions the chase aircraft lost visual contact with the missile before it reached the target, leaving some doubt about the exact outcome of the firing. There was certainly no doubt about the final missile, though. As Flt Lt Edwards' back seater, Flt Lt Hedges was, '…selected to carry out at night, a low-level, look-down, head-on shot, with the PD radar and Sparrow missile, probably the most demanding profile for the weapon system. Got a good head-on lock onto the towed Luneberg lens, and fired, I think at about 6 nautical miles, or maybe a little less. Anyhow, the missile actually hit the lens, which is about 12in diameter… ours was the shot of the MPC!' The crews returned to Brüggen on 4 February.

The RAF Germany Routine

By early 1972, the squadron had settled into the routine which would remain virtually unchanged for the next two decades. Apart from maintaining the QRA task, the unit's focus was on Taceval, the annual no-notice assessment by HQ 2ATAF that the squadron was 'combat ready' and that its personnel were proficient in their roles. Taceval involved a comprehensive evaluation of every aspect of the squadron and much hard work was needed to ensure that the entire unit functioned at the highest levels of readiness and efficiency. In order to remain on top form for the Taceval there were surprise exercises every month, either Minivals (run at station level) or Maxevals (where assessors would come from other RAFG stations). These exercises followed a familiar pattern of a day spent generating as many serviceable aircraft as possible, armed in their war fit, followed by a day or two of conventional operations and finally a strike generation followed by the 'R-Hour' mass launch. Significantly, most of the exercises were carried out under conditions of simulated Nuclear, Biological and Chemical (NBC) threat, forcing personnel to wear protective clothing (known unlovingly as 'Noddy Suits') and respirators. This cumbersome apparel turned even the simplest task into a great endeavour. Between these station exercises, came tasking for routine NATO flying exercises (such as the air-defence missile exercises 'Beer Barrel', 'Crazy Horse', 'Reno Roulette', 'Cruel Flame', the FAC exercises 'Whirlygig', 'Playboy', 'Green Pasture', or cross-servicing exercises 'Round Flag', 'Ample Gain') which might take place on 3 or 4 days of each month.

Other events which punctuated the year were the APC at Deci, and the annual checks by both the RAF Weapons Standardization Team (WST) and (separately) the NATO training division that crews were word perfect in nuclear procedures. These commitments gave some structure to the year, although of course the timing varied from year to year. Extra commitments such exercises, MPCs or trials, added to the variety. The remainder of the flying task outside all of these exercises and other external commitments was for the squadron to manage, but it would inevitably revolve around the requirements of the annual training syllabus or the conversion syllabus for crews new to the theatre.

The first few months of 1972 were spent working up the new crews from Simulated Strike Profiles (SSPs) as singletons, on to conventional operations as pairs and in four-ship formations. There was also some night flying along the pre-planned German night-flying routes and some night formation work. On 14 April, the night tasking included dropping Lepus flares as part of an army trial to see if attack helicopters were able to engage tanks under the light of the flare. It was the squadron's first attempt at dropping the Lepus flare and all went well from that aspect; as to whether it worked for the helicopters no one discovered! That month's 'Top Dog' competition was won by Flt Lt Turnill and Sqn Ldr Adams – making them the first crew to win twice.

The squadron's second detachment to Decimomannu took place during the month of May. It was divided into two phases, the first being 'Direct' (i.e. using only the pilot's gunsight) techniques for 10° strafe, SNEB and retard bombing and the second being INAS during which 30° dive bombing and 10° strafe would be practiced using sighting corrections supplied by the INAS. During the first phase, the emphasis was on tactical patterns involving a pull-up from low-level, rather than an academic pattern flown at a few thousand feet. The inter-flight competition at the end of the 'Direct' phase was won by 'A' Flight. Another competition, which was the result of a conversation in the bar one evening, was a strafing competition with the visiting *Luftwaffe* F-104 Starfighter detachment. On the day, the Phantoms scored an almost unbelievable 58 percent but alas, even this high score was not enough to beat the Starfighters and 14 Squadron's crews had to buy the beer for their *Luftwaffe* rivals! In fact the detachment proved to be an opportunity for lots of social activity, including two all-ranks barbeques and an all-ranks sports day. Weekend activities were organized and there was also a mass exodus at weekends to the Fortes Holiday Village at Pula.

The APC also provided the chance to drop some inert 1,000lb bombs and four crews were each able to drop two bombs. The profile for each attack was a pull-up from low-level and the crews noted that even with the added weight of the bombs the aircraft handled well provided that the speed was kept high! Once all the weaponry practice was complete there was the chance for a lucky few of the ground crew to have a back-seat ride in a Phantom.

The squadron was very quickly in the thick of things when they got back to Brüggen: Taceval was called at 09:40hrs on 12 June and an intensive 3½ days followed. The busy flying schedule included FAC work as well as Offensive Counter Air (OCA) & Interdiction sorties by both day and night. There were also sorties to the range

Flt Lt R.G. Turnill and Sq Ldr R.H.D. Adams celebrate 14 Squadron's 5,000th Phantom flying hour on 20 July 1972. Standing over 6 ft tall, Roger Turnill, was described by his contemporaries as, '...a brilliant and dedicated fighter pilot.' Tragically he died of cancer in 1974, aged 30 years-old. (Peter Turnill)

so that crews could demonstrate their prowess at weaponry events. All of this was concluded by the 'R-Hour' launch. The Taceval Team was clearly content with what they saw at 14 Squadron as the unit was awarded a score of '1' [excellent] for its flying and operations. There was another busy flying schedule at the end of the month for 'Exercise Sandmartin', which ran from 27 to 29 June. The squadron flew eighty sorties in the 3 days of the exercise in a programme that ranged from four-ship attack mission in France to a six-ship airfield attack at Gutersloh and on to FAC work.

Salmond Victory

The flying continued apace through the summer with a work-up for the Salmond Trophy masterminded by Flt Lts Turnill and Hedges. There was also some intensive four-ship work as the squadron looked into alternatives to the 'traditional' battle formation. A new 'Escort' formation, comprising a lead pair in loose echelon trailed by the rear pair in a wide battle formation was tried, and there were experiments with various techniques to try and get all four aircraft over a target in the minimum time. Live firing of HE strafe and SNEB rockets under control of a FAC was carried out by three crews[50] in July on the range at Bergen-Hohne. Among all this activity, during a sortie by Flt Lt Turnill and Sqn Ldr Adams on 20 July, the squadron achieved its 5,000th Phantom hour[51]. This milestone was deemed good enough reason for a much-needed 'beercall' to reward the ground crew for their hard work.

Nine days later, Turnill and Adams and Flt Lts J. Courcoux and R. Taylor set off for a 10 day detachment to Cyprus to take part in a firepower demonstration for chiefs of staff at CENTO. The profile involved carrying out pairs pull-ups for live SNEB rocket and gun attacks on a floating target (which they managed to sink twice!).

The Salmond Trophy which ran from 21 to 25 August 1972, was fought over by Brüggen's three Phantom units (14, 17 and 31 Squadrons) and XV Squadron's Buccaneers from Laarbruch. Competition sorties involved carrying out firstly a level attack on a field target, which was marked for accuracy of overflight and timing by umpires standing 50yd either side of the target, followed by a range detail. The first pass was a timed FRA lay-down pass followed by the dive pattern for retard bombing and SNEB rocket passes. After two rounds 14 Squadron was in front of the others, but XV Squadron overtook them in the next round. After a nail-biting finish, 14 Squadron were declared the overall winners after achieving a narrow lead in the 5th round. Flt Lts Edwards and Hedges scored the best individual round, while Flt Lt Turnill and Sqn Ldr Adams scored the best aggregate score. Once again, 14 Squadron's people celebrated in style!

There was no let-up in the pressure, though, for Wg Cdr Bryant or Sqn Ldr Watson. The former had been selected to command the 2 ATAF team for the forthcoming 10th Tactical Weapons Meet at Florennes and the latter was to captain the Brüggen Team. This team, which had been picked at random from all of Brüggen's crews by DCINCENT, included the 14 Squadron crew Flt Lts P. Day and B.R. Lee. Sqn Ldr Watson's harsh-training regime ensured that Brüggen's representatives were on top form for the 10 day Meet which started on 19 September. The 14 Squadron crew scored the highest national score of any of the dual-role teams and played a vital part in 2 ATAF's victory over 4 ATAF. A direct practical benefit of the competition was that 14 Squadron was able to adopt a modified profile for LADD[52] deliveries, developed by Sqn Ldr Watson, which was more accurate than the 'standard' method used until then.

The next month, birdspeeds came into force again with the commensurate decrease in the quality of low-flying until early December. The squadron split into a two-shift system to try to make the most of the flying opportunities. This approach meant that a four-wave day could be flown, with the 'early shift' flying the first two waves of day flying and the 'late shift' flying one day and one night wave. The advantages of this system were that better use could be made of the aircraft and that there was greater availability of aircrew for ground training; but on the down side it also meant that some ground training had to be duplicated and, perhaps more importantly, it split the squadron into two. However, the squadron could still work together when necessary. On 2 November, flying was cancelled early due to thick fog and not long afterwards 20 Squadron at Wildenrath were the recipients of a visit from the entire 14 Squadron aircrew, complete with bagpipes (thanks to Sqn Ldr Watson) and liquid refreshments!

The squadron's second MPC of the year was held at RAF Valley for the week beginning 7 November. Four crews led by Sqn Ldr R. Booth fired four missiles, two of which were successful launches and two unsuccessful.

The usual winter weather disrupted the flying programme through the season and the 'R-Hour' launch of the Minival on 25 January had to be a 'taxi launch' because the fog was too thick to fly. The aircraft were required to taxi out to the runway to demonstrate that they could have launched 'for real', but then taxied the length

Phantom FGR.2 XV411 on the 'pan' at Decimomannu, Sardinia with Sqn Ldr R. Booth and Flt Lt R. Crane, April 1973. (14 Squadron Association)

of the runway and back to dispersal. In the following month, seven sorties were flown on 'Exercise Black Prince' during which simulated attacks were flown against deployed mobile army headquarters units. The army sent their congratulations on the accuracy of the attacks, but little did they know that their camouflage was so good that none of the crews actually saw the target!

The squadron deployed to Decimomannu for the 1973 APC on 24 April. This year's emphasis was on flying 'operational' patterns from low level rather than the more usual 'academic' range patterns. Since the operational pattern was more demanding and less familiar to crews, the weaponry scores might be expected to suffer; however the actual results were very satisfying as the crews were able to match the scores they had only previously achieved from the 'academic pattern'. Once again the *Luftwaffe* F-104 Starfighter detachment was challenged to a strafing competition and once again the Phantoms produced a satisfyingly high score; but once again the Starfighters bettered it and again, 14 Squadron's crews ended up buying the beer! The weather was good throughout the detachment and the APC was also notable for a record-breaking 165 sorties flown in 5 days.

On 16 May, the squadron returned to Brüggen and started preparations for the forthcoming Taceval. A 3-day Maxeval on 28 May proved to be a good practice for Taceval, which was called at 05:00hrs on 15 June. In fact, this was simply a test of the squadron's reaction time and ability to generate aircraft. Once it was complete the Taceval Team left the station for a 10-day break before the flying phase. The latter proved to be disappointing, thanks to poor exercise scenarios involving long hours in NBC and too little tasking, but the squadron nevertheless achieved top ratings, so the evaluators, at least, were happy.

The Salmond Scandal

The rest of the summer was spent working up for the Salmond Trophy under the direction of Flt Lts Day and Lee. They had decided that the best way to practice would be to fly the Salmond Trophy sortie profile, but with twice the workload: there were two field targets to find, followed by an FRA and range detail during which crews had to leave the range and rejoin for another FRA before leaving a second time to find another target on the way home. This training proved to be extremely effective when the competition started on 16 July, for after three rounds 14 Squadron held an unassailable lead over the other units. At this stage, the commanding officers of 17 and 31 Squadrons decided to object formally to 14 Squadron flying the dive pattern at 400kt as opposed to the 450kt used by their squadrons. This seemed strange as both units had been informed well in advance of 14 Squadron's intention and had not raised any objection at the time. In short it was a cynical piece of gamesmanship. Unfortunately, the umpires upheld the objection and all of the points awarded to 14 Squadron for weaponry were removed, so that the lead of 120 points became a deficit of 20. Interestingly, when Wg Cdr Ord, OC 17 Squadron, led the 2 ATAF team to the 12th Tactical Weapons Meet the following year he agreed that dive-bombing should be carried out at 400kt – thus ensuring that the 2 ATAF team won!

The runway at Brüggen was resurfaced during the first 14 days of August, so the Phantoms operated out of Wildenrath during this period. The limited facilities at Wildenrath in turn meant that the flying programme would be restricted to a total of just eight sorties a day. In practice, this restriction was sidestepped by combing routine sorties with the cross-servicing 'Exercise Round Flag', thus generating an extra turn around per aircraft. Six crews were also dispatched to Cyprus for 'Exercise Red Rock II'. Apart from enjoying the Mediterranean sun they were able to drop 1,000lb bombs on the range.

At the end of the month Wg Cdr D.J. Hine assumed command of the squadron. A week of fine weather in September coincided with the aptly named 'Exercise Sky Blue'. This exercise, which had been so enthusiastically received in 1971, proved again to be a rewarding event. In the 4 days of the exercise, which started on 11 September sixty-four sorties were flown with a variety of profiles: there were attacks at ranges and airfields in the UK, France and Denmark, as well as FAC and interdiction missions within Germany. 'A four-day AFCENT exercise,' wrote Flt Lt J. Walliker, in the squadron diary, 'meant that we would do all the flying and procedures as in a Minival, but without the thrill of wearing our NBC kit or reacting to air raid alarms... there was a fair amount of FAC in [Low Flying] Area 3 on fairly large concentrations of army equipment including Chieftains, tank transporters and APCs.' A month later the picture was very different with birds and poor weather limiting the flying. The first squadron exchange as a Phantom unit took place between 16 and 26 October when Sqn Ldr D.A. Griffiths led four aircraft to exchange with the 23 Tactical Fighter Squadron (TFS) at Spangdahlem. The USAF reciprocated by sending two aircraft to Brüggen. The exchange coincided with the start of the 'Yom Kippur War' and a month later the beginnings of the 'Oil Crisis' were being felt at Brüggen. To an extent these were obscured by very cold weather, which restricted flying for much of the winter and, for example less than half the normal flying task was achieved in December. In fact, the squadron was stood down on 21 December in order to conserve fuel.

Missile Practice Camp (MCP) at RAF Valley in February 1974. From left to right: Flt Lt I. Vacha, 360 Sqn, Flt Lt A. Jones, 360 Sqn, Flt Lt B.R. Lee, Flt Lt K.G. Griffin, Dr Alfred Price, Sqn Ldr J. Watson, Flt Lt J. Feeney, Wg Cdr D.J. Hine, Flt Lt J.A. Cosgrove, Flt Lt R. Crane, two 360 Sqn, Flt Lt P. Day. (14 Squadron Association)

'NATO Beercall'

The poor weather provided a wonderful opportunity to hold a 'NATO Beercall' organized by Sqn Ldr Watson, '…so that the other nations who took part in the NATO Tactical Bombing competitions could stay in touch. The first one was at Brüggen [on 4 January 1974] and I replaced all the mess furniture with scrap furniture from the stores dump. We then had a competition to burn it all. As the bonfires started I met a grey-haired guy in flying suit with no wings or rank markings and asked him if he was visiting his grandchildren; he said no, he was C-in-C RAF Germany ('Mickey' Martin of 'Dambusters' fame). After burning all the mess furniture we did the same to the mess of Boelke Geschwader at Norvenich but the Germans had new furniture… and the same at Volkel which was the last "NATO Beercall" as the wheels [authorities] prohibited them.'

With the Low Flying Areas unusable because of the poor weather, the squadron ran an air-combat phase at the end of January, organised by Flt Lt P. Day. On 3 February, four crews[53] detached to RAF Valley for the third MPC, during which two AIM-7 Sparrow radar-guided missiles would be fired, followed by two AIM-9D Sidewinder heat-seeking missiles. To add to the interest, the missiles would be fired into a 4-mile long corridor of 'chaff' laid by Canberras of 360 Squadron. The first firing attempt, on 4 February, had to be aborted due a power failure in the range control at Aberporth, but the following morning Sqn Ldr Watson[54] and Flt Lt Feeney were ready to fire again. 'We had to lock on to a towed source,' recalled Sqn Ldr Watson, 'then break lock as it flew

Members of 14 Squadron's ground crew at Decimomannu in June 1974. (Barry Rolfe)

through chaff then attempt to lock on in chaff. The nav, Jim Feeny, could not lock on so I boresighted and fired, but my boresight had locked on to the Jindivik which broke up and spun into the sea.' Unfortunately, this success meant that there was no target available for Flt Lts Day and Vacha, much to their disappointment. After another day's delay, because of bad weather, it was time to fire the Sidewinders. The morning sortie was unsuccessful because the missiles kept locking on to the low sun rather than the target flare towed behind the Jindivik. In the afternoon, Flt Lts Griffin and R Crane[55] fired successfully at the target with an almost exact tail-on aspect and scored a hit on the flare. The next range slot was 5 days later on 12 February, and that afternoon Flt Lts Jones[56] and Cosgrove fired their Sidewinder at a high-angle off, from just behind the beam, and despite the challenging intercept geometry the missile fused as it passed the flare.

Although weather and fuel shortage kept flying hours down, some interesting weaponry events kept crews on their toes. On 26 February, three crews were each able to drop two live 1,000lb bombs at Vliehors range and on 2 April, six aircraft took part in a live strafe against old armoured vehicles on the Bergen-Hohne range under the supervision of a FAC. And despite hot rumours that APC would be cancelled to save fuel, the squadron detached to Decimomannu from 18 April to 14 May. On the way there Sqn Ldr Watson, who had organized the whole detachment, diverted into Istres with a radio problem on his way to 'Deci': unfortunately nobody else knew the master plan so the APC got off to a slow start. The weather in Sardinia was unkind, too, at the start of the detachment, but it soon cleared up and the squadron was able to complete its tasking. The joint top-scoring crews on the range during the APC were Flt Lts Day and J. Nottingham and Flt Lts S. Johnson and J. Feeney. As in previous detachments there was a strong social scene and an all-ranks barbeque on 26 April did much to cement ground and aircrew relations at the beginning of the APC. While at 'Deci' the social life for the aircrew, according to the diarist Flt Lt Griffin, '…revolved around vino rosso, spaghetti and the '*Pig and Tapeworm*'. The latter was the rudimentary bar in the officers' block which comprised an empty room and a beer fridge!'

In April, the Brüggen team for the 11th AFCENT TWM was announced. Although the team was captained by the commanding officer of 17 Squadron, whose unit provided the aircraft, the team itself was drawn from all three squadrons. It was led by Sqn Ldr Watson with Flt Lt J.A. Cosgrove and also included Flt Lt N. Brown with Sqn Ldr P.J. Goodman from 14 Squadron[57]. Sqn Ldr Watson, '…flew with each crew over three months, debriefed all their cine film and gave each an individual correction factor for toss which was very effective. We always flew operationally, never non-tactically. The deal was 14 [squadron crews] flew numbers one and three, 17 [squadron crew] the number two and 31 [squadron crew] number four…With the gunsight mod using the air-to-air sight with a different resistance in the sight for ground attack deflection (the F4 sight was fixed for strafing so you had to aim upwind to wire it normally) we achieved great averages over twelve shoots from operational attacks. The only team to do so. Eighty percent better scores than the nearest 4 ATAF team. The Meet was on at that time unseen targets on Suippes range and others, low-level toss, laydown strafe and bombing. Great fun.' The competition at Baden-Soellingen at the beginning of June was a resounding success for the 2 ATAF team, which picked up three of the four trophies and it was a victory which was largely owed to the skill and dedication of the 14 Squadron crews. Flt Lt Cosgrove later recalled: 'We were a very cohesive team, and we just got on with the job really to the normal high standard of the Brüggen Wing at that time and we all felt intensely proud to take part in the final ceremony and receive the trophy. To cap it all, the Canadian organization and hospitality at Soellingen was simply outstanding, and the social side was as challenging as the flying, but we coped manfully.'

Sqn Ldr Goodman's, '…first sortie [was] with Nick Brown on 27 May 1974, a night laydown sortie. The other events we entered were retard, strafe and LADD, all done at Suippes range in France and the sorties included a navigation content… Nick and I were the top-scoring team in the ATAF. However, there was one F-104 pilot from the Royal Bavarian Air Force [*Luftwaffe*] who out scored us! He was an ace at night laydown! The closing ceremony was on 7 June 1974 and the whole 2ATAF team took off the next morning (a Saturday) in a fairly hung-over state to fly in a formation of twenty-three assorted aircraft over Germany with elements dropping off at their airfields after a gaggle flypast. The Germans and Belgians flew F-104s, the Dutch [Northrop] F-5s and we were in Phantoms. The briefing for this sortie was carried out over breakfast and was one of the fastest briefings for a formation of this size that I had attended. The only dissent at the briefing was that Jock Watson did not want us called "Yellow" section, so he got it changed to "Gold!" The leader was running out of colours.' One of the first ports of call for

The closing ceremony of 11th AFCENT tactical weapons meet at Baden-Soellingen on 7 June 1974: the Bruggen team celebrating with the trophy won by 2 ATAF. From left to right: Flt Lt I. Grigg, Flt Lt M.W. Ball, Flt Lt J. Cosgrove, Flt Lt J. Stuttard, Flt Lt Hough, Wg Cdr G.E. Orde, Sqn Ldr J. Watson, Sqn Ldr G.E. Culpitt, Flt Lt M.J. Selves, Flt Lt N. Brown, Sqn Ldr P.J. Goodman, Flt Lt B. Hardy-Gillings. (Peter Goodman)

this impressive formation was Brüggen, where according to Flt Lt Cosgrove, '…the euphoria almost came to a very sudden end. We were on the easterly runway for the flypast, and with twenty–three aircraft in line astern we extended the flight path over JHQ Rheindahlen. Our passage did not go unnoticed! Anyway, the formation disbanded and we returned to Brüggen for a particularly sporting run and break to land. Now for the reality check! As we taxied in the Station Commander's car hove into view. As we unstrapped he shouted up from the tarmac, "…I've just had the C-in C on the 'phone. He saw your flypast, you went directly over his residence. You've got an hour to get the whole team round there." This looked like an invitation to the biggest bollocking of all time, and we were somewhat deflated to say the least. As we sloped off disconsolately towards the crew room the Station Commander called after us, "…you had better get smartened up, and pick up your wives, girlfriends and families, he's hosting an impromptu reception in your honour!" Well that put the spring back into our step, and we duly reported to the C-in-C's residence for a very unexpected but very gracious, "thank you and well done" the sincerity of which was enhanced by its spontaneity. The C-in C (Air Marshal Sir Nigel Maynard, KCB, CBE, DFC, AFC) was of course also COM2ATAF, and he was "cock-a-hoop" that 2 ATAF had thrashed the USAF dominated 4 ATAF in the competition. We certainly appreciated his hospitality.'

During the summer the squadron settled into the RAFG routine, although the fuel shortages began to be felt. The gunpods, a source of drag, were removed from the Phantoms to improve the fuel efficiency and 'bounce' aircraft were no longer flown as a further fuel-saving measure. A coincidental shortage of practice bombs also restricted weaponry sorties. However, it did not stop Flt Lts J. A. Walliker and B. Titchen detaching to RAF Leuchars with three crews from 31 Squadron to take part in a trial dropping live 1,000lb bombs. The trial involved carrying out toss deliveries of various weapon loads including a stick of seven bombs, on the range at Garvie Island (off of Cape Wrath, Scotland). Other highlights of the summer months included a visit to the Heineken brewery in Amsterdam by the ground crew on 22 September arranged by Cpl Jeff 'Dixie' Dean. Not long after this visit Cpl J. Malone, '…happened to be in stores one day when I looked out and saw (and heard) an argument in the middle of the (otherwise empty) hangar. The sergeant electrician was shouting at the JEngO [Junior Engineering Officer]. And what I heard was, "The management on this squadron couldn't organize a piss up in a brewery!" And he turned and started to walk off. He then stopped, turned back to the JEngO, pointed over at the stores where I was standing, unseen, and shouted, "In fact, on this squadron it takes a corporal storeman to organize a piss up in a brewery!"'

In October, the squadron sent two crews[58] to Ramstein to participate in the USAFE radar bombing and electronic warfare competition, 'Exercise Creek Scope III'. They won. 'Nick and I flew the Creek Scope sortie on the night of 17 October 1974,' recalled Sqn Ldr Goodman. 'This was the first and, I believe, last time we entered the USAFE radar bombing and EW competition. There were three categories of entry; F-111s from Upper Heyford, latest mark of F-4 from 4ATAF and an older mark of F-4, plus us and some Buccaneers. The competition was supposed to be held over five nights operating from Ramstein. The sorties comprised a night-radar navigation cross-country with radar scored "bombs" dropped at the Radar Bomb Scoring Units (RBSUs) at Gutersloh and Ramstein. The "bombs" were given a nominal forward throw of 3,000ft so that the pilots could not cheat and help out the nav, whose night navigation skill this competition was supposed to test. This was not something we normally practised and we got stuck into the new techniques about ten weeks before the comp. In the simulator at Brüggen we had stored away some three-dimensional scale models of the landmass of Germany. By shining a light on these models from the scale height at which we were going to fly, we got light and shade photographs of what the radar would see if we flew over the land at that height. So each leg of the sortie had a shadow map strip stuck alongside it and we navigated from these. Absolutely invaluable in the hilly country of southern Germany and the Ramstein RBSU. We hit on an incredibly Heath-Robinson method of bombing at Ramstein. After several practice sorties we chose some offsets (tops of sharp hills) which stood out on the radar and corresponded to the landmass model. From these offsets we flew an accurate track and groundspeed for a given time to cover the distance between the offset and the forward throw of 3,000ft, which was set as a cursor on the radar. The Americans had an automatic tone cut-off at the release of their "bomb" we didn't have this system and had to rely on the nav giving a countdown to "release, 3, 2, 1 NOW," when the RBSU would lift their pen off your trace and thus score your "bomb." More Heath-Robinson! The countryside around Gutersloh is fairly flat and the shadow strip is not much use here. We had to revert to the technique of finding man-made offsets in the target area. The Phantom's radar was not really optimized for ground mapping, but the Buccaneers were even worse off. The competition required that each crew should fly two sorties, in the event only one was counted because fog cancelled some sorties. Nick and I flew one sortie and Paul Day and Jim Nottingham did not fly at all. So we won on the strength of scores something like 900ft at Ramstein and 250ft at Gutersloh. I must have called "NOW" a second too early at Ramstein, travelling at about 700 feet per second!"

On 12 November, the alert hooter sounded at 04:50hrs, heralding the start of a Maxeval. After all the aircraft had been generated by ground crew wearing full NBC kit, they were launched for 'Option Delta.' In the afternoon, aircraft were launched to Vliehors so that crews could qualify to ACE standards. This they managed, despite the challenges of a 30kt crosswind! The station was stood down in the evening and there followed a 5 day break before the operational phase was evaluated. This was a busy 3-day exercise involving FAC sorties as well as tasking against airfields and surface-to-air missile (SAM) sites. The last day, the strike phase, was a German public holiday, so with no flying allowed the 'R-Hour launch' was restricted to a taxi-launch.

Shortly after take-off[59] on 21 November, Flt Lts A. M. Keane and I. D. Vacha experienced an engine fire, which soon engulfed the rear of the aircraft. The intercom failed at this point and Flt Lt Keane instructed his navigator to eject using the 'Eject' light in the rear cockpit. Keane then attempted to eject himself but his seat did not fire – possibly because his canopy was being held by aerodynamic forces caused by the empty rear cockpit. As he struggled to keep the aircraft clear of built up areas, the nose dropped and Keane's seat fired successfully, ejecting him just before the aircraft hit the ground near the village of Maasbree to the southwest of Venlo. Both crew members were uninjured and they were able to attend Flt Lt Vacha's 'Dining Out' from the squadron the following evening.

Visits to the squadron the next month included the Chief of the Air Staff, Air Chief Marshal Sir Andrew Humphrey, GCB, OBE, DFC, AFC and also representatives from the village of Maasbree, who presented the squadron with a basket of locally-grown vegetables as a way of thanking Flt Lt Keane for missing their village!

Over the autumn and winter the squadron's flying had largely been concentrated on getting new arrivals through the combat ready work-up and in training up new formation leaders. The cause was greatly helped by some unseasonably good weather in January 1975. That month there was also the opportunity to fly four-ship fighter affiliation sorties against the Gutersloh-based Lightnings and at the end of the month it was the turn of the Phantom to play fighter against 20 Squadron's Harriers. The flying moved up to medium level in February with another air-combat phase which was flown in the Gutersloh air-combat area. Crews worked up from simple one-versus-one combat to more complex two-versus-one scenarios. But air-to-ground work was not forgotten and 4 days of range work was carried out at Vliehors at the end of the month.

February 1975 also saw the 60th Anniversary of both 14 Squadron and 17 Squadron. A joint Diamond Jubilee was held on 8 February comprising a parade, flying displays and an open day. In the evening, an anniversary ball was held in the officers' mess. The reviewing officer for the occasion was SASO RAFG, Air Commodore D. G. Bailey, CBE; he was a very appropriate choice as he had previously been the station commander at RAF Wildenrath when both squadrons had been based there in the late 1960s. Amongst those guests attending the event were three former squadron commanders: Wg Cdr E.

Phantom FGR.2 XV484 seen at high-level, flown by Flt Lt J.A. Walliker. (David Farquharson)

Donovan, OBE, DFC (1944-1945), Wg Cdr T.J. McElhaw (1968-1970) and Wg Cdr D.T. Bryant, OBE (1971-1973).

Although the 1973 'Arab-Israeli War' had ended recently, it was the lessons learned from the 1967 war which were now becoming apparent at Brüggen. Hardened Aircraft Shelters (HASs) were springing up on the dispersals at the corners of Brüggen's runways. However, these concrete structures were not destined to be used by the Phantoms: a policy change in 1972 had recognized the shortcomings of the Lightning in the air-defence role and it had been decided to replace that aircraft with the Phantom. Rather than procuring new Phantoms, those used by the strike/attack squadrons would be transferred to the air-defence units and the Phantom would be replaced in ground-attack roles by the SEPECAT Jaguar GR1. In some respects the single-seat Jaguar, which had originally been intended as a tactical-training aircraft, was a step backwards in terms of performance and capability when compared to the Phantom, but it offered significant cost savings. It also gave the RAF the capability to use the British-manufactured WE177 nuclear-strike weapon rather than the previous US-supplied weapons. On 7 April, the first Jaguars of 14 (Designate) Squadron arrived at Brüggen.

Meanwhile the Phantom squadron continued with the routine of exercises and training. In April, there was live strafe and dropping 1,000lb inert bombs at Bergen-Hohne range and in May low-level tactical flying and range work was interspersed with 2 weeks of 'bouncing' 3 Squadron's Harriers. During the first week of June, the squadron hosted the CF-104 Starfighters of 441 Squadron (RCAF), for the first half of a squadron exchange. The second half took place from 16 to 24 July and was the last major event for 14 Squadron as a full-strength Phantom squadron. For Flt Lt D. Farquharson it was, '…a very memorable exchange at Baden Soellingen. Most of us got a ride in a Starfighter and most of them flew in the back of an F-4.' On the first evening in the bar, the diminutive Flt Lt Farquharson was talking to a very large RCAF ground-defence officer called Captain Davis. 'The two of us were sat together talking,' recalled Farquharson, 'and the Boss (Derek Hine) seemed to think the contrast in sizes was hilarious, and that it would be a good wheeze to get us airborne together. Getting him kitted out was tricky – he was 6ft 8in tall and weighed more than 300lb. We borrowed a flying suit from the biggest chap on the squadron and squeezed him in the back, with the canopy just touching his head. The armourer assured us that Martin-Baker [ejection seat] would cope if it came to it, and off we went round Bavaria! This was his first ride in a combat aeroplane, and probably his last. He was hugely enthusiastic for the first 10 minutes, but then broke the record for throwing up. It says a lot for the human factor design in the F-4, that two such different specimens could operate it together.'

From August, the wind-down started in earnest and the squadron was reduced to half strength with just four aircraft, eight aircrews and seventy-two airmen. Despite the loss of half of its numbers the squadron still had to maintain its normal QRA commitment, although the aircraft were provided from the Wing. The remaining Phantoms were sufficiently serviceable to mount four-ship formations and morale remained high. The squadron took part in 'Exercise Cold Fire' in mid-September and then worked up for the final Salmond Trophy. Poor weather limited the Salmond Trophy to just two waves and at the end 14 Squadron was in fourth place. When considering that the unit was by now below half strength it was a good result, especially as the squadron was leading in all events apart from laydown bombing. The final flight by a Phantom from 14 Squadron was on 14 November.

Wg Cdr Hine presented beer tankards to the ground crew at the Brüggen Rugby Club on 17 November and the squadron officers held a farewell dinner at the Chateau Neercanne at Maastricht, 5 days later. During its time operating the Phantom, 14 Squadron had flown 14,000 sorties.

Baden Solingen, July 1975. RCAF Captain Davis about to 'enjoy' his back-seat ride in a Phantom with Flt Lt D. Farquharson. (David Farquharson)

NOTES

42   Phantom FGR2 XT912 (Watson) and XT914 (Sutton).

43   Frederick Rosier (1915-1998), a wartime fighter pilot, had worked with 14 Squadron in the Western desert.

44   'Mickey' Martin (1918-1988) was one of the legendary 'Dambusters'.

45   Phantom FGR2 XT914.

46   Phantom XT914.

47   Phantom XV413.

48   Flt Lt Turnill/Sqn Ldr Coriat, Flt Lt Edwards/Flt Lt Hedges, Flt Lt D.A. Griffiths/Flt Lt A. Vosloo, Flt Lt Rhodes/Flt Lt D.C. Smith.

49   In Phantom FGR2 XV464.

50   Sqn Ldr Booth/Flt Lt P. Compton, Flt Lt J.R.J. Froud/Flt Lt G.W. Graham, Flt Lt Griffiths/Flt Lt R. Sheppard.

51   In Phantom FGR2 XV464.

52   Low Angle Drogue Delivery – a toss delivery in which the weapon was retarded by a drogue. This delivery profile gave sufficient time for the aircraft to perform an escape manoeuvre when releasing an 'airburst' weapon.

53   Sqn Ldr Watson/Flt Lt J. Feeney, Flt Lt K. G. Griffin/Flt Lt R. Crane, Flt Lt A. Jones/Flt Lt J. Cosgrove and Flt Lt Day/Flt Lt I. D.Vacha.

54   In Phantom XV411.

55   In Phantom XV421.

56   In Phantom XV411.

57   The other crews were Ft Lts M. W. Ball/Sqn Ldr G.E. Culpitt, Flt Lts Hough/I. Grigg (17 Squadron) and Flt Lts M.J. Selves/Flt Lt J. Stuttard (31 Squadron).

58   Flt Lt Brown/Sqn Ldr Goodman, Flt Lt Day/Flt Lt Nottingham.

59   In Phantom XV441.

6

1975–1985
THE JAGUAR

Single-Seat Strike Squadron

14 Squadron (Jaguar) started assembling at Brüggen at the beginning of April 1975 under the command of Wg Cdr A. Mumford. The ten original pilots included Sqn Ldr D. A. Griffiths, OC 'A' Flight, who had previously served as a Phantom pilot on 14 Squadron. Wg Cdr Mumford collected the squadron's first Jaguar from Coltishall on 7 April and during the month three more aircraft arrived directly from British Aerospace at Warton. May saw the delivery of another four aircraft and four more pilots, Flt Lts N. M. Huckins, J. V. Lawton, G. A. Miller and G. W. Pixton. Most of the first 2 months was spent carrying out engineering acceptance checks on the new aircraft and theatre familiarization sorties for the pilots, which included bombing details at Nordhorn and Helchteren ranges as well as live FAC work.

Meanwhile, a major building project which had started at Brüggen in 1974 was nearing completion. The annihilation of the Egyptian Air Force at the start of the 1967 'Six-Day War' had demonstrated the vulnerability of aircraft on the ground to a surprise attack. NATO's initial response to this lesson had been a policy of dispersing aircraft around the airfield in time of war, rather than keeping them lined up neatly on the main apron. However, it was clear that while the revetments in the dispersals at the corners of airfields such as Brüggen did offer some protection, it was very limited. That protection, too, was dependent on receiving enough notice of an impending attack to disperse the aircraft. A new policy was therefore devised which required each unit to operate at all times as it would in war, from a dispersed, hardened site. At Brüggen new accommodation, in the form of nine concrete Hardened Aircraft Shelters (HAS – each capable of housing two Jaguars), a Pilot's Briefing Facility (PBF) and a Hardened Equipment Shelter (HES), were built on the south-east corner of the airfield. After lodging with 14 Squadron Phantoms on the 'waterfront' at Brüggen for 3 months, 14 Squadron Jaguars moved across to the new squadron home in July, becoming the

SEPECAT Jaguar XX762 from 14 Squadron over Diepholz airfield in late 1975 or early 1976. (RAFM PC94-201-475)

first RAF unit to operate from a hardened site. The move itself cost a week's worth of flying, as everyone was needed to set up the accommodation and to fortify the site with sandbags and barbed wire. Another 5 days' flying were then lost to high temperatures which exceeded the operational limits for the Jaguar. This latter snag was rectified in August when the Jaguar received clearance to operate in temperatures of up to 40°C – a rather higher temperature than might be encountered on a typical summer's day at Brüggen!

By September, the squadron had settled into the routine of operating from a HAS site. It now had sixteen pilots and eleven aircraft and was well into the work-ups for both the strike and attack roles. Much of the flying was in four-ship formations, with off-range Simulated Attack Profiles (SAPs), lots of FAC work and, on most sorties, a range detail at Nordhorn or Helchteren. The squadron was now able to participate fully in the monthly station Minivals and also took part in 'Exercise Cold Fire' in September, flying twenty-six exercise sorties on 18 September.

The Jaguar was designed to simplify the pilot's workload by automating many of the functions performed by the navigator in a two-seat attack aircraft. The heart of the Jaguar was the Navigation & Weapon Aiming Sub-System (NavWASS), based around an inertial platform[60], which provided navigation information (including driving a projected 'moving-map' display) and a weapon aiming sight via the Head-Up Display (HUD). Flt Lt M.W. Ball explained that, '…there was intent to prove the aircraft and get to grips with the NavWASS and make it work from the outset. I think we were keen not to repeat the Phantom experience of only using parts of the Inertial Nav[igation] system. When [the NavWASS] worked it was great, but in those early days we were getting so many kit dumps [failures], which meant that you had to fall back on map and stopwatch for navigation. Very often the kit would dump as the [after] burners lit on take-off, so you had to use both systems. Weaponry was the same. We used the kit more often than not, but due to the unreliability of the system we practised reversionary weaponry. However, I remember getting four DHs and 80 percent [strafe] on a sortie to Vliehors when it all worked.' Flt Lt N.M. Huckins found, '…the NavWASS could be relied on to get to the Initial Point (IP) but small targets which we used for SAPs almost always relied on 50,000 [scale map] and stopwatch. This was as much about getting the Time On Target (TOT) spot on as well. I always used a 50,000 for FRAs on Nordhorn as you had to be exactly lined up so that you could still get the bomb off even if you actually saw the target at two seconds to go. NavWASS was not accurate enough for this. NavWASS drifted about 1½ miles an hour at best and could be much worse. Fixing helped but if it was running away – it was better to not bother as the effort to keep it up to date was distracting.' Flt Lt G.A. Miller also found that fixing the kit might make matters worse: '…by far the most popular form of kit management was the 'random fix'. When you identified that the Projected Map Display (PMD) was not showing your actual position, you could slew the map to put it where you knew you were. This was okay but we ended up using a very expensive NavWASS as a form of someone else holding the map for you. Also, the PMD was a roll of film that scooted around behind the screen and it stretched, hence, even if the kit thought it knew where it was and was correct, the PMD may not actually display it as such. Random fixing introduced a lot of errors into the kit which it then translated into erroneous changes in wind strength and direction, which it then regurgitated as soon as you wanted to use it for weapon aiming.'

The novelty value of a new aeroplane operating from a HAS site meant that there was no shortage of visitors, including Princess Margaret who visited the squadron on 24 September. October also brought a film crew to the squadron to record material for a RAF recruiting film entitled 'Strike Squadron.'

Salmond Success

There was a major turnover of aircraft in the autumn because the early production Jaguars were not fitted with the electrical wiring necessary for carrying strike weapons. They had been issued to the squadron as an interim measure so that the squadron could set itself up at Brüggen, but from October new aircraft with the requisite wiring started to arrive from the factory. As they were taken onto the squadron inventory the original aircraft were dispatched to the OCU. Apart from managing the exchange of aircraft, the engineers were also kept busy preparing the aircraft for the forthcoming Salmond Trophy. The squadron was very much aware that the spotlight would be on the new Jaguar's performance in the competition: 'Both Duncan Griffiths, my flight commander, and I were on Phantoms at Brüggen prior to being on the Jag and the Phantom community was not impressed with a "Pussy Cat" taking over their role!' recalled Flt Lt Ball. The work-up for the competition started in October with squadron engineers ensuring that the HUDs and the inertial platforms in each aircraft were harmonized.

The flying programme ensured that the pilots honed their skills. All sorties followed the Salmond profile comprising a field target, which had to be precisely overflown at a specific time, and a range detail at Nordhorn which started with a timed laydown FRA followed by a dive pass. Initially, the training sorties were made artificially harder than the actual competition sorties would be by including not one, but three field targets before the joining range. In the first week of November, the profile was refined and relaxed to include just one field target, but the pilots were given details only an hour before take-off. During this phase Flt Lt R. W. Lindo, one of the officers holding with the squadron while awaiting his next flying training course, was sent out to mark the accuracy of each over flight of the field targets.

The competition itself was held in the second week of November. The rules required two aircraft to fly the route on each wave, so the morning and afternoon wave which were planned for each of the 5 days generated a potential twenty competition sorties. In fact the appalling weather precluded low flying or range work for much of the week, and only two waves – or four countable sorties – were flown. However, the practice of the previous months paid off and the Jaguar pilots performed very well. Flt Lt Ball flew his first competition sortie[61] on 10 November and, '...got a hit "to the second" on the field target and then a DH laydown "to the second." Two days later he was able to repeat his success[62], thus scoring 100 percent on two sorties. With this creditable performance, 14 Squadron Jaguars won the Salmond Trophy just 7 months after receiving their first aircraft.

On 22 November, 14 Squadron (Phantom) was stood down and at a formal hand-over parade on 1 December the 14 Squadron Standard was presented to the Jaguar unit. However, the squadron was not yet combat ready and the strike work-up continued. In theory, using the British WE177 nuclear-strike weapon should have simplified procedures because there was no need for a USAF ADO. But the Jaguar brought a new and unique problem to the strike role: RAF strike procedures were founded on the 'two-man principle' whereby no person had access to a nuclear strike weapon without being accompanied by another qualified person. In the two-crew Canberra and Phantom this had been straightforward since the crew monitored and supervized each other, but once a Jaguar pilot got into the cockpit he was alone. In practice, it was relatively easy to adhere to the 'two-man principle' and Flt Lt Huckins, '...was always very proud of the fact that we were single-seat strike pilots in company with the F-104 strike pilots from other 2 ATAF forces. The procedures were worked out right from the beginning. We did all acceptances and handovers as two pilots. For example for QRA, I would go to my aircraft with the outgoing pilot and do the checks with him as second man. On exercise two pilots would go to the aircraft, one as the mission pilot, the second as the second man. For the release the policeman was the second man. He would allow one HAS door to be opened for engine start. We would get the release message that contained a release code. This was written on the back of the Combat Mission Folder (CMF) and shown to the policeman. He would have his release code in an envelope – which he opened when he saw the pilot's. If they matched – he opened the second door to allow the aircraft to taxi. If this system failed – there was a back up man (usually Sqn Ldr Ops) who would come to the HAS to resolve any problems.

Exchange with the French Air Force Jaguar Wing at St Dizier, April 1976. Left to right, standing: French Air Force (FAF), Fg Off R.A. Baron, Sqn Ldr J.B. Hill, Flt Lt J.V. Lawton, Flt Lt G.A. Miller, Sqn Ldr D.A. Griffiths, Fg Off F.L. Turner: FAF: Fg Off G.W. Pixton. Crouching: Flt Lt R.A. Kirby: FAF: Flt Lt D.J. Tester: FAF: Fg Off P. Rushton: FAF: Frank Turner later commanded 14 Squadron(Tornado). (Dusty Miller)

It seemed to work well – I never had any problems for release during exercise. The release broadcast was on radio and telebrief. If this did not work then the backup man gave the policemen the release and your release code.' A final check of strike procedures was carried out in the Maxeval which ran from 16 to 21 January, and was followed by 2 days of range work so that all pilots could qualify to ACE standards. The squadron then took its place as the RAF's first single-seat strike squadron, holding QRA from 1 March 1976.

Squadron Routine

The routine pattern of operations for the Jaguar squadron was little different from its Phantom predecessor. Outside the monthly Minivals and other major exercises, the daily-flying programme sought to use the aircraft as much as possible while filling the squadron's commitments to routine exercises. For example, the FAC 'Exercise Crazy Horse' had become a weekly task, while others such as the cross-servicing 'Exercise Ample Gain' were regular but less frequent. Most flying was carried out in pairs or four-ship formations and if there were no external commitments, the sorties were designed to fill each pilot's basic training requirements. This annual syllabus, dictated by HQ RAFG, ensured that all aircrew maintained a good all-round level of operational proficiency. Other sorties might be for the benefit of new pilots working up to combat-ready status, or be part of a work up for pilots to qualify as formation leaders. Since the Jaguar was an inherently serviceable aircraft pilots could have their fill of flying: for example, Flt Lt Huckins flew 40 hours in September 1977.

The first Jaguar exchange was with the French Jaguar Wing at St Dizier. Five aircraft with seven pilots and thirty-eight ground crew deployed to St Dizier for 9 days on 20 April. Despite the apparent reluctance on the French side to fly very much, a busy flying programme complemented the social life. Even the fact that, according to Flt Lt Ball, '…the French AF still had wine for lunch in those days did not dampen Wg Cdr Mumford's enthusiasm for flying and attack sorties were flown (after lunch!) in the French low-flying system, making use of Suippes range. However, 'The most momentous recollection,' for Flt Lt Huckins, 'was the weekend in the middle of the detachment when a group led by Anthony Mumford drove down to Burgundy. I was introduced to the delights of red Burgundy by the expert (Anthony was a connoisseur). After a number of tasting sessions, it concluded with a fantastic lunch in Gevrey Chambertin.' A simultaneous detachment by four French AF Jaguars to Brüggen was able to low fly in Germany.

With the Salmond Trophy looming in July, the squadron started to work-up for the competition in June. By now the other squadrons at Brüggen had re-equipped with the Jaguar, so there was keen competition from within the Wing. With the impending resurfacing of Brüggen's runway, the Wing moved to Wildenrath for 2 months. The QRA aircraft remained at Brüggen and would use the southern taxiway to take-off in the event of their being scrambled. Once again, 14 Squadron's pilots flew 'Salmond' profile sorties, and range details concentrated on reversionary bombing so that everyone was in practice, should the need arise on the day. Unfortunately, 14 Squadron's first fatal accident for 20 years occurred on the afternoon of 2 July. Flt Lt T. M. Bushnell crashed 5 miles northwest of Cloppenburg during a work-up sortie. The weather at the time was perfect and it appears likely that he became distracted inside the cockpit while updating his NavWASS at low level and inadvertently descended into the ground.

The Salmond Trophy was held from 19 to 23 July and once again the competition was cursed with poor weather. However, 14 Squadron's preparation paid off once more and a clear lead was quickly established over the other eight participating squadrons. Once again Flt Lt Ball was scored 100 percent on two of his three competition sorties. Flt Lt Miller flew, '…two competition sorties. The profile was two timed field targets, a timed laydown FRA on the strike target at Nordhorn followed by a shallow dive bomb on Target 3. The first competition sortie[63] scored a mere 91percent, whereas the second sortie scored 100 percent (in the same aircraft) – the second sortie was flown in two parts…with the shallow dive bomb being the sole element of the second part.' The lead was maintained to the end and 14 Squadron enjoyed its second successive Salmond Trophy victory.

With Brüggen's runway still closed in August, Jaguar flying continued from Wildenrath. This was not an altogether successful arrangement because the local population became incensed by the noise of night-flying aircraft and set fire to the runway approach lights in protest! Happily there were no such complaints the following month when 14 Squadron deployed to Decimomannu for the first Jaguar APC. Ten

Jaguar GR1s and two Jaguar T2s flew out to Sardinia on 2 September. Over the next 3 weeks the pilots practised loft and toss bombing, 5° reversionary dive bombing, laydown and strafe.

Back at Brüggen the autumn brought mixed fortunes – October was plagued by poor weather, poor serviceability and migrating birds, all of which frustrated the flying programme. On the other hand, the squadron was able to fly 500hrs in November: four-ship formations with 'bounces' were flown in Germany and when the weather on the continent was not good enough, the Jaguars flew high-low sorties into the UK low-flying system. There was also tasking for 'Exercise Spearpoint', the annual 1 (British) Corps manoeuvres on 10 and 11 November and later in the month fighter-affiliation sorties were flown against 19 Squadron's Lightnings.

Birdstrikes were an everyday hazard of operating at low-level and even a small bird could do a remarkable amount of damage to an aircraft, as Flt Lt Huckins discovered. On the afternoon of 10 December, he was flying a 'singleton' sortie[64] and looking forward to the pre-Christmas party that evening. He was, '...just approaching the Nordhorn strike run – flying into sun. I saw, very late, a flock of large birds with no time to avoid them. One very large bird hit the left side of the canopy just aft of the canopy arch and came straight through it. The remains struck me on the right arm and then went on to hit the radio-intercom connector from the seat to the aircraft, which was to the port side of the seat – which broke and removed any connection to the radio. The whole canopy shattered leaving me in a 420kt convertible and it was very cold. All the maps which were in a Simulated Strike Profile CMF (containing the target which was a German SAM site – therefore secret) disappeared out the top. The bird had given me a dead arm, so I could not use the throttle with my left hand and had to reach over to reduce power with my right. Once I slowed down – I could now here myself think, but no radio. I headed towards Hopsten and squawked emergency. (This was never picked up by any agency – probably IFF was not working). I circled Hopsten and saw a green light from tower. Presuming this was clearance to land – I did so and stopped on the runway and stood up through the broken canopy. A civilian car eventually left the Ops block and bumped its way across the grass. Subsequently, I was told by the driver (the Wing Flight Safety Officer – who was the only officer on the base – doing some catch up work before going off for the weekend) that Hopsten was in fact shut. The green light was the rotating beacon on the top of the tower. The German Air Force almost universally shut up shop at Friday lunchtime to go off for the weekend. After a quick pain killer from the duty medic I was picked up in a T2 by Flt Lt 'Rip' Kirby and made it back for the pre-Christmas party that night.'

The New Year brought more Lightning affiliation when a detachment of aircraft from 11 Squadron visited Brüggen during January. The station-alert siren sounded at 10:30hrs on Saturday morning 12 February 1977, announcing the start of Taceval. Until that moment, weekends were generally considered to be sacrosanct, but despite this unusual departure from normal expectations three-quarters of the pilots were at the squadron within 30 minutes and all were on duty within an hour of the alert being called. One of the first to arrive was Sqn Ldr Griffiths who found himself confronted by locked doors and no keys – and the watchful eye of the Taceval Team. In a piece of quick thinking, which must have impressed the team, he launched himself through a convenient window and gained access to the squadron in an unorthodox way! By 19:00hrs the Taceval Team had seen enough of the station's initial response and a temporary halt was called to the proceedings for the rest of the weekend. The exercise started again on the following Monday morning and lasted 3 days, culminating in a mass launch of the Wing's Jaguars on their 'equivalent' strike missions. The 'equivalent' routes matched the real strike routes for time, but remained well west of the Inner German Border (IGB) and all dovetailed together to generate a stream of aircraft flying through Nordhorn for an FRA at one minute intervals. Although the bomb scores achieved counted towards the station's overall Taceval rating, there was fierce competition between the Brüggen squadrons to get the best scores. With a CEP[65] of 50ft in laydown and 45ft in dive bombing, 14 Squadron's were the best on the Wing. Overall the squadron was awarded a '1' excellent rating.

Third Salmond Victory – 1977

With the formation of a fourth Jaguar squadron at Brüggen in March, the Jaguar Wing comprising 14, 17, 20 and 31 Squadrons was now complete. Despite the inevitable healthy rivalry between the squadrons the station commander, Gp Capt J.R. Walker, AFC was determined to lead a Wing which would operate seamlessly together in time of war. A number of station-run exercises were instigated to mould the Wing together, including an intensive 2 days of 'Exercise Iron Spike' on 13 and 14 April. This exercise was an opportunity to evaluate various new ideas for Close-Air Support (CAS) missions such as methods of re-tasking aircraft in flight. The Wing approach also extended into preparations for the Salmond Trophy: with victory in the trophy going to a Jaguar squadron for the previous 2 years, it was decided that every effort must be made to retain the trophy at Brüggen. 'Exercise Crooked Crab', designed to give the whole Jaguar Wing a good work-up for the Salmond Trophy started in March and filled the latter half of April. Each sortie comprised two timed field targets, and timed laydown and dive FRAs at Nordhorn. The flying was busy with three waves of six aircraft each day committed to 'Crooked Crab'. Once again, 14 Squadron's engineers carefully selected and monitored the NavWASS equipment in each aircraft.

As a means of working up the Brüggen Wing, 'Exercise Crooked Crab' was an unqualified success: Brüggen's squadrons took three of the first four places in the Salmond Trophy competition during the first week of May. Despite some very bad luck on the first day of the competition, when a practice bomb dropped by Wg Cdr Mumford did not explode (and therefore could not be scored), 14 Squadron's pilots performed admirably, winning the trophy for a third consecutive year, the first and only unit to have done so.

Over the next 2 weeks, four aircraft cycled through Lossiemouth so that the pilots could re-qualify in loft and toss deliveries on the range at Tain. 'Loft was a run-in, pull-up and stabilize in a 30° climb, then pickle off the bomb/s after an appropriate delay,' explained Flt Lt Miller, '...whereas toss was an automatic attack committing somewhere in the pull-up and allowing the kit to determine and execute bomb release under 'g'. They both depended on an accurate update just prior to the attack: for loft, to determine the pull-up point, for toss, the whole thing. Neither was terribly accurate, although there were some surprisingly good results (inside 100ft). Operationally, either lobbing in sticks of four 1,000lb bombs (to keep heads down) or a single nuke, they were accurate enough.'

The hard-won experience of the USAF in Vietnam and of the Israeli Air Force in 1973, had illustrated the vital importance of electronic warfare in offensive air operations against a modern air-defence system. Advances in radar and missile technology meant that aircraft could no longer simply rely on flying low and fast to avoid detection by radar and engagement by surface-to-air missiles (SAM). Air-defence systems could now reach into low-level airspace and aircrews now needed to avoid air defence sites and be able to manoeuvre effectively if they were detected. The means of doing this was the Radar Warning Receiver (RWR), which gave the pilot an audio-visual indication of the type and whereabouts of active radar sites. A small circular cathode-ray display in the cockpit showed a 'spike' in the direction of the relevant transmitter and a tone in the pilot's headset identified the generic type of the radar. During the mid-1970s, the RAF started to install this on the fast-jet aircraft and by mid-1977 all of 14 Squadron's Jaguars were fitted with the new equipment[66]. Training on the use of the RWR started in June with aircraft using the USAF electronic-warfare range at Ramstein and the Raytheon MIM-23 HAWK missile sites further to the east to gain experience. However, Flt Lt Miller found, '…it took immense amounts of concentration and interpretation, and sapped your capacity to do much else. Many of us thought it did little other than let you know you were about to die, principally because we had little in the way of effective countermeasures other than to fly even lower.'

There was some useful EW training in July which was coupled with the annual live HE bombing. The aircraft flew high-level to Garvie Island, off Cape Wrath on the north-western tip of Scotland to drop two live 1,000lb bombs and then recovered to Leuchars to refuel. The subsequent sortie routed through the newly-opened Electronic Warfare Tactics Range (EWTR) at RAF Spadeadam, on the border of Cumbria and Northumberland. Here various 'threat emitters', which mimicked Soviet radar systems provided more valuable experience for the Jaguar pilots before they returned to Brüggen. There was more EW training in the month both against German-based missile sites and, in the 3 days of the UK air-defence 'Exercise Highwood', against UK-based systems.

During the summer, the squadron was privileged to host a visitor from Australia. Colin Campbell, an Australian pilot who had flown the Martin Marauder and Vickers Wellington with 14 Squadron during the Second World War was passing Brüggen during a tour of Europe, so he dropped in to visit his old squadron on 26 July. Three days later, the RAF celebrated HM Queen Elizabeth's Silver Jubilee with a review and flypast at RAF Finningley. Three of the squadron's Jaguars were detached to Finningley: two participated in the flypast and the other joined the static display in which over seventy squadrons from the RAF and Commonwealth Air Forces were represented. The Squadron Standard was also paraded in front of the Queen.

The rest of the summer and early autumn was taken up with various exercises and work with FACs, which included live HE strafing both at Hohne range and against a splash target towed by a launch from Yarmouth. In the 5 days of 'Exercise Cold Fire', the annual central region exercise held in September, aircraft were tasked against conventional targets within Germany defended by NATO air-defence systems, and

Birds were a significant hazard to aircraft operating at low level in Germany, as evidenced by the extensive damage to Jaguar T2 XX847. Flt Lt G.A. Miller and the Wing Navigation Officer, Flt Lt C.F. Wrighton, hit a flock of Lapwings soon after take-off on 25 January 1978. (Dusty Miller)

included 'Exercise Blue Fox', an FAC exercise. The rest of the month was busy with other FAC work in 'Exercises Cloggy Emotion', 'Brown Falcon', 'Datex' and 'Crazy Horse'. Four aircraft from the Brüggen Wing also spent a day operating from an unopened stretch of newly-finished autobahn to test the feasibility of using roads as emergency runways. Flt Lt R. A. Baron represented 14 Squadron in this exercise.

Two of 14 Squadron's pilots were selected for the Brüggen Wing team at the RAF Strike Command bombing competition, which was held at Lossiemouth in October. The competition included teams from the Jaguar and Buccaneer units in Strike Command and RAF Germany and, for the first time, USAF teams flying Ling-Temco-Vought A-7D Corsair II and General-Dynamics F-111 aircraft. In all forty-eight aircraft participated. It was run in two phases – the first being a low-level attack phase in which teams had to fly co-ordinated formation attacks against targets at Dumfries and Otterburn while evading ground defences and a fighter threat. Then followed a weaponry phase which included strafe attacks at Tain range and laydown bombing against a towed splash target in the sea near Tarbat Ness. The USAF team from the 23 Tactical Fighter Wing (TFW) lead the way and despite Flt Lt J. Connolly dropping the best bombs of an RAF competitor, the Brüggen team came fourth overall.

The squadron was able to supply eight Jaguars for 'Exercise Fire Escape' in the first week of October. This exercise was intended to evaluate the operational limits of the Rapier SAM system and involved a twenty-four-ship attack on a Rapier site, in an attempt to overload it. Another 'Exercise Fire Escape' was run the following month, but in between these events a critical shortage of engine and NavWASS spares, combined with a high turnover of ground crew, had grounded the squadron for a few days. Unfortunately, as a result, the APC at Deci, planned for the month, had to be cancelled.

1978

The squadron 'Top Dog' competition on 26 January 1978 was won convincingly by Flt Lt Huckins with an impressive score of 100 percent. The sortie profile was similar to the pattern of previous competitions with a timed field target and FRA and also, this time, a line search for military equipment. Reasonable weather and good serviceability throughout the month had enabled the squadron to start an air-combat training work-up. This, in preparation for a forthcoming visit to Brüggen by the Lightnings of 11 Squadron, was designed to give pilots much needed experience in handling the Jaguar close to the limits of its flight envelope. For although the Jaguar's origins had been as a training aircraft, it could be a handful when manoeuvring at high angle of attack. Both confidence and practice were needed to fly safely and effectively under these conditions. According to Flt Lt F. L. Turner, '...the Jaguar handling required a safe pair of hands. Harsh handling and it would bite! It was prone to easy departure at high angles of attack and I saw at least two Jags depart briefly in front of my eyes.'

The year's Taceval started on 5 February, but unfortunately by now the weather had deteriorated. In fact there was no flying at all during the exercise and instead the pilots went through all the motions of planning, briefing and taxying out for the sortie, but the airborne part was merely simulated. For the first time the squadron was also expected to demonstrate that it could operate 24 hours a day. Despite the lack of flying the squadron was assessed as 'Excellent' in all respects.

Fighter affiliation with 19 Squadron, newly re-equipped with the Phantom and based now at neighbouring Wildenrath, provided another welcome opportunity to practise EW techniques in March. The Pulsed Doppler (PD) radar in the Phantom presented a new threat to the Jaguar: designed to find moving targets, it gave the Phantom a 'look down – shoot down' capability against aircraft flying at low level. In the days before PD radars, fighter crews generally had to find their targets visually at low level, as low-flying aircraft were invisible against the 'ground clutter' of older mono-pulse radars. The relatively small size of the Jaguar made it difficult to see and by flying very low, the Jaguar had a good chance of escaping the attentions of earlier generation air-defence fighters. However, the PD radar changed that: the Jaguar could now be found relatively easily by a Phantom, which could then launch a radar-guided missile from well beyond visual range. The first the Jaguar pilot would know would be when the missile hit him. The advent of RWR potentially gave the advantage back to the Jaguar: the RWR would show the direction of the Phantom giving the Jaguar pilot an opportunity to avoid the threat. It would also tell him if he was locked up by the Phantom radar and he could use the RWR to help manoeuvre to break the lock and defeat the missile. Success, though, would depend on the Jaguar pilots being

familiar with, and practised in, these tactics. In fact the only problem, identified by Flt
Lt M. J. Metcalf was, '…it took a long time for some of our would-be fighter pilots
to discipline themselves to progress to the target rather than engage and attempt to
shoot down every F-4 in sight!'

The emphasis for weaponry in the first few months of the year was on loft and
toss bombing. On 28 March, six aircraft detached to Lossiemouth to drop 1,000lb
bombs. Over the next 14 days, live HE bombs were dropped at Garvie and inert
bombs at Tain. Flying with these weapons loaded gave the pilots experience in flying
the aircraft at heavy weights. 'Even one 1,000lb bomb made the world of difference,'
commented Flt Lt Miller, 'especially in the early days when the engines in the Jag
were very small indeed. There was also a roll-yaw coupling issue, particularly if there
were heavy weapons on the fuselage pylon. The take-off roll was long and you had to
really pull the aircraft off the ground.' Another live drop had been carried out earlier
in the month at Tain as part of 'Exercise Tingewick', a trial of the new BL755 Cluster
Bomb. This weapon had been developed in response to the massive superiority in
numbers of Warsaw Pact tanks. Rather than having to hit each vehicle individually
with a single bomb, which was clearly impractical, the Cluster Bomb used a 'shot-
gun' effect by ejecting 147 smaller bomblets, each capable of disabling a tank, over
an area approximately the size of a football pitch. On 7 March, Flt Lt Turner, '…flew
two sorties – one as primary (when I dropped) and one as secondary pilot (who
stepped in if there was a problem with the primary). The target array was several
Soft-Skinned Vehicles (SSV) (and maybe a tank in the middle) suitably laid out. I
was very nervous as the eyes of the RAF were on us. The target was very difficult
to see but I dropped – I was determined to! The weapon went off as advertised
and I obtained reasonable coverage with the centre point a bit short. Bomblets
everywhere…several airborne bursts, too, coming quite close to the aircraft,
according to the film.'

The Salmond Trophy in April 1978 differed in format to that of previous years.
It started with an aircraft generation phase, followed the next day by a flying phase.
The sortie profile retained the field target and FRA but now also included a line
search, which gave an advantage to the two-seat aircraft with two pairs of eyes.
Once again 14 Squadron's engineers and pilots performed extremely well, however
this year they were narrowly beaten by 16 Squadron's Buccaneers. The beginning
of the following month was taken up with a work up for pilots who would be
participating in the Strike Command Tactical Fighter Meet (TFM). The sorties were
all flown in the UK, using the EWTR at RAF Spadeadam and the air-weapons
ranges at RAF Tain (Scotland) and RAF Cowden (near Hornsea, Yorkshire). Once
again, 11 Squadron's Lightnings provided opposition, as did the Phantoms of 43
Squadron based at Leuchars. Six aircraft and nine pilots, along with supporting
ground crew, deployed to Leuchars for the TFM, which lasted from 12 to 26 May.
Here they joined representatives of all of the RAF's tactical-aircraft types, as well
as a detachment of McDonnell-Douglas F-4G 'Wild Weasel' defence-suppression
aircraft from the USAF Wing at Spangdahlem. Accommodation for the exercise was
rather basic – six-man tents – but the flying was excellent. The exercise scenarios
for the TFM required aircrews to fly complex sorties: they had to plan co-ordinated

attacks by large formations against targets defended by both ground and airborne defences. The sorties, which also often included fighter escorts and 'Wild Weasel' support, usually routed through the RAF Spadeadam EWTR. There were live targets on the ranges at Tain and Otterburn and the defences included Rapier SAM and Combat Air Patrols (CAPs) by Phantoms and Lightnings. Added to all of this, the ground-attack aircraft flew on the last few missions with a realistic war-load of two 1,000lb bombs. Each sortie cycle lasted some 6 hours, including the planning and flying phases, followed by a very comprehensive debrief. The sortie rate itself was kept deliberately low so that everyone could get the most from the debrief held afterwards. The 14 Squadron detachment flew only twelve sorties during the TFM, but this apparently low utilization of the aircraft belied the incredible training value provided by the meet. Flt Lt Turner thought, 'that as a squadron we came out of it quite well. It helped to shape our tactics more in the attack role and it was here that we experimented with big 'card'-style formations.'

During the first half of the year the emphasis had been on the more experienced pilots, but the second half of the year gave the opportunity to concentrate on the more junior pilots. Six pilots and four aircraft were dispatched to Decimomannu for a mini-APC during the last week of May and first week in June. The fortnight of 'Exercise Farman', a squadron-run exercise in July, exposed the junior pilots to six- and eight-ship formations and complex scenarios which were similar in many ways to the pattern of TFM missions. Both this exercise and 'Exercise Gordon' (which was held in August) were the brainchild of Wg Cdr J.K. Sim, who had taken command of the squadron the previous November. He was concerned that by concentrating on the strike role in the early days, the squadron was in danger of losing its touch with attack flying. He was also keen to bring on the junior pilots and ensure that there was a cadre of well-trained formation leaders. During 'Exercise Farman' large formations of Jaguars practiced co-ordinated attacks on targets such as HAWK missile sites, or the airfield at Diepholz, which were frequently defended by Phantom CAPs, and ground-based systems such as Blowpipe, courtesy of the Royal Artillery. Overall the exercise, which was organized by the GLO, Maj R. Wilson, provided some excellent flying and was considered to be a resounding success.

The squadron exchange in August 1978 was, once again, with the French Jaguar Wing at St Dizier. Six aircraft, with eight pilots and thirty-six ground crew visited St Dizier where they were hosted by Escadrille 3/7; meanwhile representatives of Escadrille 1/7 visited Brüggen. In both locations mixed RAF/FAF formations were flown and the pilots at St Dizier were also able to use the range at Suippes and also fly some air-combat training sorties against Dassault Mirage IIIs.

The second squadron-run exercise later in the month, 'Exercise Gordon', was designed to give practice in the interdiction role. Pairs formations flew against tactical targets under control of an FAC while dealing with an air threat provided by Phantoms (simulating Soviet MiG-23 Floggers) or Harriers (simulating MiG-21) and ground defences provided by 37 Squadron (RAF Regiment) Rapiers. On the last two days, the Jaguars were loaded with two 1,000lb bombs so that pilots could get used to flying a heavy-weight aircraft. 'The weather was very hot,' recalled Flt Lt Turner, 'and so aircraft performance was even worse, noticeably on take-off. I

remember one occasion when one pilot just managed to scrape above the barrier at the far end of [runway] 27 and the duty pilot called out "Let!" To start with the pilots were not very successful in finding their targets in this high-workload environment, but they quickly improved with experience as the exercise progressed.

The full squadron APC, nicknamed 'Exercise Fang Grip', took place in September. Ten Jaguars and virtually the entire squadron deployed to Decimomannu. Unfortunately, the Italians decided that this year the usual 28lb smoke and flash practice bombs could not be used on Frasca range and that, instead, only inert bombs could be dropped. Perhaps it was not surprising, therefore, that with no flash or smoke to mark the impact, the vast majority of the toss and loft bombs were not seen by the range staff and therefore could not be scored. In the last week of the detachment, from 28 September to 5 October, the squadron took part in 'Exercise Display Determination', a major NATO maritime exercise in the Mediterranean. The Jaguars were tasked with anti-shipping strikes against the US Navy Amphibious Assault Group (AAG) and against the Carrier Task Group (CTG) led by the USS *J.F. Kennedy*, USS *Forrestal* and HMS *Ark Royal*. There was opportunity, too, for air-combat training against US Navy Grumman F-14 Tomcats and F-4 Phantoms and Royal Navy Phantom F-4Ks, also for HE strafing on the tactical range at Capo Teulada on the south-western tip of the island.

The squadron returned to Brüggen on 11 October and over the next 6 months of autumn and winter settled into the routine training and flying at Brüggen.

Jaguar GR1 XX958 flying at low level over the Eifel mountain range in western Germany. (RAFM PC94-201-476)

The Cresta Run

In January 1978, Flt Lt M. Metcalf had called into St Moritz on his way back from a skiing holiday. 'On his return to Brüggen,' recalled Flt Lt D. Harkin, 'Mike regaled two of the Junior Pilots (JPs), Mike Malone and me, with stories of potential daring do, gorgeous-looking women and scary-looking fun. We used annual and special leave to stay in St Moritz for 3 weeks in January/February 1979 in order to represent the Royal Air Force, along with a couple of Harrier friends from 3 Squadron Gutersloh. It was epic. We had absolutely no idea what we were doing. The St Moritz Tobogganing Club, being indulgent, warm and friendly, instructed us in the basics of the sport and watched as we crashed, smashed and generally tried to wipe out a good percentage of the RAF's young fighter pilots. We came last in the Inter-Services Cresta Championship of 1979 but we kept coming back every year, along with others.' Over the next few winters a posse of 14 Squadron pilots took extended leave to make up the bulk of the RAF Cresta Team.

The Height of the 'Cold War'

In many ways the closing years of the 1970s represented the height of RAF Germany's combat readiness in the 'Cold War'. Across the RAFG stations everyone was on a high state of alert and expected to be called in for exercise – or war – at very short notice. This relentless practice had instilled a degree of professionalism across all trades, which had not existed previously. Aircraft equipped with modern weapon-aiming systems and electronic-warfare equipment routinely operated from hardened shelters in a ground environment fully trained in Nuclear, Biological and Chemical (NBC) warfare. At Brüggen, which regarded itself as being the very forefront of RAFG, the Jaguar pilots were also pushed hard to maintain the highest levels of combat effectiveness. On 14 Squadron, one of the best illustrations of the efforts to achieve that level of airmanship and professionalism was 'Exercise Gordon', the squadron-run air-interdiction exercise, which took place in three different phases during the year. During the first in May, pairs of Jaguars flew against tactical targets under control of an FAC. The targets included inflatable dummy tanks deployed in the field, Harrier operating sites, deployed army units and static military installations. Air opposition was provided by RAF Phantoms from Wildenrath, RNLAF F-104s and USAFE McDonnell Douglas F-15 Eagles from Bitburg. In later iterations of the exercise in August and December, larger attack formations were used. Once again the Jaguars were loaded with two 1,000lb bombs. Unfortunately, despite this high-pressure training, the squadron achieved only 3rd place in the year's Salmond Trophy.

But these heights of professionalism were not won at the sacrifice of a sense of humour. Twenty-five Jaguars launched from Brüggen on an important mission on 21 June. Dubious of the capabilities of their Jaguar-flying colleagues, the Phantom squadrons at Wildenrath had challenged the Brüggen Wing to destroy a piano on the range at Nordhorn using only practice bombs. The only way that a tiny flash-and-smoke practice bomb could damage the piano would be by a direct hit; and since the piano itself was a very small target, the Phantom crews were confident that it would remain unscathed. They waited in eager anticipation for the beer which the Jaguar pilots would inevitably have to buy for them for losing the challenge! Despite some near misses, none of the six aircraft contributed by 14 Squadron to the Wing effort managed to hit the target, but a Jaguar from another squadron did so and it was the Phantom crews who had to buy the beer.

Another round of the squadron-run 'Exercise Farman' ran in the first 14 days of July. It followed a very similar format to 'Exercise Gordon', except that the targets for the exercise sorties were HAWK missile sites and both military and civilian airfields and, as in previous exercises, they were defended by Rapier missiles. All sorties penetrated at least two CAPs provided by RAF or *Luftwaffe* Phantoms, or USAF F-15 Eagles and on some missions a fighter escort was provided by the visiting Phantoms of 23 Squadron. During the second week, the Jaguars were loaded with four 1,000lb bombs, simulating a full war-load.

The following week the squadron lost its second Jaguar[67] during a Minival sortie. On 18 July 1979, Flt Lt G. A. Wardell hit a large TV mast near Iserlohn while rejoining formation. Happily, Wardell managed to eject successfully from the aircraft, which was destroyed in the subsequent crash. In the last week of this busy month, two aircraft detached to the UK for EW training. They combined simulated attacks against the radar site at Staxton Wold and the Bloodhound-missile site at North Coates and with weaponry at Donna Nook and Cowden ranges on the east coast. Sorties also included work with 5 Squadron's Lightnings, and SAM and AAA simulators on the EWTR at RAF Spadeadam.

During annual APC at Decimomannu in September, RAF Germany was tasked to provide four Jaguars for the airshow at Pisa on 7 and 8 September. So was born the 'Green Sparrows,' a light-hearted reference to the RAF's 'Red Arrows' display team. Led by Sqn Ldr P. J. J. Day (himself an ex-'Red Arrow') with Flt Lts M. Malone, D. J. Harkin and D. G. Needham who recalled, '…our simple routine was an arrival in two pairs simulating an airfield attack, followed by a join up and a three-sixty box flypast finishing with an arrow run in and break. That's all we were authorized to do – we arrived at Pisa in the same style, which constituted our official practice, but really just gave us licence to beat up the airfield.' The team appeared at a number of other displays and would reform the following 2 years for shows across Europe.

The squadron also visited Italy for the squadron exchange in the first week of November with 156° Gruppo's F-104s at Gioia Del Colle, near Venice. Between social events, the Jaguars carried out weaponry practice at Punta della Contessa range just south of Brindisi and against a splash target towed by HMS *Bulwark* which was sailing in the Adriatic Sea.

Exercise Red Flag 80-2

The focus in the last few months of 1979 was preparation for the squadron's participation in 'Exercise Red Flag' early the next year. Held on the Nevada range complex to the north of Las Vegas since 1975, 'Exercise Red Flag' was designed to expose crews as closely as possible to the experience of combat flying. US combat experience in Vietnam had shown that crews were most vulnerable in their first few combat missions and the concept of the exercise was to allow crews to gain the vital experience of those first missions in the relatively safe environment of the Nevada ranges. In UK terms, the range complex covered an area broadly similar in size to North Wales and the West Midlands. The terrain comprised large salt flats intersected by a series of mountain ridges, which ran from north to south across the area. The westerly ranges contained a number of realistic targets such full-size Warsaw Pact-style airfields, an industrial complex and concentrations of armoured vehicles. The target area was defended by an Integrated Air-Defence System (IADS) which used Warsaw Pact tactics and often utilized Soviet equipment: Northrop F-5E Freedom Fighters of the 'Aggressor Squadron' simulated the tactics and capabilities of Warsaw Pact fighters such as MiG-21 and MiG-23, while ground threats were provided by both SAM-3 and SAM-6 missile systems and ZSU-23/4 anti-aircraft guns. Some of the ground threats were radar simulators, while some of them were the genuine articles, most probably captured by the Israelis during the 'Yom Kippur War'. All of the defence systems went through the complete engagement sequence. The only departure from wartime procedures was that no missile or gun was actually fired, but all engagements were filmed on closed-circuit television (CCTV). After every mission a comprehensive debrief reconstructed every sortie and every engagement in detail so that lessons could be learned.

Thirty-five ground crew under command of the JEngO deployed to Nellis AFB, Las Vegas on 21 January to be part of the joint RAFG/38 Group ground-support party covering all 4 weeks of the exercise. Meanwhile, fourteen pilots were finishing a two-week work-up at Lossiemouth during which they qualified in ultra low-flying (down to a minimum 100ft altitude). The RAF's tactic for surviving the air-defence threat in the central front was to fly as low and fast as possible, something which RAF fast-jet crews were trained to do exceptionally well. Flt Lt Harkin thought, '…the work-up was better than the Red Flag itself because we were flying up to three times a day and the days were short due northern winter. We were finished by 3pm every day and in the Bothy Bar "early doors." It was "flat out", exciting and great fun.' On 5 February, the pilots left Brüggen for Las Vegas. The aircraft were already at Nellis having been flown there by 54 Squadron who had taken part in the first 14 days of the exercise.

Every pilot had to fly a familiarization flight on the range to qualify for the exercise and the original plan was for each pilot to then fly seven more exercise missions over the 2 weeks. Unfortunately, the weather in the Nevada was awful and in the end the pilots managed only three full-exercise sorties each. Flt Lt Harkin's experiences were typical, 'I flew one familiarization sortie on 11 February, followed by a TACAN[68] crawl around Nevada and Arizona on 19 February in order to keep current! In between, I had a couple of engine surges on take-off and aborted those sorties, so I was pretty frustrated by the time I managed two [Red] Flag four-ship sorties on 20 and 21 February.' However, the quality of those sorties still made the whole experience very worthwhile. All missions were flown in formations of up to eight Jaguars, which themselves were part of a much larger attack 'package' comprising F-4 Phantom, A-7 Corsair II, Republic F-105 Thunderchief, FB-111 and Boeing B-52 Stratofortress aircraft. The attack packages were provided with fighter escort from USAF F-15s and were also supported by F-4G and F-105G 'Wild Weasel' defence-suppression aircraft. After the first exercise sortie with practice bombs, the remaining sorties were flown armed with 1,000lb inert bombs. Two Paveway Laser Guided Bombs (LGB) were also dropped in co-ordination with laser designating F-4 Phantoms from the USAF. The exercise flying was also notable for a 'private war' between the US Marine Corps F-4 Phantoms who were the only US fighters prepared to 'mix it' with the Jaguars at low level: the USMC crews earned huge respect from the Jaguar pilots both for their aggressive style of flying and for their friendliness in the 'O-Club' bar afterwards.

Apart from providing the most exciting flying in peacetime, 'Exercise Red Flag' also offered some wonderful social opportunities. RAF personnel were accommodated in downtown Las Vegas and were able to enjoy the delights of the city; weekends were a chance to explore further afield, for example to San Francisco or Los Angeles. At the end of the exercise, 14 Squadron pilots ferried the Jaguars back across the US via McConnell AFB (near Wichita, Kansas) to Rickenbacker AFB (Ohio). From here 54 Squadron pilots (who were qualified in air-to-air refuelling [AAR]) flew them back across the Atlantic.

Back in Germany, the squadron carried out a one-way exchange with the USAF 22nd Tactical Fighter Squadron (22 TFS) based at Bitburg. Eight aircraft and forty-six support personnel detached to Bitburg on 8 April. Over the next 10 days the flying consisted of air-combat training at medium level and evasion training at low level. Not surprisingly, even when flown 'clean' the Jaguar was no match for the F-15. Flt Lt Needham, '…led a two-versus-two with Den Harkin on my wing. We split, crossed and engaged individually. I went vertical (fool) and the debrief from the F-15 pilot went something like… "Well, we engaged at high speed and went into a vertical scissors. We crossed twice and I thought 'Hey, this is going to be interesting'. I pulled back

An operational turnround carried out by 14 Squadron ground crew out under exercise conditions in a HAS in 1980. The crew are dressed in the full NBC protective clothing and wearing respirators, making the work physically challenging. Bruggen's personnel spent much of their time in their NBC suits during the frequent exercises. (Den Harkin)

for the third cross and you weren't there." Not surprising really with my two little Adours pushing out less than half the thrust than one of his P&Ws. He fell in right behind me…Fox2[69]! I called, "How are you doing Den?" "Wait", came the response, two seconds later "Dead" came the call. It lasted all of 20 seconds.' Harkin himself remembered the detachment as, '…great fun and an opportunity to get shot down by a seriously good fighter.' In the low-level environment, however, the situation was reversed and the Bitburg squadron's lack of practice in intercepting low-level intruders was as apparent as the Jaguar pilots' skills at low-level flying. Overall the exchange was greatly enjoyed by both units.

The annual APC at 'Deci' was held from 14 May to 4 June and although it was successful, flying was curtailed in the last week because of a fuel shortage in Sardinia. However, the social side was greatly enlivened by the presence of the 22 TFS from Bitburg! During the APC, pilots also had the opportunity to fly using the AR5 aircrew respirator. Until the advent of the AR5, in NBC conditions aircrew would go to their aircraft wearing the standard S6 respirator and then simply rely on the aircraft oxygen system once in the cockpit. Having to unmask and then put on a flying helmet and oxygen mask left pilots vulnerable to contamination. Comprising a neoprene hood with an in-built oxygen mask and visor, the AR5 was designed to be worn from the time the pilots left the briefing facility until they returned to it after flying their mission.

Although it provided complete protection from NBC threats, the AR5 was, in practice, hot, sweaty and claustrophobic to wear. Seven pilots flew range sorties wearing the respirator, but they did so in the two-seat Jaguar with a safety pilot on board. In fact, they were all pleasantly surprised at how quickly they got used to the mask once they were airborne, although there were still concerns about both facial comfort and peripheral vision.

Perhaps the greatest excitement of the detachment was experienced by Flt Lt Needham, who faced an almost catastrophic malfunction during a range sortie on 29 May. As he, '…banked left to turn base in the strafe pattern at Capo Frasca, the aircraft just continued to roll. Of course, the nose dropped dramatically. I ended up with what looked remarkably like pro-spin controls! Full opposite spoiler, full rudder and the stick pulled back to stop the descent. I regained some level of control as the speed reduced. With half flap, the gear down and nearly full right rudder, the stick was just off the full starboard stop. That enabled me to at least point in the direction home. I stayed over the sea and set up for a visual straight in at Deci. The weather was good, but on touch down the aircraft[70] tried to leave the runway sideways to port. Not quite sure why, I did not even have time to select the nose-wheel steering. That was more scary than the original incident because people were watching! Full right boot kept me on the tarmac thankfully.' Later investigation showed that the port spoiler failed to full deflection and Needham's subsequent recovery of the aircraft to Decimomannu earned him a 'Green Endorsement' in his logbook for exceptional airmanship.

Back at Brüggen and now under command of Wg Cdr D.A. Baron, the squadron ran another iteration of 'Exercise Farman' over the summer. September brought more opportunities to fly wearing the AR5 and the month also included more fighter-affiliation training with Bitburg's F-15s. There was also a visit by Mr H. N. Norris, a former squadron pilot who had flown the Vickers Wellesley in the Eritrean Campaign during the Second World War. He presented the squadron with a badge cut from the tail of his Wellesley after he was shot down over Harmil Island in September 1940 – exactly 40 years previously. The following month brought 'Exercise Mallet Blow', the first of what would become a regular event in the squadron's calendar in the coming years. The exercise involved attack aircraft heading up the east coast through fighter engagement zones to attack targets at Otterburn range and then fly through RAF Spadeadam, before negotiating another fighter-engagement zone heading southwards to the west of the Pennines. The exercise offered excellent training value, but in future years it gained a reputation for attracting low cloud and rain. A servicing party was pre-positioned at Leuchars for the duration of the exercise from 6 to 9 October, and as the weather this time at least was good, the Jaguars were able to fly three or four sorties each during exercise days. Unfortunately, poor weather later in the month caused some embarrassment when the squadron mounted a four-ship[71] flypast at JHQ Rheindahlen on 24 October. Led by Sqn Ldr C. McCairns they missed commandant NORTHAG (Northern Army Group), Gen Sir William Scotter, KCB OBE, departure parade as they stumbled through the murk.

The autumn brought more fuel restrictions, but despite this handicap there was more opportunity to practice attacks against realistic targets in December at Grafenwohr range, to the southeast of Bayreuth. Here pilots were able to drop sticks of inert 1,000lb bombs on armoured vehicles and were also able to strafe the targets with HE rounds.

A 14 Squadron Jaguar GR1 taxis from a HAS in heavy rain. Apart from providing NBC and blast protection in wartime, the HAS environment also sheltered both the aircraft and the ground crew from the elements during routine operations. (Den Harkin)

Another 'Exercise Mallet Blow' ran from 12 to 16 January 1981 and once again the sorties were flown via a turn-round at Waddington. On 19 January, a pair of Jaguars[72] was recovering to Brüggen when both aircraft were hit by lightning. The leader was undamaged but his Number 2 was hit three times on the pitot probe, starboard tailplane and the rear RWR housing. The port droptank also exploded, leaving just the aft section on the pylon when the aircraft landed.

During the first half of 1981, the flying programme concentrated on weaponry: toss and loft deliveries were practiced on the Wash ranges in February, live 1,000lb bombs were dropped at Garvie Island in March and the annual APC was held at Decimomannu in April. The weather in Sardinia was excellent and the year's detachment was a resounding success. Weaponry continued at nearby Helchteren for the rest of the month, while in May there were more range slots at Grafenwohr for heavy bombing. On these sorties the aircraft landed at Erding after dropping their weapons. Two aircraft also flew against a towed splash target off the coast of East Anglia. During June, the squadron flying programme concentrated on attack work-up for the junior pilots. Apart from routine pairs and four-ships, some more complex scenarios were provided by 'Exercises Mallet Blow' and 'Gordon' towards the end of the month. The 'Mallet Blow' sorties were flown via Waddington again in excellent weather conditions. 'Exercise Gordon' also included the added interest of airborne FACs in North American Rockwell OV-10 Bronco aircraft from Sembach, as well as the by now 'traditional' affiliation with Wildenrath's Phantoms. Another iteration of 'Exercise Farman' followed in August.

An 'Interesting' Exchange

Meanwhile, the squadron exchange in the second half of July was with the Greek Air Force at Larissa, about a 130 miles north of Athens. Four Jaguars under the command of Sqn Ldr Bryant deployed to Larissa, via Decimomannu, for 10 days on 13 July, while four A-7H Corsair IIs from 347 Squadron, made the reciprocal journey. The RAF party at Larissa, comprising eight pilots and thirty-three ground personnel found that the Greeks were very sociable, but they seemed to have little interest in flying with their visitors. Hampered by a general reluctance from their hosts, a lack of ranges and very limited map coverage, the detachment only managed to fly just over half of the planned sorties. They did manage to fly one wave each day, either a pair or four-ship accompanied by Greek A-7s. As Flt Lt R. I. McAlpine tactfully stated, '…it was very pleasant flying past the Greek Islands and getting to know our NATO friends; however, I suspect the tactical value was not so great.' The undoubted highlight of the visit was a weekend trip to Athens for which the Greek Air Force provided a Lockheed C-130 Hercules to transport the whole of the RAF detachment both ways.

There was a similar story at Brüggen with Flt Lt B. W. Newby noting in the squadron diary that the visitors, '…did not seem too bothered about flying, but were quite keen to do their shopping!' Indeed, after an arrival party in the mess where the guests upset the manager when they followed their tradition of smashing their plates after the dinner (unfortunately these were the mess' best crockery) they soon got stuck into the shopping. Sqn Ldr Miller, '…allocated one of the flight commander's offices for their collection of goodies, but by the end of the second day moved up to an entire HAS. They started with camping and outdoors equipment (tents and barbeques), moved up to cameras and other high value items, and finished with a mad dash to secure all the bananas (bananas?) they could carry.'

During the summer, the 'Green Sparrows' display team were enjoying their third season as RAFG's representatives at air shows. By now the formation was led by Sqn Ldr J. M. Bryant, with Flt Lts J. Taylor, Harkin and Wardell completing the line-up. According to Flt Lt Harkin, '…the squadron was cleared to perform an airfield attack then join up as a box four for wing-over manoeuvring, before splitting for an opposition pass, rejoin and break to land. It was noisy, we used part-throttle reheat throughout, and fast, we flew clean Jaguars, no tanks. We also practiced a lot and, even though I say it myself, we were pretty reasonable…We displayed at the weekend on 1 August at Giebelstadt and returned to Ramstein for a practice display for the big one the next day. On 2 August, we displayed before hundreds of thousands of people, Ramstein was a massive display. It all went well and the [Red] Arrows were all looking when our opposition pass crossed perfectly in front of the display centre. After landing and being handed the cool Budweiser, some of the Arrows were kind enough to tell us how well we'd done, particularly the timing of the cross. We had a pretty good night!'

There was a tradition at Brüggen of subjecting unsuspecting new arrivals to some sort of elaborate 'spoof,' causing much mirth among the old hands. When Flt Lt T. J. Kerss arrived on 14 Squadron in September, he discovered that his first day on the squadron would include a 'Boss check ride' which would involve leading a large formation around Germany in a Jaguar T2 with the 'Boss' in the backseat. The weather brief showed the whole of Germany to be under very low cloud and totally unsuitable for low flying, but nevertheless the duty authorizer ordered the formation to launch. Flt Lt Kerss, '…was dispatched alone to the HAS to carry out the walk-round, and strap into the T2. Needless to say I was utterly maxed out, and I remember sitting in cockpit thinking "I'm never going to survive this tour." The Boss eventually appeared, and just as I was about to close the canopy I was surprised to see Brian Newby on my left, sporting a very wide grin, holding the squadron camera. As is often the case it took a long moment for me to realize that this was a spoof, and to come down from the adrenal-pumping high that I was experiencing. I had taken it "hook, line and sinker." Some Brüggen spoofs were legendary, but to my mind, the best was that when the squadron placed one of the old decoy two-seat Lightnings in a HAS and told the unsuspecting newbie that his check-ride would be "in the Squadron Hack," and to do the walk-round, strap in, and wait for the Boss to join him.'

Fuel restrictions returned in the autumn, but even so the flying programme kept ticking along. Six more pilots flew sorties in the AR5 during October and there was another 'mini-APC' using Helchteren range. This latter event gave pilots an opportunity to try out the new 3kg practice bomb. After the lack of useful flying during the official squadron exchange, and 'alternative' exchange was carried out with 11 Squadron at the beginning of December. Six Jaguars deployed to Binbrook and for the next 4 days according to Flt Lt Newby, they enjoyed, '…a tremendous week…[with] some really excellent Lightning affiliation.' The flying also included EW training at RAF Spadeadam and weaponry against laser-marked tactical targets on the range at Otterburn.

The first two months of 1982 were busy with station exercises, two Maxevals, a Minival and the aircraft generation phase of Taceval. The squadron also made the most of the good weather with numerous weaponry sorties including a four-ship to drop HE bombs at Grafenwohr. Each aircraft was loaded with two 1,000lb HE bombs and Flt Lt McAlpine recalled, '…we had fuel for a single pass only, nobody had been to the range before and it was all a bit tense. Anyone failing to drop would have had to land away with live weapons – not good.' Happily, all four pilots dropped successfully and they returned via a refuelling stop at Furstenfeldbruck. The following month another four-ship was dispatched to Grafenwohr again, this time with four live 1,000lb bombs each. Six aircraft were also detached to Coningsby for 'Exercise Mallet Blow', which ran from 22 to 26 March. Once again, the exercise provided some valuable practice with FRAs against laser-marked targets on Otterburn range and EW training against ground threats at RAF Spadeadam and air-defence Phantoms. The emphasis remained on weaponry at the beginning of April, as all pilots had to qualify to ACE force standards prior to Taceval which was due later in the month. An intensive phase of range sorties to Nordhorn, Helchteren, Noordvader and Vliehors was complemented by a work out on the 'equivalent routes' that would be flown on the Taceval. The result of this hard work was that the squadron was well prepared for the exercise when it started on 19 April. Good weather and high tasking meant that there were almost continuous daylight operations at Brüggen over the next 4 days and at the end of it the squadron was rewarded with 'excellent' ratings in all four areas that were examined.

Meanwhile, some 8,000 miles to the southwest, the Argentinian forces had landed on the Falkland Islands on 2 April. Just 3 days later, a 'Task Force' left the UK and the Falklands War had started. Over the next 2 months Flt Lt Miller felt, '…a sense of relief that we were not mixed up in it, although the sense was tempered by a degree of feeling as though we were missing out.' RAFG's Jaguar squadrons would not be involved in any case, because they were fully committed to SACEUR in the nuclear-strike role. However, soon after 14 Squadron deployed to Decimomannu for the annual APC on 28 April, Wg Cdr Baron was told, '…a signal [had] arrived late morning from London ordering the immediate dispatch of four Jaguars to Gibraltar. With the Falklands War well under way, someone had clearly thought Gib at risk from a Spanish invasion. Our main problem was preventing Deci airfield closing at lunchtime (as was the norm to facilitate an extended Italian weekend) before the aircraft could be prepared. It took the personal intervention of the base commander to ensure the deployment, with four Jaguars on the ground at Gibraltar circa 17:00hrs.' During the APC, formations of four Jaguars were sent to Gibraltar to 'fly the flag' over each of the weekends; on the middle weekend, however, the aircraft had to return to 'Deci' as the weather at Gibraltar was unsuitable. Flt Lt Miller recalled, '…the start of the detachment [was] bracketed by the sinking of the *Belgrano* and HMS *Sheffield*. *Belgrano* confirmed that there was no backing down now, and the loss of *Sheffield* felt a lot like a body blow and was surprisingly emotional.' The squadron returned to Brüggen on 19 May.

A Jaguar Shot Down

The annual formal inspection of Brüggen was carried out 6 days later by the deputy C-in-C RAFG. After the morning parade, the squadrons resumed flying. Flt Lt McAlpine, '…was due to lead Paddy Mullen [Flt Lt T.A.F. Mullen] on a pairs SAP during which we would route past the Peheim mast and Area 2 in order to act as trade for the Wildenrath F-4s which were on Maxeval, I think. I started the day feeling under the weather and as planning progressed I felt steadily worse. Just before briefing, I decided pressing ahead was really silly, I thus phoned the duty pilot (Steve Griggs) [the wing weapons officer] whom I knew would be only too keen to swop jobs. As Steve was not in at the planning stage, Paddy took the lead and Steve became Number 2. I was by now in the tower as duty pilot.' Meanwhile, Wg Cdr Baron, along with the rest of, '…the station's senior executives assembled at 12:30hrs in the officers' mess bar before lunch with the AOC. It was then I was called away by a mess steward for an urgent telephone message. My senior flight commander, John Bryant, was at the other end of the line to tell me that we had just lost an aircraft and that an ATC broadcast to that effect was imminent. I had just enough time to notify the AOC and station commander before Brüggen and the surrounding area resounded to the words *Emergency State 1, Emergency State 1, Aircraft reported…* Without further ado, I returned at speed to the 14 Squadron site.'

'On arrival some 5 minutes later, I was briefed that, while about to cross the Rhine inbound to Brüggen, the Number 2 of a pair of aircraft[73] flown by Flt Lt Steve Griggs, had crashed without warning. The leader, Flt Lt Paddy Mullen, was due to land within the next few minutes and I went out to meet him. On climbing down from the cockpit, a shocked young Mullen told me that, whilst on recovery he had witnessed his Number 2 suddenly explode in a fireball with front and rear sections of the aircraft falling to the ground separately. He had shouted the words "Eject, Eject, Eject" over the radio and seen a parachute open a few seconds before it collapsed on coming to earth. He had then broadcast a Mayday Relay call and proceeded back to Brüggen. A short time later, news came through that Griggs was alive and well, apart from a few cuts and bruises. He had been picked up by a local farmer, filled with copious amounts of brandy, and was now en-route back to Brüggen via *Luftwaffe* helicopter.' In the immediate aftermath, the cause of the accident was still unclear at Brüggen. Griggs himself could remember that he had been flying, '…as wingman to Flt Lt Paddy Mullen on a Forward Air Controller training sortie on the North German plain. We had completed a most enjoyable sortie and were recovering to RAF Brüggen in loose fighting wing when there was a violent bang and the aircraft started yawing violently to the right and did not respond to the controls. I think that the canopy shattered and it became very noisy however, I could hear Paddy's voice from the other aircraft yelling: "Eject! Eject!" My rather confused thought processes were – he must know what is going on because I certainly don't! Result – I followed his wise advice and ejected.

'There was a violent explosion, my head was driven down to the breast plate of my lifejacket, there was a vision of the floor of the cockpit dropping away, the snatch of the parachute opening, a wrenching pain in my right hand (fool, let go of the seat handle!), and a moment of blissful quiet before I landed completely out of control into a field and it hurt. Herr Gerd Molleken (the farmer whose field I had landed in) and his daughter appeared and helped me to my feet. While gathering my parachute and various bits together a lone Phantom (F-4) flew overhead very low down. I asked the farmer if he had seen what had happened, but he had not. I had no idea myself, except that I thought that it was odd for the F-4 to be alone – they normally flew as pairs. Could I have had a mid-air with his mate? Questions for later since a bottle of brandy had now been produced and hospitality offered.' It later transpired that Flt Lt Griggs had been shot down by an AIM-9 Sidewinder missile fired accidentally by a Wildenrath Phantom crew; they had been scrambled from a station exercise and in the heat of the moment they had forgotten that they were armed with live missiles.

The squadron came very close to losing another Jaguar just 3 days later. Sqn Ldr N. C. Rusling returned from a simulated strike sortie[74], which had included a full range detail and then some circuit work when he had returned to Brüggen. Early on in the sortie, he had been aware of some commotion on the emergency frequency concerning a *Luftwaffe* F-104G which had hit something, was badly damaged and had to make an emergency landing at Gutersloh. It was only after landing that he discovered an F-104 radome-shaped hole in the port tailplane of his Jaguar.

The rest of the summer saw a busy phase of exercise flying with eight aircraft deployed to Skrydstrup from 1 to 4 June for 'Exercise Central Enterprise', and seven deployed to Marham for 'Exercise Mallet Blow' at the end of the month. In between, 'Exercise Gordon' included flying with four 1,000lb bombs loaded and airborne FAC provided by the Army Air Corps. In the second week of July, the squadron also participated in 'Exercise Argus', flying against the army's Rapier/Blindfire SAMs. On 13 July, Flt Lt McAlpine had a memorable encounter with a bird: '…John Chapman [Flt Lt J.G. Chapman] was leading me on a pairs attack sortie on a lovely hot day near the Hartz mountains. I was in arrow formation behind and offset to one side when I saw a very large bird ahead of him, but didn't have enough time to make a radio call to warn him of it. Funnily enough, I did have time to think it will make a very big bang when that hits him. It did not hit him though. The bird saw John just before he was about to hit it, the bird broke right and up, over John's wing, and straight into my left engine intake – and, yes, it was a very loud bang!

'The engine immediate wound down to 3 percent rpm and the engine temperature rose off the scale instantly – that was that. I told John what had happened and asked him to shepherd me to Gutersloh (temperature a balmy 30°C+). Now, in all the single-engine practice I had done and in all the crewroom chat I had heard, I made sure I kept a few extra knots on approach just for "Mum". And thank God, for imagine my horror when, despite the training fit of only one centre-line bomb carrier, and that I had jettisoned fuel down to about 1,000kg, and despite being in full part throttle reheat with the good engine, the speed bled off as soon as I lowered the gear. I remember being in full reheat for the last 10 seconds or so before touching down, watching the speed reduce at about 1 knot per second toward threshold speed with the runway still some way ahead.'

The summer's squadron exchange was a one-way affair: four Fiat G-91s of the Portuguese Air Force visited Brüggen for a week on 6 July. Flt Lt J. Taylor, the squadron diarist reported that, '…mixed formations were flown in the local area utilizing Nordhorn weapons range and a packed social programme ensured that the detachment was both enjoyable and successful.' 'Exercise Farman', held in the following month, included this time the added dimension of NATO Airborne Warning and Control System (AWACS) aircraft, which were able to give Jaguar formations details of the air defence fighters ahead of them.

After the Falklands War there were a large number of hastily-procured, but then unused, Paveway II Laser-Guided Bomb (LGB) kits left over and 14 Squadron was tasked to determine whether there was any tactical application for them in Germany. The targets might be designated using a ground-based Laser Target Marker (LTM) or an airborne designator such as the Pave Spike pod mounted on the Buccaneer. In each case the bombs would be delivered from a toss manoeuvre into the 'laser basket' from where it could follow the laser guidance to the target. Three pilots carried out a trial with Buccaneers from 25 to 31 August, which involved dropping sixteen inert 1,000lb bombs at Grafenwohr. The trial was expanded in September, as 'Exercise Gaff Jig', to use both Buccaneer and LTM for live drops at Garvie Island. Between 10 and 17 September, twenty LGBs were dropped at Garvie, despite some challenging weather.

Red Flag 83-2

The work-up started in the autumn for the squadron's participation in its second 'Exercise Red Flag' in February 1983. 'The work-up started in September 1982,' for Sqn Ldr Miller, 'from Lossiemouth (in area 14T) with the initial ultra low-level check-outs. I flew my first dual with Dave Baron on 14 September and later went on to check-out many other pilots. We also practiced LGB profiles on Tain and Garvie Island, using Buccaneers carrying Pave Spike marking pods. At around this time Steve Griggs ejected from a 14 Squadron Jaguar[75] when it caught fire in the air – a hot gas leak from one of the Adour combustion chambers perforated the fuel tank above the engine.' Wg Cdr Baron lamented that, 'This was the second time in 3 months that I went out to meet a helicopter recovering Griggs to base having taken off in one of my aircraft [and] he was not even a member of 14 Squadron!'

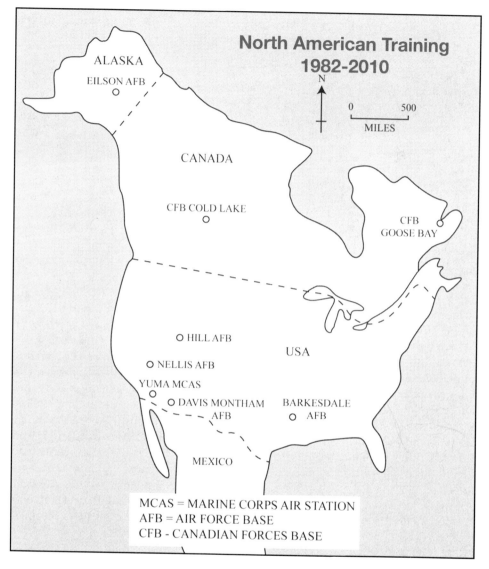

'We deployed again to Lossiemouth immediately after Christmas '82,' continued Sqn Ldr Miller, 'in order to wrap up the remaining qualifying sorties and, at the same time, gain some experience working with the 'men from Hereford' who would provide ground-based target marking. This was a particularly tricky manoeuvre because we carried a remote tone generator in the cockpit that needed to be initiated somewhere amid the complex sequence of fourteen-plus switch selections/button pushes in the loft/toss profile. The tone generator would trigger the laser target marker, but the timing was crucial – too early and the LGB would be dragged below its ideal flight path and run out of energy before reaching the target, and too late risked having too little guidance time.'

The Chief of the Air Staff with the officers of 14 Squadron on the occasion of the presentation of the new Squadron Standard on 26 November 1983. left to right Rear row: Flt Lts G.A. Case, T.A.F. Mullen, R.A. Sloan, Fg Offs J.S. Mitchell, M.J. Dudley, J. Dale (Intelligence Officer), Flt Lt J.E. Abra (Junior Engineering Officer). Middle row: Flt Lts J.N.M. Fyfe, S.A. Weatherston, Sqn Ldr J.J.E. Parr, Flt Lts J. Taylor, P.N. Martin, R.C. White, J.M. Hetherington, B.W. Newby, T.J. Kerss. Seated: Sqn Ldrs N.C. Rusling, G.A. Miller, Gp Capt C.J. Thomson (Station Commander), ACM Sir Keith Williamson, GCB, AFC, Wg Cdr D.A. Baron, AM Sir Jock Kennedy (C-in-C RAFG), Sqn Ldrs J. M. Bryant, J.H. Burgess (Senior Engineering Officer). (Dusty Miller)

During the 'Exercise Red Flag' work-up, a new Squadron Standard was to be presented to both 14 and 20 Squadrons. On 26 November, during the parade in the main hangar at Brüggen, the Chief of the Air Staff, Sir Keith Williamson, GCB, AFC presented 14 Squadron's new standard to Fg Off P. N. Martin.

Squadron personnel deployed to Las Vegas at the beginning of February 1983 ready for the exercise which ran from 8 to 17 February. For Flt Lt Kerss the exercise was, '…one of the highlights of my tour on 14 Squadron. The experience was particularly special because, as well as being able to experience the thrill of OLF[76] against 'real' threats, both in the air and on the ground. This exercise was the first in which the aircraft's Dash-10[77] ECM pod and Phimat chaff dispenser were tested "in anger." The results were impressive, and played havoc with the ground-based tracking radars. But it was not just in the air that Red Flag made its mark. This was in the "Pre Tailhook" days, and the social aspect was equally as fun.' In contrast to the squadron's previous experience in the Nevada weather, the weather was excellent for the whole exercise and the pilots were able to get the full value from the excellent flying. They were also able to carry out some more interesting weapon delivery profiles, including dropping Laser Guided Bombs on targets designated both by ground forces and also by Buccaneers. It was on one such sortie on 16 February that Sqn Ldr Miller: '…had [a] memorable moment on take-off from Nellis[78]. We were working with the Buccaneers (Pave Spike) and set off in a four-ship of two Jags (carrying LGBs) and two Buccs. We lined up ahead of the Buccs on the runway leaving (in retrospect) far too much distance between us. There was little wind and it was warm. I was leading on the left with Paddy Mullen Number 2 on the right, and the brief was to go to full burner at brake release and sort out the order once we were aloft. Paddy slowly overtook me on the runway and just as he rotated a vortex (marked by dust) drifted across the runway and went down my right intake. As my aircraft left the ground the right engine surged (big flame past my right ear and a deep cough) and the aircraft rolled violently to the right, and travelled across the width of the runway behind Paddy's aircraft, just inches off the ground. Just as I was thinking all was lost and it was time to leave, my aircraft stopped rolling right, entered the opposite vortex and rolled left, to be fully upright, but still only a little way off the ground. The surge in the right engine also cleared at the same time. Legs shaking I climbed away, raised the gear, and set off to burn off fuel before coming back to land once the rest of the stream were away – I decided that I'd had enough excitement for one day.' Miller was not the only one to have a 'hairy moment:' Sqn Ldr J.J.E. Parr was, '…leading an eight-ship into the industrial complex bang on my TOT.[79] I sensed something was not right; looking high to my 2 o'clock I could see four [Fairchild] A-10 pulling up and rolling in on the same target; they were firing live Mavericks. We aborted and returned to Nellis.' At the subsequent debrief the A-10 leader explained that he had not foreseen any problem with delivering live weapons on the target 10 minutes after his own range slot had lapsed!

Gibraltar Incident

After a month at home, the squadron set off once again for the year's APC, which started at Decimomannu on 18 April. Over the weekends of the detachment aircraft were sent off on lone-ranger flights and on 29 April four Jaguars left for Gibraltar. Flying one aircraft was Sqn Ldr Parr: 'After about an hour with the externals [tank] and wings empty, fuel started to feed from the front collector tank, not the centre. Puzzled, I tried to think how to fix it, then remembered the Jaguar adage "if the fuel system stops working as advertized get on the ground asap[80]". I calculated that to press on would see me in my dinghy about 50 miles from Gib and with Alicante 10 minutes away on my right I elected to divert there and Mick [Hetherington] came with me. We were talking to ATC, I think I had declared a Pan, nonetheless, after a short time we were intercepted by two Mirages who stayed with us all the way. I landed at Alicante uneventfully with fuel all over the aeroplane except in the right place; now the fun begins.' Diplomatic relations between the UK and Spain were at a low point because of the question of Gibraltar and by the time Sqn Ldr Parr managed to contact Sqn Ldr Bryant at 'Deci' there was already great agitation both at Brüggen and HQ RAFG. However the British Ambassador, who was also involved by now, was very calm about the whole incident. Unfortunately, things then got worse when Flt Lt Hetherington took off from Alicante ostensibly bound for Faro, but flew instead straight to Gibraltar! Sqn Ldr Parr found himself in the midst of a major diplomatic incident with, '…red hot phones…Number 10 involved – you name it! The Ambassador – still unfazed – suggested people would calm down over the weekend and he was leaving for the hills. While all this was going on the engineers had offered some advice, but after refuelling and ground runs the problem was still there. I agreed that I would 'puddle jump' the aircraft back to Brüggen overland, but not over a weekend with many en-route airfields closed. This I subsequently did, having scrounged a map from a Boeing 737 crew, after a most enjoyable weekend in the sun courtesy of HMG. The political bit rumbled on a bit, but then a young Sub Lt 'Soapy' Watson [RN] landed his Sea Harrier on a container ship which took the heat off me.'

Wg Cdr Baron handed over command of the squadron to Wg Cdr D.F.A. Henderson in June and the following month there was a two-way exchange with the *Luftwaffe*'s FBW 32 at Lechfeld. Six F-104Gs visited Brüggen from 25 to 31 July. Apart from a lively social side to the exchange, the two squadrons flew some mixed-formation attack sorties including an airfield attack against Husum. For Flt Lt Kerss, '…the highlight was a back-seat ride over Northern Germany in an F-104 Starfighter. A great aircraft with plenty of punch, even in dry power. The wings were tiny, and the resulting handling was brought home to me when, as I was flying it, I found that I set off the stick shaker with what seemed to be the lightest pulls to climb over the Osnabruck Ridge.' The summer also brought the usual range of exercises, including the squadron's own 'Exercise Farman' working up against F-4, F-15 fighter and HAWK missiles while attacking small airfields across northern Germany. 'Exercises Cheerful Challenge' and 'Cold Fire' took place in August, while in early September range slots were available at Garvie Island for live bombing. Formations flew via-Machrihanish to drop live 1,000lb bombs, although the weaponry was almost brought to a halt by fishing boats passing close to the island. Throughout the month there was also a work-up with the Buccaneer squadrons at Laarbruch for LGB profiles, in which, as previously, the Jaguars would toss a LGB towards a target marked by a trailing Buccaneer equipped with Pave Spike.

On 12 September, Flt Lt Kerss and Sqn Ldr Miller were climbing out[81] of one of the Dutch coastal bombing ranges for the return to Brüggen. 'The weather was stunning,' recalled Sqn Ldr Miller, 'great visibility and bright blue sky beneath and around a field of towering cumulonimbus along the Dutch coast…on recovery Tim decided rightly to climb up to medium level and asked Dutch Military [air-traffic control] for a service, adding that he needed to avoid the bank of huge clouds directly ahead of us. Dutch Mil acknowledged the request, identified us, then fed us straight into the biggest cumulonimbus I ever recall seeing.'

'As we approached our transit altitude,' continued Flt Lt Kerss, 'the sky darkened and I noticed St.Elmo's fire appearing on the pitot probe – a sign that we were approaching an area of electrical storm activity. By this time Dusty [Miller] had closed into close formation on my right wing. Suddenly there was a massive bang on my airframe, and I immediately realized that I had experienced a lightning strike. As I checked my instruments Dusty informed me that I had lost the drop tank on my right wing.' Meanwhile, as Sqn Ldr Miller, '…edged closer and closer in formation on the

Flt Lt C.F. Allan drops a stick of 1,000lb retard bombs at Vliehors rage on 28 January 1985. In capturing the moment, Sqn Ldr J.J.E. Parr found himself too close to photograph all eight bombs in the stick! (Jerry Parr)

starboard side of Tim, the cloud surrounding us got darker and darker, and I can recall hearing the sound of rain beating on the windscreen above the very noisy Jaguar air conditioning. There was then a tremendous flash (and I swear I heard a bang) and a great fork of lightning attached itself to the end of Tim's pitot probe. A few seconds later I transmitted a call to Tim to ask if he was okay when, before he could answer, another great flash and bang, another fork of lightning into the pitot probe, and the debris from an exploding under-wing fueltank disappearing up and behind Tim's aircraft. Moments later we emerged from the side of the cunim into the stunningly clear blue sky.' Although the under-wing tank had been completely destroyed the aircraft was otherwise undamaged and Kerss was able to recover safely to Brüggen. Some months later Kerss heard that the remains of the tank had been found in the grounds of a stately home!

Eight days later, 14 Squadron hosted a visit by the prime minister, Mrs Margaret Thatcher, who was treated to a demonstration of a 'scramble' launch by two Jaguars flown by Flt Lt Mullen and McAlpine. This was made all the more spectacular when Flt Lt Mullen inadvertently selected part-throttle reheat as he taxied out of his HAS and he shot past the VIPs at an impressive speed.

On 27 and 28 March 1984, part of the newly-built A29 autobahn to the west of Ahlhorn was made available for use by NATO aircraft before it was officially opened to traffic. The 2km stretch of straight road had a removable central reservation and hard standing for an ORP at each end. Jaguars of 14 Squadron 'cycled' through the highway

strip on both days: Sqn Ldr Parr landed there on the first day and found the experience, '...interesting but not exciting. It would have been a great beer call if we had not had to fly out! The whole of 2 and 4ATAF were there.' The next day Sqn Ldr Miller landed there and found, '...being north-south(ish) orientation and nestling in a deep cutting, a strong south-westerly [wind] created significant turbulence at around one hundred feet on the approach.'

After the Taceval Team visited in April and declared the squadron once again to be 'Excellent,' the unit prepared for two detachments in the summer. The first was the squadron-strength APC at Decimomannu in May and the second, smaller one, was mounted to Gibraltar in early June so that the squadron could take its turn manning the permanent force of three Jaguars there. Diplomatic relations with the Spanish were still strained and although Spain was by now a full member of NATO, the aircraft were

Jaguar GR1 XX756 flies past the 'waterfront' at Bruggen on 3 July 1985. The squadron had vacated the HAS site in preparation handing it over to 14 Squadron (Tornado). The aircraft is in an air-combat fit with no under-wing tanks and an AIM-9 Sidewinder air-to-air missile carried on the outboard pylon (Geoffrey Lee)

there to remind the Spanish that Gibraltar was a British territory. A large part of the role of the Jaguars was 'flying the flag' and with low overshoots along the runway, in Flt Lt Kerss' words, '…we left the Spaniards in no doubt of our presence! We were frequently tracked by missile radar on the top of a local hill (as revealed by our RWR gear). Our sorties out of Gib comprised "ship recce", one v one combat and splash firing against targets towed by the RN. For me it was fascinating to seek out Russian naval shipping and to see "the enemy" at first hand!' From 3 to 18 September, 14 Squadron took over the Gibraltar task.

As the runway at Brüggen was due for some resurfacing work at the end of June and beginning of July, the squadron decamped to Akrotiri via Brindisi on 21 June for a 3-week air-combat training camp. The squadron was divided into three shifts so that a suitable balance could be struck between flying and enjoying the beach! Sqn Ldr Parr,

Jaguar GR1 XZ356 returning from Vliehors range on 2 July 1985. (Geoffrey Lee)

who ran the detachment, had arranged, '…some DACT and F-4 affiliation plus night flying. That was an eye opener for the young first tourists who had never flown in true, pitch-black night! Clean, the Jaguar was a good combat aeroplane – many F-4 crews in particular were forced to eat humble pie. Because it was so small – ergo difficult to pick up – we could often gain an advantage early despite having no thrust and a small wing it turned well.'

The previous autumn, Sqn Ldr Parr had discovered some old tandem-beam bomb racks which were being used to hold up the awning over the squadron barbeque site. He told the armourers that if they could get the racks to work they could have the pleasure of loading up eight 1,000lb bombs, which could then be dropped on the range in a single stick. The squadron armourers duly got the racks into working order and on 28 January, Flt Lt C.F. Allan took off[82] for Vliehors loaded with eight 1,000lb bombs. On his wing[83] was Flt Lt D.A. Earp with Sqn Ldr Parr sitting in the back with his camera. Although the drop was successful Sqn Ldr Parr ended up too close to be able to capture the whole eight-bomb stick on film!

The squadron was in Gibraltar again in February 1985 and mounted a flypast on 4 February, the day the Spanish formally ended the 16-year-old blockade and opened the border to Gibraltar. Another flypast took place 14 days later, this time by five Jaguars, to celebrate the squadron's 70th Anniversary.

By the beginning of March, 14 Squadron was the only Jaguar squadron left at Brüggen. The other squadrons on the Wing had already re-equipped with the Tornado and 20 Squadron had also moved to Laarbruch. Much of the responsibility to meet Brüggen's QRA strike commitment therefore fell to 14 Squadron.

On 1 April, a three-ship formation was on a routine training sortie to the Munsterlager range. They transitted to Hanover at medium level and then let down to low-level under radar control. Having broken cloud at 3,000ft, just to the northeast of Celle, they dropped to low-level and headed towards the range in a loose trailing formation. The leader then called them across to the range frequency. After looking into the cockpit to tune his radio manually Flt Lt G. Brough, in the Number 3 aircraft[84], looked up and found himself in a steep descending turn extremely close to the ground. Although he instinctively rolled the wings level and pulled hard, he realized that the aircraft would hit the ground and he ejected almost on impact. Very luckily the ejection seat saved him.

Later in the month, the squadron was honoured to host Gp Capt W.S.G. Maydwell, DSO, DFC who had commanded the unit for much of its time as a Martin Marauder squadron during the Second World War. Gp Capt Maydwell was guest of honour at a dining-in night on 20 April, an occasion which was also attended by AVM D. Bryant, the former CO in Phantom days and Wg Cdr J.J. Whitfield, commanding 14 (Designate) Tornado Squadron.

The squadron's last deployment to Decimomannu as a Jaguar squadron ran from 14 May to 4 June. However, this particular detachment was not limited to the APC: this was also the first ever use of the ACMI range by an RAF ground-attack unit. The Air Combat Manoeuvring Instrumentation (ACMI) range comprised an air-to-air range off the western coast of Sardinia equipped with a full-telemetry system which tracked data-link pods carried on each aircraft within the range. The pods were carried on one of the missile pylons, while the other pylon was loaded with an AIM-9L Sidewinder missile acquisition round. Apart from giving the capability to watch each engagement in real time and to assess 'kills' accurately, the system enabled a full debrief to be carried out so that all the participants could learn from their experience. During the debrief, each engagement could be replayed – and paused at any time – giving a 'God's-eye' view of the fight, or the view from any of the aircraft cockpits. It was indeed a powerful training tool. While on the deployment 14 Squadron took the opportunity to carry out Dissimilar Air Combat Training (DACT) against *Luftwaffe* F-4 Phantoms and Fleet Air Arm (RN) Hunter T8Ms.

Wg Cdr Henderson led another detachment to Gibraltar on 15 June. During the fortnight there, the detachment carried out more air-combat training as well as low-level attacks against RN ships (HMS *Amazon, Penelope* and *Naiad*) as well as splash bombing and strafing. The final squadron detachment was to Fassberg from 30 August to 5 September for 'Exercise Treaty', an annual exercise with the French and US forces to test contingency plans for the reinforcement of Berlin. The flying involved some work with FAC on Sennelager range (to the east of Gutersloh) and routine attack profiles as pairs or four-ships across northern Germany. Flt Lt K.G. Noble , '…managed to sand-bag a ride in a French Mirage IIIb [with] a real bandit pilot flying much lower than we were supposed to!'

The Jaguar squadron was formally disbanded at the end of October and the Squadron Standard was handed over to 14 Squadron (Tornado) on 1 November.

NOTES

60   The Elliott E-3R inertial platform was at the heart of the NavWASS in the Jaguar GR1. Although advanced for its day it was prone to 'dumping' and was eventually replaced in the Jaguar GR1a by the improved Ferranti FIN 1064 platform.

61   In Jaguar GR1 XX751.

62   In Jaguar GR1 XX827.

63   In Jaguar GR1 XX836.

64   In Jaguar GR1 XX963.

65   Circular Error Probable, is a measure of the accuracy of a ballistic weapon and is measured as the radius of a circle centred on the target into which half of the weapons will fall. The smaller the CEP the more accurate the weapon delivery.

66   The Marconi ARI 18223 RWR was mounted in the tailfin of the Jaguar with a display in the cockpit.

67   Jaguar GR1 XX960.

68   TACtical Air Navigation radio beacon.

69   Fox 2 was the radio call to indicate a kill using a heat-seeking missile.

70   Jaguar GR1 XX767.

71   Sqn Ldr McCairns, Flt Lts Wardell, W.R. Hartree and I.D. Hill.

72   Jaguar GR1s XX760 and XX 826.

73   Jaguar GR1 XX963.

74   In Jaguar GR1 XZ382.

75   Jaguar GR1 XX760 on 13 September.

76   Operational Low Flying (ie down to 100ft).

77   The Westinghouse AN/ALQ-119(V)10 Electronics Counter-Measures (ECM)pod.

78   In Jaguar GR1 XX369.

79   Time Over Target.

80   As Soon As Possible.

81   Flt Lt Kerss in Jaguar GR1 XX956, Sqn Ldr Miller in Jaguar GR1 XX750.

82   In Jaguar GR1 XX352.

83   In Jaguar T2 XX845.

84   Jaguar GR1 XZ388.

7

1985-2001

THE TORNADO
IN GERMANY

The Canberra Replacement (Continued)

When newly-qualified Tornado navigator Fg Off J. J. Payne arrived at RAF Brüggen to report to 14 (Designate) Squadron at the end of May 1985 he discovered that it only comprised two other personnel: the squadron commander, Wg Cdr J. J. Whitfield, and another navigator, Flt Lt R. J. Turner. However, over the next few months the rest of the aircrew and ground crew arrived, and factory-new aircraft were delivered. The aircrew came from a mixture of backgrounds: some had previous Tornado experience gained at Marham or Laarbruch, while the majority came straight from the Tornado Weapons Conversion Unit (TWCU). Of these graduates of the TWCU, there were a number of ex-Jaguar pilots (including Flt Lt I.B. Walker who had previously flown the Jaguar on 14 Squadron) and a large contingent of first-tourists fresh from flying training. By mid-1985, the three other Jaguar squadrons at Brüggen had already re-equipped with the Tornado and since 20 Squadron had moved to Laarbruch, their old HAS site, on the south-west corner of the airfield, became temporary home for the newest Tornado unit. By the end of October, a complete Tornado squadron had formed on the site and was well on the way to being declared combat ready. The unit took part in the station Minival in mid-July and a number of squadron-run 'Op Days' in August and September helped to get into the rhythm of the strike and attack roles.

The Panavia Tornado was almost as large a step in capability from the Jaguar as the Phantom had been from the Canberra: equipped with state-of-the-art electronic-warfare equipment it could carry a heavier weapons payload further and, crucially, it could do so at night or in bad weather. The heart of the Tornado was its Terrain Following Radar

(TFR) system enabled the crew to fly at high speed and low level without even being able to see the ground, while the Ground Mapping Radar (GMR) also bestowed on them the ability to attack a target accurately, again, without seeing it. For the first time, the RAF had a true day and night all-weather attack capability at low level. It was a capability that was long overdue: it had been needed since the 1960s and it was the role for which TSR2 had originally been designed. In fact the Tornado was, by a circuitous route, a direct descendant of the TSR2 and therefore perhaps the true replacement for the 1950s-vintage Canberra. In the aftermath of the cancellation of the TSR2 and F-111K projects the government had kept aspirations for a low-level strike aircraft alive, firstly as the Anglo-French Variable Geometry (AFVG) aircraft and then, when the French lost interest, as the Multi-Role Combat Aircraft (MRCA), a collaboration with the Germans and Italians. The MRCA had evolved into the Tornado, which would eventually equip eight squadrons in RAF Germany: four each at Laarbruch and Brüggen. However, despite the formidable capability of this new machine, experienced Tornado navigators like Flt Lt D.H. Steer, who had completed a tour with 27 Squadron, thought, '…that RAFG was still operating as it had done in the Hunter era and thus looked upon navigators as spare baggage, and TF radar and bombing as completely superfluous…there was still a large Jaguar/Hunter mentality which meant, unlike the UK squadrons, the Tornado was not being used to its full potential.'

On 1 November 1985, 14 Squadron officially became a Tornado squadron when the Squadron Standard was handed from Flt Lt P.C.H. Rogers of the Jaguar squadron, to Fg Off Payne. The parade, like so many of the Squadron's Standard parades, was held in the hangar. Appropriately the reviewing officer was the Deputy C-in-C RAF Germany, AVM D.T. Bryant, OBE who had commanded the squadron in Phantom days. At a dining-in night that evening, the Jaguar squadron made another presentation: they had decided that it would be amusing to reinstate the squadron's tradition from 88 Squadron days of having a python as a mascot. The new python, a 3-inch baby, was christened 'Flt Lt Eric Aldrovandi' and 'Eric', who was eventually to grow to the respectable length of 22 ft, would become the only squadron member to serve with the unit throughout its 25 years as a Tornado squadron.

The first priority was for the RAF's newest Tornado squadron to be declared combat ready in the nuclear-strike role. This had to be achieved despite a particularly cold winter during which snow sometimes brought operations at Brüggen to a halt. On one such occasion, when it was obvious that nothing could be done at Brüggen, the entire squadron closed down for a few days to go skiing at Winterberg. However, a series of exercises through the winter months culminated in a successful Initial Taceval, which finished with a mass-strike launch on 12 February. The reward for passing this first test was that the squadron took its turn, once more, manning the aircraft on nuclear QRA!

Tornado Operations in 'Cold War' Germany

The Tornado took the place of the Jaguar seamlessly in the RAFG Order of Battle in 'Cold War' Germany. The priority for all NATO strike-capable squadrons was to cover the strike commitments dictated by SACEUR. On a day-to-day basis this meant the QRA comprising one or two aircraft from each squadron at 15 minutes' readiness to

A 14 Squadron Tornado GR1 (ZD707) at low-level over Germany in early 1986. (RAFM X003-2603-0150)

launch against the most important targets. As a crisis developed, so the force generation level would increase, requiring more aircraft to be held at high readiness to cover a greater number of targets. In the last resort, all strike-capable aircraft (over fifty aircraft at Brüggen) would be held at cockpit readiness for release in the Composite Launch Sequence Plan (CLSP), a master plan which co-ordinated the release of the whole of NATO's tactical-nuclear arsenal in Northern Europe. This escalating commitment was practiced on every exercise, always ending (after long, boring hours at cockpit readiness) in an impressive mass launch of every aircraft on the Wing. In parallel with the coverage of pre-planned targets covered by the CLSP, Tornado crews might be called upon to carry out a Selective Use (Seluse) of a nuclear weapon as a demonstration to the enemy of the political resolve to use such weapons. Again, Seluse planning and launch procedures were practiced in every exercise.

In parallel with the nuclear commitment, Brüggen's Tornado squadrons were also declared to SACEUR as attack (that is non-nuclear) assets. Whenever the station's hooter sounded, which it did quite frequently in the late 1980s, everyone rushed to their place of work and the Tornados were loaded with live weapons in the expectation of a launch for 'Option Alpha'. This pre-planned operation, which included all of SACEUR's attack aircraft, was designed to neutralize the Wasaw Pact airfields and strategic SAM systems in Eastern Germany. The Brüggen squadrons were tasked against the MiG-29 ('Fulcrum') bases at Zerbst, Jutebog and Kothen and the SAM-5 site at Altengrabow, all just to the east of Magdeburg. The squadron was responsible for providing eight aircraft to cover the SAM5 site – a popular choice since it would involve dropping 1,000lb bombs,

14 Squadron's first Tornado Armed Practice Camp (APC): Flt Lts M.J.W. Napier and D.M. Dolan strapping into Tornado GR1 (ZD718) on the line at Decimomannu on 27 May 1986, before a 20° dive-bombing sortie at Frasca range. (Mike Napier)

rather than the JP233 runway-denial weapon, which had been developed for use against airfield targets. The JP233 had been designed by someone with very little tactical sense, for although it might damage a concrete runway more than would a traditional free-fall bomb, its delivery involved flying directly along a runway at 200ft. Most Tornado crews recognized that this would be suicidal! A more tactical compromise was developed later involving use of the JP233 to cut across runways instead, but as crews were later to find in the Gulf War, even this was pretty 'hairy'.

Like the Phantom and Jaguar units before them, the Tornado squadrons deployed to Decimomannu every year for an APC. For 14 Squadron the first Tornado APC took place from 12 May to 3 June. Most of the squadron aircrew spent 10 days at 'Deci', but the first tourist crews[85] were there for the entire 3 weeks. The sun shone every day for the whole of the APC, which was a great success and served to bond the new squadron together. It was also the first opportunity to fire the Mauser 27mm cannon, which had only just been cleared for use. The summer months brought the usual fare of NATO exercises such as 'Central Enterprise' and 'Blue Moon' in June and the squadron was kept busy in its work-up to combat ready status in the attack role. After a busy Maxeval in the second week of September, half of the squadron deployed to Spangdahlem for an exchange with the 81st TFS (USAF). The flying was limited by weather and also, according to Flt Lt Steer, because, '…the USAF idea of co-ordination seemed to be "same day same way."The social was no more successful at Spang as we were invited to the squadron CO's house for drinks and we were not too impressed by the party ending at 8pm after one drink. All the Americans obediently trooped out but we insisted on taking a crate of beer with us in exchange for exiting the house at that ridiculously early hour!'

Throughout the year the squadron's air and ground crews had mounted QRA, just as their forebears had done for almost 25 years. The QRA site was a securely fenced-off area adjoining the south-westerly HAS site which had four HAS and a hardened accommodation block. Apart from carrying out the daily servicing required for each aircraft and its weapon, there was little to do and the tedium was relieved with videos and boardgames. The QRA also had its own cook, so at least crews knew that they would eat well while they were on duty! However, it is unlikely that the junior crews, who seemed to bear the brunt of QRA manning, spent much of their enforced freetime thinking about the gradual political rapprochement between East and West during the mid-1980s: so they were very pleasantly surprised at the announcement in October that QRA would cease at the end of the month. As festivities across the station celebrated the end of this tedious chore, few people realized that this momentous event marked the beginning of the end of the 'Cold War'; in fact the 'Cold War', which had dominated military life since the Second World War, would be over in just 2 years.

In any case, QRA was soon forgotten in the excitement following news that the squadron's next visit to Decimomannu would be to use the ACMI Range. The air-combat work up started in November and by the time the squadron deployed to 'Deci' on 7 January 1987, most of the crews had almost completed the qualification syllabus. The first few ACMI sorties enabled everyone to qualify, after which some more interesting scenarios were introduced. A detachment of Harriers from 3 Squadron provided enemy forces and as the Tornado crews worked up from one-versus-one engagements with the Harriers to a spectacular four-versus-two finale at the end of the detachment.

By 20 January, the squadron was back at Brüggen and caught up in the working-up towards the next Taceval. A Minival followed at the end of the month and there was Maxeval in the last week in February. The sound of the alert hooter marked the start of a Taceval on 30 March. Early in the exercise, Flt Lts J.P. Moloney and J.A. Hill were Number 2 of a formation of three aircraft tasked with an interdiction mission. After take-off Moloney thought that his aircraft's[86] controls seemed less precise than usual, but he attributed this to the fact that he had just returned from leave and had not flown recently. The formation continued the departure route towards the Rhine at around 700ft and as it approached the boundary of the LFA, the three aircraft widened into tactical formation. Moloney made a gentle right turn, but as he rolled back to the left to straighten out of the turn, the aircraft continued rolling to the left. The nose dropped and when the aircraft reached an inverted attitude both crewmembers realized that they would have to eject. They did so as the aircraft rolled upright again. Although Flt Lt Moloney was largely unhurt, Flt Lt Hill broke his arm during the ejection sequence and then suffered further bad luck when he landed at the top of a large fir tree. Unfortunately the tree complicated his rescue because when a *Bundesheer* (German Army)

CH-53D helicopter arrived on the scene, its downwash caused the tree to swing violently backwards and forwards, much to the alarm of Hill – and the hilarity of Moloney who was watching from the safety of the ground.

The Taceval continued despite the loss of the Tornado and finished on 2 April. During the remainder of the month, the squadron took part in 'Exercise Mallet Blow' with four-ship formations, which refuelled at Cottesmore or Coningsby between sorties. This profile, which enabled each formation to get the most out of the low-level phase of each mission, was also repeated in 'Excercise Mallet Blow' during August.

Once again the APC at Decimomannu in mid-May was blessed with sunshine. After some years of negotiation, the Italians finally agreed to the use of the Laser rangefinder at Frasca Range. The honour of using the equipment for the first time fell to Flt Lts Napier and Turner who led[87] a formation of three aircraft for a bombing and strafe detail on the morning of 19 May. After dropping all their bombs successfully, they joined the pattern for a laser-ranged strafe run. 'Instead of "No 'its" or even (dream on) "Ten 'its" as the range safety officer scored my first pass,' recalled Flt Lt Napier, 'there was silence. "Paris 2 – In Hot, Lima." Silence. "Paris 2 off dry…Paris 3 – In Hot, Lima." Silence. "Paris 3 off dry." My turn again, "Paris One – In Hot, Lima." This time it is met by an urgent cry of horror: "Paris Lead, you 'ave keel-ed two 'orses!"' The combination of poor tracking and a software bug, which put the aiming pipper in the wrong place when the laser was fired, caused the untimely deaths of two horses which had been (perhaps foolishly) grazing near the strafe panels.

RAFG Routine

At Brüggen the routine was, typically for the squadron, to mount three flying waves of some six aircraft. A four-ship would be mounted whenever possible and the squadron would also frequently provide a 'bounce' aircraft. Other profiles included pairs or singleton sorties (the latter designated simulated-strike profiles) and the plethora of periodic checks and instrument ratings required for each pilot. A typical Tornado attack sortie would take 2 hours to plan and would invariably be produced as an IMC-capable plan. This was done by planning 'parallel tracks' for each pair of aircraft, so that the auto-pilot/Terrain-Following Radar (TFR) could fly each aircraft on its own discreet route; a four-ship was flown as two pairs, with the rear pair flying some 40 seconds behind the lead pair. In visual conditions the leader would fly his own track and the other aircraft would fly a much tighter visual 'card' formation. A typical Tornado route in Germany might head eastwards at 500ft past the EW training range at Borgholzhausen to the south of Osnabruck, before heading into the 250ft low-flying system for (usually) two simulated attacks against ground targets. With much of northern Germany home to NATO army units there was no difficulty in selecting realistic military targets. The attacks were usually planned as an IMC-compatible laydown profile, simulating 1,000lb bombs. The problem with attacks by multiple aircraft on the same target was that each successive aircraft risked being damaged by debris blown into the air by the bombs dropped by the one ahead. The solution was to attack from different directions with 40 second spacing between each aircraft. Although this was tactically feasible at night or in poor weather, there was always a question – that was never really addressed – about whether it would be tactically sound to attack a defended target at such wide intervals in good visual conditions. The route would often take in known fighter engagement zones, or pass close to landmarks used by fighters as 'anchors' for their CAPs. The best known of these was the Peheim mast, northwest of Ahlhorn which was a favourite haunt of the F-4 Phantoms from Wildenrath, and the F-15 Eagles from Soesterburg. Routing via Peheim also led naturally onto the attack track at Nordhorn range. Most Tornado sorties included a range detail, either at Nordhorn, Helchteren, or Vliehors, or occasionally at Siegenburg, way down to the south of Regensburg. On occasions the UK ranges in the Wash, at Donna Nook, Cowden, or even Jurby might also be used, while closer to base range slots at Bergen-Hohne were sometimes available.

The summer of 1987 was filled with many such sorties, and there were also the usual run of summer exercises including 'Mallet Blow', and 'Cold Fire'. There was also an opportunity for selected crews to fire an AIM-9G during a MPC at RAF Valley from 7 to 22 July. In October, the squadron deployed for what would become an annual feature in their calendar: Goose Bay, Canada.

North America

Goose Bay at the foot of Lake Melville in Labrador, had its heyday in the 1940s and 1950s, firstly as an important staging post on the North Atlantic ferry route and later as a forward operating base for strategic bombers. By the 1970s, the advent of longer-range aircraft and ballistic missiles had left a large and underused airfield amid a vast, almost unpopulated terrain: in other words, ideal low-flying country. The RAF's Strike Command had used Goose Bay as a low-level training area for its Avro Vulcan bombers and when these were replaced in the UK by the Tornado the latter type also started to use the facilities at Goose Bay. Then, by extension, the RAFG Tornados were also included. Eight aircraft were ferried across the Atlantic by one of the (air-to-air refuelling qualified) UK-based Tornado squadrons: they would remain in North America for the 'training season', which included Goose Bay detachments for RAFG units and participation in 'Exercise Red Flag'.

Goose Bay's isolation was a double-edged sword: on the one hand the emptiness of the training areas meant that apart from avoiding some small fishing settlements there were virtually no restrictions on low flying which could be carried out down to 100ft throughout the area. With exclusive use of the training areas, too, the Tornados could practice automatic terrain following in low cloud and fog without fear of hitting anything else – something that was not possible in Europe. However, all this freedom came at a cost: there were no targets and no defences to practice against. To an extent the target problem could be solved for IMC[88] attacks using a bit of imagination: eskers (winding ridges of stratified sand) became runways, small islands became command bunkers, while larger islands became ships, but none of these were particularly realistic in good visibility. Nor were there any other fighters to train against. The latter would not be a problem for long as the RNLAF would bring their General-Dynamics F-16 Fighting Falcons to Goose Bay in future years, but it did limit the value of the detachment in 1987 as a work-up for 'Exercise Red Flag'. For 14 Squadron this first detachment between 4 and 19 October was also a precursor to the squadron's first 'Red Flag' exercise as a Tornado unit. On the positive side, though, all the crews were able to qualify at operational low flying in time for 'Red Flag'. Sqn Ldr T.P. McDonald found that, '…the flying in Canada was amazing. There was something quite unreal about flying at low level, covering hundreds of miles without seeing anything that was man-made. The flying at 100ft and 480kt or more was also very exhilarating.' One landmark, which everyone enjoyed, was Harp Lake, a long finger of water a mile wide, sandwiched between 1,000ft cliff walls, which ran in a straight line for 25 miles. It was an incredible thrill to be in a Tornado speeding along the bottom of the chasm, just 100ft above the surface of the lake. The night terrain-following radar certainly sharpened Sqn Ldr McDonald's mind, '…the weather was not brilliant and with no surrounding towns, villages or lighting of any description it was very, very dark. On my first night mission with the TFR and the aircraft being flown by the autopilot, we began to climb up one side of a ridge, which was the first in a series of ridges and valleys that crossed our track at right angles. Then we went into cloud! The aircraft continued to gently climb toward the crest of the ridge and then it began to descend down the other side, still in cloud. Our minds were concentrated a little more. Then we broke clear of the cloud as the aircraft descended into the valley before pulling up toward the next ridgeline and entering cloud once more. And so it went on, up and down, in and out of cloud, in pitch darkness, with a constant commentary from Jeremy [Payne] describing what he could see in plan view on his Ground Mapping Radar [GMR], while I described what I could see on the E-scope which gave an elevation-view of the terrain ahead… it certainly gave us a lot of confidence in one another and in the capability of our kit.'

The squadron's senior crews, led by Sqn Ldr H.W. Price and Flt Lt Steer, flew the aircraft to Nellis AFB via Griffiss AFB (near Utica, New York) and Offut AFB (near Omaha, Nebraska), to be ready for the start of 'Red Flag' on 26 October. Meanwhile, a team of more junior aircrew had managed to escape for a week of sightseeing in California, thanks to a USAF Lockheed C-141 Starlifter which had fortuitously staged through Goose Bay on the day after they had qualified!

'Exercise Red Flag 88-1' started with the mandatory range familiarization flights on 26 October. On the subsequent days the squadron flew as many aircraft as possible on each wave, typically flying six or seven-ship formations. Like the Jaguar and Buccaneer crews before them, the Tornado crews found some difficulty in locating the targets which were, for the most part, bulldozed in the sand to make them stand out from 20,000ft, rather than 100ft! With little vertical extent and with the dubious accuracy of some of the range maps, finding targets could be a challenge even with the Tornado's formidable navigation kit. However, the training value of the exercise had been increased further by the introduction of the 'Red Flag' monitoring and debrief system, akin to the ACMI system at Decimomannu, which recorded the movement of each individual aircraft via a data-link pod carried on the missile pylon. For Sqn Ldr McDonald the flying on 'Red Flag' was, '…brilliant, the best I have ever taken part in, then or since. The weather was good and we were able to practice all of the tactics that we would need to use for real.' Every 'Red Flag' sortie was flown as part of a 'package' of around fifty aircraft comprising the strike aircraft supported by fighter escort, 'Wild Weasel' defence suppression aircraft, EW jammers, reconnaissance aircraft and tankers. The exercise was the first time that many of the aircrew had worked closely with the USAF and seen the way that massive packages were all co-ordinated in the strike plan. It was an experience which would prove invaluable a few years later during operations in the Middle East.

Sadly the weather broke towards the end of the second week and on the last mission the weather on the ranges was so poor that only the 'crazy Brits' equipped with TFR, were able to participate. What the Americans did not realise was that not all of the TFR equipment was working and the ingress (entry) tactics used by some crews on that day owed more to their experience flying in marginal European weather than using their radar.

With the inevitable postings that followed the 'Red Flag' detachment, there was a large changeover of personnel over the winter. The squadron settled back into a training regime at the beginning of 1988, which would last most of the year. Detachments to Decimomannu for ACMI in February and APC at the end of June bracketed a Taceval in mid-February and another trip to Goose Bay in April. Among the new joiners to the squadron was Wg Cdr R.V. Morris, who took over as CO in April. The squadron exchange in the September was with the Greek Air Force F-4 Phantom Wing at Andravida: like those who had exchanged with Greeks before them, the 14 Squadron 'away team' found that the operational side of the exchange was somewhat limited. However, the Greeks did plan a mixed-formation sortie which included a simulated attack on a target on a small island in the Aegean. The plan was for an almost simultaneous attack by eight aircraft heading due east. It was only when the RAF crews looked at the map more closely that they realized that the target lay almost on the border with Turkish airspace and the Greeks were intending to provoke the Turks. In the end a more diplomatic line of attack was chosen, running parallel to the border!

The End of the 'Cold War'

The New Year of 1989 started disastrously with the loss of two of the most popular and talented members of the squadron in a fatal flying accident. Friday, 13 January 1989, was the last day of the station Minival, which ended with the 'traditional' CLSP mass launch of thirty aircraft. After the usual long wait at cockpit readiness Flt Lts M. P. S. Smith and A.G Grieve were released and took off[89] at 08:31hrs, the 23rd aircraft to get airborne. After successfully attacking a field target northeast of Bremen their route joined the stream of Brüggen Tornados heading westward at one-minute intervals to join the strike run at Nordhorn range. As they passed some 10 miles south of Wittmund they would have found it difficult to see southward, which was 'up-sun' in the haze; they were busy, too, setting themselves for the bombing run at Nordhorn. At the same time a flight of four *Luftwaffe* Dassault/Dornier Alpha Jets was heading due northward to carry out an airfield attack at Wittmund. The Tornado hit the lead Alphajet in an almost perfect 90° interception and although the German pilot was able to eject, both members of the Tornado crew were killed instantly.

There was little time for mourning as the squadron started its work-up for 'Exercise Red Flag 89-3' the following month. This, the squadron's second participation as a Tornado unit, ran between 3 and 14 April. Then the familiar pattern followed through the rest of the year: detachments to Decimomannu and Goose Bay were interspersed with NATO exercises such as 'Central Enterprise'. There was also an MPC at RAF

Decimomannu, June1989. A formation returns from the Frasca range, with the practice bomb carriers visible on the under-fuselage shoulder pylons. The 'flat turn' was something of a tradition – and usually a debriefing point – for recoveries into 'Deci'. (Mike Lumb)

Valley during the summer for selected crews, including Flt Lts J.J. Burrows and M.G. Oldham who fired an AIM-9G Sidewinder missile on 31 July.

As the year progressed, news reports were full of accounts of the growing unrest in Eastern Europe. A new policy in the DDR to let East Germans leave the country was discernable in the West by the large number of Trabant cars, which were to be found usually at the head of both a traffic jam and a cloud of black smoke, on the autobahns. However, most personnel at Brüggen were surprised at the sudden end to a divided Germany when the 'Berlin Wall' was breached on 9 November. There was no particular euphoria at the prospect of having won the 'Cold War': instead everyone found that the whole reason for being in Germany had suddenly vanished. The purpose of RAFG had been to oppose the large Soviet army in Eastern Germany, which was poised to advance westwards at any moment. With no more 'Red Peril' across the IGB, the British Forces in Germany had apparently been made redundant. For the time being, however, the status quo at Brüggen remained unchanged.

The squadron celebrated its 75th Anniversary in style on 3 February 1990, with a parade and flypast at Shoreham. A reunion dinner in Brighton that evening was well attended by former squadron members, with a particularly high turnout of ex-wartime members.

Operation Granby – Muharraq Detachment

The annual detachments to Goose Bay and Decimomannu took place in May and July respectively and the squadron was also tasked with missions on 'Exercises Elder Joust' in April and 'Central Enterprise' in June; in the latter exercise the Brüggen Wing mounted a twelve-ship formation on one task. However, the busy summer activities had taken place against a backdrop of growing political tension in the Middle East. When Iraqi forces invaded Kuwait on 2 August 1990, it quickly became clear that the UK would become involved. It was obvious, too, that RAFG's squadrons would make up the bulk of any contribution by the RAF's Tornado force: their role to hold back the mass forces crossing the Elbe was by now largely redundant and the aircraft in Germany also had the more powerful Turbo-Union RB 199 Mk103 engines and Radar Homing & Warning Receiver (RHWR) fitted, neither of which was the case with the UK-based aircraft.

The first signs that things were moving was when the Brüggen Wing received instructions to carry out Air-to-Air Refuelling (AAR) conversions for combat-ready crews. Up until then there had been no tactical requirement for RAFG crews to be AAR qualified and it had been the jealously-guarded preserve of UK-based crews. On 8 August, conversion sorties started with Flt Lt M.J. Murtagh as the squadron's only AAR instructor. His first convertee was Flt Lt S.H. Cockram and because of a shortage of dual-control training aircraft their first mission was in a 'strike' aircraft (i.e. with no controls in the rear cockpit). Flt Lt Cockram recalled, '…Murts was our only AAR Instructor (as his previous tour had been on 27 Squadron). I recall he was simply superb and always made me at ease when moving around and towards the tanker, but the [Lockheed] TriStar (my first sortie) was awful (long hose, low wing, poor perspective and only taking fuel off the centre hose, so no ability to refuel two aircraft at a time). The Victor on the other hand had a shorter hose, high wing and wing pods as well as fuselage, so it was much more flexible.' Cockram himself was almost immediately signed off as an AAR Instructor and by the time he had finished his own conversion he had already cleared another four navigators on the tanker. In this way, the whole squadron was swiftly AAR qualified and was ready to deploy to the Middle East by 25 August; AAR and combat ready.

Meanwhile, Brüggen's engineers had prepared twelve Tornados for deployment to the Gulf region. The aircraft were painted in a desert pink camouflage scheme. Twelve crews had been selected from across the Wing: the crisis had broken over the summer leave period so there was not one complete squadron with enough combat ready AAR-trained crews available as a single unit. This pattern continued into the Gulf War, where the Tornado Wings were manned by crews from across the Tornado force. For this deployment 14 Squadron, which provided five-and-a-half crews[90], was designated the lead unit. On 27 August, all twelve aircraft, led by Flt Lt Cockram and Wg Cdr Morris, left Brüggen for Akrotiri in three four-ship formations, each supported by a tanker. The following day, pausing only to incur the displeasure of the station commander at Akrotiri by delivering a rousing 'beat up' as they left, they continued to Bahrain. Here they were based at Muharraq under the command of Gp Capt R.H. Goodall, AFC who had previously been Brüggen's station commander. Almost immediately four aircraft were loaded with JP233 and held at readiness to attack airfields in Kuwait.

In-theatre training started almost immediately: extensive use was made of low-flying areas in Saudi Arabia and Oman as well as the King Fahd Range (just to the south of Dhahran) and the Qarin range on Masirah. The crews also familiarized themselves with flying the aircraft at heavy weights, loaded with two JP233 canisters, the new larger 2,250ltr fuel tanks and two AIM-9L Sidewinder missiles. However, carriage limitations for live weapons (they were designed to be carried once and dropped, rather than flown repeatedly) meant that each crew received only a limited exposure; the heavier weights were later simulated by carrying two 1,500ltr drop tanks under the fuselage instead of weapons. The heavyweight flying was not without incident: on 28 October, Flt Lts T.J. Marsh and K.A. Smith suffered an engine failure while flying with two JP233 and discovered that they needed to use reheat on the other engine during the landing! To an extent the training carried out in Nevada, involving operational low flying over desert, was a good preparation for low flying in the Gulf region and crews were soon very comfortable at flying operational heights. Evasion training was provided by RAF Tornado F3 aircraft as well as USAF F-15s and Omani Air Force Jaguars. Crews also practiced night flying, using TFR. Previously they had been restricted by peacetime rules to 400ft, but they were now authorized to the lowest selectable height of 200ft. During this practice, it was discovered that, rather worryingly, the TFR could not detect some types of sand.

Fairly early into the detachment, Gp Capt Goodall told the crews that it was time to let the Gulf region know that the Tornados had arrived and intimated that a 'punchy' arrival at Muharraq would be in order. On the next sortie the crews took him at his word. Flt Lt Marsh was Number 4 as they recovered towards Muharraq at very low level, '...I could not see the airfield but do remember easing up over the lights around a five-aside football pitch as we coasted into the airfield and then back down along the taxiway with Numbers 1 and 2 down the runway. Lead and Number 2 broke up and to the right and eventually so did [Flt Lt Hogg] all I could see though was the ATC tower in front of me since the taxiway deviated slightly at a corner just before it. Now I didn't have time to count my bananas so I decided to break just before the tower. Never having flown a run in and break from such extreme low level before my natural reaction was to pull the stick and push the throttles forward into reheat as though in a low-level abort! I quickly sorted things out, coming out of reheat and landed without further ado...And so into the debrief...all the operational stuff was being discussed, when the briefing room door was kicked open practically flying off its hinges. A very red-faced and extremely irate Group Captain berated us for several minutes and then made his exit... unbeknown to us at the time of our run in and break, on the pan just next to ATC was a VIP sheikh being waved off by the airport's commercial manager (Muharraq was mainly commercial still at this time, and I vaguely remember all the jumbo [Boeing 747] tails just to my left as we sped down the taxiway). So we had blown him over in a cloud of dust: this had caused a diplomatic incident, and the ambassador had come down hard on [the Group Captain] – hence his ire!'

While flying practice continued apace, plans were being drawn up for the increasingly inevitable war. Wg Cdr Morris with Flt Lts Cockram, Cookson and L. Fisher (from IX Squadron) were frequent visitors to both the neaby Bahraini Air Base at Sheikh Isa and the aircraft carrier USS *J.F. Kennedy*. Bahrain was home to a US Marines Corps Air Wing and USAF 'Wild Weasel' units from Spangdahlem. Here, they planned the initial stages of the air campaign, which would follow the declaration of hostilities. As one of the few aircraft with an anti-runway weapon, the RAF's Tornados were tasked against Iraqi airfields. In the case of the Muharraq-based aircraft the target would be Tallil airfield, to the southwest of An Nasirah on the Euphrates river. However, the JP233 had been specifically designed for use against Warsaw Pact airfields in the Central Region and the stick length of 2,400m coincided with the typical length of runways in East Germany. And here was the problem: Tallil's two parallel runways were almost twice that length, as were the taxiways on an airfield that was even larger than most international airports. The plan was, therefore, to use the JP233 to 'bottle up' the Iraqi aircraft by cutting off the taxiway access from the HAS sites to create minimum operating strips which would be too short for their aircraft to use.

Apart from their 'in-house' work-up sorties, the Tornados participated in a number of exercises, including the huge 'Exercise Imminent Thunder' in Saudi Arabia on 15 and 16 November. The latter exercise involved over a thousand aircraft, as well as naval and ground forces from the Coalition that had formed in the Gulf over the previous 2 months. On the two nights of the exercise, eight-ship formations of Tornados from Bahrain were tasked to simulate JP233 attacks against the airfield at King Khaled Military City. The exercise was intended as a 'final warning' to the Iraqis that the Coalition meant business and was also an opportunity for the forces to practice working together en masse.

By late November, the crews at Muharraq had been in theatre for 3 months and with no immediate indications of when the war might start, it was decided to start rotating crews back to Brüggen. On 18 November, the original crews left Bahrain. While there might have been some disappointment at the possibility of missing out on some real action, the overwhelming feeling for most of the returning personnel was one of relief that they were getting back home to some form of normality. Some also believed that they might not actually be missing much – suspecting that the crisis would blow over without any fighting. Meanwhile, two more 14 Squadron crews[91] had deployed to Bahrain to cover the period from 7 October to 8 January, but as mid-January approached most of the crews based at Muharraq were provided by the newly-arrived XV Squadron.

Operation Granby – Dharhran Detachment

As the 14 Squadron presence at Muharraq wound down, the squadron's commitment in the Gulf region was bolstered by the establishment of another Brüggen-led Tornado detachment at nearby Dhahran, in Saudi Arabia. The Dhahran detachment, which was led by Wg Cdr J.J. Witts from 31 Squadron, included three crews[92] from 14 Squadron who arrived in theatre by C-130 Hercules on 28 December. Along with a IX Squadron crew (Flt Lt R.S. Goodwin and Sqn Ldr D.G. Catterson) as Number 2 these three crews had flown together as a constituted four-ship since mid-November and would continue to do so for the next 3 months. During the first week at Dhahran everyone was busy setting up the base for Tornado operations. Sqn Ldr Coulls recalled, '…they had a mountain to climb to be ready to receive the aircraft in a few days' time, prepare operational, engineering and domestic accommodation, get ourselves integrated into

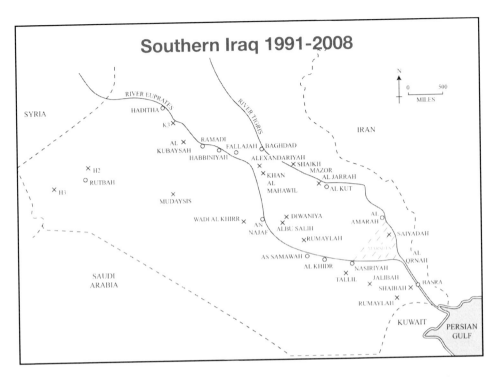

the base and plan an in-theatre work-up. These situations usually bring out the best in people and against the odds we managed to get things into some semblance of order. The facilities were rough and ready, but excellent initiative was being demonstrated everywhere. The squadron adjutant was quite literally walking the streets of downtown Dhahran with a suitcase full of cash, buying the things that we needed and signing contracts for more complicated services.' The detachment also included another 14 Squadron navigator, Flt Lt M. J. Wintermeyer, although he crewed with Flt Lt G.G.M. Harwell from IX Squadron, was part of a different four-ship team.

The detachment's twelve aircraft arrived at Dhahran in the first week of January and with a deadline of 15 January to be ready for action, the crews settled into a brief in-theatre work-up. Each crew was allocated five sorties, designed to familiarize them with the local procedures and to get them used to flying with a full weapons load including either two JP233 canisters or eight 1,000lb bombs. 'The next major issue,' explained Sqn Ldr Coulls, 'was to get ourselves tasked onto the Master Air Attack Plan, which was being prepared by a very secretive organization in Riyadh under US leadership. As usual, the UK had excellent access to the planning process due to our position as "ally of choice" (although we do sometimes test their patience) and we had people in key roles in the heart of the organization. However, by this stage there were in excess of 3,500 USAF, USN, USMC and US Army aircraft in-theatre, and the arrival of twelve more Tornados was not necessarily the biggest news in town. The political process had made us very late, albeit welcome, additions and we needed to find our way into a plan that had been under development for nearly six months. But first both OC 31 and [I] needed to be read-in, which necessitated a trip to Riyadh. We were led into the bunker

Tornado ZD744, armed with live JP233 canisters, at low level over the Arabian Desert on 6 January 1991. The aircraft is flown by Flt Lts K.J. Duffy and N.T. Dent, who were killed in a flying accident exactly one week later. This photograph is a poignant reminder of two popular young officers. (Andy Glover)

and received a full brief on the phases, aims and objectives of the air campaign and our likely part in it. It transpired that, because of our late arrival, we had only been tasked for a single, night four-ship for the first 3 days. This was extremely disappointing, if understandable, but there was a promise of expanding our participation, bringing it up to two, eight-aircraft formations per day, one timed to be on target just after dusk and the second just before dawn.'

'Back at Dhahran,' continued Sqn Ldr Coulls, 'preparations were proceeding apace. The crews had been arranged into three distinct eight-ship formations, one under the leadership of the 14 Squadron team, and the mission planning tasks were allocated on a strict "need to know" basis. Not surprisingly, the 14 Squadron eight-ship was tasked to plan the Night 1 mission, with a minimum number of people being made aware of the detail. The training flying was progressing very well; we had enough AAR support, the engineers were turning out serviceable aircraft in a range of unusual weapons fits, and the hosts were providing us with the airspace that we needed. We had flown with JP233, drummed up some fighter opposition to practise our air-to-air tactics and were getting used to the idiosyncrasies of low flying in the desert, by day and night. For training we were cleared to fly at 100ft by day and 200ft at night and it transpired that the desert was conducive to both, particularly when compared to the more rugged

terrain in the north of UK or Canada. However, there were very dangerous traps for
the unwary and visual illusions abounded. After about a week of intense training, it was
directed that we were to cease flying on 13 January and prepare the aircraft for the first
missions. On 13 January, the 14 Squadron four-ship was programmed to fly a practise
AAR trail south through Saudi Arabia and into Oman, leave the tanker using night/
poor weather procedures, carry out a simulated attack and then return to Dhahran.
We had also planned to conduct some additional training events, including the use of
flares at very low-level to test their effectiveness against infrared air-to-air missiles in
that environment. We had planned to involve a segment of valley flying in the northern
part of Oman, before returning to the tanker for the trip home. We knew that this was
to be our last training sortie and were feeling comfortable in the desert environment
after four reasonably demanding trips in quick succession. Our Number 3 (Gibson/
Glover), unfortunately, did not manage to get airborne, but other than that the early
part of the sortie went to plan: we rendezvoused with the tanker and made our drop-off
point in Oman in good order. Having settled at low-level we completed the exercise
with the flares and a few minutes later our Number 2 started calling over the radio for
the Number 4 to check-in. After several attempts with no reply, and still with no sign
of the Number 4, we spotted a large plume of black smoke several miles behind us.
We immediately turned around and headed for the smoke. To our horror, we found a
very obvious scrape across the desert floor several kilometres long, the smoke rapidly
dispersing and numerous unrecognizable items of debris scattered along the line.'
During a hard left-hand turn at very low level, the wing of the aircraft[93], flown by Flt
Lts K.J. Duffy and N.T. Dent, had hit the ground at around 500kt with inevitable results.
Both crew members were instantly killed. A replacement crew, Flt Lts Murtagh and
Wain, who had been part of the original Muharraq detachment, were swiftly dispatched
from Brüggen: '...whoever had selected Murts and Stu to join our formation under
those circumstances,' declared Sqn Ldr Coulls, ' had made an inspired choice. Their
temperaments were perfect – relaxed, confident and unflappable – just what we needed.'

The air war started in the early hours of 17 January and naturally Wg Cdr Witts
wanted to lead from the front. Sqn Ldrs Moule and Coulls, who had carried out the
original mission planning, helped to explain the plan during the briefing and assisted
the team get ready for the sortie, including starting up the spare aircraft. However, the
squadron was represented on this first mission of the Gulf War by Flt Lt Wintermeyer.
Armed with JP233 they were tasked against the airfield at Wadi al Khirr. Unfortunately,
soon after take-off Flt Lts Harwell and Wintermeyer discovered that their TFR and
radar altimeter (radalt) were not working: 'We tried everything to get it sorted out,'
reported Wintermeyer, 'even waiting until after we had tanked before realizing that it
was not going to happen – we could not proceed to the target without our TFR or
Radalt, so we had to turn back for Dhahran. From that point onwards I think we were
completely silent in the aircraft[94] until Gordon called three-greens on approach; what
was there to say?'

The following night's sortie was led by another formation and after two false
starts when operations were cancelled at late stages in the planning process, Sqn
Ldrs Moule and Coulls led their team airborne on the night of 20 January to harass
Jalibah south-east airfield. Their plan was for the first four aircraft to loft five 1,000lb

airburst-fuzed bombs onto the anti-aircraft defences to keep their heads down while the second four-ship attacked the runways and taxiways with JP233 from a different direction. The eight Tornados would be part of a larger package attacking other targets in the vicinity, which would be supported by fighter escort and defence suppression assets. However, things soon started to go wrong. Flt Lt Murtagh hit his head while performing his walk-round check on the aircraft and received a nasty gash which needed medical attention and then, shortly after take-off Moule and Coulls were faced with major problems with the aircraft's[95] navigation equipment. Firstly it failed completely, but came on line again a short time later and then worked intermittently throughout the rest of the flight. Sqn Ldr Coulls, '…had been given "no-go" criteria, i.e. if certain systems were not working correctly, we were supposed to abort the mission…Two of the key items had failed (the RHWR and the jamming pod), but after a short discussion, and considering what had gone before throughout the previous 20 hours, we had a severe case of "pressonitis" and decided to keep going. Probably not our best ever decision!' After topping up from a tanker on the Iraqi border, Moule and Coulls let down to low-level, and at 200ft they found themselves in a layer of fog. Almost immediately their autopilot failed and Sqn Ldr Moule had to fly the aircraft manually, close to the ground in fog and in darkness. After soldiering on for a while, both crewmembers realized that they were a hazard both to themselves and the rest of their formation, so they returned to Dhahran. Meanwhile, Flt Lts Gibson and Glover, the sole remaining representatives of 14 Squadron, pressed on to Jalibah. Here they discovered that rather than keeping heads down, the air-burst bombs merely gave the gunners notice to start firing! As they completed their loft manoeuvre in the ensuing barrage, Gibson and Glover sustained battle damage to the starboard underwing fuel tank[96]. Wintermeyer visited Jalibah the following night.

After the first week of operations, during which the RAF had lost a number of Tornados during low-level operations, the US-led Coalition headquarters decreed that future offensive operations would be carried out from medium-levels above the reach of anti-aircraft guns and SAMs. In Sqn Ldr Coulls' words, '…to say that this was something of a culture shock to us is an understatement; medium-level tactics had not been widely practised by the Tornado force and the majority of the crews had no experience whatsoever.' Their first chance to try out the new tactics was on 23 January when they were tasked against the runways at Al Taqqadum (just west of Baghdad). This time the whole operation ran much more smoothly. After refuelling they ran in to the target area at medium-level, supported by four HARM-equipped F-4G 'Wild Weasels', four EF-111 Raven jamming aircraft and a fighter sweep of eight F-15Cs. 'As we proceeded north,' recalled Sqn Ldr Coulls, 'with about 60 miles to run to the outskirts of Baghdad, all hell broke loose below us. We had some collective experience of ground fire at this point, but had seen nothing like this. We could make out AAA[97], with numerous colours of tracer and trajectory. There were missiles, presumably unguided, again with different coloured trails, fortunately all topping out below us; it looked like the intelligence might be right after all. Some of the fire looked like they might only be flares, fired for effect, but we had no real way of knowing. This intense display continued for at least the next 15 minutes, until we were well clear of the target, and is a sight that we will never forget. We were also happy that our bombs had impacted close to the aim point; there was enough ambient light to see the ground and make out the features on the airfield and we managed to arrange our off-target manoeuvre in order to see the bombs strike. To help, there was some low-lying mist on the airfield and we could see the shockwaves travelling outwards from the impact points. As we manoeuvred off target, we were locked-up by an SAM-3 target-tracking radar, which we knew was there, but our procedures seemed to work and the lock was broken.'

The 14 Squadron crews at Dhahran were in action again on almost every night over the next week. The targets included the power station at Nasirayah on 25 January, various ammunition storage facilities (Khan al Mahawil south of Baghdad on 26 January, Ar Rumaylah southwest of Basra on 27 January and Ar Ramadi on 31 January), the petrol production facilities at Saiyadah on 29 January and the maintenance facilities at Al Jarrah airfield near Al Kut on 30 January. Each aircraft dropped five 1,000lb bombs against these targets, but the results from this unfamiliar height were not especially accurate. Even so, there were some spectacular results, with Flt Lt Glover noting that the attack against the Nasiriyah power station had caused a major fire. Five nights later, when their radar failed, Flt Lts Gibson and Glover had to resort to formating on the Number 4's wing and dropping their bombs when they saw his bombs being released.

By now the strength of the anti-aircraft barrages had diminished and the greatest threat was probably that of a mid-air collision with other aircraft. Typically all eight aircraft would be constrained in a narrow-height box of only 2,000ft, offering only a 250ft sanctuary block for each aircraft. Sqn Ldr Coulls had a narrow escape with Sqn Ldr Moule when, '…we were heading north towards our target on an inky-black night with very little ambient light. The countryside below us was completely blacked out, except for a few fires that we could see burning, which we assumed were the result of previous attacks. I was looking at a fire to the west of us, trying to gauge how far away it was, and therefore how big, when I spotted a small, stationary blue light on a similar azimuth but not associated with the fire. I discussed this with Douglas, but we could not work out what it was. It then started to increase in size and took on more of a blue glow and a slim, triangular shape, but it still had no real shape. Then, in an instant, a Tornado in full reheat "bloomed" just to the left of us and at the same level. I yelled, "push", followed by "bunt" and Douglas bunted the aircraft hard. Our formation member, which is undoubtedly what it was, passed just over the top of us in a hard right turn allowing me to see right into the cockpit and the glow of the displays. It is impossible to say exactly how close we got, but it was less than a wingspan.'

Part of the solution to the inaccuracy of medium-level bombing was to be found in daylight operations, which started at the beginning of February. During daylight, a 30° dive profile enabled the pilot to see the target and mark it accurately for the weapon-aiming computer. However, the main solution to the problem of hitting targets from medium-level was to be provided by laser-guided bombs (LGB). At the end of January, six Buccaneers arrived at Muharraq, equipped with Pave Spike laser-designation pods. The job of developing tactics to use this new equipment fell to Sqn Ldrs Moule and Coulls. Although the Tornado crew had no experience of LGB operations and the Buccaneers had only used Pave Spike from low-level before, a workable set of tactics soon evolved and after a practice sortie on 30 January they were ready to go.

However, it was still a few days before the go-ahead for LGB operations was given and in the meantime medium-level daylight sorties continued. For the 14 Squadron four-ship these involved a level attack on a fuel-storage area at Al Kut on 1 February, a dive attack against the storage warehouses at As Samawah on 3 February and the oil refinery there on the next day. The latter sortie started a large fire. Flt Lt Wintermeyer also saw action on that date, flying a night mission against Shaykh Mazhar ammunition depot. After refuelling from a VC-10, they crossed into Iraq but, '…just across the border our aircon failed! This meant there was no cooling either to us or to the avionics, the cabin pressure fell and we had to quickly go onto 100 percent oxygen. We had a quick chat and decided to push on to the target…after all we had come this far and it was not a huge problem! The only hassle was that the snag was intermittent, so our ears were going through hell. The change of pressure from our operating height to the normal cabin pressure height was quite dramatic, over a "millisecond". Anyway we had to concentrate on the task in hand, which was to drop eight 1,000lb bombs on the ammo dump southeast of Baghdad! About 5 minutes from target we saw two orangey glows, which we later decided were missiles, but well out of the way! Onto the target run…unfortunately my kit was not very good at this stage so I relied on the Euphrates breaking out on the radar to help me find the target. It was a very long 2 minutes as we sped towards the target with no definite picture. I was playing with all the controls trying to get the best paint when at the bottom of the screen the shape I was looking for turned up. It was with great relief that I moved the cursor, changing the picture and refined my mark to ensure the bombs had a good chance of hitting the target, which I think they did – give or take a few feet or so! We turned off target and Gordon overbanked to get a good look at the bombs going off underneath. They did! We turned for home and slowed down a little – without aircon we were using emergency ram air to cool the kit and we were flying about 80kt above the recommended speed. Since we were at the back of the stream we could afford to slow down a little without fear of hitting someone else in the formation. We gave the code word for being off target so that our escorts could follow us out and we concentrated on getting back to Saudi in one piece. Just off target our kit gave an indication that we were being looked at by a radar-guided missile, but one of our four-ship was locked up, fortunately not fired at! Some 5 minutes off target we saw some rather heavy flak [AAA] just below us and to one side so we carried on sauntering home bravely!'

Wintermeyer's first daylight sortie came 3 days later, dropping free-fall bombs against the SAM support facilities at Al Jarrah; however, the other 14 Squadron crews had already carried out their first LGB sortie by then. On 5 February, Mission 0201G comprising four LGB-armed Tornados, supported by two Pave Spike equipped Buccaneers, headed for a large roadbridge over the Tigris at Al Kut with a time-over-target (TOT) of 05:30hrs GMT. 'The rendezvous, tanking and target ingress went like clockwork,' recalled Sqn Ldr Coulls, 'and we settled on the target run. All was going well shortly before weapons release, when there was a radio call from our designator, asking which bridge we were aiming at; with seconds to go until weapons release, confusion reigned! However, we were cleared to drop just in time and as we manoeuvred off target, it was suddenly apparent what the problem had been. The target bridge had already been hit and one end of it was lying in the river. The Buccaneer navigator had

been able to see all of this with his targeting pod. There was another large bridge in
the city, about a kilometre from ours. In the event, our bombs were guided into the
bridge's buttresses at one end, completing the job that somebody else had started.' The
effect of precision-guided weapons was immediately noticeable: accurate results could
be achieved so that the destructive effect of a formation of four aircraft each dropping
three LGBs far exceeded that of formations of up to twelve aircraft dropping sticks of
five or more free-fall bombs.

With air supremacy over Iraq and the ability to destroy point targets at leisure, the
air campaign now entered two distinct phases. During the first phase, in the second
week of February, the Tornados from Dhahran were tasked against the bridges over the
Tigris and Euphrates rivers as part of a wider campaign to disrupt the Iraqi resupply
and reinforcement routes. The bridges attacked with LGBs included those over the
Euphrates at Al Khidr (7 February), Albu Salih (8 February), As Samawah (10 February),
and the Tigris at Al Amarah (on 11 February). However, where larger target arrays did
not need the same precision, some sorties were flown with free-fall, rather than laser-
guided bombs. The oil-storage depot at Basra, was bombed in this way on 10 February,
as was the Latifyah liquid-propane plant two days later.

In the second phase of LGB operations, from 13 February until the end of the
month, the airfields of the Iraqi Air Force were systematically destroyed. The initial
targets were the HAS, each one of which was individually targetted. The first such
sortie was against the huge airbase at Al Asad, to the south of Haditha (around 120

A pair of Tornados armed with Paveway II Laser Guided Bombs (LGB) refuel from Victor tanker on 8 February 1991, while en route to attack the bridge over the Euphrates at Albu Salih. The nearest aircraft is crewed by Sqn Ldrs D.E. Moule and C.J. Coulls and the other by Flt Lt R.S. Goodwin and Sqn Ldr D.G. Catterson. Their supporting Pave Spike-equipped Buccaneer is in the background. (Andy Glover)

miles northwest of Baghdad) and in the following 2 days Al Jarrah and Tallil were attacked. The sortie against Tallil on 15 February was typical of a LGB mission. The 14 Squadron four-ship took off from Dhahran at 11:28hrs GMT. Each aircraft[98] was armed with two Paveway II LGBs. The formation rendezvoused with their VC-10 tanker near the Iraqi border 30 minutes later. Here they also met up with the Bucaneer designators. After refuelling they headed to Tallil, escorted by F-4G 'Wild Weasel' and Grumman EA-6B Prowler electronic warfare aircraft and a fighter sweep of F-14 Tomcats. Each aircraft then delivered two bombs onto an individual HAS, marked by the Buccaneer. The Tallil mission was the last one by Dhahran crews that was targetted against HAS sites: once these and other hardened airfield buildings had been destroyed, the attention turned to the airfield operating strips. The technique was to crater the runways and taxiways into short unusable strips and to crater every taxiway junction. The airfields at Al Amarah and nearby Qal'at Salih, Shaibah and Ar Rumaylah (both near Basra), and Habbaniyah were all attacked by 14 Squadron crews between 16 and 27 February. Towards the end of the month, just as the ground war was starting, weather conditions over Iraq made laser operations difficult. Another hazard also appeared. Sqn Ldr Coulls was, '…northwest from Dhahran on a track that was becoming very familiar, when we entered an area of very poor visibility in what was otherwise a beautifully clear day. We even noticed an unusual smell inside the aircraft as we flew through it. As we climbed above it, it became clear that it was an enormous plume of smoke, stretching back to the northeast as far as the eye could see.

The 'Dhahran Seven' – the 14 Squadron aircrew who flew operations from Dhahran during the Gulf War. Left to right: Flt Lts M.J. Murtagh, A.J. Glover, Sqn Ldrs C.J. Coulls, D.E. Moule, Flt Lts M.J. Wintermeyer, M.A. Gibson, S. Wain. (Douglas Moule)

Obviously, something catastrophic had happened. We flew our mission and on our return to Dhahran the conditions had deteriorated further; the plume had become much larger, both laterally and vertically, and was already causing some distress to some of the locally-based crews trying to recover to the airfield. We had reported the phenomenon to AWACS during our sortie, and also included the details in our post-mission report, but nobody seemed to know what had caused it at that point. It was later in the afternoon that the news broke that the ignition of the well-heads in Kuwait, by the now retreating Iraqi forces, had caused this environmental disaster.'

As they prepared to go into work to fly their next mission, the ceasefire was announced. 'After a few days of uncertainty while the negotiations were taking place,' recalled Sqn Ldr Coulls, 'we were finally taken off readiness and it became clear that it was over…our formation was the first to leave Dhahran [on 11 March] and trail our aircraft back to Brüggen, an 8½ hour trip with four AAR brackets. At the western end of the Mediterranean, we were given a sharp reminder of the fact that we were now back in a different regime when we met a tanker that had been flown out from the UK by a crew that had not been involved in the operation. During 'Desert Storm', we had, of necessity, rewritten many of the routine peacetime procedures, not least for AAR. Therefore, we joined the tanker in a tactical formation and radio silent, and promptly (and quite rightly) received a severe ticking off from the tanker captain, insisting that we use the published procedures. Back to normality!'

Operation Granby – Tabuk Detachment

Having returned from Bahrain at the end of November 1990, Flt Lts Marsh and Smith settled into a quiet routine on the squadron, including Christmas leave and, for Marsh, the RAF Ski Championships. However, in the new year they were tasked to deliver replacement aircraft to the Gulf. Leaving Laarbruch on 16 January with the first aircraft, they arrived at Dhahran just in time for the start of hostilities, so there was a short delay before they could return to Germany. Flt Lt Marsh reported that they spent that night, '…in a basement somewhere, masked up due to SCUDs.' On 21 January, (having also said their farewells on the two previous mornings before being cancelled each time) they repeated the exercise, flying from Brüggen to Dhahran in a pair with Flt Lts Hogg and Fisher. The latter crew had decided that they ought to be involved in any action in the Gulf and had moved their names to the top of the list of crews ready to deploy. Both crews were expecting to stay in theatre, but when they arrived they were told that they were to return to Germany. However, that night two aircraft from Tabuk were lost on operations and the two crews were detailed to fill the vacant spaces. Flt Lts Marsh and Smith joined a four-ship led by Flt Lts A. Edwards and J.B. Klein; the previous leaders had been killed during the recovery from a low-level loft attack.

Flt Lt Hogg was in action on the night of 23 January, attacking Al Taqaddum airfield to the west of Baghdad, while the following night Marsh and Smith flew their first mission against the barracks on the airfield at H3, to the west of Rutbah in western Iraq. They were Number 8 of an eight-ship formation, each dropping eight 1,000lb bombs from medium level and were greeted by heavy anti-aircraft fire. The attack package was supported by two ALARM-armed Tornados and an EA-6B jamming aircraft, along with a fighter escort comprising a pair each of F-15 and F-14. Between them, the 14 Squadron crews were in action on every night for the rest of the month, carrying out further medium-level raids in large formations against the cable-relay stations at Ad Diwaniyah and Ar Rutbah, fuel storage at H3 and airfield facilities at Al Taqqadum. Unexpectedly, their fourth mission was flown[99] at low-level against an electronic warfare site at Wadi Al-Khirr, some 20 miles west of An Najaf. After refuelling from a VC-10 tanker, they let down to low-level, the last in a formation of twelve Tornados. Luckily there was only light anti-aircraft fire. Flt Lt Marsh found, '…this attack was extremely distracting being at the back of the package and experiencing the reflections and flashes in the HUD and on the canopy, plus all the AAA. I treated it like the range and maybe was a bit slower than I might have been but we did not hit the ground!'

Marsh and Smith carried out two more medium-level night missions, on 2 and 3 February against the oil-pumping facility at H2 (northeast of Rutbah) and an ammunition storage area at Al Alexandariyah (a heavily-defended airfield 20 miles south of Baghdad). Meanwhile Hogg, who had bombed Habbaniyah airfield on 1 February, flew the first daylight mission two days later against the ammunition storage depot at Al Kubaysah, some 50 miles west of Habbaniyah. This raid resulted in some spectacular secondary explosions and the smoke from the ensuing fire was visible virtually all the way back to Tabuk. On each day through the next week, sorties were flown against Iraqi fuel production or storage facilities. The target on 7 February was the oil refinery near K3, on the Euphrates near Haditha. As part of a ten-ship formation, Marsh and Smith[100] were armed with five 1,000lb bombs, which they delivered from a steep-angle

Off target at Haditha oil refinery on 7 February 1991. As Flt Lts Marsh and Smith recover from their steep-dive attack, the impact of their stick of five 1,000lb bombs can be seen just above the wingtip. (Tim Marsh)

dive attack. No anti-aircraft fire was seen during this mission. 'Our target,' recalled Flt Lt Marsh, 'was a small pumping station, which we thought that we had hit with the centre bomb because we could see black smoke, compared to light grey from bombs either side in the stick. Battle damage assessment shows a miss with the stick spacing, but clearly it hit something and ruptured it causing the black smoke. If this pumping station had been taken out the whole refinery became unserviceable; the rest of the package got all the fuel containers! Smoke was visible from this target 3 days later from over a hundred miles away!'

Three days later, Marsh and Smith were tasked against installations on the airfields at Habbaniyah and H3, again using steep-angle dive profiles. During this time LGB operations had started at Dhahran and Muharraq and the crews at Tabuk had been waiting impatiently for laser designators to support them. However, all the available Pave Spike pods were already in use, so the Tornados from Tabuk would instead have the GEC Ferranti TIALD[101] pod, which had been hastily accelerated into service and was declared operational on 9 February. TIALD crews from 13 Squadron had arrived some days beforehand, accompanied by engineers from the manufacturers. 'There were two pods,' recorded to Flt Lt Marsh, 'Sharon and Tracy, after the "Fat Slags" in *Viz* magazine. The two pods were different inside and there were no spares. The boffins were good at fixing them in rapid time if there were snags…the UK crews had been testing like mad and came to theatre wanting to test them on a Saudi range first! We pointed out

Tabuk Detachment TIALD crews, left to right: Flt Lts T.J. Marsh, K.A. Smith (14 Squadron), A. Edwards and J.B. Klein (16 Squadron). James Klein would later serve as a flight commander on 14 Squadron at Bruggen before commanding the squadron at Lossiemouth. (Tim Marsh)

that the biggest unrestricted range possible was just north over the border. However, they still took their time.' Apart from the limitations of having just two TIALD pods, there were only four aircraft with the requisite wiring to mount them, so the TIALD operation would require careful management. The first TIALD-designated attack was flown on 11 February when Flt Lt Hogg dropped three LGBs onto the highway bridge over a tributary of the Euphrates at Hachama (just north of As Samawah). The following day Marsh and Smith[102] dropped three LGBs on the hardened operations building at Ar Ruwayshid airfield on the Jordanian border.

After this successful operational debut, the two TIALD pods were programmed for round-the-clock use, but first, more TIALD-qualified crews would be needed to act as designators. Flt Lts Edwards and Klein's four-ship was selected for this honour and after a few days to learn the ropes and practice using the equipment, they were ready. Flt Lt Marsh explained, '…the way it worked was each sortie was planned and led by the four-ship leader, with input from us with respect to the "laser basket" position. The navs concentrated heavily on pre-sortie target study, working out how to march the cursor along taxiways etc to the Desired Points of Impact (DPI), considering there were quite often two lots of bombs in the air at any one time. The pilots' job was mainly heads out, but also helping with the timing, so that if no splash was seen within a tight timescale, then the laser was to be switched off and the next target acquired. Our four-ship was split into two pairs of TIALD crews and we then operated with the four as a six-ship.

Typically each TIALD would "spike" for two of the four-ship. The split and manoeuvring at the target had to be quite carefully thought out since the pod had gimbal limits and so a gentle turn was best otherwise the fuel tanks got in the way.' Marsh and Smith were in action with their TIALD on 17 February[103], taking out the HAS on H3 airfield. The next night their target was a buried fuel storage at Tallil. On the way to the target area, the lead TIALD crew suffered a gearbox failure and had to divert into a Saudi airfield, leaving Flt Lt Smith as the only TIALD operator for four bomber aircraft. Over Tallil they encountered heavy anti-aircraft fire, including a missile launch. However, despite such distractions and the fact that this was only his second operational sortie with the pod, he was able to score a direct hit on each of the four targets.

Over the next week, sorties were flown against Iraqi airfields. On 19 and 20 February, a six-ship from Tabuk made the long flight across the width of Iraq to attack the operating areas at Shaibah, near Basra, by cratering all of the taxiway junctions. Unfortunately, the weather was unsuitable, so they returned to Tabuk, to try again the next day. This third sortie, on 21 February, was successful, as were those against Al Jarra and Mudaysis (halfway between Rutbah and An Najaf) on the following 2 days. By now the Iraqi resistance had all but crumbled: there was no defence suppression-support for the Mudaysis mission, but nor was any defensive fire observed. However, a mission against buried fuel storage at the huge Al Asad airbase, south of K3, supported by 'Wild Weasel' aircraft, was met by light anti-aircraft fire.

The last operational mission which Flt Lts Marsh and Smith flew was on 26 February, but they were unable to attack Habbaniyah airfield because of the weather and heavy smoke from burning oil wells. Two days later the war was over and a massive party ensued at Tabuk. Flt Lt Marsh remembered, '…we were all woken from our beds at five in the morning by the four-ship who had been cancelled due to Saddam's capitulation. The party continued at the Lightning Club all day!'

Back at Brüggen

In the immediate aftermath of the Gulf War, the crews who had flown operationally returned to Germany for a well-deserved rest. In the meantime, from 20 March to 22 May, four crews[104] from the squadron were detached to Muharraq to maintain a presence in the Gulf region..

In Germany, effects of the 'Options for Change' defence review, which had followed the end of the 'Cold War', started to be felt with the disbandment or relocation of Laarbruch's Tornado squadrons. However, Brüggen's squadrons, which for now were untouched by the review, continued with the normal routine. The exception to this 'normality' was that low flying below 1,000ft was no longer possible on continental Europe. As a result, almost all the flying comprised high-low profiles in the UK to use the UK low-flying system and a Tornado Turn-around Facility (TTF) was set up at Leuchars to provide some engineering support for Brüggen's Tornados. Apart from routine low-flying training, exercises like the UK air defence 'Exercise Elder Joust', which took place between 23 and 25 April and 'Exercise Mallet Blow' (from 15 to 19 July) provided some extra interest. Two detachments to Decimomannu in quick succession for ACMI during the first week of May and APC for the first half of June also served to bring the unit together with a sense of normality. The summer also saw a new CO, with Wg Cdr F.L. Turner, who had previously flown Jaguars with 14 Squadron, taking over in June. Wg Cdr Turner was the first CO since wartime days who had also flown on the squadron as a junior officer.

The annual detachment to Goose Bay, which took place from 27 September until 8 October, provided an opportunity to re-qualify in OLF, in readiness for the work-up for 'Exercise Red Flag'. Most of the work-up was carried out in January 1992, using the tactical low-flying area in the Scottish borders and the EWTR at RAF Spadeadam. Tornado F3 squadrons from both Leeming and Leuchars acted as the enemy fighter force. The work-up sorties followed a high-low profile to the TTF at Leuchars and then a low-high profile for the return trip. The exercise itself ran from 3 to 14 February, but poor weather made it a washout: most crews managed only three or four sorties. At the end of the exercise, 14 Squadron crews ferried the aircraft back via Offut (Omaha, Nebraska) and Griffiss (Utica, New York State) to Goose Bay.

Operation Jural

The rest of the year followed the usual pattern, with APC at Decimomannu from 29 April to 15 May (when some crews returned via Naples), 'Exercise Central Enterprise' in June, 'Exercise Western Vortex' (the detachment to Goose Bay) from 25 July to 6 August. However, from mid-summer all this activity had continued under the shadow of further developments in Iraq. At the end of the Gulf War, a 'No Fly Zone' was established over the north of Iraq, north of the 36th Parallel, in order to prevent the Iraqis from interfering with Kurds. The RAF contribution to this operation (mainly by the Jaguar and Harrier squadrons) was named 'Operation Warden'. Meanwhile in the south of the country, the Iraqi armed forces had been used to quell an uprising by Shia Marsh Arabs. The crisis developed and in August the UN imposed another 'No Fly Zone'(NFZ), this time south of the 32nd Parallel. The British contribution, called 'Operation Jural', was initially planned to comprise six reconnaissance Tornado GR1A operating from Dhahran: the intention was that these aircraft would fly low-level reconnaissance sorties just as they had done during the Gulf War. However, the US-led Coalition policy was for no flying below 10,000ft over Iraq. Unfortunately, the reconnaissance sensors on the Tornado GR1A were designed for use at low-level and did not work at this altitude; instead the Tornado GR1As were replaced by Tornado GR1 aircraft, which would patrol the skies using the new TIALD pod as an 'airborne-security camera.'[105] Each of the RAF's Tornado units was to provide personnel for the operation for 3 months and within that period of responsibility there would be a 'roulement' of crews, each of whom would spend 6 weeks in theatre. During November, December and January, 14 Squadron was assigned the duty of maintaining 'Operation Jural'.

The task of organizing the operational side of the forthcoming detachment fell to Sqn Ldr Coulls, while Sqn Ldr Napier and Flt Lt K.A. Ward arranged a work-up for the squadron. All crews were given AAR practice to get them up-to-speed, and live 1,000lb bombs to drop at Garvie Island from medium-level profiles. There was also medium-level fighter affiliation with the Tornado F3 squadrons at Leuchars and an ACMI detachment to Decimomannu from 13 to 20 November gave further practice at medium-level manoeuvring. At that stage there were only three TIALD pods in

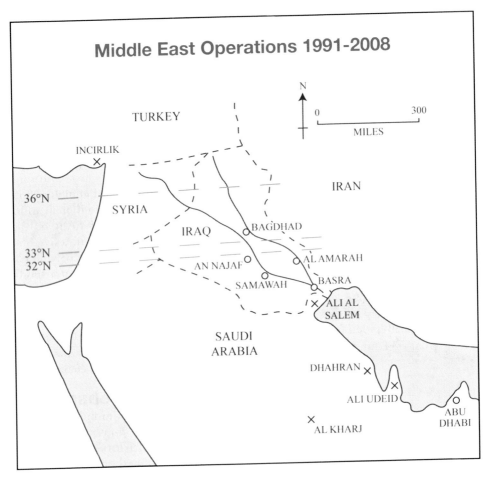

Middle East Operations 1991-2008

existence and all three were in use in Dhahran, so with no way for crews to familiarize themselves before they left, the introduction to the pod would have to be done in theatre. However, with great prescience, Wg Cdr Turner insisted that everyone practice the weapon delivery profile for TIALD attacks so that crews would at least be familiar with the geometry of co-operative designation drops. This practice also ensured that the navigators were familiar with finding ground features using the radar from a much higher altitude than they were used to.

The first crews arrived at Dhahran in early November. They were accommodated in the nearby 'Khobar Towers' complex, which was also home to the large US and much smaller French detachments. Before crews were declared 'theatre combat ready' they had to fly four familiarization sorties: two in Kuwait, which included an introduction to the TIALD pod, then two sorties over Iraq, firstly as wingman and secondly with the TIALD pod. Low flying in Kuwait was an education for all crews, as they saw at first hand the destruction left behind by the Gulf War, from destroyed bridges and a smashed satellite-tracking station, to the piles of burnt out vehicles on the Basra road. Sqn Ldr Napier recorded, '…we also flew over two very large military airfields which had been

'Shooter' on recovery to Dhahran after a reconnaissance of Ghalaysan New airfield on 31 December 1992. Tornado GR1 (ZA452) is flown by Sqn Ldr M.J.W. Napier and Fg Off C. Platt – this crew would see action 14 days later over Al Amarah. (Mike Napier)

devastated during the war. Each HAS (of which there were quite a few) had a large hole blown in it – the whole place had been well and truly trashed.'

The squadron's first operational sortie was flown by Wg Cdr Turner and Sqn Ldr Coulls on 27 November, although 14 Squadron did not assume the lead role for the operation until the end of that week. The high tempo of operations and relatively long sortie lengths brought the landmark of 1,000hr flown by Tornado GR1s on 'Operation Jural' quite swiftly: this milestone was achieved on 29 November during the first trip in theatre by Flt Lts D.K. Roxburgh, D.J.A. Potter, K.A. Ward and Fg Off L.P. Williams. Sorties over Iraq were nominally flown as a four-ship, although in practice once they were in Iraqi airspace each four split into autonomous two pairs to cover the various line searches or points of interest in the tasking signal. Within each pair of Tornados the element leader carried the TIALD pod and concentrated on the reconnaissance task, while the wingman, or 'shooter', covered the leader by keeping a good look out for SAM launches or fighters. Both aircraft were armed with AIM-9L Sidewinder anti-aircraft missiles in case of the latter. The navigator in the 'shooter' also had a hand-held video camera with which to film any areas of interest on the ground. At Dhahran, there were two second-generation TIALD pods available for operations, named 'Rachel' and 'Becky', plus another, which was used as a source of spare parts for the others. On most days, four aircraft would be tasked for an operational sortie over southern Iraq and the other two aircraft would be readied as reserves. If they were unused by the operational wave, these would be used later in the day for a 'Kuwaiti Trainer' flight.

Crews quickly became used to the geography of southern Iraq and in particular the marshes between the Euphrates and Tigris rivers. Here they could see evidence of the massive engineering project to drain the marshes. The military installations (including airfields, barracks and engineering depots) in the region also became familiar landmarks over the next few weeks. A typical 'Operation Jural' sortie entailed a transit to the air tanker 'tow-lines' just south of the Iraqi border and AAR with a Victor which was based at Muharraq. Occasionally the Victor would be replaced by a USAF McDonnell Douglas KC-10 Extender. After refuelling, the two pairs of Tornados would push across the border to carry out their reconnaissance tasking. On 16 December Sqn Ldr Napier described how the task, which was typical for an 'Operation Jural' sortie, involved, '...flying across to the marshes to run up the road to Al Amarah then back across the marshes, back up to Al Amarah to check out a barracks, across to look for a SAM-2 site in the middle of the desert, down to Nasiriyah to look for another troop concentration and home.' A flight like this would last around 3 hours. The Tornado detachment flew almost every day, including Christmas Day and New Year's Day, which was a new experience for the crews that flew on each of those days! As a result most crews flew some 40hr a month during the detachment: well over twice the typical total for flying at Brüggen. The winter weather was not altogether helpful for reconnaissance operations and sorties frequently had to be curtailed or re-tasked when cloud obscured the ground.

Operation Ingleton

Although Coalition forces enjoyed air supremacy over southern Iraq, the Iraqi forces still represented a credible threat to individual aircraft operating in the 'No Fly Zone'. There were SAM-3 sites around some of the larger airfields, for example Basra and Tallil, which were 'no go areas' for Coalition aircraft and Iraqi air defence radars monitored operations in the zone. Iraqi fighters also periodically flew into the NFZ, in the hope perhaps of finding an unescorted reconnaissance aircraft. It was for this reason that Coalition aircraft were always armed and flew in pairs while over Iraq. During December, the political tension mounted as the Iraqis declared an intention to take back the skies south of the 32nd parallel. More SAM sites were moved into southern Iraq and incursions by Iraqi aircraft into the NFZ became more persistent. Then on 27 December, an Iraqi MiG-25 ('Foxbat') was shot down by a USAF F-16D – the first air-to-air kill both for a USAF F-16 and for an AIM-120 missile. Although reconnaissance tasks continued, planning started for an air attack by Coalition aircraft to force the Iraqis to withdraw their air-defence systems from the NFZ.

On the evening of 13 January 1993, a force of some 100 Coalition aircraft, including the escort and support aircraft, set out from airfields in Saudi Arabia and Bahrain and from the aircraft carrier USS *Kittyhawk*, to attack the nodal points of the Iraqi air-defence system south of the 32nd Parallel. Among this force were four Tornados[106], led by Sqn Ldr Napier and Fg Off C. Platt, which took off from Dhahran just after dusk. This first mission of 'Operation Ingleton' was tasked against the Al Amarah Integrated Operations Centre (IOC), a large complex near Musay'idah around 10 miles south of the city of Al Amarah. The targets within the IOC included the headquarters building, several control bunkers and a number of radar systems and radio-relay antennae. The lead pair of Tornados was detailed to attack the headquarters building while the target for the second pair was the radar control bunker; other targets within the complex would be dealt with by USAF and USN assets. After refuelling from a Victor on the Iraqi border the Tornados pushed northwards as two pairs towards Al Amarah. There was some sporadic anti-aircraft fire from Tallil as they passed abeam and the lead aircraft was also illuminated by a SAM-2 missile-guidance radar, although no missiles were seen. After crossing the Euphrates, the route turned onto their north-easterly attack track, with the Number 2 in each element ahead of the bomber so that the navigator could find the target with the TIALD pod. Approaching Musay'idah in darkness, Sqn Ldr Napier was looking ahead through the HUD: 'With no lights showing, the target is invisible in the darkness and the target bar hovers over a black void. Suddenly there is a bright flash next to the target bar as the last F-15E drops his bombs. At least I know that the computer position is pretty accurate. It is certainly accurate enough to drop a laser-guided bomb, but the rules of engagement say that we must identify the target positively ourselves before we can drop. Chris [Platt] is working hard on the radar. He is trying to identify the offsets which we planned beforehand to help us find the target. The first is a road bridge in the marshes, but high floodwater after all the rain masks it on radar. The second offset proves useless, too. The pressure is on. If Chris cannot find the third offset, we cannot drop. That really would make us a laughing stock.

'"Got it!" a yell of triumph from Chris as he finds our last offset, a bridge over the river 2 miles beyond the target…

'Thirty seconds out. An exchange of code words tells Steve [Kennedy] that we are on our way, and he lets us know that he has found the target with the pod and is happy for us to drop. Chris and I run through our final checks and make sure that all the right switches have been made. As the time-to-go runs down in the HUD, my thumb is clamped on the attack commit button on the stick top. Thump, Thump, Thump! Just like driving fast over three large cobblestones. The bombs have come off.

'"Stores away!" I transmit, pulling back on the stick and rolling right to barrel away from the bombs in case they explode below the aircraft as they arm. The aeroplane is much lighter now and responds much more crisply as we wheel off to the southwest to clear the Triple-A sites along the Tigris. Behind us as we turn I am aware of the flash as the bombs explode.' Both attacks were successful and in each case the three Paveway II LGBs scored direct hits on their targets.

After several more plans for attacks on Iraqi installations, which came to nothing, another offensive mission was launched 5 days later. This second 'Operation Ingleton' sortie was a daylight raid against the IOC at An Najaf and was part of a larger strike designed to finish off some of the targets which had not been hit on 13 January. All four Tornados[107] were tasked against the radar control building and again they were supported by Victor tankers from Bahrain. Before setting off from Dhahran, the Tornado crews had been warned that they had to take special care in identifying the target because of its proximity to the important Moslem shrine at An Najaf: they were not to drop if there was any doubt about target identification, or any chance that the weapons might fall into the area of the shrine. Unfortunately, much to the frustration of both crews, Flt Lt Kennedy in the lead pair was unable to identify the target with

Tornado GR1 (ZA490) flown by Flt Lts A.J. Coope and P.L. Ward, low over the sea on 18 January 1993. The 'photoship' was flown by Sqn Ldr S.G. Reid. (© Crown Copyright 1993)

his TIALD pod, so Sqn Ldr Napier and Fg Off Platt did not drop; however in the second pair, Flt Lt Craghill, whose pod benefited from a better optical sensor, found and marked the target ensuring that it was hit by three LGBs dropped by Number 3.

The responsibility for 'Operation Jural' was handed to 31 Squadron and all the 14 Squadron crews were back at Brüggen by the end of January. After flying almost exclusively at medium-level in the Gulf, the aircrews had to adjust back into their more accustomed low-level environment. An early opportunity was 'Exercise Northern Banner', carried out in northern England and Scotland in late February. By now, virtually all routine low-flying from Brüggen took place in the UK and AAR support was available more regularly to support the day-to-day flying. The TTF at Leuchars was another useful asset enabling crews to make the most of the UK low-flying system for routine training.

On 1 April, Brüggen's Tornados were involved in the RAF's 75th Anniversary Flypast at Marham. Practices on 26 and 30 March illustrated the problems inherent in a large formation of aircraft of widely differing performance and on the day itself the weather provided an added dimension of excitement, with the Tornados coming uncomfortably close to the trees as they clung onto their formation positions under a lowering cloud base! There were monthly Minivals at Brüggen during the first few months of the year in preparation for the station Taceval, which took place from 4 to 6 May. With the communist threat in central Europe now gone and with very different 'real' operations taking place in the Middle East, Taceval had lost the edge that it had once had at the height of the 'Cold War'. In the latter half of the year, the squadron enjoyed the usual detachments to Decimomannu for both APC (in July) and ACMI (in November) and Goose Bay (in August to September). A new squadron commander, Wg Cdr T.L. Boyle took over in January just in time for the work-up for 'Exercise Red Flag'. In a departure from previous 'Red Flags', this exercise, which ran from 8 to 16 February 1994, comprised an afternoon wave and a night wave, giving crews exposure to multi-aircraft operations in complete darkness. With almost no artificial light in the Nevada desert, the effect was very different to night training over Europe, or even operating over Iraq. The crews flew a mixture of low-level sorties using the TFR and medium-level sorties (sadly without the benefit, on this exercise, of laser-guided weapons). Sqn Ldr Steer remembered his two night sorties as, '…being challenging but not so much fun.'

Back in the UK low-flying system 'Exercise Brilliant Invader' provided some high-quality training in the last week of March. Sorties for this exercise, which was the successor to 'Exercise Mallet Blow', were tasked as four-ship formations. Supported by VC-10 tankers and flown as high-low missions to Marham in the first wave, returning to Brüggen later in the day following a low-high profile. The air weapons ranges at Otterburn (Northumbria) and Luce Bay (south of Stranraer) provided both novelty and challenge during the exercise. On 6 April, 14 Squadron's Tornados deployed to Decimomannu for the annual APC, which this year included some work with ground-based LTM. The aircraft recovered to Brüggen on 20 April, but the squadron's personnel departed again the next month to Goose Bay.

The post-Gulf War period saw increased complexity in the weapons systems available for the Tornado and in the operational use of the aircraft. The RAF's Tornados retained their low-level role, but were also expected to prosecute operations from medium level in the Gulf; laser-guided weaponry using the TIALD pod was becoming a routine requirement and the ALARM anti-radiation missile had recently entered squadron service. It was decided that the best way to gain expertise in these new areas was for Brüggen's squadrons to specialize in one discipline. Thus 14 and 17 Squadrons would become the TIALD experts while IX and 31 Squadrons would concentrate on ALARM. In practice, of course, this was more easily said than done, mainly because of the acute shortage of TIALD pods. Apart from the pods required to support 'Operation Jural' (and 'Operation Warden' when the UK-based Tornado units took on that responsibility) most of the production pods were diverted to the Jaguar force.

'Operation Driver'

On 24 August, the main 14 Squadron party deployed to Dhahran; the start of its planned period covering 'Operation Jural'. The missions into the NFZ followed the same pattern as the previous time on 'Jural', but with the major difference that 14 Squadron had the honour of being the first Tornado unit to use the Vinten Vicon pod operationally. This new photographic reconnaissance pod gave the Tornado a far more effective medium-level reconaissance capability. Meanwhile, political tension had been building in Iraq once again and at the beginning of October the Iraqi army deployed a large number of ground forces into the south of the country, under the NFZ. Much of the intelligence about this movement came from the images collected by the squadron during the patrols of the NFZ, which showed heavy military equipment such as tank transporters heading towards Basra. The British response to this was 'Operation Driver', which included the deployment of six additional Tornado GR1s into the region. On 6 October, RAF Brüggen was notified to prepare to dispatch the aircraft, and 5 days later the Tornado reinforcements, accompanied by a VC-10 carrying additional ground and aircrew, arrived at Dhahran. The new aircraft and crews started to fly operations on 13 October. 'Operation Driver' sorties were usually flown as six-ships and apart from the continued reconnaissance tasking, most sorties took the form of a simulated LGB attack on military installations. However, the situation died down quickly and the extra aircraft trailed home on 9 November. Wg Cdr Boyle believed, '…that subsequent analysis revealed that errors can be made and perhaps the [transporters] were actually going north, towards the ex-marshes, that's why nothing much ever came of it. It all went from flash to bang in about a week, then took a month to die down.'

1995

The year 1995 was remarkable in that it was the only year in the decade in which 14 Squadron was not involved in an operational detachment. Sadly it also marked the nadir of Tornado serviceability, which affected all the routine flying from Brüggen. An ill-conceived cost-saving measure made by the engineering authority and supply chain left Brüggen critically short of RB199 engines throughout the mid-1990s. The squadron's engineers did their best, but engines had to be robbed from unserviceable aircraft so that a few serviceable ones could be preserved. During the year, a number of Tornado airframes at Brüggen literally had no engines in them. Serviceable aircraft were pooled across the Wing to ensure that the major detachments had enough, but this was at the cost of routine training: it was not unusual for there be only one or two serviceable Tornados left at Brüggen. For Flt Lt M. J. Sharp who joined 14 Squadron during the year, '…the lasting memory of my time on 14 [Squadron] was no aircraft and, aside from detachments, a struggle to get minimum hours and even then mostly low quality [flying].' The crisis was even worse than the experience with the Venom some 40 years earlier. Furthermore, if crews could not, for some reason, use the UK low-flying system they were faced with the very limited value of 1,000ft flying in Germany. Apart from the frustration caused to combat-ready crews, the lack of aircraft also impacted on new arrivals to the unit who had to undergo the work-up before becoming combat ready themselves. One additional duty which deflected the squadron further from this task was the provision, by the Brüggen Wing, of sixteen Tornados for a diamond formation flypast over Buckingham Palace for the Queen's official birthday. According to Sqn Ldr J. B. Klein, '…the various practices around RAFG nearly ended in disaster as Clutch [radar] failed to mention a Cessna 172 that almost flew co-altitude through the formation as we headed north-bound toward Nordhorn and then also failed to mention the same said Cessna on our return leg. Just as well no one actually saw it because the emergency split brief was a nightmare and was more akin to "every man for himself evasion!" Twenty-four Tornados deployed to Leeming at the beginning of

Ex-'Scorpion Wind', 1 December 1995 – Tornado GR1 (ZA399) flown by Flt Lt D.A.C. Legg and Sqn Ldr J.B. Klein over the desert near Yuma. (Darren Legg)

June for the work-up, representing a massive drain on resources at Brüggen. However, the flypast on 17 June, which was led by Brüggen's station commander Gp Capt G.L. Torpy, DSO and Sqn Ldr Klein, was a great success.

The squadron had managed to gather enough aircraft for a deployment to Turkey for 'Exercise Distant Thunder' in mid-April. It was, effectively, a squadron exchange with the Turkish Air Force F-104 Wing at Akinci Air Base, some 20 miles northwest of Ankara. Sqn Ldr Klein recalled, '…the flying was mixed tactical four-ships at low-level around south-west Turkey,' adding that, '…planning was done on 1941 vintage Russian low-level charts!' With little flying at Brüggen, the routine deployments to Decimomannu and Goose Bay which followed in the summer at least provided an opportunity for crews to maintain some degree of proficiency at low-level flying and weaponry.

However, the early winter brought a uniquely interesting detachment. Five years after the end of the 'Cold War' for which they were intended, there was a stockpile of unused BL755 Cluster Bombs (CBUs) which were coming to the end of their life and, since they could not be dropped on any range in Europe, they would have to be destroyed. When Sqn Ldr S. Kinnaird at HQ 2 Group heard that plans were being drawn up for transporting them to be dumped at sea, he came up with a better idea. Having just returned from an exchange posting with the US Navy, Kinnaird knew that live cluster bombs could be dropped on the Chocolate Mountain and Barry M. Goldwater Ranges near Yuma, Arizona: he suggested that dropping the bombs would be a more cost-effective way of disposing of them. Thanks to his intervention, on 20

November, 14 Squadron arrived at the US Marine Corps Air Station, Yuma to find a large number of cluster bombs to be dropped over the next 10 days. Although single BL755s had been dropped in the past (for example by Flt Lt Turner in March 1978), the detachment to Yuma was the first opportunity not only to drop sticks of weapon,s but also to do so from a tactical-delivery profile as part of multi-aircraft co-ordinated attacks.

'The first week,' explained Flt Lt K.R. Rumens, 'was spent dropping live CBUs in a very narrow valley/gorge with a dead end. The valley was in the Chocolate Mountain Range. It was a dedicated CBU-style ordnance range where there were known to be hundreds of unexploded ordnance so it was totally closed off to all human traffic. We all got to drop in the region of twenty live CBUs. The first sortie we dropped single CBUs. The QWIs wanted to see good safe patterns and releases before we started dropping sticks. The valley was very tight and it had an 800ft cliff at the end of it. After the last CBU came off you needed four-to-five 'g' to pull up before you hit the end wall. Sortie 3 was interesting because you had to start to pull out of the valley before the fourth CBU came off. Sortie 4 and 5 were flown as a pair with one aircraft laying down a stick of four whilst the other aircraft tipped in from the ridge of the valley and flew a 5° dive profile. Very exciting and a lot of fun.' One of the first lessons learnt was that the assumptions about 'self damage' from cluster bombs was rather over-optimistic. Unlike 'traditional' high-explosive bombs, which threw a large amount of debris into the air when they exploded (meaning that a following aircraft attacking the same target at low-level had to wait until the debris subsided), cluster bombs were thought to pose little risk to subsequent aircraft. However, the lightweight covers which held the bomblets in place until the bombs were dropped caused an unexpected hazard: early in the detachment Flt Lt Sharp found himself with, '…a HUD full of BL doors on a slash attack.' Flt Lt I.R. Walton also found, '…how big the skins looked as they flew past when I was Number 2.'

The exercise also included FACs who provided LTM on the range, although Flt Lt Walton reported that, '…Lasers [proved] unworkable on the range with all the smoke, which, was a real shock. It was a tactic transforming detachment.' On the last 2 days of the detachment, the squadron was also invited to participate in the US Marine Corps 'Exercise Scorpion Wind'. This involved working with – and against – the USMC McDonnell Douglas F-18 Hornets. The sorties were flown as six Tornados against four F-18s. Flt Lt Rumens remembered that initially, '…we generally ran in low across the flat desert training area out to the east of Yuma. There was nowhere to hide so we got shot every time by the AMRAAM shooters. After a couple of days we limited the F-18s to AIM-9Ls and then the fun began. Each sortie thereafter saw the six-ship of Tornados hitting the burner and climbing up to merge with the F-18s for basically six-versus-four ACT. It was awesome…the F-18 drivers could not get their heads around six Tornados fighting them. The ACMI debriefs were a sight to behold. I had one of my shots discounted because while I was in the process of tracking and firing another F-18 flew through my HUD chased by Tom Boyle!' Sqn Ldr Klein felt, '…the detachment overall was excellent fun, but probably of limited tactical value due to range and airspace constraints, but highly revealing in that many crews missed the target even with a long stick of four CBUs! (Radar Altimeter [as a height sensor] over lumpy terrain does not work even with an area weapon): a good lesson for all. Socially, the 'Cactus Moon' bar in town was a winner with all concerned – giving away free Stetsons provided enough beer was consumed.'

On 11 January 1996, 14 Squadron unfortunately suffered its fourth Tornado crash when an Italian exchange pilot Capt A. Spinelli lost control while acting as the 'bounce' for a pair of Tornados on a training flight over Germany. With Flt Lt C. J. Donovan in the back seat, Capt Spinelli was attempting to intercept the pair from above as they flew to the southwest of Munster. After exceeding the angle of attack limit, the aircraft descended rapidly towards the ground, but fortunately Flt Lt Donovan was able to command eject himself and Spinelli moments before impact; both crew members survived, although Donovan was plagued by back problems afterwards. Later in the month, the squadron hosted the annual visit by the Tornado Standardization Unit (TSU). Sqn Ldr T. M. Anderson and Flt Lt S. J. Lloyd decided to use their TSU check on 25 January to try out one of the old 'Cold War' pre-planned 'Option Alpha' attacks. Before setting out for a simulated attack on the old SAM-5 site at Altengrabow, they rang the *Luftwaffe* MiG-29 ('Fulcrum') base at Preschen to arrange some fighter affiliation. During the 'Cold War', the agile and capable MiG-29 had been much feared by NATO strike/attack crews, but on that day in 1996 and despite a lot of help from the Tornado crews flying at 1,000ft, the German fighters proved incapable of intercepting the four Tornados. Sqn Ldr Anderson and Flt Lt Lloyd were also busy at the end of the month with sorties for 'Trial Ganoid', an investigation into the tactical use of the TIALD pod at low-level.

Operation Jural Again

The squadron covered 'Operation Jural' from February to early May. Flt Lt Rumens recalls, 'The squadron had four months in Dhahran to cover. Everyone did half the detachment with a week's handover in the middle, so effectively about nine weeks each.' Just as previously, the sorties were all flown in four-ships at medium-level with AAR support. The formations were made up of two pairs each with a Vicon aircraft and a TIALD aircraft 'shooter' to warn of missiles or fighters. The reconnaissance runs were complex, comprising between ten and fifteen points of interest. Sqn Ldr Anderson was proud that the squadron, '…had a really good success rate with points of interest…and were very highly regarded by the planners – we delivered in quantity and quality (the Vicon pod had no equal in theatre – we were the recce asset of choice).'

Shortly after the squadron left Dhahran, the 'Khobar Towers' complex was attacked by Hezbollah terrorists using a truck bomb. Although some USAF personnel were killed there were no RAF casualties, but as a result of the attack the air operation supporting the southern NFZ was moved to Al Kharj, some 70 miles southeast of Riyadh. The NFZ was extended up to the 33rd Parallel, just to the south of Baghdad, in September, as a response to Iraqi action in the north of the country.

Wg Cdr P. W. Rycroft took command of the squadron in July, as the unit prepared for 'Exercise Red Flag' in October. At the beginning of December, 14 Squadron returned to the Middle East for another 2 month period in the southern NFZ. The excitement of low-level flying and the attractions of Las Vegas were replaced by the tedium of medium-level reconnaissance and the dubious delights of Al Kharj. Political tensions and military posturing in Iraq had largely, if temporarily, settled down, so there was little excitement for the squadron. Instead, the daily patrols over the extended NFZ became something of a tedious chore, and without even the prospect of escaping to Bahrain (as had been the case at Dhahran) Al Kharj had all the appeal of a prison. The accommodation was in tents and Flt Lt Walton remembered, '…morale was pretty average and Christmas was miserable!'

After a brief lull on returning from Al Kharj, the routine detachments started in February 1997 with APC. This was the last detachment at Decimomannu by 14 Squadron as the RAF support unit closed in September 1997. The ACMI range which had been set up in the North Sea meant that the RAF no longer required the facility and it was thought that the UK coastal ranges would offer a cheaper alternative to Sardinia. Although operating out of Decimomannu over the previous 25 years had not been without its frustrations, the loss of somewhere that had been such a fundamental part of life in RAF Germany for 25 years was keenly felt. If 'Deci' was regarded with great affection, the same could not really be said of Goose Bay which the squadron visited in mid-May. At least Goose Bay still offered good flying, though, in the form of operational low flying and terrain following in IMC.

On 14 June, four Tornados from 14 Squadron led a twenty-six aircraft formation over Buckingham Palace to mark the Queen's official birthday. The aircraft had deployed to Marham on 6 June to carry out the practice work beforehand. A week after the flypast, 14 Squadron's personnel were heading for Alaska to take part in 'Exercise Distant Frontier'. The squadron was based at Eielson AFB, to the southeast of Fairbanks, for the exercise which ran from 23 June to 7 July. 'Distant Frontier' was very similar in concept to 'Exercise Red Flag', but with an exercise area roughly ten times larger than the Nevada ranges. Paradoxically, the Tornado crews found themselves operating at low-level over a temperate landscape of forests and trees at the very time that their operational flying was being done at medium-level over a desert that was not entirely dissimilar to that in Nevada! Like 'Red Flag', the targets for 'Distant Frontier' included full-size replicas of airfields defended by Russian-made defence systems. Typically, the Tornados flew in six-ship formations as part of larger 'packages' of aircraft, which, in US style, included fighter sweep and escort, other attack aircraft and the suppression of enemy air-defence assets such as 'Wild Weasel' aircraft, jammers and other electronic warfare aircraft.

Operation Warden

Set up in the immediate aftermath of the Gulf War, the northern NFZ was much smaller than the zone in the south. It covered the area to the north of the 36th Parallel, including the city of Mosul and, to the north, the Zagros Mountains, which marked the borders with Turkey and Iran. Policing the northern NFZ in Iraq had originally been the responsibility of the Harrier and Jaguar squadrons, but when they were needed for operations over the Balkans in the mid-1990s, the Tornado force replaced them. Having previously served exclusively over southern Iraq, 14 Squadron assumed responsibility for 'Operation Warden' during August and September. Flying operations were mounted from the Turkish Air Force Base at Incirlik, just outside Adana in the central south of the country. Without the restrictions of the strict Islamic laws in Saudi Arabia, and a rather more favourable climate, Incirlik was a far more pleasant location than the Saudi bases used for 'Operation Jural'.

The sorties over the northern NFZ followed a similar pattern to missions over southern Iraq, but there were some notable differences. Firstly, the crossing point into Iraq involved a 400-mile transit eastwards along the border between Turkey and Syria, much longer than the transits in the south. Secondly, the terrain was markedly different: in the south it was pretty much a flat desert, but in the north the Zagros Mountains rose to 13,000ft, with Mosul sitting in the plain on the headwaters of the Tigris. Lastly, the Iraqi forces were less active in the area.

A typical 'Operation Warden' sortie might last between 2½ and 3½hr. Tanker support was provided by a VC-10, which was also based at Incirlik, and the Tornados carried out reconnaissance with both the TIALD pod and the Vicon pod over various points of interest. The flying was somewhat tedious, but at least the mountain scenery added some interest. On their return to Brüggen, the squadron could at least look forward to an air combat work-up and an MPC after Christmas.

Operation Bolton

At the end of the Gulf War, UNSCOM's[108] team of inspectors had been investigating Iraq's compliance with UN directives on biological and chemical warfare, but during late 1997 the Iraqis stopped co-operating with UNSCOM. As part of the diplomatic response to Iraq, the UK initiated 'Operation Bolton' in October to reinforce British presence in the region. The Saudis were unwilling to allow offensive operations to be carried out from their territory, so initially the operation comprised the deployment of HMS *Invincible*, augmented by the Harrier GR7s of 1 Squadron, to the Persian Gulf. They arrived in theatre in late January. In the meantime, however, the Kuwaitis had expressed a willingness to host combat aircraft and on Friday, 6 February, after just 3 months back home at Brüggen, 14 Squadron was given 48 hours' notice return to the Middle East. Crews were immediately recalled from leave and detachments. Flt Lt S.E. Reeves, '…was skiing in Val d'Isere when I got a call saying "come on back" so I had to hire a car and drive back;' Flt Lt Rumens, '…was at RAF Leuchars taking part in a night TLT exercise when the TLT staff came and instructed the two 14 Squadron crews to return to Brüggen immediately. At the time we had absolutely no idea why. The next day back at Brüggen the boss briefed all of the 14 Squadron aircrew and engineers and informed us that first thing Monday morning we would be taking nine Tornado GR1s out to a base in Kuwait. We were to get ready for war immediately.'

After a working weekend for the whole station, nine Tornados left Brüggen on 9 February 1998 heading for Ali Al Salem Air Base. The air base, which lay some 25 miles to the west of Kuwait City, had been reoccupied by the Kuwaiti Air Force after the Gulf War, but details about the airfield were scant. 'As Squadron QFI,' recalled Flt Lt Rumens, 'I was tasked with briefing the squadron with what facilities the airfield had. The brief was pretty lean. We had no charts/plates, no information on radar services or approach aids. I had worked out from satellite imagery the rough runway direction and length and it looked like concrete! In fact the only thing we knew was phoned through to us from Tom Boyle, our former boss, who was already in theatre. Tom informed us that Kuwait City International Airport would see us into the area

on their radar and then chop us to Ali Al Salem tower for which a frequency was provided.' After a 7½hr direct transit the Tornados crossed into Kuwait. 'We did not really know where we were going to,' continued Flt Lt Reeves, 'it was getting dark, we were worried about not being able to see the airfield and then saw the biggest set of runway lights and running rabbit[109] that you have ever seen! But after we landed on the runway we found that the the taxi pattern and the taxiways were just a minefield of debris and holes and all sorts of stuff.' The airfield was still in the semi-destroyed state in which it had been left after the Gulf War. Along with the other crews, Flt Lt Rumens discovered, '...there were no lights anywhere else on the airfield so we were waved off of the runway by a few engineers who had torches and we shut down and chocked nine Tornados in a tight "gaggle" on a bit of concrete just off the end of the runway. The next day, in the light, the engineers had to tow aircraft to the parking places.'

Wg Cdr P.W. Rycroft with members of 14 Squadron at Ali A Salem Air Base, Kuwait during the squadron's detachment for 'Operation Bolton' in early 1998. Damage dating from the Gulf War is evident on the HAS in the background. (Steve Reeves)

Over the next two days, the squadron established a dispersed operating base in one of the HAS sites. Each of the large HASs had an enormous hole in the roof, thanks to the attention of Coalition aircraft during the Gulf War. Despite the holes, the HAS buildings provided ideal storage space for engineering equipment. In one HAS, the operations and engineering facilities were set up inside long tents, each of which was protected with sandbags. Initially, the aircraft were parked in the open outside the HAS, but later on, as the temperatures rose, lightweight shelters were constructed to protect airframes, engineers and aircrew from the sun. Weapons were delivered to Ali Al Salem and the TIALD pods being used by 17 Squadron, who were still on 'Operation Jural', were flown in from Al Kharj. As Flt Lt Rumens commented, '...this upset the 17 Squadron boys because they now realized that if hostilities broke out we would be doing all of the bombing and they would be taking photos!' Just 48hrs after arriving in Kuwait, 14 Squadron declared itself ready for operations.

Although the diplomatic initiatives had largely defused the crisis soon after it had erupted (a new agreement between UNSCOM and Iraq was signed on 17 February) the squadron remained in Ali Al Salem until the beginning of May. Over the next 3 months, 14 Squadron's crews carried out operational sorties in the southern NFZ. The aircraft were armed: in Flt Lt Rumens' words, 'Numbers 1 and 3 carried TIALD and two Paveway II, and Numbers 2 and 4 did the photography, using the Vicon pod.' With a much reduced transit time to Iraqi airspace, when compared to Dhahran or Al Kharj, sortie times were much shorter than on previous detachments, typically being around 2hr. Flying continued around the clock and most crews flew a mixture of day and night missions. As previously, Coalition aircraft took the opportunity of being in Iraqi airspace to carry out practice attacks on military installations and on occasions the Tornados were partnered with 1 Squadron's Harrier GR7 aircraft which were now operating ashore from Ahmed Al Jabbar Air Base south of Kuwait city. AAR support was provided for some sorties and with little activity on the ground it was the opportunity for AAR with unusual tankers which offered most of the interest. These tankers included a RAAF KC-707 and a RCAF KC-130 Hercules.

Between the operational sorties, there was an opportunity for some training, low-flying in Kuwait and using the ranges at Al Abraq and Udari. There were also aircombat training sorties as well as fighter affiliation training with Kuwait Air Force F-18s and more combined training sorties with the Harriers. Another attempt to bring some variety into the flying was the mounting of two flypasts. On 1 April the squadron launched eight aircraft as part of a flypast over Kuwait to commemorate the 80th Anniversary of the RAF. The formation also included a VC-10 and a pair of Kuwait Air Force F-18s. By now, the number of Tornados at Ali Al Salem had been increased to twelve and another flypast by all twelve aircraft on 19 April marked 3 months of 'Operation Bolton'. The following month the squadron's personnel were able to return home.

Over the summer, there was only the briefest respite from operations in the Gulf and even so the squadron's personnel were away from Brüggen for some of that time to participate in 'Exercise Maple Flag'. This exercise, which was similar in style to 'Red Flag' and 'Distant Frontier', was run by the Canadians from Cold Lake in Alberta, some 150 miles northeast of Edmonton. The 14 days of exercise flying started on 15 June using the large range complex to the north of the airbase, which straddled the border between Alberta and Saskatchewan. Here, target arrays including a number of dummy airfields were defended by Soviet-style defences. The Tornados operated in six-ship formations at low-level in the, by now, familiar large packages of offensive aircraft. Apart from a large contingent of US and Canadian, the friendly forces included other NATO members such as the Germans and Italians. After the exercise, 14 Squadron's crews flew the Tornados back to Goose Bay where the aircraft were needed for the remainder of the North America training season.

The squadron resumed 'Operation Bolton' from Ali Al Salem Air Base on 3 September 1998. The operational pattern was much as it had been earlier in the year, except that political tension was mounting once more after Iraq declared in August that it would not, after all, co-operate with UNSCOM. But even so there was very little activity below the NFZ over the next 2 months, making the flying over Iraq pretty dull. Apart from 'counting flies by the thousand, interspersed with particularly uninspiring (and very definitely alcohol free) evening meals at the Kuwait officer's mess,' Flt Lt D. W. Hales thought, '…operational highlights were 45° dives with [inert] PW II at Udairi Range and a few opportunities for HE strafe at Al Abraq. It goes without saying that the RAF Regiment were distinctly uneasy with the lack of action [so] they soon arranged a few random sprints across the gravel for practice air-raid warnings. Indeed, I'm pretty sure they arranged extra simply to show their displeasure at the fact we had turned the air-raid shelter adjacent the pilots' barrack block into a recreation room, complete with squadron artwork left by every detachment passing through. Before one could gasp 'gas, gas, gas', there were spare sofas down there and a large sheet making best use of the squadron's projector to play four-man deathmatch on a Playstation using discs from the computer souq downtown.' One project taken on by Flt Lt Reeves during the detachment, was the development of tactics for using the Paveway III 2,000lb bomb, which had recently entered service. Examples of this new and more complex weapon had been sent to Ali Al Salem, although the operational techniques for using it still needed to be worked out. Once again the squadron used the time outside the operational sorties for useful practice in various disciplines: there was air-combat training, the opportunity to drop LGBs at Al Udairi range and more affiliation training with the Kuwaiti Air Force F-18s. Flypasts featured again, with two eight-ship flown, one on 15 September to commemorate 'Battle of Britain' day and another on 26 October after an operational mission. At the beginning of November, the squadron handed over to 12 Squadron, who were to be involved in offensive action over Iraq during December. In another development in early 1999, the Al Kharj detachment was handed over to the Tornado F3 force, when the commitment from Tornado GR1 aircraft became unsustainable as more aircraft were sent back to British Aerospace for the mid-life update programme.

Operation Engadine

While the Tornado GR1 Force operated over Iraq throughout the 1990s, other British aircraft were called in to support UN and NATO operations in the Balkans. In the mid-1990s RAF Jaguars, Harriers and Tornado F3s, as well as RN Sea Harriers, had intervened in the war in Bosnia-Herzogovina and in late 1998 another war erupted in nearby Kosovo. After attempts to resolve the conflict diplomatically had failed, NATO commenced air operations against Serbia in March 1999. The RAF fixed-wing contribution to NATO forces comprised initially of a detachment of Harriers based at Gioia del Colle (near Bari). On 24 March 1999, the Harriers flew the first offensive sorties of 'Operation Engadine' over Kosovo. Just 4 days later, Parliament decided to increase the number of RAF aircraft available for the operation: on Sunday, 28 March, RAF Brüggen's Tornados were earmarked for this commitment and 14 Squadron's new CO, Wg Cdr T. M. Anderson, was tasked with leading the transition to war. After a few days of frenetic activity, including some 'engineering miracles,' ten Tornado GR1s and six TIALD pods, were ready for action. TIALD-qualified crews were selected from across the Wing and divided up into four teams of six. Each formation comprised two pairs of TIALD-equipped bombers and two 'spotters' equipped with Night-Vision Goggles (NVG). The majority of TIALD crews were provided by 14 Squadron, which

was the lead TIALD unit, while other TIALD crews came from 31 Squadron. IX and Squadron provided the 'spotters'. One of which flew either unarmed or, later, loaded with ALARM missiles, would accompany each pair to warn the bombers of SAM launches.

Apart from getting crews, aircraft and weapons ready, there was another problem to be overcome in the few days available. Although Brüggen had spent the 'Cold War' decades of the 1970s and 1980s practicing wartime operations from the station, all that expertise and infrastructure had been dismantled during the 1990s, as the emphasis shifted to deployed operations like those over Iraq. Secure communications, which had been removed from the squadron operations building over the previous 10 years, had to be reinstalled. Photographic interpreters and equipment to link to the satellite imagery would also be needed for target planning. With no time to follow the usual ponderous official channels, acquaintances were contacted and favours called in: Sqn Ldr S.P. Rochelle called a friend at the Tactical Imagery Wing (TIW) to get a mobile reconnaissance interpretation centre driven across from the UK to Brüggen.

Another arrival at Brüggen during the next few days, were three VC10 tankers from 101 Squadron, which deployed to operate with the Tornados. This arrangement worked extremely well and Flt Lt I. J. Cosens later commented, '...it was great having them at Brüggen, as you all felt like one team.'

The first airstrike, led by Sqn Ldrs J.K. Hogg and Rochelle, was flown by the 'Green Team'[110] on the night of 4/5 April against targets on the periphery of Kosovo. This long-range mission would involve a flight time of nearly 8hr and would include a number AAR brackets. The first three aircraft took off from Brüggen at 21:30hrs following their VC-10 tanker, with the second wave, comprising three more Tornados and another VC-10, getting airborne 5 minutes behind them. No diplomatic clearance had yet been received for the operation, so instead the tankers filed a flight plan for a routine training flight to Aviano Air Base, in north-east Italy.

Flying southwards through eastern France to the Mediterranean coast, the formations then routed via Corsica eastwards across Italy. Throughout this long transit the aircraft were in and out of thick cloud, including cumulonimbus, and carried out two refuelling brackets. The first scare came during the flight across the Adriatic when the crews discovered that the whole of the airspace was filled with tankers and other NATO aircraft: the Brüggen crews had not received the airspace co-ordination instructions detailing the positions of these tanker tracks! However, the Tornados managed to find a way through the mêlée and made a rendezvous with pre-strike tankers to the south of Macedonia prior to the attack. But the problems were far from over, as Wg Cdr Anderson later described: '...this was actually a pair of TriStar tankers, operating in cell (formation) for the first time. The AAR was a nightmare – the Tornados were heavily laden and draggy with their weapons on board; the tankers were at the top of the Tornados' effective operating altitude; and the tankers, which had much more excess thrust than the Tornados had apparently forgotten about the need to make gentle power corrections! I have never before or since experienced such a heart-stoppingly difficult AAR event – the Tornados were in and out of combat power just trying to get engaged and then to stay in, all in the inky black and as the clock ran rapidly down to "push" time – in the event, Rocky [Sqn Ldr Rochelle] made one of the ballsiest calls I have witnessed and [delayed] the whole night mission of goodness knows how many aircraft for 10 minutes to enable the Tornados to tank!'

After taking on fuel, the Tornados crossed the border into Serbia and headed towards their targets, where they were greeted with heavy anti-aircraft fire. The first pair attacked the highway bridge at Jezgrovice (along the shores of Lake Gazivoda 40 miles northwest of Pristina) with PW IIs, while the second pair delivered PW IIIs onto the rail tunnel near Mure (some 50 miles north of Pristina) on the boundary between Kosovo and Serbia. The NVG-equipped spotters were able to act as pathfinders for the bomber crews: '...for example,' explained Sqn Ldr Legg, 'cloud structure and gaps are clearly seen miles ahead on goggles in the dark – this allowed the IX [Squadron] crews to give direction for best attack to 14 [Squadron] with TIALD.' Each bomber dropped its weapons, using the TIALD pod to self-designate. All NATO aircraft shared the same planned weapon impact time with the objective of achieving a simultaneous cutting of all road and rail links into Kosovo. 'As our weapons impacted,' recalled

The 'Green Wave' in the crew room after the first mission over Kosovo. Back row left to right: Sqn Ldrs J. K. Hogg, D.W. Gallie, Wg Cdr T.M. Anderson, Flt Lts R.A. Howell, K.A. Gambold, G. Page. Seated: Flt Lt E.C. Fraser, Sqn Ldr P.J.D. Lennihan (IX Sqn) Flt Lts D.R.W. Wood (IX Sqn) K.R. Jones (IX Sqn) Sqn Ldrs S.P. Rochelle, D.A.C. Legg (IX Sqn). (Keven Gambold)

Sqn Ldr Rochelle, 'the whole of Kosovo lit up. There must have been a 150 major explosions around Kosovo.' After completing their attacks, the aircraft returned home via the same route, having first rendezvoused again with the RAF TriStar tankers for post-strike AAR. The Tornados landed back at Brüggen in daylight after a 7½hr flight.

The following night Flt Lts Reeves and I.D. Hendy led their 'Red Team'[111] against Pristina Barracks, each bomber armed with two Paveway IIs. In Flt Lt Cosens' view, '...probably the most challenging aspect of the whole thing was the tanking on the way down during the early part. Pretty much the whole period was stormy across Southern Europe...and at our levels you spent a lot of time on the transit [in cloud] on a tanker getting bumped all over the place. It was a relief at the Adriatic to get dropped by them and go on your own.' On this second night, turbulence, cloud and refuelling were not the only hazards: a drama was unfolding in the rear cockpit of Flt Lt Hales Tornado: '...we were zig-zagging through France somewhere near Lyons, hanging for grim life onto the VC-10 as it negotiated a thick band of embedded cumulonimbus, when Boulty [Flt Lt M. S. Boulton] announced that he needed a pee. This was little more than an hour into a 6¼hr sortie. Anyway, seats safe, rubber bag out, and I soon heard Boulty's sighs of delight turn to squeals of disgust as he realized he had missed and evacuated himself into his woollen bunny suit!'

After leaving the tanker and crossing into Serbia, Flt Lt I.J. Cosens, found, '…there was a lot more AAA [than over Iraq], especially as you crossed the border – it was like fireworks night with the tracer rounds going up much higher than I expected.'

Although NATO was operating over Kosovo virtually round-the-clock, typically mounting about 600 sorties each day, the rate of flying for Tornado crews was relatively low. With tasking for six aircraft each day, but crewing for three or four constituted six-ship formations, they might expect to fly once every 3 to 4 days. Theoretically the operational crews worked on a four-day cycle, commencing on the evening of Day 1 with the main-mission planning, which began after the issue of the air tasking order for the following night. During the night, the plan would be revized as the intelligence from the previous day's operations was fed back. That evening (Day 2) the crews would report for a meteorology and intelligence brief at around 21:30hrs, followed by sight of up-to-date target imagery and any final alterations to the plan, before a formation briefing at 22:05hrs. After a final weather update the crews would go out to the aircraft just after 23:00hrs to be ready for the formation check-in at midnight, with the first take-offs some 10 minutes later in the early hours of Day 3. After the mission they would stand down for a day and then start the process again on the evening of Day 4. In practice, however, the flying rate was less regular as the weather over the Balkans affected tasking. Laser-guided weapons needed a clear line of sight between designator and target, and bomb and target, so any substantial cloud in the target area would preclude Tornado operations.

On 12 April, the 'Green Team' carried out an attack on the ammunition storage facility at Cacak and targets on the nearby airfield at Obvra some 70 miles south of Belgrade. Two nights later, it was the turn of the 'Red Team', who bombed Nis airfield. Although hits were scored on both of these attacks, neither mission was entirely successful, a reflection both of the lack of practice because of the shortage of TIALD pods at Brüggen in the previous years and of the practical difficulties of laser-guided operations in cloudy skies. Over the next 14 days, the weather over the Balkans deteriorated further and Tornado missions were cancelled. In the meantime, the UK government was looking into the possibility of a land invasion and at Brüggen, 14 Squadron crews were stood down from medium-level operations and tasked with becoming current at operational low flying to support ground forces. The plan was for IX Squadron to lead a forward deployment to Solenzara, Corsica at the end of May to continue the medium-level air campaign with 31 Squadron, while 14 Squadron prepared to support the ground war. During late April a number of training sorties were flown in the UK low-flying system, before the plan changed again and laser operations resumed over Serbia on 28 April. On that day the airfield at Podgorica was attacked, followed two nights later by the POL storage depot at Vitanovac, a few miles southeast of Obvra.

Before 'Operation Engadine', Tornado crews had only flown offensive operations during deployed operations in the Middle East. The Kosovo war was the first time that they had done so from their home base. For most squadron personnel, both air and ground crew, it seemed bizarre that while they were fighting a war, the rest of the station continued as normal with the peacetime routine! This was also true of family life, and while some aircrew found living at home while flying on operations to be comforting, others found it difficult. Some of the wives, too, found the situation very stressful.

During late April, a second, more direct route to Serbia was authorized. This northerly route through the Czech Republic, Slovakia, Hungary and Croatia reduced sortie times to around 5 hours and required just one pre and one post-strike AAR bracket. On 2 May, the route was used for the first time for an attack on the airfield at Obvra. Although the name Obvra was marked on the NATO map, the airfield was more properly Ladeveci Air Base, home to a wing of SOKO J-22 *Orao* (Eagle) ground-attack aircraft and Aérospatiale Gazelle attack helicopters. For this mission, all four bombers[112] were armed with two Paveway II LGBs: the first two were tasked against a hangar and the control tower, while the second pair were to bomb aircraft parked on hard-standings on the south-easterly end of the airfield. The two spotter aircraft were flown once again by IX Squadron crews. The airfield was well defended, with at least three known SAM sites in the area. Reflecting this high threat, defence suppression in the target area was provided by the four USAF F-16CJ 'Wild Weasels' and a pair of US Navy EA-6Bs. After overflying Croatia and Bosnia towards Sarajevo the formation turned onto an easterly heading for the attack. The Tornados met with heavy anti-aircraft fire as they approached the target area and then, just after the first weapons impacted, two SAM-3 were also launched. The missiles were aimed at Number 2 of the lead pair, forcing Wg Cdr Anderson into a hard defensive manoeuvre to escape them. The 'Wild Weasels' responded to the SAM launch by firing a HARM at the radar, but in the next few seconds three more SAM-3s left the launchers. Flying 8 miles behind the first pair of bombers, the leader of the rear pair saw what was happening ahead: Sqn Ldr Rochelle recalled, '…see the missiles going for the leader…we continued to prosecute our attack and you see on my TIALD video this SAM-3 screeching across the screen.' At this stage a SAM-3 missile guidance radar locked onto the spotter aircraft flown by Flt Lt Wood, who was forced to jettison his tanks and run out to the north. The rear pair was also on the receiving end of the SAM site: '…as we were coming off the target there were missiles coming up behind us,' recalled Sqn Ldr Rochelle, 'and as we started to defend against those, one exploded not far behind our jet – so it was pretty hair-raising.'

Meanwhile, the crew of the fourth bomber found themselves in the midst of the action. Five SAM-3 and two HARMs had already been fired during their target run. Flt Lt Gambold, '…saw one [missile] come after us and then explode below, I assumed we would just ditch the bombs and go home, but I heard Otis [Flt Lt Page] say "right then, let's go drop 'em" and I thought, alright then, why not?' After completing its attack, the aircraft was engaged by two more SAM-3s. Flt Lt Gambold found himself inverted as he manoeuvred to break the radar lock, but he still found time to call 'busy tonight!' over the radio, to the amusement of the other crews. However, the excitement was not over yet: another SAM-3 was launched from a second site and to escape it he had to jettison his fuel tanks and perform a last-ditch break, before running out from the target area at low-level. According to Wg Cdr Anderson, '…the 'Wild Weasels' later reported that they had never seen their HARM targeting system scopes light up with so many radar emitters and target tracking radars simultaneously.' Once clear of the missile engagement zone, the six Tornados gathered back together and made their rendezvous

Flt Lts G. Page (pilot) and K.A. Gambold (navigator) preparing to leave Bruggen for a sortie over Serbia. The crew, who were caught in the midst of the missile engagements over Obvra on the night of 3/4 May, flew more missions during 'Operation Engadine' than any other 14 Squadron crew and were 'Mentioned in Dispatches' for their courage.. (Keven Gambold)

with the tanker in Hungarian airspace. During the course of 'Operation Engadine', the Tornado and VC-10 crews had developed a code system to make communication amongst themselves easier. Known as 'Eric Codes' after 14 Squadron's python mascot, they comprised a list of pre-agreed messages which could, in a few seconds, clarify exactly the fuel requirements of the Tornados. After passing his codes, Sqn Ldr Rochelle was surprised to receive the response 'Eric 99.' It was not a code that he was familiar with, so he checked the list, which by coincidence had been re-issued that night. There he read the decode, 'Eric is in the Tanker!' The 101 Squadron crews had decided that it would be good for morale if 14 Squadron's mascot also joined them for an operational sortie! On the recovery to Brüggen, instead of the usual instrument approach to land, Sqn Ldr Gallie led the six Tornados for a low-level break into the visual circuit, to announce to the world that they were back from what had been the most difficult sortie thus far. Battle-damage assessment later showed that all four bombers had achieved direct hits on their aiming points.

After 6 weeks of concentrating on the Serbian air-defence system, NATO began targeting Serbian weapon and ammunition stores. The target on 10 May was the storage at the barracks at Leskovac, some 45 miles northeast of Pristina and 4 days later Sjenica airfield. The latter mission was notable for a 'guest pilot' flying with the team: the station commander, Air Cdre I.W. McNicholl, under the supervision of Sqn Ldr Rochelle, joined them on this last sortie to use the long southern route. Although the attack was generally successful, cloud in the target area led to at least one miss. Subsequent missions later in the month utilized the shorter northern route. On 24 May, the Batanjnica petrol-storage site was attacked, as was the ammunition storage at Ralja, 30 miles southeast of Belgrade on 26 May. On 27 May, the Belgrade SAM support facility was bombed and the following day the ammunition storage sites at Boljevac, 100 miles southeast of Belgrade and Sremska Kamenica, near Novi Sad, were also bombed.

Flt Lt Cosens reported, '…strangely enough, the further into Serbia you went, the less intense the air defence, maybe there was not much left of it after those early days. The first time we were given a target in Belgrade area surrounded by a fully-integrated air defence system, we were all a little surprised by the fact it was probably the quietest night we had.' However, this was not true of Ralja, which was particularly heavily defended: apart from heavy anti-aircraft artillery fire, Wg Cdr Anderson recorded that three SAM-6s were launched during his attack. For Flt Lt Gambold it was the, '…first night I saw a SAM-6 and I nearly overstressed the jet. It was so fast there was no way to tell the aspect angle, so I just front-sticked the jet with expletives and it was gone before the aircraft even moved!'

The Boljevac/Sremska Kamenica mission on 28 May, marked the end of direct operations from Brüggen. A forward-operating base was established by IX Squadron at Solenzara on the east coast of Corsica at the end of May and the remaining Tornado operations over Serbia were mounted from there. In fact, the air campaign lasted only another 10 days and 14 Squadron crews were not involved. During the war, the squadron had hosted two VIP visitors in the persons of the Prime Minister Tony Blair, on 20 April and Prince Andrew, the Duke of York, on 7 May. From 14 Squadron's perspective, 'Operation Engadine' had been a great success: the results of the bombing by the squadron's crews demonstrated remarkably high accuracy with the LGBs, despite the challenges of heavy target defences and weather which was less than ideal. As Flt Lt Hales put it, '…life after that was a bit of an anti-climax – like the inevitable January after a roaringly good Christmas.'

Tornado GR4

Plans for a mid-life update for the Tornado had started almost as soon as the first aircraft arrived at Brüggen in 1984. Various improvements were mooted, including a Terrain Contour Matching (TCM) navigation system, similar to the guidance system for cruise missiles, which would offer a more stealthy system for night or IMC low-flying. However, it was not until the mid-1990s that a much more modest programme was finalized and aircraft were rotated through the British Aerospace factory at Warton for modification. The first of the modified aircraft, known as Tornado GR4, reached Brüggen in early 1999. Wg Cdr Anderson flew his first GR4 familiarization flight on 29 March. Externally the only difference between the GR1 and GR4 aircraft was that the latter mounted a FLIR[113] turret under the nose, alongside the LRMTS[114] fairing. However, the avionic fit inside the aircraft was markedly different from the older variant: in particular a new data-bus in the weapons system allowed for more complex weapons to be used. Amongst these was the Enhanced Paveway II, which incorporated a GPS-guidance system to back up the laser-guidance. On the Tornado GR4, individual weapons could be programmed by the navigator and dropped accurately without laser-guidance if necessary. For the first time the RAF had an all-weather precision-guided munition capability from medium-level, so that clouds would no longer limit operations as they had over Serbia.

After a quiet summer the squadron deployed to Goose Bay on 3 September for the usual operational low flying and TFR training in Labrador. An APC had been planned over Easter, but it had been overtaken by the Kosovo campaign, so another detachment was organized for mid-November. On 12 November, four Tornados were detached to Akrotiri for a week-long weaponry and air-combat camp. Each day waves of aircraft would get airborne in pairs, loaded with eight practice bombs and go straight into the range pattern at Episkopi. After dropping their bombs they would then climb up for air combat manoeuvring until they had used their fuel and then recover to Akrotiri after a short but very intense sortie. The detachment included the squadron bombing competition, which was won by Wg Cdr Anderson and Sqn Ldr Rochelle.

Operation Bolton 3

January 2000, marked the beginning of another 3 months of operations in the Middle East. On 11 January, the squadron resumed 'Operation Bolton' at Ali Al Salem and found Iraqi forces being much more active. Not long after the squadron's previous time in Iraq during autumn 1998, the Coalition had launched 'Operation Desert Fox', a series of air and cruise-missile strikes against Iraqi targets, after which Iraq stated that it did not recognize the legality of the NFZs. From then on attacks on Coalition aircraft became commonplace over southern Iraq, with both anti-aircraft guns and SAMs being fired. As a result of this provocation, limited offensive action over Iraq was authorized. On 19 February, Wg Cdr Anderson led an airstrike against a S-60 anti-aircraft gun battery at Al Turbak and again on 11 March when another S-60 battery at Tallil was attacked. The squadron celebrated its 85th Anniversary while on operations, with a dinner at the Safir Hotel in Kuwait City on 3 February.

The year's Goose Bay detachment, which took place in June, marked the start of a work-up for 'Exercise Green Flag'. This exercise, held at Nellis AFB, followed very similar to 'Red Flag', but with an emphasis on electronic warfare. This 'Green Flag' was the last of its kind: the EW was included in future 'Red Flags' and the 'Green Flag' name was later reused for an entirely different close air-support exercise.

Meanwhile, RAF Brüggen was winding down and 14 Squadron prepared to move to home. The end of the 'Cold War' had been followed almost immediately by massive political pressure to deliver a 'Peace Dividend:' by reducing the defence budget, funds could be diverted to more popular areas of government spending. The contraction of the armed forces had started with almost indecent haste immediately after the Gulf War. In Germany, the RAF lost the flying stations at Wildenrath and Gutersloh in 1991. Wildenrath's Phantom squadrons had been disbanded and Laarbruch's Tornado squadrons were either re-deployed, or disbanded, to make room for the units, which in turn had been displaced from Gutersloh. Although Brüggen and Laarbruch survived this first phase of cuts, it was clear that the RAF's presence in Germany would end sooner rather than later. Laarbruch closed in 1999 and the final drawdown came 2 years later with the closure of Brüggen.

NOTES

85   Pilots: Flt Lts N.R. Aldersley, J.A. Butler, A.P. Jeremy, M.J.W. Napier, Fg Off P.K. Comer. Navigators: Flt Lt A.G. Grieve and Fg Offs N.T. Cookson, Payne, S. Walker and R.J. Wesley.

86   In Tornado GR1 ZD894.

87   In Tornado GR1 ZD710.

88   Instrument Meteorological Conditions (or 'in cloud' in layman's terms).

89   In Tornado GR1 ZD891.

90   Flt Lt S.G. Cockram/ Wg Cdr R.V. Morris, Flt Lt J.K. Hogg/Flt Lt N.T. Cookson, Flt Lt T.J. Marsh/Flt Lt K.A. Smith, Flt Lt M.J. Murtagh/Fg Off S. Wain, Flt Lt D.A. Bentley/Flt Lt S.R. Sayers and Flt Lt A.S. Linstead.

91   Sqn Ldr J.A.J. Rimmer/Flt Lt G. Harrison, Flt Lt H.S. Turner/Flt Lt D.M.V. Lumb.

92   Sqn Ldr D.E. Moule/ Sqn Ldr C.J. Coulls, Flt Lt M.A. Gibson/ Flt Lt A.D. Glover, Flt Lt K.J. Duffy/Flt Lt N.T. Dent.

93   Tornado GR1 ZD718.

94   Tornado GR1 ZD895.

95   Tornado GR1 ZD895.

96   In Tornado GR1 ZA457.

97   Anti-Aircraft Artillery.

98   Sqn Ldrs Moule/Coulls (ZD745), Flt Lt Goodwin/Sqn Ldr Catterson (ZD740), Flt Lts Gibson/ Glover (ZA374), Flt Lts Murtagh/Wain (ZA490).

99   In Tornado GR1 ZD719.

100   In Tornado GR1 ZA446.

101   Thermal Imaging And Laser Designator.

102   In Tornado GR1 ZD746.

103   In Tornado GR1 ZD739.

104   Sqn Ldr Rimmer/Flt Lt Lumb, Flt Lt Bentley/Fg Off L. P. Williams, Flt Lts M. J. Baverstock/ D.A.W Evans, Flt Lts D.N.S. Ritch/D.J.A. Potter.

105   This use of targetting pods pre-dated the USAF concept of Non-Traditional Intelligence Surveillance and Reconnaissance (NTISR) by 10 years.

106   Sqn Ldr M.J.W. Napier/Fg Off C. Platt (ZA492), Flt Lts M.J. Hudson/S. Kennedy [617 Sqn] (ZD849), Flt Lts C.D.A.F. Bearblock/N.P. Francis (ZA462), M.J. Cook/C.M. Craghill (ZA472).

107   Sqn Ldr Napier/Fg Off Platt (ZA452), Flt Lts Hudson/Kennedy [617 Sqn](ZD472), Flt Lts J. Stockings/J. Calder [31 Sqn] (ZA492), Cook/Craghill (ZD849).

108   UN Special COMmission.

109   A runway approach-lighting system using strobe lights.

110   Bombers (14 Squadron crews): Sqn Ldrs Hogg/Rochelle, Flt Lts K. A. Gambold/G Page, Sqn Ldr D.W. Gallie/Flt Lt E.C. Fraser, Wg Cdr Anderson/Flt Lt R.A. Howell; Spotters (IX Squadron crews) Sqn Ldrs D.A.C. Legg/Flt Lt K.R. Jones, Flt Lt D. Wood/Sqn Ldr P.J.D. Lenihan.

111   Flt Lts Reeves/I.D. Hendy, Flt Lts I.J. Cosens/C. Platt, Flt Lts D.W. Hales/M.S. Boulton, Flt Lt V.J. Hargreaves/M.J. Letch.

112   Sqn Ldr D. Gallie/Flt Lt E. Fraser, Wg Cdr T.M. Anderson/Flt Lt C. Platt, Sqn Ldr Legg/Flt Lt D. Howett, (IX Sqn), Sqn Ldrs H.F. Smith/S. P. Rochelle, Flt Lts K.A. Gambold/G. Page, Flt Lt Wood/Sqn Ldr Lenihan (IX Sqn).

113   Forward Looking Infra-Red.

114   Laser Rangefinder and Marked Target Seeker.

8

2001-2011

THE TORNADO
AT LOSSIEMOUTH

Farewell to Germany

For 14 Squadron the closure of Brüggen, its home for 31 years, meant a move to Lossiemouth in north-east Scotland and the end of an era: having spent 55 years in the country, 14 Squadron was the longest-serving RAF squadron in Germany. Wg Cdr Klein, who had previously served on the squadron as a flight commander returned to take command of the squadron in December 2000. He, '…arrived in Germany shortly before Christmas 2000 to find I had half a squadron (half already in transit back to UK), an office with a cardboard box for a chair, and much of the planning for the move itself already complete and underway. I led a three-ship formation as the squadron formally arrived at Lossiemouth on Friday, 5 January 2001 to a piper's welcome.

'Since the squadron accommodation at that stage was still under construction the squadron initially had to operate out of the old alternate COC[115] hard (no windows and only limited office space – I think my office was actually the crypto safe – it certainly had a combination lock on the steel door), and the ground crew operated out of the 'soft' offices attached to one of the waterfront hangers. Not an ideal situation, compounded again by the other half of the squadron going on leave to effect their respective domestic moves back to the UK, so effectively we operated as half a squadron for about 3 months. We eventually moved into the brand new purpose-built accommodation on the waterfront in April 2001 with aircraft operating off a line (in the wet). The aircrew accommodation was one side of the hanger with ground crew in a mirror image set-up on the other side of the hanger. The op[eration]s set-up was downstairs with offices and a crewroom upstairs and, being a new build, there was even handicapped parking outside (but nothing for the station commander!) and a lift to get upstairs for all those disabled aircrew or for specialist aircrew who could not carry their wallets upstairs without assistance…at least that is how we looked upon it at the time. The lift survived about a week before the aircrew broke it.'

Representatives of the squadron returned to Germany for Brüggen's formal closing ceremony on 15 June. During the parade 14 Squadron, along with Brüggen's other squadrons, was presented with a *Fahnenband*, a traditional German battle honour, as a mark of appreciation by the German government for the role which the unit had played in the 'Cold War'.

As the squadron settled into its new home the flying was not without incident. On 21 February, Flt Lts M. W. Roscoe and M. J. Elsey took off for an inverted-flight check, but shortly after getting airborne Roscoe encountered a major control restriction which prevented him from pushing the control column forward of neutral. Displaying, 'excellent handling skills and exemplary airmanship', the crew managed to recover the aircraft safely back to Lossiemouth by juggling trim and power settings with undercarriage and flap selection. Both crewmembers were awarded a 'Green Endorsement' for their handling of this potentially catastrophic incident.

The first major detachment from Lossiemouth was to Hill AFB, near Salt Lake City, Utah, for 'Exercise Torpedo Focus' in March. This exercise had become the (eventual) successor to the APCs, which the squadron had previously carried out in Libya (in Canberra days) and more recently at Decimomannu. The ranges at Hill were cleared for dropping live LGBs using the TIALD pod, a rare opportunity given the large safety area required for such weapons. In the US training areas, Tornado crews were also able to carry out night flying at low-level using electro-optics (the Tornado GR4's FLIR system as well as Night-Vision Goggles [NVG]). To all this first-class training was added fighter affiliation with F-5s and F-16s flown by the Aggressor Squadron from the Naval Fighter Weapons School (TOPGUN) at Naval Air Station Fallon in nearby Nevada, as well as work F-16s from Hill AFB. A short detachment to RAF Valley (Anglesey) for an MPC followed in May and at the end of June the squadron spent a week at Goose Bay for operational low flying and night/IMC work. All of these exercises proved to be a useful work-up for the deployment to Kuwait at the beginning of August.

Operation Resinate (South)

By 2001, all the operations of all three British services in and over Iraq had been amalgamated into 'Operation Resinate'. This operation was further divided into 'Resinate (North)' and 'Resinate (South)'. The situation in southern Iraq had worsened noticeably in the months since the squadron's previous deployment to Ali Al Salem and it was not unusual for Coalition aircraft to be fired upon by the Iraqis or for Coalition aircraft to attack targets in Iraq. As previously, the operational missions mainly consisted of climbing into a holding pattern over Kuwait and waiting to be called for a strike. However, the tedium of these sorties was offset by the opportunity for training flights over Kuwait or the Gulf, with low flying, air combat and range work all included in the flying programme. On most days, aircraft would take-off from Ali Al Salem for TIALD or Vicon training over Kuwait or range work at Al Abraq. There were also a number of pre-planned missions. Sometimes these sorties were the cause of frustration

Flt Lts C.J. Stradling and J.A. Freeborough in front of their Paveway II-armed Tornado on 28 August 2001, before an 'Operation Resinate' strike against the anti-aircraft headquarters at Umm Khayyed. One of the Tornado Force's most experienced navigators, Chris Stradling would fly his 4,500th Tornado hour over Afghanistan while serving with 14 Squadron in 2010. (James Freeborough)

and disappointment: on 25 August, Flt Lts J. A. Freeborough and C. J. Stradling had to turn back from a strike on An Numinyah when their Skyshadow ECM pod developed a fault. They were escorted back to Kuwait by Flt Lt Smith and Wg Cdr Klein. Then 3 days later Freeborough and Stradling were part of a four-ship[116] tasked against the anti-aircraft headquarters at Umm Khayyed to the south of Basra. On this attack, Flt Lt Stradling could not find the target with the TIALD pod and so once again they brought their bombs home. On landing they found the reason that they could not find the target: it had already been obliterated by the Number 2's weapons!

The next month started off quietly, but on 11 September the terrorist attack on the Twin Towers of the World Trade Center in New York changed the whole attitude of the US government to events in the Middle East. For Wg Cdr Klein, '…disbelief at the time was followed by waiting to see whether we would be involved in any reprisals or retaliatory action. In the end we just upped the security state at Ali Al Salem and continued "normal ops" which included recce, and the continued and fairly frequent TIALD/Paveway II LGB bombing of targets in Iraq.' Two such missions, against ZSU-57/2 self-propelled anti-aircraft guns at Shahban, north of Basra, followed on 18 and 20 September and were described by Wg Cdr Klein as, '…bombing various relatively cheap AAA pieces with a very expensive bomb, usually under SAM and AAA fire.'

During the first mission, Flt Lt Smith and Wg Cdr Klein led a four-ship[117] for two runs across the target area and were able to destroy three out of four of the guns. Two days later, Smith and Klein led another four-ship[118] back to Shahban and destroyed one of the guns, but this time the rear pair of aircraft were engaged by multiple SAM launches and anti-aircraft fire. At the back of the formation, Flt Lt Freeborough spotted the missiles, '…it was very pretty and looked like a firework display – then I realized what it was!' One missile detonated a kilometre away from the Number 4, as the formation retired across the border. A week later Smith and Klein were in action again, attacking an S-60 anti-aircraft gun near Shahban with a Paveway II bomb.

Apart from offensive sorties, the Tornados were also busy with reconnaissance sorties using the Vicon pod. The particular quarry for these sorties were the P-18 ('Spoon Rest') early-warning radars, which were associated with the SAM-2 system. A number of Vicon searches were flown in the first week of October, looking for 'Spoon Rest' deployed in the areas of Basra and As Samawah. Another strike was flown on 3 October by four crews[119], including Flt Lt R.E. Mannering who in his words, '…finished the OCU in July and arrived on the squadron during the work-up for Resinate. I was allowed to deploy (after much chiselling on my part) limited combat ready ops only. I think it is the first time a squadron Boss used his discretion on this type of waiver.' The formation set off in two pairs and carried out a Vicon run first; then the Vicon aircraft acted as 'shooters' for the two bomber aircraft, the Numbers 1 and 3. Unfortunately, the target intelligence was out of date and the guns had been moved, so although both aircraft successfully dropped on their designated aiming points, no damage was done to the Iraqi artillery. The remainder of the squadron's time in Kuwait was routine, with Vicon searches over Iraq, but with no further offensive action despite much time spent in the holding pattern.

Lossiemouth routine

The routine at Lossiemouth was very similar to that of the early days of the Tornado in Germany before the shortage of spares and aircraft had hampered flying from Brüggen in the mid-1990s. By now the squadron had its full complement of Tornado GR4s and was able to mount a full flying programme from its home base. Sorties were usually flown as pairs or four-ships, making full use of the UK low-flying system as well as the air-weapons ranges at Tain, Otterburn and Garvie Island, the electronic-warfare tactics range at RAF Spadeadam. Regular fighter affiliation was available with the Tornado F3 squadrons at Leuchars and Leeming and the BAe Hawks of 100 Squadron, as was air-to-air refuelling with VC-10s and TriStars. There were also sufficient TIALD pods available for use at Lossiemouth, so crews could perform both low-level and medium-level designating profiles. Overseas training flights, descendants of the 'Exercise Lone Rangers' of previous days, were also included in the flying task; in March 2002 the destination was Prague.

Apart from operational deployments to the Middle East, which came around each year, 14 Squadron's personnel might expect annual detachments to Goose Bay for night/IMC low flying and OLF and the US either for APC or an 'Exercise Red Flag'. Having been based at Hill AFB in Utah for 'Exercise Torpedo Focus' in 2001, the squadron was based at Davis-Montham AFB, near Tucson, Arizona, in April the following year. Flt Lt Mannering summed up the Davis-Montham detachment, '… great ranges, great social and great flying from Paveway II self-designating high dive to OLF to air-combat Training to affiliation with F-16 chaps from Tucson International (Air National Guard flyers) and from Luke AFB.' The emphasis of the detachment was on heavy-weapons training which included dropping live 1,000lb HE bombs both retarded and free-fall, BL755, Paveway II LGBs and the larger Paveway III 2,000lb LGB on the nearby Chocolate Mountain and Barry M. Goldwater Ranges. The Goose Bay detachment took place in June, to be followed at Lossiemouth later in the same month by 'Exercise Garlic Lemon', flying mixed four-ships with French Air Force Dassault Mirage 2000s and by participation in some of the thirty-aircraft combined air operations formations organized by the combined QWI course.

When the squadron deployed to Kuwait for 'Operation Resinate (South)' in early November 2002, it found that the pace of operations had quickened. During the year, the UN and Iraq had moved into an impasse about 'Weapons of Mass Destruction' (WMD) and the US had started moving towards another war with Iraq. Iraqi forces were markedly more aggressive to Coalition aircraft operating in the southern NFZ: on 14 November, three SAMs were launched and anti-aircraft guns were fired at Sqn Ldr Entwistle and Wg Cdr Klein on a reconnaissance sortie. The Tornado detachment at Ali Al Salem now had a new reconnaissance sensor in the Raptor,[120] a long-range electro-optical and infra-red sensor pod which was carried under the aircraft. Imagery from Raptor could be transmitted by data-link in realtime to analysts on the ground, making Tornado an incredibly powerful reconnaissance asset for the Coalition. Unfortunately, pilots were not overly impressed with the effects of the weight and drag of the large pod on the Tornado's handling characteristics at medium-level! One of the Raptor tasks was to try to locate the exact positions of the Iraqi SAM systems within the Baghdad 'Super-MEZ.'[120] Flt Lts Mannering and A.T. McGlone flew two such sorties on 27 November and 8 December: Mannering remembered, '…we tickled the Super MEZ to identify the SAMs using the Raptor – I believe this information was passed up the chain for use by other assets. I do remember the headquarters at the time being very impressed and the squadron getting a pat on the back for that one.'

Another innovation since the squadron's previous time on 'Operation Resinate' was the Enhanced Paveway II (EPW II) system, which had been introduced into service the previous year. EPW II included provision for GPS guidance if there was no laser designation for the weapon. The squadron had occasion to use the new weapon in anger on several occasions as it took part in a concerted campaign against the Iraqi air-defence system in the run up towards an increasingly inevitable war. On the first such strike on 18 November, Sqn Ldr Entwistle and Wg Cdr Klein, led six aircraft against the air-defence operations centre at Tallil. The lead crew dropped a single 2,000lb Paveway III on the operations bunker, while the rest of the formation attacked other targets in the complex with EPW II. At this stage the Paveway III was still something of a novelty and as Wg Cdr Klein stated, '…it was certainly unusual and out of the ordinary compared with the "normal" run of the mill drops of EPW II…on that particular sortie the IR conditions were not great and TIALD did not produce the greatest picture on the TV TAB and the bunker just about appeared out of the murk before weapon release. Paveway III drops were always at greater range than their smaller PW II counterparts, which always increased the pressures in target identification.'

Usually a formation of six aircraft would include four bombers and two Raptor aircraft, who could transmit real-time battle-damage assessment to the air tasking agency. Four consecutive days of offensive missions started on 20 November, with an attack by another six-ship on the cable repeater station at Al Kut; a USAF KC-10 tanker supported this longer-range mission. Over the following days, formations of six aircraft bombed the 'Spoon Rest' radar at Shaibah and the fibre-optic cable repeater station at Al Uzayr (to the south of Al Amarah). Another strike against a 'Spoon Rest' on 23 November was called off after the formation carried out its initial Raptor sweep of the area. All of these last three missions were supported by USAF KC-10 tankers.

Over the next 3 weeks, Raptor sorties were flown over Iraq, but the aircraft in the hold were not called into action. However, on 14 December, Sqn Ldr W.P. Bohill and Wg Cdr Klein led the six aircraft[122] against a cable repeater station at Abu Zawbah, between Basra and Al Amarah. In the Number 5 aircraft Flt Lt Stradling saw that his wingman, Flt Lts C. Kidd and A.R. Fisher, '...had to run for a spare aircraft and were still starting up when we were getting the details and the clearance to proceed to the target. While in the hold waiting to press north, I got onto the squadron chat frequency and told them (words to the effect) that they might want to hurry up and join us as the party was about to get started!' Kidd and Fisher managed to catch up with the rest of the formation, but their troubles were not over, as they were locked up by a Roland missile as they approached the target. 'It was a perfect opportunity to bang the tanks off,' recalled Flt Lt Fisher, 'but we did not. After the event it was most likely a spurious lock on warning and we were probably above its maximum height capability anyway. What it did do was put us off the attack run – let's just say the attack was successful, but the video was not pretty, we only dropped one weapon because that's all we were asked to do – one weapon on one target.' The rear pair marked their arrival back at Ali Al Salem with a low pass in close formation before breaking into the circuit.

The next day, after refuelling from a KC-10, another four-ship[123] attacked a 'Spoon Rest' radar at Al Kut. The destruction of the radar with a single EPW II dropped by the lead aircraft stirred up a hornets' nest of anti-aircraft fire, so the formation was re-tasked to bomb the nearby cable repeater station in response. A third consecutive day of offensive action followed with an attack on cable repeaters at An Nasiriyah by four aircraft.[124] The sortie had originally been a reconnaissance mission, but the formation was re-tasked to bomb the cable repeater station, leaving them, as Flt Lt Freeborough noted, '...very tight on gas.' After a relatively quiet 14 days, the squadron was called into action again on 30 December. Sqn Ldr Bohill and Wg Cdr Klein led another formation[125] on a night-time strike on the air-defence operations centre at Al Kut. This was the last offensive action by 14 Squadron crews before the end of the deployment. By now it was obvious that war was imminent and that the next unit at Ali Al Salem would see the action. Wg Cdr Klein commented that the squadron

A Tornado GR4 on recovery to Ali Al Salem Air Base, after an operational sortie on 14 December 2002. Tornado GR4 ZD790 is flown by Flt Lts C. Kidd and A. Fisher and is armed with two Paveway II; a third weapon had been dropped on cable repeater stations at Abu Zawbah. (Chris Stradling)

returned to Lossiemouth, '...just before hostilities began, much to the squadron's extreme disappointment especially those who had missed out on the first Gulf War.'

The beginning of the 2003 was a busy period with a number of exercises, as well as the routine training. At the end of January, two Tornados deployed to Jever for two days on 'Exercise Ulan Owl'. During this army exercise, run by 7th Armoured Brigade, the aircraft flew CAS sorties on Munsterlager range. During March, a night tactical leadership training course was held at Lossiemouth. The squadron was able to join the other participating aircraft including other Tornado GR4 units, Harrier GR7, Tornado F3, RNAF F-16, BAe Nimrod MR2 and Lockheed P-3 Orion maritime patrol aircraft, and Boeing Chinook, Aérospatiale Puma and Augusta Westland AW-101 Merlin helicopters for large Combined Air Operations (COMAO) formations, all flown at night using the various electro-optical sensors carried on each type. March also brought the 'Joint Maritime Exercise', which involved a large number of NATO aircraft and ships. Exercise missions included CAS tasks in Scotland and anti-shipping strikes. The new month started with an MPC at RAF Valley. A number of AIM-9L missiles were fired, including a night firing by Flt Lts Mannering and Stradling on 3 April. 'It was a successful firing,' reported Mannering, 'with the biggest issue being the gogs [NVGs] getting massively bloomed out by the AIM-9L rocket firing. The profile was a beam intercept with a radar handover to visual acquisition flown with Stradders – fab night.' The missile scored a direct hit on the target flare pack towed by a Jindivik.

Wg Cdr J.B. Klein hands over command of 14 Squadron to Wg Cdr C. Basnett at Lossiemouth in July 2003. They are under the watchful eye of the squadron mascot, Burmese python 'Sqn Ldr E.C. Aldrovani.' (James Klein)

On 9 May, HM Queen Elizabeth visited RAF Lossiemouth including 14 Squadron. Wg Cdr Klein recalled, '…amongst others, Her Majesty was introduced to Sqn Ldr Eric Courtney Aldrovandi, who, I am pleased to say, behaved impeccably.' Quite what Her Majesty thought of the 20ft Burmese Rock Python remains a mystery. In July, Wg Cdr Klein handed command of the Squadron to Wg Cdr C. Basnett.

Operation Telic

The invasion of Iraq, named 'Operation Telic', had started on 20 March 2003. Although 14 Squadron had returned from 'Operation Resinate' 3 months earlier, the unit was represented in the conflict by one of its navigators, Flt Lt Bury. Additionally, Sqn Ldrs Platt and Fraser acted as 'Warlords', running the operations desk for the Tornado detachment at Al Udeid. Flt Lt Bury was sent to Al Udeid at short notice to fly with Flt Lt T. J. Lindsay whose navigator had returned home for compassionate reasons. 'I arrived, read [the order book], slept and then the air war kicked off,' recalled Flt Lt Bury, 'so my first 'famil' trip was into the Western Desert.' The attacks by

Coalition aircraft, including 14 Squadron's Tornados, had largely dismantled the Iraqi air-defence system before the invasion began. So once formal hostilities began, air power was concentrated against Iraq's Republican Guard units. Flt Lt Bury's first sortie on 22 March was a night-time strike on the Republican Guard barracks at Saribadi, some 30 miles to the southwest of Baghdad. 'We were fragged as a four-ship,' continued Bury, 'with Flt Lts Howie Edwards (squadron QWI) and Gary Partridge as my element lead. The flow in to Iraq was a simple system of height and direction de-conflicted corridors from Kuwait, along the Saudi border, with arms leading off at various points into Iraq. Our task was to drop EPW IIs on a Republican Guards barracks on the south side of Baghdad and on paper the transit in looked reasonably simple until you hit the "Super MEZ" of Bagdad. Unfortunately, we were not briefed on the possible location of a SAM-3 battery, which had been reported by intelligence but not corroborated. We pressed east from the Saudi border as two pairs split by about a minute and had not gone particularly far before all hell broke loose on the radio. Our leader was calling SAM engagements followed by prepare for…an ejection. As the rear pair, we had seen the flare up on our NVGs and at this point assumed that the lead pair had been shot down. A disappointing start to my first mission! As the rear element we kicked right to sidestep the apparent threat. As it turns out, this actually directed us into the threat – a modified SAM-3 system. We were subsequently lit up by a SAM-3 Missile Guidance (MG) radar with what appeared to be missile launches as well. Luckily for us, the battery had adopted the [inaccurate] technique of launching and then delaying illuminating with MG. This minimized our warning of a shot but resulted in a reduced chance of hitting us. We reacted to the threat with the upshot that our [element] leader elected to take us home due to a lack of fuel to complete the mission. Tankers were at a premium so there was no scope for a top up pre or post target. It was at this point that we heard our [formation] leader had not actually ejected, but had been forced to divert in to Ali Al Salem. All in all, an exciting first sortie. It all seemed a bit tame after that!'

Over the next week the tasking comprised CAS and Killbox Interdiction (KI) sorties, but as Flt Lt Bury explained, '…the limiting factor for success was nearly always communications. Finding the correct frequencies to contact the relevant E3 for tasking or subsequently to talk to a FAC, mean that engagement opportunities in the areas we were tasked to were scant, KI provided a much more target rich environment. The whole of the airspace was split in to Killboxes (KB), which had an alpha-numeric identifier and associated frequencies. As long as you were tasked to a given box, and it was designated as open…you could employ weapons against the cleared target sets (armour, military equipment, etc). Often, there was a handover of targets between formations if you arrived to find an aircraft working your KB already. Once [they had expended all their weapons] they would assume SCAR (Strike Co-ordination and Reconnaissance) commander role and handover any unserviced targets.' These missions were flown at both day and night, including a 6hr night sortie on 26 March. The previous night a CAS mission was curtailed due to heavy electrical storms.

On 29 March, Flt Lt Bury returned his attention to the Republican Guard, this time the barracks at Shaykh Mazhar, to the southeast of Baghdad, where the pair of Tornados dropped two EPW II and four RBL755s[126] on buildings and armoured vehicles. A KI sortie the next evening was frustrated by poor weather over the target areas and by difficulty with communications. By the beginning of April, US forces were approaching the outskirts of Baghdad and on 4 April, US infantry units captured Saddam International Airport. Flt Lts Lindsay and Bury were involved in this action: they dropped two EPW IIs on tanks which were firing on US forces. More KI sorties were flown over the next 10 days to the north of Baghdad, including one mission on the night of 9 April, when vehicles and artillery in berms (earth wall and ditch) were engaged with three EPW II. On his last sortie over Iraq 5 days later, Flt Lt Bury located missiles mounted on trucks to the north of Baghdad but was unable to get clearance to attack. However, by now the land war was virtually over.

The squadron returned to Ali Al Salem at the beginning of August 2003. With the invasion completed the situation in Iraq was very different from the squadron's previous visit: Flt Lt P.D. Froome felt, '…there was a much more relaxed feel to the detachment in terms of tension with the medium-level threat removed, although there was risk on approach if you diverted in country. The tempo was still there though – amount of recce tasking …This detachment was entirely recce – every jet with a JRP[127], every sortie involved recce of some description, as well as route searches/show of presence. The Main Supply Routes (MSRs) were divided up across Iraq, and time and direction allocated to avoid nasty encounters. The guns were loaded though, in case you were called on to support a ground callsign.' The daily reconnaissance flights were flown in pairs, with both aircraft fitted with a JRP. Since there was no air-to-air threat, the Tornados no longer carried AIM-9L Sidewinder missiles and the original LAU7 pylons were replaced with a BOL rail, a more modern missile pylon which had the benefit of incorporating extra chaff and flare countermeasures. From Ali Al Salem the Tornados ranged all over Iraq and covered all the borders.

With the immediate threat from Iraq removed, the Kuwaitis were keen to reclaim Ali Al Salem for themselves and the RAF was informed that the airfield would be closed to RAF aircraft, ostensibly for runway resurfacing, from the end of August. For the rest of 'Operation Telic', the Tornados would operate from Al Udeid Air Base in Qatar, just to the southwest of Doha. The move to Al Udeid was made on 25 August. According to Flt Lt Froome, '…we completed the move without any break in operational tasking and actually flew the jets down off the back of op sorties. We had six aircraft deployed and we flew three pairs that day. I led one pair with Colin Basnett (OC 14 Squadron). We were the last pair to leave Ali Al Salem, and joined up with the previous pair after tasking to arrive at Al Udeid as a four-ship.' During this sortie, Wg Cdr Basnett completed his 2,000th Tornado flying hour. Although the new base was comfortable enough, it was an hour's transit time to and from the Iraqi border, so operational sorties would require AAR support and would last considerably longer than had been the case from Kuwait. The main source of AAR support was a VC-10 tanker, but other tankers such as KC-10s and KC-135 Stratotankers were also used. Flt Lt Froome spent many hours, '…photographing pretty much all of the borders of Iraq during that detachment. The sorties were mostly 5 hours long, and involved at least two tanking

Tornado GR4 ZA596 flown by Flt Lts B.C.B. Thorpe and M.J. Bressani refuelling from a VC-10 tanker over Iraq during an 'Operation Telic' sortie in September 2003. (Bev Thorpe)

brackets, mostly with VC-10s.'

One novelty was that airfields in Iraq could be used as diversions. Flt Lt Freeborough and Wg Cdr Basnett diverted into Basra on 9 September and 10 days later Lt Williams and Flt Lt Glover landed at Tallil after an engine vibration warning. With little to do in Al Udeid while not flying, a number of 14 Squadron's personnel found some original ways to amuse themselves. Flt Lt Froome recalled, '…Yorkie Beevers[128] organized a night in the desert in Qatar during a down day or two. Pretty much the whole aircrew detachment went. It involved dune driving, sand skiing, a BBQ, and sleeping out under the stars. Pretty damn good and a nice relaxing time considering.'

After returning from Qatar at the end of September, the squadron headed for Goose Bay at the end of October for what Flt Lt Froome called, '…a normal (but oh too long!) detachment to Goose Bay. We did the full range of flying: OLF, night – both traditional and EO, heavy weapons, and normal convex flying. The weather was cold (probably an understatement!) with snow appearing during the detachment. This was also our Tornado Standardization Visit (TSV) preparation period ahead of their visit in December, so there was plenty of ground training…The weaponeering we did in the training area was a variety – 28lb practice bombs, inert 1,000lb bombs (free-fall and retard) and some inert Paveway II with both airborne and ground-based designation.

We had an RAF Regiment TAC(P) team deploy with us who were ferried out to the range on the Monday morning, and brought back on the Friday evening. The team lived on the range to do FAC work as well as the designating. All very challenging in the weather – for us and them! Matt Bressani and I dropped one PW II from a loft profile in marginal conditions: we had anticipated this and worked out what the minimum cloud base we could release the weapon with, but it was unnerving to release it knowing we would go into cloud, come out with the minimum time to acquire and guide. But it did and it worked!' Night flying in the weather at Goose Bay involved using the full flexibility of the Tornado's systems. Flt Lt Mannering explained, '...typically you would let down on automatic TF or prove the system and then fly around using a combination of NVGs and FLIR (dependant upon environmental conditions). If the weather turned bad we would [select] the TF and take it out again when it improved. [On] our OLF [sorties at] Goose one would OLF until you hit cloud and then TF through and then back to OLF when the weather permitted.' The squadron was tasked with ferrying the Tornados back to UK at the end of the 'North American season', but things did not go well: after launching in three waves most of the aircraft ended up stuck in St John's because of weather in the Azores. When they were eventually able to continue, some of the aircraft had to return to Goose Bay because of unserviceabilities. Eventually, everyone made it home in time for the Tornado Standardization Visit in December.

In January 2004, the squadron sent two crews[129] to the AAFCE Tactical Leadership Programme (TLP) at Florennes Air Base, Belgium. The flying programme was affected by the weather, which included a lot of snow and ice. Flt Lt Froome was particularly impressed by the 14 Squadron ground crew, '...we (14) did not lose a single sortie due to aircraft availability. They worked flat out to make sure we were always up and ready. On one sortie, I remember getting to the jet whilst they were still clearing it of snow and ice and I did my walk round as they continued, trusting them to clear the tailplanes as I was strapping in (always against the timeline!). But they did. Amazing support from them'

The following month the squadron set off for 'Exercise Red Flag'. As this was the first exercise of the 'North American season' 14 Squadron was responsible for ferrying the aircraft out to Nellis AFB. The trail started on 20 February via Lajes in the Azores and then on to Bangor, Maine, the next day. Here the weather closed in, with a heavy snowfall. The aircraft were only able to leave on 23 February, after they had been de-iced – a very unusual procedure for a Tornado! On 1 March, the exercise started and comprised an afternoon wave and night wave. On previous exercises the squadron's shifts had swapped over in the second week so that everyone was exposed to both day and night flying, but on this detachment the day and night shifts were maintained for both weeks. Flt Lt Mannering, '...was on the night wave for the exercise but there was a day and night wave. As I was EO Combat Ready I was able to do the low-level manual flying on NVGs. Exercise scenarios were based upon expected threats scenarios at the time, namely a 'North Korea-esque' threat. Another pilot on the night wave was Flt Lt Froome who found, '...as the only low-level EO fast jet players we had a fair bit of freedom once we were down at low-level. The scenarios we were working in meant a variety of medium-level/low-level (sometimes driven by the heavy weapons we were carrying for training). There were some live 1,000lb Retards to be dropped at night, as well as some Paveway IIs and 1,000lb free-falls (both inert and live).' Although the weather intervened on some days, most crews managed to get five or six high-value sorties under their belts during the fortnight.

Two months later, the squadron returned to the US for another 'Exercise Torpedo Focus', which was held once more at Davis-Montham AFB. For Flt Lt Froome the detachment was, '...probably the highlight of my QWI tour. A 3 week detachment for no other reason than to do weaponeering! We had stacks of live and inert of all types, something like: ten Paveway III live, ten Paveway III inert, twenty Paveway II (various), twenty or so of each retard and freefall live, thirty-plus inert of the same, hundreds of 27mm rounds, and sixty-odd BL755! The Barry M. Goldwater Range complex on the doorstep had an incredible series of target arrays for everything, but the Paveway III live and the BL755 (we went to Chocolate Mountain for them). The targets ranged from old tanks and vehicles, through to ISO containers laid out in complexes, and old aircraft as well. It allowed us to practice the full variety of weapon delivery profiles. I had the job of allocating weapons to crews, based on when they last dropped each weapon. Some of the junior crews had not dropped anything like this so they got to drop everything! The exercise allowed us to drop sticks of live retard weapons (not normally allowed) because we were using training fuses, so the youngsters were getting to drop sticks of four live 1,000lb retards.' The exercise was also an opportunity for two of the crews[130] to operate as airborne FACs. As part of a wider experiment, 14 Squadron had sent the crews to qualify as FACs in the UK. Flt Lt Mannering, '...was lucky to be part of the team. We qualified as ground FACs at JFACTSU[131] at RAF Leeming and then we did the USAF FAC-A course with the A-10s albeit we were flying in our own jets. It was done as a test case as we, the RAF, were considering bringing this qualification with our Fast Jet community.' In practice it proved too difficult to keep the crews current enough in the role to remain qualified, so the idea was later dropped. 'Exercise Torpedo Focus' ended on 22 May and over the next 2 days the aircraft were delivered to Goose Bay. The squadron personnel returned briefly to Lossiemouth before themselves starting the annual two-week Goose Bay detachment on 25 June.

Operation Telic 2004

In the 11 months since the previous visit to Al Udeid, conditions at the airbase had improved greatly thanks to a massive influx of US money. The tented accommodation had been replaced by 'Portakabins' and during the detachment the squadron moved into a new operations building. The situation in Iraq had also changed: the insurgency had started and as Flt Lt Froome remarked they were, 'supporting the guys on the ground in a more direct manner, flying in pairs. This meant that one jet would have the recce pod and the other would have the bomb and TIALD pod. We ended up split into a day and night shift, and there was careful management of who flew because we all rapidly approached the 90hr per month limit imposed by GASOs[132]. When the US surged into Fallujah, the British Army moved up to cover the gap to the south of Baghdad left by the USMC going into Fallujah. In early November, we spent a lot of the night tasking covering that move north and subsequent operations. Later November sorties were further north than Baghdad.' Most sorties lasted in excess of 6hr and despite the interesting developments on the ground, the flying was usually rather mundane in nature.

For Flt Lt Froome on the night shift there were, '…surges of adrenaline for the tanking', but little else of interest; however the day shift, seemed to have a more exciting time. On 13 October, Flt Lt Kidd and Sqn Ldr D.J.A. Potter responded to a Troops In Contact (TIC) incident during an 8hr sortie and delivered two EPW II on an arms dump being used by insurgents. On 3 November, Sqn Ldr J.N. Tiddy and Flt Lt Glover were leading a pair of aircraft on a pipeline search over northwest Iraq. The sortie profile included training for a JTAC, but they were also called upon to provide a show of force to support Coalition troops. 'We were flying airborne CAS as a pair for a team of US Joint Terminal Air Controllers (JTACs), when they reported a large group of people moving towards their position.' recalled Flt Lt Glover: 'At that time conducting a Show of Force (SoF) was a fairly commonly used tactic. One aircraft would perform the low-level SoF while the other aircraft remained high to provide cover looking out for [missile] launches, etc. Following our 550kt [low-level pass] directly overhead, with live EPW II's clearly visible, the group seemed to lose interest in the US JTACs and dispersed!' But the excitement was far from over: on recovery to Al Udeid the formation was unable to land there because of heavy thunderstorms over Qatar. They flew a holding pattern for as long as they could, waiting for the storms to clear, but no improvement came. Running critically short of fuel the formation had little choice but to divert to Al Dhafra, nearby in Abu Dhabi. Unbeknown to them, however, they had chosen the day of the funeral of the UAE's president to make their unplanned visit to Abu Dhabi and most of UAE airspace was a no-fly zone. As they entered the airspace the pair of Tornados was intercepted very aggressively by two Mirage 2000s, who clearly suspected that these fully-armed aircraft were up to no good. Eventually they were

A panoramic view from the navigator's seat of a pair of Tornados tanking from a Boeing USAF KC-135 Stratotanker, 'somewhere over Iraq', on 21 October 2004. (Paul Froome)

able to land at Al Dhafra to refuel. Six days later, Sqn Ldr Tiddy and Flt Lt Glover were called in for another show of force, during a 7hr CAS sortie over north-west Iraq, which included three AAR brackets.

90th Anniversary

The beginning of 1995 was dominated by the preparations to celebrate the squadron's 90th Anniversary, masterminded by Sqn Ldr Potter, who was enjoying his third tour with the squadron. The project culminated on the weekend of 8/9 April with an open day followed by an all-ranks dinner, which was attended by a large contingent of former squadron members. The dinner was held in the squadron hangar, which had been decorated in the blue and white squadron colours and a Tornado, painted in a special anniversary colour scheme, as an impressive backdrop.

Earlier in March there had been an MPC, mounted from Lossiemouth and flown as hi-lo-hi sorties. This was amongst the first MPCs to be operated from a home base, rather than deploying to RAF Valley, as had been the case in the past. It was also one of the first firings against the new Mirach target drone, which had replaced the Jindivik in late 2004. With 2 years' allocation of missiles to use up, Flt Lt Froome found, '…it was a busy period for the QWIs, working out the crewings, the profiles, briefings, practices and then supervising the actual sorties themselves.' Once the anniversary celebrations were over the squadron concentrated on the work-up for 'Exercise Maple Flag', which ran from 30 May to 10 June at Cold Lake, Alberta. The exercise was very similar in content to the squadron's participation 7 years previously and most crews managed to complete six or seven exercise sorties. During one of these sorties, on 6 June, Flt Lt Stradling achieved his 3,000th Tornado flying hour.

Tornado GR4 ZG756 flown by Flt Lt P.D. Froome and Sqn Ldr R. Barrett, on 17 March 2005, has the special 90th Anniversary colour scheme; a dark blue spine and tail incorporating the squadron's blue and white diamonds. The aircraft is carrying two Storm Shadow missiles. (Geoffrey Lee)

Apart from 14 Squadron's anniversary, 2005 also marked the 200th Anniversary of the Battle of Trafalgar. The Royal Navy was understandably keen to commemorate this historic victory, so the International Festival of the Sea, held at Portsmouth between 28 June and 3 July, incorporated celebrations of Trafalgar. On 28 June, the royal review of the fleet was followed by spectacular shows and demonstrations in the days that followed, including a daily flypast by RN, Army and RAF aircraft. Four of the squadron's Tornados took part in the display, operating from RNAS Yeovilton for the week. Unfortunately, the weather was not to kind to the event and in the end it was only possible to carry out the full flypast on 3 July. Just 3 days later the squadron was fully involved in 'Exercise Dacian Wolf', a ten-day exercise hosting four MiG-21ML aircraft from 861 Escadrille of the Romanian Air Force. The exercise involved flying mixed sorties with the Romanians, including complex scenarios such as four Tornados, plus four MiG-21s, against a pair of Tornado F3s. In the autumn, Wg Cdr Basnett handed command of the squadron to Wg Cdr A.S. Frost.

Operation Telic 2005/6

'The two-month stint in the Gulf provided new experiences for both old and new members of the squadron,' reported Flt Lt E.B. Williams, 'Tasked in support of coalition forces, a typical sortie would last for approximately 8hr. This could involve photo-reconnaissance and Close Air Support (CAS) anywhere across Iraq. This would also involve air-to-air tanking from UK or US tankers. Whilst long and often mundane, there were short periods of high intensity that served to keep the crews on their toes. A 14 Squadron crew dropped a 1,000lb bomb on Christmas Day – the first UK bomb dropped since 14's last stint in the region! New Years Eve celebrations involved an American dog handling demonstration and an Australian Naval band…New Year's Day saw crews back on task happy to be the RAF's main strike asset in on-going Iraqi operations.'

After returning from Qatar in early February, the squadron's next detachment was to Hill AFB for the annual 'Exercise Torpedo Focus' in March and April. Apart from the exercise being, 'a very worthwhile detachment with some excellent training, especially for the younger squadron members,' Flt Lt Williams also pointed out, '…the area also happens to have some of the best skiing in North America, allowing squadron personnel to experience the joys of downhill skiing!' Over the early summer the squadron carried out two visits to Gibraltar and sent four crews to attend the AAFCE TLP at Florennes, Belgium. The squadron also hosted five McDonnell Douglas F-18 Super Hornets from the US Navy's own '14 Squadron,' VFA-14, for 10 days in June. Flt Lt Williams recorded, '…this [visit] generated some valuable training missions, both with and against the F-18s, and a reasonable amount of socializing.'

Other exercises and detachments included 'Exercise Templar Forge' in September, an air combat training camp, run on similar lines to the old Air Combat Manoeuvring Instumentation (ACMI) camps at Decimomannu in the 1980s and 1990s and a month-long exercise in Abu Dhabi in November. Against this back-drop, 14 Squadron was extremely busy helping to bring into service the Rafael Litening III targeting pod. The pod had been procured to fulfil an Urgent Operational Requirement (UOR) for operations over Iraq as it was clear that the TIALD was not sufficiently effective for the Close Air Support (CAS) and over-watch tasks being undertaken in Iraq. According to Flt Lt R.J. Boardman, 'This step-change from the TIALD pod gave much greater definition of what was happening on the ground (for example from our normal operating height we were able to see if personnel were carrying weapons rather than just about being able to make out a tank from a building with TIALD!) and had the ability to beam, via a data-link, the pictures we were seeing in cockpit directly to the troops on the ground. They used a ruggedized [laptop] called a ROVER[133] to view the full motion video and it gave them a tremendous amount of information and situational awareness.' The Fast Jet Operational Evaluation Unit (FJOEU) had carried out the initial trials with the Litening, but it was left to 14 Squadron, as the Tornado force's experts on designator pods, to determine how best it should be used.

Operation Telic 2007

When the squadron deployed to Al Udeid in January 2007, they were the first unit to use the Litening pod operationally. The situation in Iraq had deteriorated further since the squadron's last visit a year previously and the new pod soon came into its own. Flt Lt Williams described, '…a typical sortie lasted between 7 to 8 hours in duration, with three air-to-air refuelling brackets. We would transit from Al Udeid (Qatar) up into Iraq, where our tasking would typically be in or around the Baghdad area, although missions in support of ground operation elsewhere, such as in support of UK forces in Basra, were not uncommon. The flexibility offered by a pair of

GR4s, meant that we would often end up working as single aircraft on different taskings – typically in support of coalition convoys, armed over-watch of a specific area or to support a TIC (Troops In Contact). The latter would involve an immediate re-tasking in support. The FAC could request a SoF (often specifically requesting a Tornado) – which involves a low-level pass (100-200ft) at something like 550kts plus. This technique is a very effective method of dispersing crowds around any hostile situation. If the situation required further involvement then the GR4 would typically be armed with the [EPW II] and the 27mm gun for strafe attacks. The feedback we received from the FACs within theatre was very positive and the quality of picture delivered by our new capability was the best from any fast air asset. This fact, coupled with the flexibility that we offered, meant that we found ourselves in situations that we would have never previously been utilised in with the TIALD pod.' In fact on the second day of Litening operations, Wg Cdr Frost was asked by the FAC, '…hey, what pod have you guys got there? You are by far the best in theatre; I'm going to request Tornados for all sorties from now on!'

Unfortunately, however, there were still not enough of the new pods to go round, so some sorties were still flown using TIALD. 'This was particularly frustrating on 28 Jan 2007,' recalled Flt Lt Boardman, 'when I was flying in the vicinity of Baghdad with Flt Lt Yeoman[134] and we were called to a TIC that was developing someway to the southwest. On arrival we heard a single F-16 being cleared to conduct a strafing run against a building, having expended all of his bombs already! Taking over from the F-16 as second on the scene we had a paltry load of one Paveway II 1,000lb bomb, the aforementioned TIALD pod to guide it, and about 100 rounds of 27mm HE shells. We were given a very brief update on the situation from [a] ground commander who was in a Humvee positioned in a walled compound to the south of a fairly large village. He said something along the lines of; "the entire village has been overrun by insurgents and anything to the north of my position is hostile – I need you to clear the village!" He could see a hostile "bongo" truck approaching his Humvee and asked us to take this out with our bomb as a matter of some urgency. Having located it on the TIALD pod, Dan said he was captured and, having positioned the aircraft on an attack run, I made the armament switches live. Just about a second before I was about to "commit" the bomb from the aircraft, Dan rather animatedly told me to "stop, stop, stop" as he had seen two [Hughes] AH-64 Apaches fly through his screen, over the vehicle we were about to bomb. Rightly worried about blowing up friendly aircraft, he quickly asked if the FAC had control of the rotary aircraft in the area and he answered in the affirmative. We therefore immediately set-up for another bombing run on the pick-up truck when the same thing happened again. On our third attempt, with the insurgents getting ever closer to the FAC, the pick-up truck entered a small set of trees and disappeared from Dan's TIALD display. Rather frustratingly he would have been easily able to track the vehicle and deliver our bomb onto the target had we been carrying the new Litening III pod. Very soon after this, two "Sandy" (specially trained in the on-scene-commander role) A-10 aircraft arrived on scene and, having many advantages over our single, TIALD equipped Tornado (a Sniper Pod, more fuel, many more weapons and a phenomenally powerful cannon to name but a few) we departed the area to get some more fuel and continue our

'Operation Telic', 25 March 2007. Tornado GR4 ZA589 banks away displaying the typical operational fit comprising a Litening III targeting pod on the left-shoulder pylon, a Joint Reconnaissance Pod on the centreline and an Enhanced Paveway II LGB on the right-shoulder pylon. The flares are being ejected from the BOZ pod on the starboard outer-wing pylon. (Sam Williams)

briefed tasking to the north.' This major action, which was later called the Battle of Najaf, was eventually brought to an end by US reinforcements, but not before one of the Apaches had been shot down by the insurgents.

Two weeks later, two Litening-equipped Tornados were tasked to carry out an IED[135] sweep of a tactical landing ground 12 miles north of Al Amarah just before it was used by a C-130J Hercules. After the operation was delayed because of a problem with the aircraft, the C-130 was fixed sooner than had been anticipated. It therefore set off on task, but unfortunately the Tornado crews had not been updated on the situation. As a result one Tornado was still refuelling when the C-130 started to make its approach and the other (flown by Sqn Ldr Tiddy and Wg Cdr Frost) reached the area just before the transport aircraft touched down. Wg Cdr Frost was able to record the last 30 seconds or so of the transports' approach. As it touched down a massive explosion ripped through the aircraft almost destroying it; miraculously it did not kill anyone on board. Wg Cdr Frost immediately became the on-scene commander and was able to co-ordinate the response to this major incident. The crew and passengers were rescued by another C-130 and since the damaged aircraft was beyond repair, an attempt was made to render it useless to the enemy by blowing it up with explosives. However, this was

A 14 Squadron Tornado GR4 taking part in CAS Exercise at Castle Martin Range, Wales, in late 2008. The aircraft is carrying a 1,500ltr fuel tank and a CBLS on the shoulder pylons. (Sam Williams)

not entirely successful and the following day a 14 Squadron Tornado (flown by Flt Lts C.J. Butterfield and G.E. Bundock) finally destroyed the hulk with an EPW II.

While at Al Udeid the squadron was visited by HRH the Prince of Wales. The other highlight of the operational tour was a violent storm which struck Al Udeid. Winds of up to 80kt destroyed one of the sun shelters and seriously damaged the aircraft inside; other aircraft on the airfield were also damaged, but luckily only one Tornado was affected. The machine was so badly damaged that it had to be returned to UK for repair inside a Boeing C-17 Globemaster II transport aircraft.

After a month of block leave, the squadron's year continued with 'Exercise Neptune Warrior' in the last week of April, and two crews attending AAFCE TLP at Karup, Denmark, in the following month. The routine flying at Lossiemouth included the combat ready work-ups for newly-arrived navigators Flt Lts T.J.B. Dugan and S.B. Williams. June brought 'Exercise Fox Path', a proving exercise for Ground Alert Close Air Support (GCAS) and Emergency CAS (ECAS) and also 'Exercise Anatolian Eagle' in Turkey. The latter was predominantly an air-defence exercise and as Flt Lt Dugan put it, '…we felt we were bulking up other peoples' training!' There was better value training in late July at Davis-Montham AFB, Tucson, the new home for 'Exercise Torpedo Focus'. This exercise gave the crews some useful experience using the TIALD pod to deliver laser-guided weapons, with most crews being allocated several PW IIs to drop. At the end of the exercise on 22 August, the squadron trailled the aircraft home. Crewed with Flt Lt Williams; Flt Lt Boardman, '…led the four-aircraft trail home, suffering a cabin conditioning failure in full hot shortly after leaving Davis-Monthan[136] enroute to Eglin AFB in Florida. We elected to continue the transit but the cockpit had become a greenhouse and we literally baked in the cloudless skies over the southern United States. On arrival we had lost a considerable amount of our bodyweight in sweat and only really cooled down once we had jumped into the frenzied waters of the Gulf of Mexico, stirred by the ferocious Hurricane Fay. We were joined at Eglin by a VC-10 and they provided tanker support for the legs between Eglin and Bermuda, Bermuda to Lajes in the Azores, and Lajes to Marham, arriving home on 25 August.'

September gave the squadron a good workout for what might be expected over Iraq during their next stint on operations. 'Exercise Fast Mover' at the beginning of the month involved working with ground forces on Salisbury Plain, while later in the month the squadron hosted a number of visitors participating in 'Exercise Sky Lance'. Held between 17 and 28 September, 'Exercise Sky Lance' was one of the largest RAF exercises for several years and was run concurrently with the autumn iteration of the naval 'Exercise Neptune Warrior'. Aircraft types taking part in the exercise included BAe Typhoon, Tornado GR4, Harrier GR7/9, Tornado F3, E3D, and Nimrod MR2, along with NATO aircraft such as Rafale, Mirage 2000D, F-15Cs. The exercise involved working within a Coalition framework – in much the same way as the RAF was operating over Iraq – and the sorties were part of large combined air operations packages. During the exercise, the squadron was also able to participate in 'Exercise Flying Rhino', a CAS exercise run by 1 (UK) Armoured Division working with FACs deployed in the area around Loch Ewe, near Gairloch, Scotland.

Operation Telic 2008

The winter months gave the squadron an opportunity to consolidate with routine training at Lossiemouth, although during February 2008 it was also involved with a trial to investigate the effects of flying extended (in excess of 4hr) sorties with the Brimstone anti-armour missile. The following month, Wg Cdr S. E. Reeves took command of the squadron, just 4 days before the unit deployed to Al Udeid to take over responsibility for 'Operation Telic' from 12 Squadron on 23 March. The major difference in this detachment from previous ones, was that being a little later in the year it was considerably hotter, with temperatures reaching 40°C towards the end of the detachment. Another change since the squadron's previous visit was the start, in late March, of 'Operation Knight's Charge', an offensive by the Iraqi Army to reclaim Basra from the militias who had largely wrested control of the city from the British Army. Many of the squadron's sorties were flown in direct support of this operation, providing CAS and tactical reconnaissance for Iraqi Army units. However, despite this activity on the ground, Flt Lt Dugan found that most sorties were routine, '…you prepared for the worst but the worst would only happen once every hundred flights so for the rest were actually the same procedure time after time after time.' The challenge for the crew was to stay alert to what was happening on the ground while they were on station overhead for up to 6hr at a time. Most sorties were flown as pairs with the Tornados carrying a Litening pod and EPW II, although for some missions the Raptor or the new Digital JRP (DJRP) might be carried. As previously, the sorties began with a transit northwards past Bahrain and Kuwait to the tanker 'tow lines' on the Iraqi border south of Basra. From here the Tornados would continue to the operating area, which would usually be around Basra, but tasking as far away as Baghdad, or even Kirkuk, was not unknown.

The nature of the task meant that Tornado crews had to be adaptable: CAS work over urban areas was difficult enough, but it was further complicated by the variable standard of some FACs. Sqn Ldr I.A. Davis described a sortie over Basra on 1 April with Flt Lt Williams: 'The sortie was relatively uneventful for the first part. We were 40 minutes into our first CAS tasking over Basra and although the city was busy with ground callsigns scattered around there were no major incidents and I was just starting to think of tanking and having a well-needed pee when we were tasked to search for a group of personnel who had been firing RPGs at Iraqi forces. The grid reference we were given was poor and the talk-on from the FAC was also rather poor, which does not build a huge amount of confidence between the aircrew and the chap on the ground. All of a sudden Sam [Williams] identified a group of three personnel running away from the grid we had been passed and [then] hiding in a building. He generated co-ordinates for this building and passed them to the FAC. The FAC instantly requested we strafe the insurgents if they left the building! This was downtown Basra and our gun has some collateral damage implications…we handed over [to a US aircraft] and climbed to the tanker. We filled to full, I managed a pee after we had left, and we descended into the melee again.

'The previous event had all but ended by the time we finished filling with fuel but… [in the meantime a] UAV had identified a rocket pointing at Basra Air Base and was trying to get someone to bomb it before it went off. The co-ordinates he generated were in error by up to 300m and a Predator UAV and a US Apache helo were attempting unsuccessfully to get "eyes on" the target. We orbited several times over the area and it was clear that the other assets were the main focal point for the JTAC, but as we orbited Sam highlighted a linear feature that when we looked closer could well have been a rocket. We told the FAC and after a short confirmatory talk-on he was happy we had the rocket. He quickly cleared the other assets out of the area and …[authorized our attack] with all the details including our updated co-ordinates, which was amusing as he had to get the co-ordinates from us to then pass them back to us to make the attack legal. The target was on the edge of the "Shia flats" and when I requested the Line of Attack (LOA) for the strike the FAC was happy for us to nominate our own. We went to 20 miles from the target and spun round…there was a massive thump as the EPW II sailed off to the sand below. A few seconds later Sam made every WSO's favourite call, "Splash". The bomb worked according to Raytheon's promotional manual and hit the target spot on. There was an almighty explosion.'

For Flt Lt Dugan the 'once every hundred flights' came around on 4 May, when he was also flying with Sqn Ldr Davis. By then the Iraqi Army had cleared most of Basra and was pushing through the northerly outskirts of Al Latif. Sqn Ldr Davis and Flt Lt Dugan had taken off from Al Udeid alone[137] after their wingman ground aborted with a hydraulic snag. After refuelling south of Basra they carried out a pre-reconnaissance of two buildings, which were about to be searched by Iraqi troops, and were then handed over to another JTAC. The new task was a typical one: to perform a sweep along a route to ensure that it was clear of suspicious activity before it was used by an Iraqi Army convoy. Starting at one end of the road, which ran just to the west of Al Latif, Davis and Dugan began to search its length. They were looking for anything that seemed out of place, although as Dugan commented, '…one person's perspective of "out of place" is different from another person's.' Not far along the route Flt Lt Dugan found, '…what looks like a pillbox…the size of four portaloos together…with a person moving around it. It looks odd because the person has a jacket over his head…he looks as if sheltering from the sun, going in and out of the pillbox – it looks a bit odd.' Sqn Ldr Davis kept the Tornado overhead while Flt Lt Dugan monitored this unusual individual over the next few minutes. After wandering around the pillbox, he walked a few metres to a culvert under the road. Sqn Ldr Davis was also able to watch the unfolding events from the front cockpit: '…all of a sudden, someone appeared from the outlet pipe which got our interest. Initially we thought they may be trying to plant an IED under the road and called all the details in to our FAC who was already watching via the ROVER link on our pod. He in turn informed us that a local Iraqi Army (IA) unit was on its way. Within 5 minutes another bloke appeared walking down the road and chatting with the three existing personnel. This got more suspicious when, after walking between the building and the pipe for 10 minutes, a car pulled up and all the personnel climbed in and drove off. I was frustrated at this time because it looked like the IA would not make it in time to pick these fellas up and we could quite easily lose them if they entered a town.' By now the Tornado was running short of fuel, but Sqn Ldr Davis managed to persuade their TriStar tanker to leave the towline and come towards them so that they could refuel over Basra itself. 'We were not going to leave this vehicle until we had to,' continued Davis. 'Our luck was in; the suspects drove about 800m and then reversed up to a crossroads. A yet unseen man walked down one of the roads and was greeted by his colleagues as another unseen man walked out of a field to be greeted by the suspects.' Dugan tracked the suspected terrorists as they started to walk to various discrete points in the open area beyond the road, apparently retrieving items. The Litening pod enabled him to copy down the exact co-ordinates of each of the locations that were visited. 'By this stage,' Davis continued, 'the tanker was above us, but we could not leave the vehicle. The IA passed the static vehicle twice before they confronted the suspects. You can imagine the language in the cockpit after they drove past the suspects we had been tracking for the last hour.' A Predator UAV arrived on the scene to relieve the Tornado so that it could refuel. While they took on 16,000lb of fuel Sqn Ldr Davis reported, '... Trev managed to keep the pod on the target and kept me updated on the progress and we weaved through the bubbling cumulonimbus clouds that were hampering the tanker crews' efforts to maintain VMC. When we arrived back on station the area was crawling with IA searching the vehicle and surrounding area.' With the help of the Litening pod and the co-ordinates that Dugan had copied down, the crew was able to help the Iraqi Army unit carry out an effective search. Shortly afterwards, the FAC reported that they had found a major weapons cache. Hidden in the ground near to the road were a heavy machine gun with twenty boxes of ammunition, seventeen 50mm mortars and twenty 82mm mortars.

Other highlights of the detachment included, on 4 April, a spectacular 'fireworks show.' Flt Lt Boardman described how, '...after a routine landing a USAF [Rockwell] B-1B Lancer aircraft suffered some sort of a failure to its steering that caused it veer off the taxiway onto the rough, desert ground. This meant its undercarriage collapsed and it subsequently came to rest on some concrete blocks that both ruptured one of its fuel tanks and set off its self-protection flares. The crew managed to get out of the aircraft and their mad dash to safety alerted a group of Australian engineers working on a nearby Hercules to the danger and they too managed to leg-it away as the fuel caught light. The fire made short work of the B-1B and cooked-off its 22,000lb bomb load over the next few hours to give the majority of the camp an incredibly spectacular fireworks display (although I managed to sleep through the lot).' On 28 April, the squadron was also privileged to host HRH Prince William when he stopped off at Al Udeid while returning from a brief visit to Afghanistan. The operational deployment came to an end in early June and 14 Squadron's personnel were relieved to leave the heat of Qatar for the cooler temperatures of a Scottish summer.

The deployment to Al Udeid in 2008, proved to be the squadron's last participation in 'Operation Telic.' Tornado operations over Iraq ceased in May 2009, ending almost 20 years of involvement by 14 Squadron. However, as the requirements for air support over Iraq waned, so those over Afghanistan waxed. British forces had been involved in Afghanistan since 2001 and RAF Harrier aircraft had been operating over the country since September 2004. With the end of 'Operation Telic', it was decided to replace the Harrier detachment at Kandahar during 2009 with Tornado GR4. Thus 'Operation Herrick', the British commitment in Afghanistan, became the squadron's operational focus over the next 2 years.

On returning from Iraq, the squadron started practicing tactics for using the new Brimstone Dual Mode Seeker (DMS) weapon which had been developed for use in 'low collateral' environments where a 1,000lb bomb was too destructive. Intended originally as a 'fire and forget' weapon with its own millimetric radar seeker, the Brimstone DMS was also fitted with a laser receiver, so that it could be directed onto its target by the Litening pod, thus ensuring a very high degree of accuracy. The squadron would later use this weapon in Afghanistan. The annual air-combat training camp, 'Exercise Templar Forge' took place for 14 days in September at Akrotiri, Cyprus, where, apart from the flying, the notable event was the 'Navigators' Union Dinner'. This function was arranged by Flt Lt Dugan. Non-navigators were given their invitations on large heavy objects – and they had to bring their invitation with them to be able to attend. Aircraft steps, 1,500ltr drop tanks, filing cabinets, fire doors and Tornado main wheels were among the items which were manhandled to the venue by pilots, engineers and administrative staff.

The autumn brought with it 'Exercise Joint Warrior' (in October) and a tactical-leadership training exercise the following month. As the year's end approached a new Squadron Standard, the squadron's third, was presented by HRH the Duke of York at a parade on 10 December and the old Standard was laid up at St Aidan's Church, Lossiemouth.

Afghanistan

As part of the preparations for 'Operation Herrick', most of 14 Squadron deployed to Barksdale AFB, on the outskirts of Shreveport, Louisiana, in January 2009, to participate in 'Exercise Green Flag East'. The aircraft started the trail out on 9 January, arriving 3 days later in time for the start of the exercise on 15 January. Although this exercise shared the same name as the EW-orientated exercise run from Nellis AFB in the 1980s and 1990s, it was in fact completely different: this exercise was specifically designed to train aircrew, JTACs and ground forces in the techniques of urban CAS. Exercise flying took place both over the local towns of Oakdale and DeRidder, where scenarios included convoy support, route sweep and counter IED missions and also over a purpose-built 'CAS town' on the nearby weapons ranges. In the latter, ground troops were given various scenarios which mirrored what they might expect on operations; invariably the scenario developed so that air support would be required, ranging from SoF to dropping EPW II. Another novelty for the Tornado crews was carrying out strafe attacks on moving targets on the US Army range at Fort Polk. Here, remote car-sized targets could be driven along rails to expose crews to a little-practiced weapons profile. As Wg Cdr Reeves put it at the time, '...this has been a fantastic exercise that has enabled crews to train in a realistic joint environment for the full range of airpower tasks – from presence right through to lethal force – that we face on current operations. Green Flag-East has provided the best CAS training facility I have seen.'

The beginning of 2009 marked a fundamental change in the employment of the Tornado. From the early days of the 'Cold War' through the Gulf War, the subsequent operations in Iraq and the Kosovo campaign, the aircraft had been used in the interdiction role as part of larger packages of aircraft on pre-planned missions. These multi-aircraft Combined Air Operations (COMAOs) were usually independent of ground operations, with a clear demarcation between ground and air forces. Even during the later phases of 'Operation Telic', aircraft launched on a pre-planned route and although they would generally work with a JTAC or FAC, the air operations were not fully integrated into the land campaign. In Afghanistan, all that would have to change and the squadron's routine flying changed from the pre-planned interdiction flying of the previous 25 years to a much more fluid CAS role where there was no 'line on the map' at the start of the sortie.

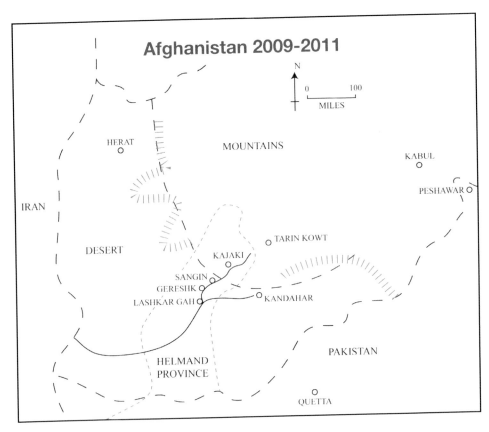

Crews had to understand what was happening on the ground and also had to know how to interpret the Rules of Engagement (RoE) in complex and dynamic situations.

The first Tornado detachment in Afghanistan, planned for the spring of 2009, was to have been led by 14 Squadron. Wg Cdr Reeves and Sqn Ldr A. MacDonald had visited Kandahar for 4 days in November 2008 to make the initial preparations for the Tornado deployment. However, during the visit Sqn Ldr MacDonald could see, '...the field was undergoing radical development, and at the time the main roads on base were dirt tracks. The [base] was being prepared for Tornado, complete with sun shelters and support ops areas. When we visited, the first layers of concrete were being laid, but the temperatures at night were falling fast and there was an expectation that winter would slow work. We stood on one of the large berms, separating Tango ramp from the neighbouring Dutch F-16 ramp and I realized then that it was going to take longer than two months to get the Tornado in country... And, of course, this was right. Before Christmas, possibly on the strength of the visit (attended by some higher ranking decision-makers from air command) the Tornado deployment was put on delay, mostly due to infrastructure, but such a delay also allowed some of the "new" stuff we were due to receive to come on line. This included Brimstone DMS and PW IV. Both were undergoing trials, and the longer we waited, the greater the certainty that Tornado would deploy with them from the off.' In the event, the task of leading the Tornado deployment to Kandahar in the summer of 2009 fell to 12 Squadron, but it would be supplemented by a number of experienced Tornado crews from across the Lossiemouth Wing: 14 Squadron provided four crews. Flt Lt Boardman, '…worked closely with 12(B) Sqn throughout the year and I flew a passenger sortie with the Brigadier of 19 Light Brigade who would be commanding the troops on the ground when the Tornado took over in Afghanistan. We also deployed to Marham in January 2009 and Lyneham in March 2009 in support of 19 Light Brigade, who were conducting their Mission Rehearsal Exercises (MRX) on Salisbury Plain at those times.'

Meanwhile, the squadron participated in 'Exercise Joint Warrior' from Lossiemouth in May and 'Exercise Templar Forge,' the annual air-combat camp at Akrotiri which took place the following month. This year, the squadron also took some FACs with them to Cyprus so that crews could perfect some urban CAS techniques in addition to the air combat. There were also some dissimilar air combat sorties against Harrier GR9s. Wg Cdr Reeves, who arrived in Cyprus on 19 June (in time for an air combat sortie before the 'Navigators' Union Dinner' that evening), had just returned from Afghanistan where he and Sqn Ldr MacDonald oversaw the final preparations for the transfer from Harrier to Tornado at Kandahar.

Sqn Ldr MacDonald, '…spent around 4 weeks sorting the handover, preparing the ops rooms, planning computers, lockers, living accommodation, all of the trivia required to ensure that the arriving personnel could start flying immediately, as the Harrier would fly a couple of joint missions with the Tornado and then depart almost immediately.' On 14 June, eight Tornados left Lossiemouth to join the 904 Expeditionary Air Wing (EAW) at Kandahar. They arrived in Afghanistan 2 days later after a night stop at Akrotiri and flew their first operational sortie on 24 June. 'When the Tornado force arrived,' continued Sqn Ldr MacDonald, 'we in-briefed to the theatre and started flying almost straight away. I was crewed with Charlie Butterfield [Flt Lt C. Butterfield]. We crewed up with a 12 Squadron crew and flew as a dedicated pair, which meant eating, sleeping (same four-man room) and working together. This worked really well. The flying task was interesting and busy. CAS stacks ended up being just that, and without data-link to see the other players in the area, it was sometimes a little unnerving as an unexpected player shot through our allotted airspace. Reapers [UAV] and helicopters below us, F-16s and B-1Bs above us, all itching to get involved. I remember seeing an awful lot of burning APCs at the TICs we were called to; it was quite depressing, and there was often nothing we could do to help.'

Much of the work of the Tornado detachment was in western Kandahar Province, only a few miles away from Kandahar City, where the Taliban was pressing ISAF[138] forces and attempting to extend its control. Most sorties were in direct support of ground patrols, frequently providing armed over-watch for troops engaged by Taliban groups; they were also often re-tasked to cover ISAF convoys which had been involved in roadside IED incidents. Often a Show of Presence flypast would deter the enemy, but if necessary this tactic could be escalated into the more intimidating Show of Force and, ultimately, the use of weapons, known colloquially as 'going kinetic.' Missions over Afghanistan were flown in pairs, in aircraft usually equipped with the Litening pod and armed with the new PW IV 500lb laser-guided bomb and the Brimstone anti-armour missile. Traditional reconnaissance sorties were also routinely flown using the Raptor pod. Most sorties were supported by air-to-air refuelling, often from KC-10 and KC-135 tankers, giving typical sortie lengths of between 3 and 5hr.

Apart from the flying task, the Tornado detachment also mounted ground-based CAS (GCAS), which involved the crews sitting at readiness awaiting the order to scramble if emergency air support was needed at short notice. On 29 June, Flt Lt Stradling led the detachment's first operational GCAS scramble to respond to two TIC incidents involving the Dutch contingent. During the sortie they carried out a SoF over enemy positions near Tarin Kowt, some 70 miles north of Kandahar in the province of Urozgan. The low pass over the enemy positions proved enough to break the contact. This province was actually in the area of responsibility of Australian forces, illustrating that although the British Army's operations were largely confined to Helmand Province, the RAF aircraft were tasked over a much wider area. Stradling completed his 4,000th Tornado flying hour[139] the following day while leading a CAS sortie, firstly over Kuhak, some 95 miles south of Herat and then Nad-e-Ali, near Laskar Gah in Helmand Province. On 8 July the crew was scrambled from GCAS again, as the Number 2 in a pair to support a TIC near Shamaz, near Gereshk, some 70 miles west of Kandahar.

Flying almost daily sorties meant that crews soon racked up the flying hours, and 40 or 50 hrs a month were usual on operations. Operations continued in the hours of darkness and on the night of 31 July, a 14 Squadron crew was called in to support a TIC in the semi-rural area some 60 miles north-west of Kandahar. The navigator described the unfolding action as, '...a night drop against a group of two or three insurgents who were hiding against a compound wall, having previously been [firing] against friendly forces in the Kajaki area. We had previously been supporting a group of British forces on a night task and were called off to go and assist with a possible TIC. We were given confirmation of the position by a B-1B, and then set up for the attack. It took about 20 minutes for us to get permission to drop so close to a compound, but once it was received we dropped a single PW IV against the position. On completion of the task we then returned to the previous task before returning to KAF[140], with a sortie duration of about 5hrs.' Over the next 3 weeks the crew flew a variety of daylight missions, including Raptor, CAS and GCAS sorties, which took them over much of Kandahar Province as well as Helmand to the west. Their last sortie of the tour was flown on 20 August during which they intervened in two TICs, carrying out two strafe attacks on enemy positions near Sangin where insurgents were using the cover of a hedgerow to fire upon ISAF troops: '...20 August 2009 was election day and one of the busiest sorties I have ever flown in a Tornado,' reported the navigator, 'We were sent to a number of different tasks as TICs developed and closed with amazing speed. The last event of the sortie was to support a TIC near Sangin, where the Brits had taken casualties earlier in the day and they were again taking incoming fire from an unknown position. We did two high angle strafe attacks against small wooded areas close to a friendly Patrol Base. Our Number 2 also did three attacks against similar positions, in the hope of flushing them out, although nothing was seen. We were extremely low on fuel when we eventually handed over to a pair of A-10s.'

Meanwhile, Flt Lt Boardman and Sqn Ldr Abbott had arrived in theatre. Flt Lt Boardman recalled that they, '...flew thirty missions on Operation Herrick, all bar three being at night, and we soon found that the sorties were remarkably similar to those we had flown over Iraq on Operation Telic, without the lengthy transit at the start and end of each sortie. Indeed, instead of spending nearly 1½hrs transiting up the North Arabian

A Tornado GR4 accompanied by a US Navy Grumman EA-6B Prowler over Helmand in August 2009. (Chris Stradling)

Gulf and then refuelling, you could get your tasking on the ground prior to take-off at Kandahar and be "on-task" a couple of minutes after that… .

'The nights were generally quiet in Afghanistan and the main sortie of note for us came on 15 September 2009 when we were called to a convoy that had struck an IED, had lost their FAC and were convinced they were being ambushed! We were the only aircraft[141] anywhere near their location so we were vectored to their last known position. This grid reference turned out to be massively in error and there was nothing to be found on the Litening III pod when we arrived. The soldier on the radio (untrained in talking to aircraft) was somewhat shaken, did not know his location and had difficulty describing to us where he was. We ascertained that he was near a burning vehicle on a single-track road near a wadi. Given that none of these features were present on the Litening III pods considerable field of view, we were at a bit of a loss as to where the convoy actually was. Under my Night Vision Goggles (NVGs) I could see two lights in the desert that could potentially have been something burning. One was many miles to the east, the other even further to the northwest. Looking on my map I thought there was more likely to be a road to the northwest so plumped for that one and flew towards it. As we approached the light source it seemed that it was indeed likely to be from something burning and I directed Phil's Litening III pod onto it using the infra-strobe facility that is only visible through NVGs. We attempted to calm the soldier down by letting him know we had found the convoy and were directly overhead. The noise of our jet went some way to convincing him and he then said that they were coming under small arms attack from the south. We let him know we would be doing a thorough search of the area with the Litening III pod and that we had not seen anyone or anything in the immediate vicinity during our transit to them. Over the next few minutes, Phil expanded his search and found nothing within 5 miles of the convoy, but they still felt they were under attack and were firing into the night with their weapons. We flew low over the top of the area to increase the noise from our aircraft and this seemed to quieten the situation down. Back at height, Phil spotted a vehicle approaching the convoy some 10 miles down the road from where they had come and his headlights would have occasionally shone through the trees to the south of the convoy, potentially giving them the impression that they were being fired upon. We relayed this information to the soldier on the ground and he asked us to stop the vehicle from getting too close to their stricken vehicles. We thought about how to achieve this and we ended up diving down in front of the vehicle, turning our lights on and dropping flares. We then made some noise over the top of the vehicle in order to attract the driver's attention if he had failed to see us initially! This seemed to have the desired effect as the vehicle stopped straight after we flew over it and soon afterwards turned off its lights. We conducted a second pass over the vehicle to make him aware we could still see him and on this occasion he put on his hazard warning lights and remained stationary throughout the rest of the time we were in the area. The rescue helicopters arrived shortly afterwards and picked up the casualties from the convoy and we helped escort the remaining vehicles to the relative safety of their compound.' Boardman and Abbott flew their last 'Operation Herrick' sortie on 12 October.

In contrast, Flt Lt P. T. Rossiter flew almost exclusively by day, with much of the tasking in the area of the Tangi Valley, to the northeast of Kabul. Here, Shows of Presence and SoF were regular features of daily flying. 'We did quite a few SoF there as they were pretty nervous. They had been receiving mortar fire [into the base] over a fairly sustained period of time. We found ourselves conducting a SoF at the end of sorties over anything suspect. This was because, unlike Helmand, they did not have a stack of aircraft over their location the whole time. This meant that when you were leaving they were often on their own for a while, although jets could get to them fairly quickly if required.'

Back at Lossiemouth, the rest of the squadron had been involved in CAS training with 'Exercise Flying Rhino' near Loch Ewe during the month of September and 'Exercise Joint Warrior' in October. Except for the four crews who had been selected to augment the 12 Squadron detachment, 14 Squadron's personnel found themselves to have an extended break from operations, as the next roulement for them to Afghanistan was not scheduled until October 2010. This breathing space gave the squadron the opportunity to concentrate on its routine training task over the next 12 months. For newly arrived squadron QWI Flt Lt J. A. J. Robins-Walker, '...this meant a good tempo of training and every hour flown had to really count. I was acutely aware of the value required each time a junior member flew.' The APC, 'Exercise Torpedo Focus', was held at Davis-Monthan AFB from 19 February until 10 March. 'We had a great selection of weapons available to us,' continued Flt Lt Robins-Walker, 'and although only the PW IV and strafe were the Afghanistan relevant weapons (unfortunately every DMS Brimstone was required in theatre and I do not think we would have ever got a range clearance for it!) it meant everybody got to experience flying a heavily-laden aircraft, with live weapons on board from an airfield at a similar altitude to KAF and with similar temperatures. Although seen as "old school" and soon due to be dropped from the inventory, nothing developed trust in your weaponeering plan and respect for the limits better than being in a four-ship all dropping live 1,000lb retard weapons at

Sqn Ldr T. Hill and Flt Lt B.J. Dempster over the Chalap Dalan mountains, to the north of Kandahar, during a mission to the north-west corner of Afghanistan on 13 November 2010. The aircraft, Tornado GR4 ZD801, is in a typical 'Operation Herrick' fit, equipped with a Litening III pod and armed with two Paveway IV laser-guided bombs and Dual-Mode Seeker Brimstone missiles. (Jameel Janjua)

minimum release height and minimum safe separation between aircraft. Sometimes the old stuff really is the best for teaching!!

'Although there were not many hours going around this was the best flying I had ever experienced, as I could teach and assess all aspects. There was plenty of OLF, EO low-level, complex CAS developing our moving target tactics with DMS Bimstone, night strafe as well as the more traditional Tornado strike sorties using PW III, Stormshadow and ALARM. 14 Sqn was thriving with high morale amongst both the aircrew and the engineers.'

The next major detachment was to Namest in the Czech Republic, about 20 miles west of Brno. This iteration of 'Exercise Flying Rhino', held between 29 April and 21 May, was the eighth joint exercise with the Czech armed forces and included the co-ordination artillery firing with CAS sorties. It involved more than 2,000 UK troops, as well as personnel from the Czech Republic, Denmark, Lithuania, Slovakia and the US. The object of the exercise was to simulate the operational environment over Helmand and many of the FACs were being trained to deploy to Afghanistan soon afterwards.

Operation Herrick 2010

During the summer of 2010, the ISAF had started a campaign, known as 'Operation Hamkari', to take back western Kandahar from the Taliban. This fertile region, extending from Kandahar City some 30 miles westwards, lies on either side of the Arghandab River and is bounded in the south by the Dowry River (with desert beyond) and to the north (with mountains beyond) by Highway 1, the main roadway between Kandahar and Herat.

Heavy vegetation gives some cover from aerial surveillance and the maze of compounds and villages had made it ideally suited for the Taliban to convert into strongpoints and IED factories. They also defended the area with extensive IED belts and booby-traps. From this secure base the Taliban was able to control most of the region, including most of Highway 1. However, by the beginning of October, ISAF ground forces were starting to clear Zhari and Panjwai, two districts lying roughly 15 miles west of Kandahar City. Much of the task during 14 Squadron's deployment to Afghanistan would be in support of 'Operation Hamkari' and ISAF ground forces.

Although the squadron officially assumed responsibility for the 904 EAW Tornado component on 16 October, the units crews had started to arrive in theatre in the weeks beforehand. It was quickly apparent that operations over Afghanistan would be very different from anything that the squadron's crews had previously experienced. As Flt Lt Robins-Walker explained, '…the software, weapons and tactics were developing quickly as the [Tornado] force transitioned from what was suitable in Iraq to the demands of Afghanistan. The game was changing fast. No more droning up the North Arabian Gulf for a predictable 8hr sortie over Iraq, [with little] chance of "going kinetic" and even if you did get the opportunity the EPW II was usually just too big for the urban environment. Now you were in the country, the sorties were shorter but far more dynamic and you needed to be ready from the moment the wheels were in the well as holding QRA meant you could be dropping a weapon within minutes of being airborne. Whilst [that] now gave us a lot more room for manoeuvre we really needed to understand the detail to ensure we could make it work for us. Plenty of time was spent discussing scenarios with advice from the legal team to ensure we were empowered to make decisions when the time came.'

The squadron's first sortie of the detachment, a Raptor mission over Helmand, was led on 6 October by Sqn Ldr Kidd and Flt Lt Stradling, with Flt Lt Robins-Walker and Flt Lt P.J. Todhunter on their wing. Five days later, the Canadian exchange officer, Capt J.J. Janjua's first sortie took him over Panjwai, where by coincidence his own countrymen were on the ground. He noted in his diary afterwards that he, '…was particularly happy to see that the mission was in support of 1 Royal Canadian Regiment Battle Group, operating within Task Force Kandahar. There was not much going on in that area today, and most of the mission was spent searching roads for IEDs or anything else suspicious. However, despite the lack of 'action,' I was pretty pleased to be "supporting" Canadian soldiers on the ground. Another thing that I noticed on my first trip was how this part of Afghanistan is quite pretty actually. It is not a whole lot like home, but it is kind of like parts of the States that I have flown in. It is very populated around Kandahar City and all of the buildings and compounds look very similar. Just adjacent to Kandahar City are really neat mountains and sharp hills in almost all directions. South of KAF[142], there is a line in the sand that runs northwest-southeast that is the boundary between a "Red Desert" to the south and KAF and the city to the north. So, in its own right, this place is beautiful. It is easy to forget that it has been ravaged by war for the last several decades, at least. I guess that is the difference of perspective in this case – it is easy to forget where you are from the sanctuary of the cockpit.'

Each day the ground forces from the whole of ISAF put their bids for air support to the Combined Air Operations Centre (CAOC) in Al Udeid, which then decided which units would receive air support – and which would not. Apart from manning

GCAS, the squadron launched three pairs daily to cover the tasking from the CAOC. Typically, a pair of Tornados would be assigned to a JTAC to provide armed over-watch, much as they had been over Iraq, using the Litening pod for surveillance and being ready to intervene directly if needed. The usual weapons fit for an 'Operation Herrick' sortie was two PW IV and one or two Brimstone DMS rounds as well as the gun. The small PW IV was much more suited to low-collateral operations than had been the case with the heavier EPW II and its accuracy was further enhanced by the ability to use hybrid laser/GPS guidance. The Brimstone DMS had also proven to be the ideal weapon in theatre because of its accuracy and also because the shaped-charge warhead limited its lethal effect to a very small area.

While operating as a pair, the Tornados 'flip-flopped' between the tasking area and the tanker to ensure that at least one aircraft was always on scene. Within each aircraft the pilot took responsibility for safety, deconfliction with other airspace users via the local air controller and kept track of the fuel state and the relative position of the tanker; the back-seater communicated directly with the JTAC or FAC and was the person who received the 'Nine-Line' or legal authorization to attack. Sqn Ldr T. Hill reckoned that each crew might expect at least one 'kinetic' event during their operational detachment and, '…no matter your experience, you could still feel the hairs on the back of your neck standing up when you heard the Nine-Line, knowing that this was for real and that on the ground someone's life could be depending on you.'

In addition to routine armed over-watch missions, crews might expect to be tasked for three Raptor sorties each week. Again these were flown as pairs and since the 'stinger' in the Number 2 slot was not critical, as had been the 'shooter' in the early days over Iraq, that crew would often free-call nearby JTACs to see if they might be used. This is exactly what happened on 20 October when Capt Janjua was flying, '…my first Raptor Reconnaissance flight in theatre. The recce task is very boring, and the most fun was trying to tank in this bitch of a fit on a KC-135 BDA[143] – the Iron Maiden. It was a little work, but workable. As this was going on, [Number 2] were pimping themselves out to the nearest JTAC. To my surprise, they contacted me letting me know that they were going kinetic…Post-flight, I learned that they had conducted two strafe passes into a tree line where British troops were taking fire from.'

The eyes of the whole RAF detachment at Kandahar were glued to the television on 19 October, waiting for the announcement of the decisions taken in the government's strategic defence and security review. There was jubilation amongst the Tornado crews that the Tornado GR4 had survived the review in favour of the Harrier. This decision was, for anyone who had been involved with Tornado from its earliest days, the long-overdue recognition of the aircraft's incredible versatility. However, any elation was muted by the realization that the statement included a reduction of the Tornado force by two squadrons, which might well include the loss of their own unit.

A week later another crew used the gun for the first time in anger, having carried out their first show of force the previous night. They were Number 2 of a pair, which was providing over-watch for a routine night patrol in Kandahar province for ISAF troops. 'We worked as pairs, only really splitting to pop to the tanker for some fuel,' recalled the pilot. 'Whilst at the tanker you would try and keep a radio on the JTAC's frequency to maintain some awareness of what was happening. Unfortunately we were out of range, so refuelled and headed back to hear our formation mates taking a Nine-Line for a strafe attack! So we arrive slightly on the back foot, trying to quickly get up to speed on the situation. The ground forces are taking fire from insurgents in a tree line and request a strafe attack from each aircraft. RoE discussed and confirmed, Eddie and Dan are in first and Jim and I follow about 30 seconds back. It is extremely dark, the NVGs help but are struggling with the low light levels. The WSOs[144] have the target on the Litening III pod and once you are in the dive as a pilot you have to have complete trust in the WSO as the point he is marking is shown as a cross in the HUD. By day and on a good night, you can obtain the target visually and adjust as required, but on this occasion it was a case of putting the strafe pipper in the cross and trying to fly the rest on numbers in the HUD! I see the lead aircraft rounds striking the ground and that helps confirm the location of the target area. I tip into the 30° strafe attack and pull the trigger, the gun fires and then stops, in the split second it takes to register this, the gun fires again, so I carry on down the dive… I recover at the minimum range as best as I can judge it and the GPWS warning goes off adding to the drama…What a rush! The JTAC is satisfied with the result, the firing has stopped and it has enabled his troops to move into a better position. Our [time] with this JTAC is over and we move onto another area to provide over-watch. A much quieter area to the south of KAF and the visibility is much improved. The troops are suspicious of some activity nearby and request a show of force, we oblige and the culprits disappear not to be seen again.'

Apart from using the gun in anger, crews were able to practice night-strafe attacks using the range at Tarnak, just south of Kandahar airfield. The range comprised a large complex of buildings which had been used as a training camp by Al Qaeda. Flt Lt Robins-Walker commented, '…the range is so close to the airfield that when sat outside the accommodation block at night you could watch a [Tornado] in the strafe pattern at Tarnak and hear the impact of the HE shells. Even better when there was an AC-130 gunship in there firing its 105mm cannon!'

When the Tornado was originally introduced into service, the heart of the machine was the TFR and the night/all-weather capability that it endowed. Thirty years on the TFR might have seemed to be archaic and outdated by medium-level tactics and modern electro-optical equipment; however, in Afghanistan, the TFR provided the Tornados of 904 EAW with a uniquely useful capability. Flying among hills and with weather or visibility frequently very restricted it would be impossible for other types to get to low-level safely to perform a show of force, but the TFR provided an ideal way of doing so. One of the squadron's navigators, Flt Lt C. W. Baber, pointed out, for example, '…if somebody asks you to do an over-flight at the bottom of a valley, in the dark at 250ft, there is absolutely no other way of doing it. Other folks flying at 1,000ft do not get the same kind of impact.' This technique was put to good use on the nights of 3 and 8 November by Flt Lt Robins-Walker, who confirmed, '…the TFR is as useful as it has ever been. To still achieve the effect of a show of force at night/IMC/very low light levels is invaluable and was of great comfort to the coalition troops. Although over the flat terrain of Kandahar province both these were on particularly dark nights with low visibility due to mist/dust supporting the Canadians to the southwest of KAF who were concerned about IED teams laying a trap for their route the following morning. The insurgents knew when the weather was poor at night there was less aerial activity, except for when the mighty Tornado GR4 was down in the dust at 250ft and 600 kt! Flt Lt Roughton was with me on both occasions and we elected to use the TFR to get us down to 250ft and then monitor with the NVGs, and if we could take over manually we would to allow us greater manoeuvre freedom should there be any small arms fire. Our wingman provided over-watch by monitoring the area with the Litening pod and the JTAC had informed us of some large unlit masts in the area so arranged a line of attack that would keep us clear. Even then we felt a long way from the robust obstruction warning database available in the UK, so our eyes were on stalks for anything that the TF might not pick up! During the sortie we swapped roles and our wingman also completed shows of force to maintain the noise and presence footprint for the duration of our [time on station].'

On 10 November, Capt Janjua was once again flying a Raptor sortie when, '...for the second time running, my wingman was briefed to go and do something useful with his fuel rather than follow me around like a lost dog. Well, for the second time in a row while on a recce mission, my wingman did just that. They ended up dropping a PW IV on a compound that was a known weapons cache. It was funny, because Sausage and I had been flying nearby at the beginning of the flight, and [he] had noted some smoke out the window. He asked if I thought it was a fire. I replied that that was not a fire, and that it was definitely a bomb. I knew that [Number 2] was working close by. Upon landing, we learned the details…the video footage and subsequent BDA was great, and the bad guys are seen returning to the scene to find out what is left of their [weapons].'

One mission 4 days earlier illustrated how the technology of modern electro-optical targeting pods and precision-guided low-collateral weapons had changed the face of CAS work over Afghanistan. A pair of Tornados was, 'tasked to North Helmand to check out a High Value Target. It was the end of the day and night time was closing in. There was also a UAV[145] on station. We identified a vehicle with multiple personnel in. We tracked the vehicle to several locations. Finally we got the call to strike, we waited as the car approached and passed through villages, it made its way through windy lanes and areas of high ground until there was an area we could strike in. Due to the difficulty of the terrain it was hard to assess the exact best time to strike. On getting clearance I waited for an opportune moment to release a DMS Brimstone. Unfortunately, on tipping in the picture was not ideal due to some terrain masking the target, by the time it cleared I decided not to release as we were approaching minimum range. I knew our Number 2 would be lining up to support our attack behind us and would be in a better position. I hauled off, called clear and [Number 2] engaged with a DMS Brimstone. The target exploded and came to a halt, at least three people managed to escape and starting running in various directions. We positioned ourselves and engaged on the running individuals, we were now down to using the 27mm cannon. This was a busy period with aircraft repositioning in the air, switching height blocks and contracts. All of this whilst sorting out the targeting between the formation and carrying out individual weapon checks in order to carry out successful attacks. Our final attack was a strafe attack; again this is not a straightforward procedure at night and in mountainous terrain. The target sets were in the bottom of a valley, so a careful selection of [attack direction] was required. There are numerous things that can go wrong with an attack: the outcome can be anything from an aborted attack to flying into the ground. The light levels were very poor, so based on the fact that we had a good GPS position

I dived steeply at the floor in the centre of the valley. Stu was marking the target with the Lightening III pod. We fired well over 100 rounds in the one pass. It was a busy, exhilarating and frantic period, the attack was a successful one and we returned home. Personally, it was a period of personal reflection, I had conducted attacks before, but this was the first time I definitely knew I had taken someone's life. I am not sure if everyone feels the same, [but] I think it is worth considering the fact that you have taken a life, how you think you should feel and how you actually feel. There are very few people in this country who are authorized to use lethal force and even fewer who have to use it. It is something that will always be with you, it can never be taken back. Overall it is a mixed feeling of doing the job that you have been trained to do and the fact that rightly (or wrongly depending on your viewpoint) that you have taken a life.'

An almost identical scenario occurred just a few days later, on 11 November, when another pair was scrambled from GCAS in the late afternoon. After engaging a car with a DMS Brimstone, the pilot observed that, 'incredibly, the back doors of the car open and three insurgents appear and start running in three different directions. As briefed, the Reaper UAV follows one, [Number 2] another and us the third.' The three insurgents were hunted down in the fading light of evening, leading the pilot to consider that, '…the most interesting aspect of this experience which I still think of from time to time is how the targeting became so personal. Often fast jets are tasked with targets that do not have a human angle to them a radar, a weapons storage facility, a HAS. Often faceless targets that may or may not have people in or around them, but you very rarely are exposed to that aspect. After this sortie it really brought home how different some of these scenarios are from the traditional strike missions we had often spent hours training for.' On the night of 22 November, another Brimstone DMS was fired at a band of insurgents who had been positively identified laying IEDs.

Meanwhile, routine sorties continued and non-kinetic techniques were often sufficient to persuade enemy groups to disengage from Coalition forces. Capt Janjua recalled a show of force near Anjir Shali, to the west of Sangin in Helmand Province on 10 December: '…shortly after starting work [with the JTAC] he informed us that they had just had an IED strike a convoy in his area [of responsibility]. He passed the co-ordinates and requested a Show of Force to ensure that any planned ambush of the convoy while it was stopped waiting for helicopter MEDEVAC of wounded was thwarted. Macca and I quickly sorted out the kit and airspace, and developed a reasonable plan… so, down we went to fly over the friendlies at 225ft and 500kt. We came off target into the sun. In the climb back to our working altitude, the JTAC informed us that the troops on the ground had heard AK47 fire as we approached and flew overhead. Turns out the Taliban would take great pride in downing a fast jet with small arms fire; I guess that I can not blame them. The rest of this scenario involved us looking for bad dudes in adjacent compounds because the friendly FOB nearby was now taking a little [fire]. We could not ascertain positive identification, but we did see some suspicious groups moving around in treelines. As we [left for the tanker], a British AH-64 approached to escort the medevac choppers and get a handover from us. After the flight, we reviewed the DVR footage from both Litening pods. You could clearly see the convoy, stopped in its tracks as the lead vehicle has been disabled. We hoped that nobody was seriously injured. Stradders was our element mate, the flight lead, and he did a great job of tracking our approach and egress. The DVR clearly shows [countermeasures] being dispensed as we raged into the area and then got the heck out of Dodge…Macca and I also joked about checking the fin for bullet holes as we got out of the jet. And we both took a little look as we walked away.'

Ten days later a pair of Tornados was supporting US forces in a mountainous area to the northwest of Kandahar, as they attempted to head back to their base under cover of darkness. The lead aircraft was on the tanker and Number 2 was overhead the convoy when, in the pilot's words, '…all hell broke loose and the convoy came under heavy machine gun and mortar fire from the high ground to the north. [We] were requested to employ a PW IV onto the area where the fire was coming from, which we located but could not make out any individuals. RoE satisfied, collateral damage estimate satisfied, I position the aircraft on an 8 to 10 mile run in. [My back-seater] is very busy marking the target with the Litening pod as individuals can now be seen firing down onto the convoy. We keep the laser firing on the Litening which is constantly updating the coordinates in the PW IV until release when we stop the laser and let the PW IV use GPS aided navigation to hit the target. It is a direct hit with the instantaneous fusing neutralizing three insurgents and their weapons systems. The convoy is able to extract from the situation without further incident. [The WSO] did an excellent job in a high-tempo scenario with a very tricky target at night.'

Operations carried on through Christmas Day, which was marked by virtually every member of the detachment wearing Santa hats while on duty. One landmark which passed on Christmas Day itself was the completion of the 'Earth Challenge' in which members of the squadron had taken it in turns in the gym to run the equivalent distance of the Earth's circumference. This diversion was one of a number of projects to keep everyone amused when they were off duty. Another was a mini-Ashes series of cricket matches played against the Australians.

New Year's Day was another working day, which found a pair of Tornados working with a US Forces team in southern Afghanistan. The US troops were particularly excited to hear the voice of one of the female navigators and a low-level beat up of their compound also helped to bring some cheer to their remote outpost. Ten days later, Wg Cdr Reeves handed over command of the Tornado detachment to Wg Cdr J.K. Frampton, MBE (officer commanding 12 Squadron) during a 2¾hr Raptor sortie. 'And that,' added Wg Cdr Reeves wistfully, 'was my last trip in a Tornado.' During the next week, 14 Squadron's thirteen crews and 120 engineers returned to Lossiemouth after a highly-successful detachment during which the squadron's crews had dropped four PW IVs and fired eleven Brimstone missiles and 427 rounds of 27mm HE.

Wg Cdr J Moreton assumed command of the squadron on its return from Afghanistan, but sadly his command was to be short-lived: on 1 March the Air Force Board announced that 14 Squadron would be disbanded on 1 June 2011. Flying operations ceased on 15 April with a flypast by six Tornados over the squadron's flightline and 4 days later HRH Prince Andrew took the salute at the Disbandment Parade. Most of the personnel were absorbed into XV Squadron until they could be redistributed among the remaining Tornado Force. Although the squadron had ceased to exist 2 days beforehand; on 3 June, three 14 Squadron aircrews flew together for one final flypast by three-ship 'Vic' formation over the officers' mess at RAF Lossiemouth.

NOTES

115 Combat Operations Centre.

116 Sqn Ldrs M.J. Entwistle/C. Platt, Flt Lt Cooper/Sqn Ldr J.W. Ross, Flt Lts M.G. Spencer-Jones/ Elsey, J.A. Freeborough/C. J. Stradling.

117 Flt Lt M. Smith/Wg Cdr Klein, Flt Lts R.A. Caine/Elsey, Spencer-Jones/N.P. Bury, Freeborough/N. Johnston..

118 Flt Lt Smith/Wg Cdr Klein, Flt Lts Davis/A.R. Fisher, Spencer-Jones/Bury, Freeborough/ Johnston.

119 Flt Lts Caine/P.J. Richley, J.A. Davis/Fisher, Mannering/R. Barrett, Sqn Ldr Hales/Flt Lt Johnston.

120 Reconnaissance Airborne Pod for TORnado (RAPTOR).

121 Missile Engagement Zone.

122 Sqn Ldr W. P. Bohill/Wg Cdr Klein, Flt Lts Freeborough/M. Bressani, Sqn Ldr P.B. Binns/Flt Lt McGlone (RAPTOR), Flt Lt A.S. Lord/Sqn Ldr J. Ross (RAPTOR), Flt Lts Davis/Stradling, Flt Lts Kidd/Fisher.

123 Flt Lts Davis/Stradling, Smith/Fraser, D.C.D. Berris/N.S. Thomas (Raptor), Kidd/Fisher (RAPTOR).

124 Sqn Ldr Bohill/Wg Cdr Klein, Flt Lts Freeborough/Bressani, Binns/McGlone (Raptor), Berris/Thomas (RAPTOR).

125 Sqn Ldr Bohill/Wg Cdr Klein, Flt Lts Freeborough/Sqn Ldr Francis, Flt Lt Lord/Sqn Ldr Ross, Flt Lts Smith/Fraser.

126 A BL755 Cluster Bomb with a radar fuse to enable it to be dropped from medium-level.

127 Joint Reconnaissance Pod – broadly similar to the Vicon pod which had been used previously.

128 Flt Lt P.D. Beevers.

129 Flt Lts Froome/Thomas, Mannering/Stradling.

130 Flt Lt Mannering/Flt Lt Elsey and Sqn Ldr P. Binns/ Flt Lt N. Thomas.

131 Joint Forward Air Controller Training and Standards Unit.

132 Group Air Staff Orders.

133 Remotely Operated Video Enhanced Receiver.

134 In Tornado GR4 ZD844.

135 Improvized Explosive Device.

136 In Tornado GR4 ZA546.

137 In Tornado GR4 ZG707.

138 International Security and Stabilization Force.

139 In Tornado GR4 ZA607.

140 Kandahar Airfield.

141 Tornado GR4 ZA560.

142 Kandahar Airfield.

143 Boom-Drogue Adaptor which converted the KC-135's boom so that it could be used by probe-equipped aircraft (as used by most non-USAF operators). The small drogue on a very short hose made this a particularly challenging operation for the receiver pilot.

144 Weapons Systems Operator – a more accurate description of the role carried out by the Tornado navigator.

145 Unmanned Aerial Vehicle, or 'Drone'.

9

2011-2015

THE SHADOW

On the Seniority of Squadrons

During the massive expansion of the RFC, and later the RAF, during the First
World War, such issues as the relative seniority of the flying squadrons or what
might happen to those units once peace was resumed were a long way from the
thoughts of those who were responding to the national emergency. The possible
future size and shape of the RAF was not a problem that needed to be addressed
until the war was won. However, when the war had been won, it was followed by a
contraction in the size of the RAF which was even more rapid than the expansion
had been and some sort of policy on squadron numbers was quickly needed. This
was provided in January 1920 when Lord Trenchard directed that certain squadron
numbers would be preserved in the post-war RAF and that from then onwards
these would be established as the core units of the RAF of the future. Even so,
the post-war RAF would have twenty-seven squadrons, compared with the pre-
war RFC's seven. Amongst Trenchard's original twenty-seven squadrons was 14
Squadron, thus placing the unit, in numerical order, as the seventh most senior
flying squadron in the RAF. The squadron was also amongst the first to be awarded
a Standard in April 1943. After the Second World War a similar contraction of the
service was managed using a similar process and once again 14 Squadron's position
among the most senior of the RAF's fighting units was confirmed. At various times
over the next 60 years the rules concerning the seniority of the RAF's squadrons
were reviewed by the Air Force Board (AFB), including a review in September
2008 by the Assistant Chief of the Air Staff, AVM T.M. Anderson, CBE, DSO.
On 1 November 2010, the AFB's own 'List of Active Numberplates' confirmed the
position of 14 Squadron as the RAF's sixth most senior flying squadron as measured
by accrued years of active service, sitting above the other Tornado units (at that time
IX, 12, 13, 31 and 617 Squadrons) in the order of seniority.

Unfortunately, the AFB was unable to abide by its own rules when, in late 2010, it had to select two Tornado squadrons for disbandment; instead, it was forced to follow a political directive that units which were either on, or preparing for operations in Afghanistan were not to be disbanded. As a result of this politically driven decision-making 14 and 13 Squadrons were disbanded in 2011 while more junior units continued in service. Fortunately for 14 Squadron, a champion emerged in the shape of Air Marshal Anderson, by now Director General of the Military Aviation Authority, who wrote to the Chief of the Air Staff (CAS), on 7 April 2011, pointing out the injustice of the decision. 'The recognition of seniority, measured as it is by front-line service,' wrote Air Marshal Anderson, 'is of itself a critically important acknowledgement of those units down the years that, by virtue of the length of their service, have hosted and given purpose to very large numbers of Royal Air Force airmen and women engaged in discharging their loyal duties and who, in doing so, have not infrequently made the ultimate sacrifice. Such acknowledgement cannot be easily set aside – if it were to be, what would that say about the modern air force's principles and core values?' He further pointed out that, 'the fact that decisions have now been made as they have, counter-intuitively and, through at least some eyes, essentially for short term political expedience, has been taken very hard in many quarters.' Air Marshal Anderson was able to persuade CAS that 14 Squadron's distinguished 'numberplate' should be allocated to a unit which was beginning to make an impressive impact on the RAF's operations in Afghanistan.

The Shadow

Sadly, the seed of 14 Squadron's good fortune in autumn 2011 had been sown in the disastrous crash of a Nimrod MR21[146] in Afghanistan in 2006. The Nimrod was primarily a maritime patrol aircraft, but the type was being used to great effect over both Iraq and Afghanistan in the Intelligence, Surveillance, Target Acquisition and Reconnaissance (ISTAR) role. The aircraft's communications suite and optical sensor[147.] which could be used to relay real-time imagery to ground troops, made the aircraft an essential part of the army's operations. However, as a result of concerns about the Nimrod's airworthiness after the accident, the Nimrod fleet was grounded, leaving a gaping hole in the RAF's capability to support army operations.

The army quickly raised an Urgent Operational Requirement (UOR) to fill the operational ISTAR role over Afghanistan and so was born the Shadow R1 aircraft. Four of these aircraft[148], which is based on the Beechcraft KingAir 350 airframe, were ordered and the responsibility for operating them fell to a flight on 5 Squadron. In July 2009, the first operational Shadow sorties were flown from Kandahar and the aircraft quickly showed that it was more than capable of filling the role vacated by the much larger and more expensive Nimrod. A fifth aircraft[149] was added in December 2011.

In its operational fit the Shadow carries an extensive communications suite giving it the capability to operate as a communications relay station over the mountainous terrain of Afghanistan. Crucially, the aircraft is also equipped with

A Beechcraft Shadow R1, seen at RAF Waddington. With this aircraft 14 Squadron returned to its roots, working closely with Army units. (© Crown Copyright 2011)

the same optical sensor as Nimrod, which enables high-resolution imagery to be acquired. This data can be interpreted by an on-board operator or securely down-linked to troops on the ground. A laser 'sparkle' facility gives operators on board the aircraft the capability to identify points of interest to troops on the ground.

Re-forming 14 Squadron

Initially the Shadows were flown by crews who were detached temporarily to the flight for the duration of an operational tour in Afghanistan. The pilots were provided by 45 Squadron, the multi-engine training school at nearby Cranwell, which flew the similar Beechcraft KingAir B200. The instructors on 45 Squadron provided the aircraft captains, while co-pilots were recent graduates from the training course. Rear crew came from the pool of ex-Nimrod crews, who were awaiting new postings after the demise of the aircraft. Although this ad hoc arrangement worked well enough to get Shadow into service quickly, clearly it was not sustainable. The unit lacked cohesion and hard-won operational experience was being lost as soon as it was gained.

Furthermore, the peculiarities of the Shadow's engineering arrangements meant that maintenance engineering was already entirely separate from 5 Squadron. Because of the speed with which the Shadow was introduced into service, it was done with Civil Aviation Authority (CAA), rather than military, airworthiness certification. Additionally, the requirement to keep the aircraft as close as possible to the operational theatre meant that routine servicing would have to be carried out in the Middle East. The result of these requirements was a partnership between the Shadow Flight and Gama Support Services to support the engineering side of Shadow. Despite their military training and experience, RAF engineers had to qualify for CAA licences in order to supervise servicing on the aircraft. This was achieved by sending them on day-release courses while they were seconded to the Gama facility at Farnborough.

Beechcraft Shadow R1 (ZZ419). The turret housing for the Westcam is clearly visible on the underside of the aircraft. (Mike Powney)

The solution to bring all the various operational, engineering and administrative areas together was to give the Shadow unit its own identity as a squadron, under command of Wg Cdr R.H. Moir. On 14 October 2011, a ceremony was held at Waddington to present the Shadow Flight with the Standard of 14 Squadron. The parade commander for this occasion was Sqn Ldr F.C.J. Parkinson and, appropriately, the reviewing officer was Air Marshal Anderson, the former CO who had done so much to ensure that 14 Squadron continued its existence.

Operation Herrick

Like 14 Squadron's Tornados previously, the unit's Shadows operated in Afghanistan from the airbase at Kandahar. Each of the squadrons four flights took its turn to man the permanent detachment in theatre. Unlike the Tornados, which were ISAF rather than purely national assets, the Shadows were specifically tasked in support of UK land forces. With the operational area in Helmand less than 30 minutes flight time away from Kandahar, the Shadow could be on task swiftly. Although the aircraft has a nominal endurance of around 7 hours, actual sortie lengths depend on the fuel load. The hot and high conditions of the Afghan summer could limit the maximum take-off weight of the aircraft; however, refuelling facilities at Camp Bastion, some 90 miles west of Kandahar, meant that an aircraft could remain in the operational area almost indefinitely. Operating at medium–altitude, the aircraft's small size and noise footprint, in comparison to a fast jet, made it almost undetectable from the ground.

On 19 July 2012, Shadow operations passed a significant landmark with the achievement of the squadron's 10,000th operational hour. This was, in the words of Wg Cdr Moir, '…a significant milestone, and stands as testament to the hard work, dedication and determination of all those associated with the success of this unique platform.' The squadron had been transferred from 2 Group to 1 Group just a few months beforehand and further testament to 14 Squadron's achievements was the presentation of the AOC 1 Group, 'Operational Performance Award' for 2012. This trophy is awarded to the individual, or unit, who has displayed the most notable contribution to operations throughout the year. During 2012, the RAF had been heavily involved in high-profile and highly-successful operations in Libya (involving the Tornado GR4 and Typhoon forces), and Afghanistan (involving the Tornado GR4 and support helicopter forces) so the selection of 14 Squadron above all these units was praise indeed. The citation for the award stated, '…in providing unique and enduring support to UK forces in Afghanistan, No 14 Squadron has earned an unparalleled level of respect by those forces with which it has operated. In addition to its mandated commitment, the squadron has supported numerous high-profile tasks as directed by the highest echelons of government, receiving unanimous and resounding critical acclaim. In developing key relationships with DE&S and Industry, the squadron has worked tirelessly to overcome obstacles and adapt to rapidly changing circumstances. The monthly output has more than doubled, the mission system has evolved to meet an adaptable and dynamic threat, and the desire for the capability, from tactical to strategic users, remains insatiable.

Shadow R1 (ZZ418) on final approach to RAF Waddington. (Matt Jessop)

Deploying rapidly, to remote and austere locations, and often operating with a "broad church" of partners, the squadron has significantly enhanced its own and the service's reputation.'

Having been procured under a UOR specifically for operations over Afghanistan, the Shadow aircraft were originally intended to be dis-established in 2015 at the planned end of the UK commitment in Afghanistan. However, the squadron proved so effective in its support of the army that it was incorporated into the mainstream funding in 2013 and a sixth aircraft was procured in late July. On 4 October 2013, Wg Cdr R. J. Bousfield took command of the squadron.

The Future

Although the Shadows continue to be heavily committed to operations in Afghanistan, 14 Squadron also supports the army as it looks ahead to possible future contingencies. When they can be spared from operational flying, the aircraft are occasionally released to participate in army training exercises around the world. Other roles being proposed for the aircraft include maritime surveillance, for which the Shadow's sensor fit could be easily modified. Thus, the second century of 14 Squadron's existence reflects both its beginnings as an army co-operation unit in the First World War and the unique contribution in the Second World War with the Martin Marauder in the coastal reconnaissance role.

NOTES

146   Nimrod XV230 exploded in mid-air after an on-board fire on 2 September 2006; all 14 crew members were killed.
147   The Wescam MX-15 electro-optic/infrared sensor.
148   Shadow R1s ZZ416, ZZ417, ZZ418 & ZZ419.
149   Shadow R1 ZZ504.

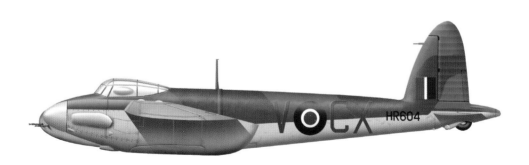

DH Mosquto FBVI HR604 Cambrai 1945

DH Mosquto B35 VP202 Wahn 1950

DH Vampire FB5 WA109 Fassberg 1951

DH Venom FB1 WE362 Fasberg 1954

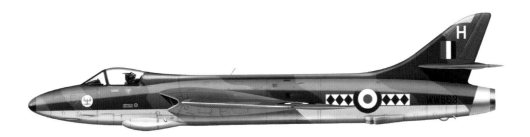

Hawker Hunter F4 WW663 Oldenburg 1957

Hawker Hunter F6 XJ642 Gutersloh 1962

English Electric Canberra B(I)8 WT345 Wildenrath 1963

English Electric Canberra B(I)8 WT 368 Wildenrath 1966

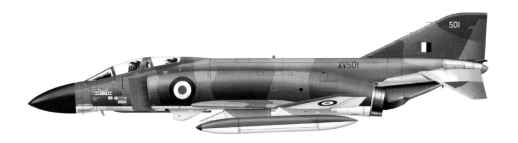

McDonnell Douglas Phantom FGR2 XV501 Bruggen 1970

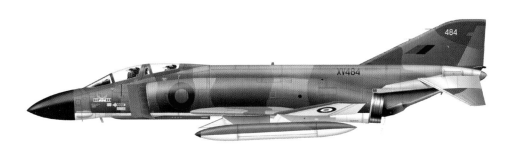

McDonnell Douglas Phantom FGR2 XV484 Bruggen 1975

Sepecat Jaguar GR1 XX958 Bruggen 1980

Panavia Tornado GR1 ZD744 Bruggen 1987

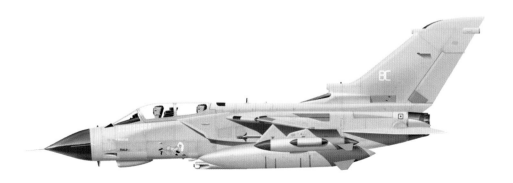

Panavia Tornado GR1 ZD848 Tabuk 1991

Panavia Tornado GR4 ZA560 Lossiemouth 2002

Panavia Tornado GR4 ZD810 Kandahar 2011

Beechcraft Shadow R1 ZZ419 Waddington 2012

Abbreviations and Acronyms

2 ATAF	Second Allied Tactical Air Force
2 TAF	Second Tactical Air Force
4 ATAF	Fourth Allied Tactical Air Force
AAA	Anti-Aircraft Artillery
AAFCE	Allied Air Forces Central Europe
AAR	Air-to-Air Refuelling
ACAS	Assistant Chief of the Air Staff
ACE	Allied Command Europe
ACM	Air Chief Marshal
ACMI	Air Combat Manoeuvring Instrumentation
ADIZ	Air Defence Identification Zone
ADO	Alert Duty Officer
AFCENT	Allied Forces Central Europe
ALARM	Air Lanched Anti-Radiation Missile
AMRAAM	Advanced Medium Range Air-to-Air Missile
AOC	Air Officer Commanding
APC	1. Armament Practice Camp,
	2 Armoured Personnel Carrier
Asap	As Soon As Possible
ATC	Air Traffic Control
AWACS	Airborne Warning And Control System
AWTI	Air Weapons Training Facility
BAFO	British Air Forces of Occupation
CAOC	Combined Air Operations Centre
CAP	Combat Air Patrol
CAS	1. Close Air Support,
	2. Chief of the Air Staff
CBLS	Carrier Bomb Light Store
CBU	Cluster Bomb Unit
CEP	Circular Error Probable
CLSP	Composite Launch Sequence Plan
CMF	Combat Mission Folder
COC	Combat Operations Centre
COMAAFCE	Commander Allied Air Forces Central Europe
DACT	Dissimilar Air Combat Training
DCINCENT	Deputy Commander-in-Chief Central Europe
DFCS	Day Fighter Combat School
DJRP	Digital Joint Reconnaissance Pod
DMS	Dual Mode Seeker
EO	Electro-Optical
EW	Electronic Warfare
EWTR	Electronic Warfare Tactics Range
FAC	Forward Air Controllers
FLIR	Forward Looking InfraRed
FRA	First Run Attack
GAF	German Air Force
GASO	Group Air Staff Orders
GCA	Ground Contolled Approach
GCAS	Ground-based Close Air Support
GCI	Ground Controlled Intercept
GLO	Ground Liaison Officer
GMR	Ground Mapping Radar
HAS	Hardened Aircraft Shelters
HE	High Explosive
HES	Hardened Equipment Shelter
HUD	Head-Up Display
IAS	Indicated Air Speed
IED	Improvized Explosive Device
IFREP	In-Flight REPort
IGB	Inner German Border
ILS	Instrument Landing System
IMC	Instrument Meterological Conditions
INAS	Inertial Navigation and Attack System
IOC	Integrated Operations Centre
IP	Initial Point

ISAF	International Security and Stabilization Force	QWI	Qualified Weapons Instructor
		R/T	Radio-telephone
ISTAR	Intelligence, Surveillance, Target Acquisition and Reconnaissance	RAFG	Royal Air Force Germany
		RBSU	Radar Bomb Scoring Unit
JEngO	Junior Engineering Officer	RHAG	Rotary Hydraulic Arrestor Gear
JRP	Joint Reconnaissance Pod	RHWR	Radar Homing and Warning Receiver
JTAC	Joint Terminal Air Controller		
LABS	Low Altitude Bombing System	RoE	Rules of Engagement
LADD	Low Angle Drogue Delivery	RP	Rocket Projectiles
LFA	Low Flying Area	RSO	Range Safety Officer
LGB	Laser-Guided Bomb	RWR	Radar Warning Receiver
LOA	Line Of Attack	SACEUR	Supreme Allied Commander EURope
LRMTS	Laser Rangefinder and Marked Target Seeker		
		SAM	Surface-to-Air Missile
LTM	Laser Target Marking	SAP	Simulated Attack Profile
MEZ	Missile Engagement Zone	SASO	Senior Air Staff Officer
MPC	Missile Practice Camp	SATCO	Senior Air Traffic Control Officer
MRCP	Mobile Radar Command Post	SEATO	South East Asia Treaty Organization
NAAFI	Navy Army Air Force Institute		
NATO	North Atlantic Treaty Organization	SoF	Show of Force
NavWASS	Navigation and Weapons Aiming Sub-System	SOP	Standard Operating Procedure
		SSP	Simulated Strike Profile
NBC	Nuclear Biological & Chemical	SSV	Soft-Skinned Vehicle
NFZ	No Fly Zone	TACAN	TACtical Air Navigation (radio beacon)
NVG	Night Vision Goggles		
OCU	Operational Conversion Unit	TACEVAL	TACtical EVALuation
OLF	Operational Low Flying	TFM	Tactical Fighter Meet
ORP	Operational Readiness Platform	TFR	Terrain Following Radar
OTR	Operational Turn Round	TIALD	Thermal Imaging And Laser Designator
PAI	Pilot Attack Instructor		
PAR	Precision Approach Radar	TIC	Troops In Contact
PBF	Pilots' (later Personnel) Briefing Facility	TLP	Tactical Leadership Programme
		TOT	Time On Target
PD	Pulsed Doppler (Radar)	TTF	Tornado Turnaround Facility
PI	Practice Interception	TWM	Tactical Weapons Meet
PMD	Projected Map Display	UAV	Unmanned Aerial Vehicles
POL	Petrol Oil & Lubricants	UNSCOM	UN Special COMmission
PW	Pave Way (Laser -Guided Bomb)	UOR	Urgent Operational Requirement
QFI	Qualified Flying Instructor	USAFE	United States Air Force Europe
QRA	Quick Reaction Alert	WST	Weapons Standardization Team

Appendix 1
Biographic Notes

Adams, Sqn Ldr R. H. D.	Phantom navigator. Robin Adams, who left the RAF to join industry in 1984, had previously flown in photo-reconnaissance Canberras with 31 Squadron. After 14 Squadron his staff tours included the Central Trials and Tactics Organization, HQ 38 Gp and MoD OR.
Adams, Fg Off R. J.	Vampire, Venom and Canberra pilot. Richard 'Dicky' Adams (d.2005) also flew Canberras with 14 Squadron in the 1960s; he left the RAF in 1976 to become CFI of a flying club and later ran a Skoda car agency. However, he rejoined the RAF in 1980 to serve as a QFI on Southampton UAS.
Airey, Flt Lt I. S.	Canberra pilot. Flt Lt Stewart Airey left the RAF in 1972 to fly Viscounts with Northeast Airlines and later Boeing 747-400 with Cathay Pacific.
Aldersley, Flt Lt N. R.	Tornado pilot. Neale Aldersley, who left the RAF in 1989, joined Britannia Airways, then British Airways and was a captain on the Airbus A320 and Boeing 767.
Aldrovandi, Flt Lt E. C.	Squadron mascot. 'Eric Androvandi', a Burmese rock python, retired from the RAF with the rank of Sqn Ldr when the Tornado squadron disbanded. At 22ft long he had established a record for a python in captivity and he retired to 'Amazonia' near Glasgow.
Allan, Flt Lt C. F.	Jaguar pilot. A keen photographer, Chris Allan also flew Lightnings and has published a number of books featuring air-to-air photographs taken from the cockpit of a Lightning.
Allan, Flt Lt K.	Canberra pilot. Ken Allen left the RAF in 1974 and joined AST at Perth as a QFI. He was killed, aged 45 years-old, in a flying accident in a Cessna 310 in March 1976.
Anderson, Fg Off	Mosquito navigator.
Anderson, Flt Lt B. M.	Canberra navigator.
Anderson, Sqn Ldr T. M.	Tornado pilot. Air Marshal Timo Anderson, KCB, DSO, who retired from the RAF in 2013, served two tours on 14 Squadron as a flight commander and as OC 14 Squadron. He commanded RAF Bruggen and was the first director of the Military Airworthiness Authority. He is the President of the 14 Squadron Association.
Anderton, Fg Off M. D.	Canberra navigator. Plagued by airsickness, Mark Anderton left the squadron after a year to fly in the Varsity. He left the RAF shortly afterwards to become a grain trader before setting up a promotional clothing company with customers ranging from rock stars to Formula One teams.
Ball, Flt Lt M. W.	Jaguar Pilot. Gp Capt Malcolm 'Raz' Ball, AFC, flew Phantoms, Jaguars and F-111s before becoming one of the first Tornado instructors at the Tri-National Tornado Training Establishment. He later commanded the Tornado Operational Evaluation Unit and was station commander at RAF Cottesmore. He retired from the RAF in 1997.
Barlow, W/O B. J. F.	Mosquito pilot.
Barnett, Fg Off M. J. R.	Canberra navigator. Formerly a Vulcan navigator, Martin Barnett remained on Phantoms in the air-defence role and spent 10 years as the organizer of the RAF Leuchars Battle of Britain Open Day; he retired as a Sqn Ldr 1993.
Baron, Flt Lt R. A.	Jaguar pilot. Roy Baron left the RAF in 1980.
Baron, Wg Cdr D. A.	Jaguar pilot and OC 14 Squadron. An ex-Hunter and Phantom pilot and QFI, Gp Capt Dave Baron, OBE commanded RAF Church Fenton. He retired from the RAF in 1996. He was appointed chairman of the Tangmere Military Aviation Museum in 2006.

Barrett, Sgt J. F.	Mosquito pilot.
Barrett, Fg Off T.	Hunter pilot. Wg Cdr Tim Barrett's RAF career included exchange tours with the USAF and Singapore Air Force and command of 2 Squadron. His last tour before leaving the RAF in 1983 was Air Attaché in Cairo where he was present at the assassination of President Sadat.
Barrett, Flt Lt S. A.	Vampire pilot. Sqn Ldr Selwyn 'Bill' Barrett, who was commissioned in 1943, later commanded Edinburgh UAS and retired from the RAF in 1965.
Bartley, Sqn Ldr I.K.StC.	Canberra navigator. Ian Bartley.
Batt, Fg Off B.B.	Hunter pilot. Air Cdre Brian Batt was Director of Flying Training. He also served as the Deputy Lieutenant for Havering, Essex.
Baugh, Plt Off S. A.	Hunter pilot. Flt Lt Stanley Baugh retired from the RAF in 1969.
Baverstock, Flt Lt M.J.	Tornado pilot. On leaving the RAF in 1999, Mike "Grouty" Baverstock joined British Airways and flew the Boeing 777.
Bearblock, Flt Lt C.D.A.F.	Tornado pilot. After leaving the RAF in 1999, Chris Bearblock joined British Airways to fly the Airbus A320.
Beasley, Sqn Ldr C.W.	Hunter pilot and OC 14 Squadron. Charles 'Hank' Beasley was commissioned in 1943 and flew Spitfires with 92 Squadron, 1944-1945. He retired from the RAF in 1962 with the rank of Sqn Ldr.
Belfitt, Flt Lt F.	Mosquito navigator. Flt Lt Frank Belfitt retired from the RAF in 1969; he won the DFM while serving with 50 Squadron in 1941.
Bentley, Flt Lt D. A.	Tornado pilot. Gp Capt Dave Bentley commanded 19 Squadron Hawks and became commandant of the Central Flying School.
Benwell, Sqn Ldr R.H.	Vampire pilot and OC 14 Squadron. Commissioned in 1943, 'Reggie' Benwell went on to command 16 Squadron. He retired from the RAF as a Wg Cdr in 1969.
Bergh, Flt Lt M.O.	Mosquito pilot. A South African, Wg Cdr Oelof Bergh, AFC (1930-1983) was shot down and taken PoW in Korea. He commanded 93 Squadron in 1960 and retired from the RAF in 1974.
Bigland, Lt J.R. (RN)	Canberra navigator. After leaving the Royal Navy, Lt Cdr Roy Bigland joined BAe and was killed in a Buccaneer crash at West Freugh in 1978.
Bishop, Flt Lt I.P. (DFC)	Mosquito navigator. Ian Bishop was killed, aged 30 years-old, in the crash of a Hastings in September 1949.
Bolger, Fg Off T.J.	Venom and Hunter pilot. An Irishman described as 'a very charming ladies' man,' Thomas 'Pat' Bolger retired from the RAF as a Flt Lt in 1961.
Bolton, Nav II	Mosquito navigator. 'Nobby' Bolton, joined the RAF in 1942 and flew Mosquitoes with 109 and 139 Squadrons during the war. Although he made an almost full recovery from the injuries he sustained in abandoning a 14 Squadron Mosquito, he was invalided out of the RAF.
Bond, Nav III W.D.R.	Mosquito navigator. Don Bond was posted to 100 Squadron. After leaving the RAF he qualified as a flight engineer and enjoyed a long career in civil aviation.
Bonsoni, Sgt A.J.	Mosquito pilot.
Booth, Sqn Ldr R.	Phantom pilot. A former Hunter pilot, Roy Booth retired from the RAF in 1975 and joined Britannia Airways. He retired in 1993.
Boulton, Flt Lt M.S.	Tornado navigator. Mark 'Bolty' Boulton retired from the RAF in 2003.
Bourne, Sgt A.	Hunter first-line servicing. Arthur Bourne, who had been awarded an AOC's Commendation from Transport Command, was also presented with an engraved tankard by the squadron pilots as a mark of their appreciation of his good work when he left 14 Squadron in July 1961.
Boyle, Wg Cdr T.L.	Tornado pilot. After retiring from the RAF in 2001, Gp Capt Tom Boyle OBE spent 3 years flying Tornados as a full-time reservist, before joining BAe in Saudi Arabia. He then joined Thales to run the Tornado simulator at RAF Marham.

Bredenkamp, Flt Lt J.	Hunter pilot. Wg Cdr John Bredenkamp (b.1934) retired from the RAF in 1989.
Brewer, Flt Sgt	Mosquito navigator.
Broad, Flt Lt R.N.	Vampire, Venom and Hunter pilot. A Cambridge graduate, Sqn Ldr Bob Broad, MA retired from the RAF in 1967 and joined IBM. Originally at Fassberg on 98 Squadron he joined 14 Sqn as OC 'A' Flight in 1954 after returning from exchange with the USAF flying the F-84 in Korea. He subsequently served on the Air Fighting Development squadron before staff tours at HQ Bomber Command and 6ATAF in Turkey.
Brockbank, Plt II	Mosquito pilot.
Brook, Flt Lt D.C.G.	Hunter pilot. AVM David Brook, CBE retired from the RAF in 1990; he subsequently chaired a number of inquiries on behalf of the Department of Transport. Brook commanded 20 Squadron and was station commander at Wittering.
Brough, Flt Lt G.	Jaguar pilot. Sqn Ldr Gary Brough later flew Tornados and retired from the RAF in 1997.
Brown, Flt Lt N.J.	Phantom pilot. Flt Lt Nick Brown, AFC was killed in a flying accident in a Jaguar in December 1979.
Browne, Fg Off J.A.	Hunter pilot. Flt Lt James 'Nosher' Browne transferred to the reserve in 1963.
Bryant, Wg Cdr D.T.	Phantom pilot, OC 14 Sqn. AVM Derek Bryant, CB retired from the RAF in 1989, having commanded RAF Coningsby and latterly been Commandant of the RAF Staff College.
Bryant, Sqn Ldr J.M.	Jaguar pilot. An ex-Lightning pilot, Wg Cdr John Bryant retired from the RAF in 1990.
Burgess, LAC R.E.	Vampire and Venom armourer. Ron Burgess joined 14 Squadron as an armourer in May 1952, aged 25 years-old. After his national service, Ron Burgess joined Percival Aircraft (later British Aircraft Corporation), where he became shop steward. When BAC closed he became production supervisor at Murphy Chemicals of Wheathampstead.
Burrows, Flt Lt J.J.	Tornado pilot. After leaving the RAF in 1990 'JJ' flew with Air 2000 before joining Virgin Atlantic Airlines, eventually becoming Airbus fleet manager.
Bushnell, Flt Lt T.M.	Jaguar pilot. Terry Bushnell was killed in a flying accident on 2 July 1976 aged 29 years-old. He was an experienced pilot who had previously flown Lightnings and had been a Gnat QFI.
Butler, Flt Lt J.A.	Tornado pilot. John Butler left the RAF in 1990 and flew for Air 2000 and Royal Brunei before flying for Thompson Airways as a B737 captain.
Cameron, Fg Off I.A.	Canberra navigator. Wg Cdr Ian Cameron retired from the RAF in 2002.
Carder, Fg Off A.S.	Venom and Hunter pilot. Sqn Ldr Alex 'Tubby' Carder (b.1933) retired from the RAF in 1967 and became the personal pilot of the Sultan of Brunei.
Cassells, Flt Lt J.R.	Mosquito pilot. Sqn Ldr James 'Jock' Cassells (1922-2008) retired from the RAF in 1965. He had been awarded the DFC for operations with 106 Squadron and a bar to the DFC for service with 139 Squadron.
Champniss, Flt Lt P.H.	Hunter pilot. Gp Capt Phil Champniss, AFC retired from the RAF in 1978 and joined British Aerospace in Saudi Arabia, becoming chief executive of the Al Yamama project. He had commanded 43 Squadron in Aden and two Harrier squadrons.
Chapman, Flt Lt J.G.	Jaguar pilot. After retiring from the RAF in 2009, Gp Capt John 'JC' Chapman joined the defence business arm of Dell.
Checketts, Plt Off D.J.	Vampire pilot. Sir David Checketts, KCVO (b.1930) retired as a Sqn Ldr in 1967. He served as Equerry to the Duke of Edinburgh (1961-66), Equerry to the Prince of Wales (1967-70), and Private Secretary to the Prince of Wales (1970-78).
Chick, Flt Lt R.	Hunter pilot. Sqn Ldr Roger Chick (1932-2012) who later flew Lightnings and was a QFI retired from the RAF in 1990.
Christie, Flt Lt D.	Canberra pilot. Don Christie (1936-2002) retired from the RAF in 1974.
Clark Flt Lt F.D.G	Hunter pilot. AVM David Clark, CBE, (d.2006) was AOC Training Units and commandant of the National Defence College.

Clarke, Plt II P.J.   Mosquito pilot. Flt Lt Peter Clake was killed in a flying accident in a Canberra near Exeter in October 1953.

Clause, Flt Lt D.M.   Mosquito pilot. Gp Capt Donald Clause, AFC, later commanded 500 Squadron RAuxAF in 1954.

Cockram, Flt Lt S.H.   Tornado pilot. Gp Capt Steve Cockram commanded II (AC) Squadron and later served with the Royal Air Force of Oman.

Cocks, Plt III R.L.   Mosquito pilot. Raymond Cocks (1925-1975) joined the RAF in 1944 and left in 1952 to join Gillette as a sales representative.

Coleman, Flt Lt D.E.   Mosquito navigator. Derrick Coleman (1923-2007) had served in the Pathfinder Force with 35 Squadron during the Second World War and was shot down and taken PoW. He was promoted to Sqn Ldr in 1957.

Collins, Fg Off A.J.   Canberra navigator. Sqn Ldr Alan Collins retired from the RAF in 2001.

Comer, Fg Off P.K.   Tornado pilot. Wg Cdr Paul Comer commanded 208 Squadron Hawks at RAF Valley.

Commander, Fg Off R.J.   Canberra navigator. Flt Lt Robert Commander retired from the RAF in 1985.

Compton Flt Lt P.J.   Phantom navigator. Sqn Ldr Phil Compton (b.1948) retired from the RAF in 1994.

Connolly, Ft Lt J.   Phantom and Jaguar pilot. Jerry Connolly, AFC commanded 6 Squadron Jaguars and RAF Wittering. He retired from the RAF as an Air Cdre in 2001.

Cook, Fg Off M.J.   Tornado pilot. After a short time with Monarch Airlines, Marcus Cook became an Inspector at the Air Accident Investigation Branch.

Cook, Flt Lt P.W.   Mosquito pilot. Gp Capt Phillip Cook later commanded 98 Squadron; he retired from the RAF in 1968.

Cookson, Fg Off N.T.   Tornado navigator. Later Wg Cdr Nigel "Cookie" Cookson, who flew two tours with 14 Sqn, was Naval & Air Attaché in Ankara and in Pretoria.

Cooper, Fg Off K.G.   Hunter pilot. Flt Lt Kenneth Cooper (b.1931) retired from the RAF in 1970.

Cooper, Nav II T.W.   Mosquito navigator. Sqn Ldr Thomas 'Bill' Cooper, AFM retired from the RAF in 1963 but remained active with the RAFVR (Training) branch until 1979.

Cope, Flt Sgt   Mosquito navigator.

Coppard, Flt Lt E.G.   Canberra navigator. After retiring from the RAF in 1967, Ernie Coppard qualified as a civilian navigator and flew with Invicta Airways and Nigerian Airways. He then worked in an operational role for several units at Manston before finally retiring in 2001.

Coriat Sqn Ldr H.   Phantom navigator. Hubert Coriat (b.1937) was commissioned in 1957 and was later OC operations at RAF Honington.

Cornwall, Fg Off N.O.   Mosquito pilot. Neville Cornwall, a graduate of Queens College Cambridge, was commissioned in 1946 and was killed, aged 22 years-old, in a flying accident off Gozo, Malta in October 1948.

Cosens, Flt Lt I.J.   Tornado pilot. Ian Cosens served two tours on 14 Squadron. After leaving the RAF he joined British Airways as a Boeing 777 pilot.

Cosgrove Flt Lt J.A.   Phantom navigator. Gp Capt John Cosgrove, CBE (d.2013) - later OC Ops at RAF Honington, retired from the RAF in 1998.

Coulls, Sqn Ldr C. J.   Tornado navigator. A cornishman, Air Cdre Chris Coulls commanded 17 Squadron Tornados and RAF Waddington. Inexplicably this gifted Tornado QWI did not feature in the post-Gulf War honours list.

Courcoux Flt Lt J.   Phantom pilot. Sqn Ldr Ian Courcoux retired from the RAF in 1978.

Cousins, Fg Off D.N.   Hunter pilot. After leaving 14 Squadron, Derek Cousins (d.1979) was a QFI at Syerston. He later flew Whirlwinds in the Far East and Pumas at Odiham. His final tour was as the support helicopter expert at JWE Old Sarum. He retired from the RAF as a Sqn Ldr.

Cox, Wg Cdr R.W.	Mosquito pilot and wing leader. An ex-Halton apprentice, Gp Capt Reginald Cox (AFC) who retired from the RAF in 1977, had won both the DSO and DFC while flying with 7 Squadron during the war.
Cracroft, Plt Off H.G.	Hunter pilot. Wg Cdr Hugh Cracroft, who retired from the RAF in 1985, flew Hunters with 14, 2 and 8 Squadrons and Buccaneers with the Fleet Air Arm as an instructor on 736 Training Squadron and with 800 Squadron RNAS on HMS *Eagle*. He also served as OC operations wing at RAF Honington. After leaving the RAF he joined BAe Systems.
Craghill, Fg Off C.M.	Tornado navigator. Wg Cdr 'Mal' Craghill completed an exchange tour with the USAF flying the F-15E.
Crane, Flt Lt R.	Phantom navigator. Wg Cdr Bob Crane retired from the RAF in 1993, but rejoined 5 years later. He was dismissed the service by Court Martial in 2003.
Crellin, Sgt W.M.	Mosquito and Vampire pilot. Murray Crellin was commissioned in 1953 and retired from the RAF as a Flt Lt in 1969.
Cribb, Gp Capt P.H.	Station commander at Oldenburg. Air Cdre Peter Cribb, CBE, DSO★, DFC (1918-2011) was a distinguished wartime bomber and pathfinder pilot. After resigning from the RAF in 1967, he emigrated to Australia.
Crocker, Flt Lt R.G.	Mosquito pilot. Ronald Crocker won the DFC while serving with 622 Sqn; he retired from the RAF in 1947 and was the Mayor of Warrington in 1969-70.
Crook, Fg Off C.	Venom pilot. Described as 'the most charismatic of all the pilots' on 14 Squadron at the time, Sqn Ldr Cecil 'Ces' Crook, MBE commanded 209 Squadron in Malaya during the Indonesian Confrontation and transferred to the RNZAF. He was a member of the RNZAF 'Red Checkers' display team in the 1970s.
Cross, Fg Off E.J.	Venom and Hunter pilot. After being injured in a Venom accident in 1954, Flt Lt Edwin 'Chris' Cross rejoined the squadron in September 1956; he left the RAF in 1961 and joined British European Airways.
D'Arcy, Fg Off S.H.R.L.	Vampire and Venom pilot. Sam D'Arcy (1929-2012) survived the first live ejection from a Venom; he left 14 Squadron to be flight commander with 4 Squadron on F-86 Sabres, and then qualified as a test pilot. D'Arcy, who was the son of the 6th Count D'Arcy, retired from the RAF as a Sqn Ldr in 1987.
Dachtler, Flt Lt A.H.	Phantom pilot. Alan Dachtler, BSc, retired from the RAF in 1981.
Davies, LAC F.	Hunter electrical mechanic. Frank Davies left the RAF in 1960 and joined Thorn EMI defence division as the government accountant. After redundancy he ran a stationery business in West Sussex.
Davies, Flt Lt G.E.D.	Mosquito pilot. Sqn Ldr George Davies who won the DFC with 102 Squadron in 1944 retired from the RAF in 1962.
Day, Flt Lt P.	Phantom pilot. Sqn Ldr Paul Day later commanded the Battle of Britain Memorial Flight and flew over 1,000hrs in Spitfires and Hurricanes. He retired from the RAF in 2004.
Day, Sqn Ldr P.J.J.	Jaguar pilot. An ex-Red Arrows pilot, Wg Cdr Pete Day commanded 617 Squadron (Tornado).
de Torre, Corporal M.E.	Venom instrument fitter. Self confessed 'Aviation Nut' and keen glider pilot, Michael de Torre joined the RAF as a boy entrant and after serving with 14 Squadron he was posted to RAF Waddington to work on Vulcans. After leaving the RAF in the late 1950s, he was commissioned into the RAFVR(T) and commanded an ATC Squadron before retiring in 1994.
Deck, Sqn Ldr A.G.	Mosquito pilot. Originally commissioned into the RASC, Arthur Deck transferred to the RAF in September 1941. He won the DFC with 227 Squadron in 1943 and the DSO with 143 Squadron in July 1945. After retiring from the RAF in May 1956 he died in Kenya 1950.

Deluce, Fg Off W.   Hunter pilot. William 'Bugs' Deluce was killed, aged 24 years-old, in a flying accident on 18 August 1955 and is buried in the Ohlsdorf Cemetery in Hamburg.

Dent, Flt Lt N.T.   Tornado navigator. Norman Dent (1963-91) from Washington (Tyne & Wear) was killed in a flying accident in Oman on 13 Jan 1991 during the work-up for the Gulf War.

Donaldson, Gp Capt E.M. Station commander at Fassberg. Air Cdre 'Teddy' Donaldson, CB, CBE, DSO, AFC★, (1912-1992) a renowned Second World War fighter pilot established the world-speed record in a Meteor in 1946. After retiring from the RAF in 1961 he became the air correspondent for the *Daily Telegraph*.

Donovan, Flt Lt C.J.   Tornado navigator. Having flown his first tour on Javelins with 60 Squadron in Singapore, 'CJ' Donovan (d. 2000) became a simulator instructor at Bruggen after his ejection from a 14 Squadron Tornado.

Duffy, Flt Lt K.J.   Tornado pilot. Originally from Stourbridge, Kieran Duffy (1966-1991) was killed in a flying accident in Oman on 13 Jan 1991 during the work-up for the Gulf War.

Dunn, Flt Lt J.L.W.   Mosquito and Vampire pilot. A New Zealander, Bill Dunn retired from the RAF in 1966 with the rank of Sqn Ldr; he had been awarded a QCVS. After leaving 14 Sqn he flew F-86 Sabres with 149 Squadron and Javelins with 72 Squadron.

Earp, Flt Lt D.A.   Jaguar pilot. Sqn Ldr Derek "Wyatt" Earp retired from the RAF in 1991.

Edmunds, Fg Off A.C.   Hunter pilot. Tony Edmunds later flew for British Airways.

Edwards, Flt Lt P.   Phantom pilot. Gp Capt Peter 'Ted' Edwards commanded 31 Squadron Jaguars and retired from the RAF in 2001.

Ellis, Sqn Ldr P.C.   Mosquito pilot. Gp Capt Peter Ellis, DFC retired from the RAF in 1970; he had won the DFC with 613 Squadron, and commanded 6 Squadron in 1954.

Elsby, Fg Off R.C.   Hunter pilot. Flt Lt Robert Elsby (d. 2008) had originally joined the RAF as a radio fitter. He left the RAF in 1964 and became a dentist.

Evans, Flt Lt D.A.W.   Tornado navigator. An ex-member of the RAF Bobsleigh Team, Wg Cdr Don Evans left the RAF in 2011.

Farquharson, Flt Lt D.   Phantom pilot. David Farquharson instructed at the Tactical Weapons Unit at Brawdy, then left the RAF in 1986 and joined IBM.

Feeney, Flt Lt J.   Phantom navigator.

Field, Fg Off C.P.   Hunter pilot. Colin Field (d. 1980) medically retired from the RAF in 1959 and joined BP.

Field, Wg Cdr J.   Canberra pilot. OC 3 Squadron. Air Cdre John Field (d. 2002).

Finch, Plt Off D.V.   Vampire pilot. David Finch BSc(Eng) had just graduated from Imperial College before National Service.

Fitzgerald, Fg Off P.J. Vampire and Venom pilot. Patrick Fitzgerald was a national service pilot, who later transferred to a Short Service Commission.

Forrester, Fg Off R.A.   Canberra navigator. Wg Cdr Bob Forrester, OBE retired from the RAF in 1998.

Foulkes, Sqn Ldr A.S.   Hunter pilot and OC 14 Squadron. Sqn Ldr Stan Foulkes retired from the RAF in 1977.

Foxley-Norris, Wg Cdr C.N. Mosquito pilot, OC14 Squadron. A former Battle of Britain pilot, Air Chief Marshal Sir Christopher Foxley-Norris, DSO (1917-2003) retired from the RAF in 1974 having served as C-in-C RAF Germany.

Francis, Flt Lt N.P.   Tornado navigator. Working on the Shadow R1 project with Raytheon, Paul 'Taff' Francis continues his link with 14 Squadron.

Fraser, Flt Lt E.C.   Tornado navigator. Later Wg Cdr Ewen Fraser.

Froud Flt Lt J.R.J.   Phantom pilot. Sqn Ldr Jim Froud later flew Jaguars and retired from the RAF in 1991.

Fry, Flt Lt B.J.   Mosquito navigator. Sqn Ldr Basil Fry retired from the RAF in 1967; he won the DFC in 1945 while serving with 105 Squadron.

Fulker, Nav II A.A.	Mosquito navigator. 'Bert' Fulker was killed, aged 27 years-old, in a flying accident on 30 Aug 1949.
Furze, Wg Cdr R.McA.	Canberra pilot and OC 14 Squadron. 'Mac' Furze (1928-2011) had been the RAF's youngest Canberra captain and flew in the 1953 London-Christchurch Air Race in which he took third place. The following year he also flew on a covert reconnaissance mission over Western Russia in an RB-45C Tornado. Mac retired from the RAF in 1983 and settled in Much Hadham where he ran an antiques restoration business.
Gallie, Sqn Ldr D.W.	Tornado pilot. Dave Gallie is one of the RAF's most experienced Tornado pilots.
Galyer, Fg Off J.T.	Canberra and Phantom pilot. After leaving 14 Squadron, John Galyer was posted to CFS and was a member of the 'Gemini Pair' aerobatic team. He returned to 14 Squadron flying Phantoms as flight commander. He left the RAF in 1981 and joined Orion Airways when it started up, becoming Boeing 737 fleet manager. After the take-over by Britannia Airways he went on to the fly the B757 and 767, before retiring in 2003.
Gambold, Flt Lt K.A.	Tornado pilot. Keven Gambold volunteered to be among the RAF's first UAV pilots and after settling in the USA became chief operations officer of Unmanned Experts.
Gibson, Flt Lt M.A.	Tornado pilot. Flt Lt Mike Gibson left the RAF in 1992. He joined Virgin Atlantic Airways and became a training captain on the Boeing 747.
Gillanders, Fg Off D.C.	Canberra pilot. Sqn Ldr Doug Gillanders retired from the RAF in 1979.
Glover, Flt Lt A.D.	Tornado navigator. 'Andy' Glover served two tours on 14 Squadron, in the late 1980s and the early 2000s.
Golightly, Sqn Ldr R. H.	Mosquito pilot. Commissioned in 1941, Wg Cdr Robert Golightly, OBE, DFC, AFC retired from the RAF in 1972; he won the DFC while serving with 333 Squadron in July 1945.
Gooch, Flt Lt M. J. C.	Mosquito pilot. Michael Gooch RAFVR, was killed in a flying accident on 6 December 1945.
Goode, Sqn Ldr G.E.	Mosquito pilot and OC14 Squadron. Sqn Ldr George Goode won the DFC with 105 Squadron (Blenheims) for an attack on Rotterdam in May 1941, during which he was attacked by five fighters; he was later shot down over southern Italy in August 1941 and taken PoW. He retired from the RAF in 1958.
Goode, Plt Off R.A.E.	Vampire pilot. Roy Goode was a national service pilot.
Goodman, Sqn Ldr P.J.	Phantom navigator. 'Pete' Goodman later flew with 27 and 31 Squadrons on Tornados and left the RAF in 1996. He then served as a retired officer at RAF Innsworth.
Goodyear, Plt I.S.	Mosquito navigator. Sidney 'Geordie' Goodyear, AFM had been a Beaufighter pilot during the Second World War.
Gorman, Fg Off E. B.	Canberra navigator. Ted Gorman (d. 2010).
Graham, Flt Lt G.W.	Phantom navigator. Granville Graham (b.1932) retired from the RAF in 1986.
Graham, Flt Lt H.	Mosquito pilot. Herbert Graham had already completed two tours with 143 Squadron - one on Beaufighters and one on Mosquitoes.
Grange, Flt Lt M. J.	Canberra navigator. Wg Cdr Michael Grange (b. 1938) retired from the RAF in 1993.
Greenleaf, Sqn Ldr E. J.	Mosquito pilot and OC 14 Squadron. An ex-Halton apprentice, Sqn Ldr John Greenleaf, DSO, DFC (1915-2010) retired from the RAF in 1958. He won both the DSO and DFC while flying Pathfinder Mosquitoes with 571 Squadron in 1944.
Gregory, Flt Lt A.	Canberra pilot. Sqn Ldr Tony Gregory retired from the RAF in 1977.
Greig, Fg Off A.	Mosquito pilot. Sqn Ldr Archibald Greig, DFC AFC retired from the RAF in 1963; he won the DFC while serving with 576 Squadron.
Grieve, Flt Lt A.G.	Tornado navigator. A gifted QWI navigator, Alan Grieve from Forres, was killed aged 28 years-old in a flying accident on 13 January 1989. He was married, with a baby daughter.
Griffin, Flt Lt K.G.	Phantom pilot. Sqn Ldr Keith Griffin (b. 1948) retired from the RAF in 1987.

Griffiths, Sqn Ldr D.A.	Phantom and Jaguar pilot. Gp Capt Duncan Griffiths, OBE, AFC flew Phantoms and Jaguars with 14 Squadron and retired from the RAF in 1986.
Guy, Flt Lt	Mosquito navigator.
Hales, Flt Lt D.W.	Tornado pilot. After leaving the RAF in 2004, Sqn Ldr Dave 'Buster' Hales joined British Mediterranean Airways, before transferring to Emirates Airlines as a Boeing 777 pilot.
Hall, Fg Off A. N.C.M.	Canberra pilot. After QFI tours, 'Nick' Hall flew Wessex helicopters in Northern Ireland and Cyprus and UH-1Ds on exchange with the *Luftwaffe*. He was instructing at Shawbury when he retired from the RAF in 2000 as a Sqn Ldr, but continued there as a civilian instructor until 2007.
Hammond, Nav II	Mosquito navigator.
Hanson, Flt Lt J.H.	Canberra pilot. After flying Canberras with 213, 88 and 14 Squadrons, Flt Lt John Hanson was posted to Transport Command. He flew the Britannia with 99 Squadron and instructed on the OCU. On leaving the RAF in 1973, he joined Cathay Pacific Airways where he flew the Convair 880, Boeing 707, Lockheed TriStar and Boeing 747 aircraft, eventually being appointed as the chief check captain, Boeing 747 fleet.
Harbison, Plt Off E.R.	Vampire pilot. Eric Harbison was killed, aged 25 years-old, in a flying accident on 21 Jan 1952. He had previously served with 502 Squadron.
Harding, Plt III R.R.	Mosquito pilot. Ronald Harding, who later flew Vampires, Hunters and Lightnings was commissioned in 1952 and promoted to Gp Capt in 1967.
Harkin, Flt Lt D.J.	Jaguar pilot. An experienced Jaguar pilot, Sqn Ldr Den Harkin also flew F-16 on exchange with the RNLAF. On leaving the RAF he joined British Airways where he was captain on both the Airbus 320 and Boeing 777.
Harper, Fg Off F.J.	Mosquito navigator. Frederick Harper won the DFM while serving with 578 Squadron in 1945.
Harreld, Flt Lt J.J.	Canberra navigator. Flt Lt Jeffrey Harreld, who left 14 Squadron to become an OCU instructor, retired from the RAF in 1972.
Harrison, Flt Lt G.	Tornado navigator. Sqn Ldr Gary Harrison left the RAF in 2001 and joined Thales before moving into the property rental business.
Hartree, Flt Lt W.R.	Jaguar pilot. Since retiring from the RAF, Wg Cdr Bill Hartree has been the organizer of the annual Cosford Air Show.
Hawkins, Fg Off R.L.	Canberra navigator. Sqn Ldr Rod Hawkins, MBE who retired from the RAF in 2006 was Mentioned in Dispatches during the 1991 Gulf War.
Headley, Plt Off D.G.	Vampire and Venom pilot. After going on to fly Javelins with 64 Squadron Don Headley, MBE (b. 1932) left the RAF in 1963 and joined the RN Civil Ferry Flight. He subsequently joined Hawker Siddeley, becoming chief test pilot at Holme-on-Spalding Moor in 1975. After management posts within BAe he served as chief test pilot at Slingsby Aviation 1995-2004.
Hedges, Fg Off R.W.	Canberra and Phantom navigator. Gp Capt Bill Hedges, CBE also served on 14 Squadron as a Phantom navigator. He later commanded the Tornado detachment at Tabuk during the 1991 Gulf War. He retired from the RAF in 1992 and joined BAe and later Adams Offshore, supporting military and civil aviation in Saudi Arabia.
Henderson, Wg Cdr D.F.A.	Jaguar pilot and OC 14 Squadron. Originally a Wessex helicopter pilot and later an instructor on the Jaguar OCU, David Henderson, CBE commanded RAF Marham and left the RAF in 1996 with the rank of AVM.
Hendy, Flt Lt I.D.	Tornado navigator. Ian Hendy retired from the RAF in 2008.
Hill, Flt Lt I.D.	Jaguar pilot. Flt Lt Ian "Iddy" Hill was killed, aged 41years-old, in a Jaguar flying accident during 1987.
Hill, Flt Lt J.A.	Tornado navigator. Later Gp Capt John Hill.
Hine, Wg Cdr D.J.	Phantom pilot and OC 14 Sqn. Air Cdre Derek Hine retired from the RAF in 1989.

Hodgson, Flt Lt J.	Hunter pilot. Wg Cdr John Hodgson (b. 1932) retired from the RAF in 1987.
Hogg, Flt Lt J.K.	Tornado pilot. John Hogg flew two tours with 14 Squadron; he retired from the RAF with the rank of Sqn Ldr in 2002 and joined British Airways to fly the Boeing 777.
Holme, Flt Lt M.	Mosquito navigator. Maurice Holme, from West Boldon Co Durham was killed, aged 24 years-old, in a flying accident on 6 December 1945.
Holmes, Sqn Ldr W.G.	Canberra pilot. Wg Cdr Bill Holmes retired from the RAF in 1980.
Honey, Fg Off R. J.	Hunter and Phantom pilot. AVM Bob Honey, CB CBE was Air Secretary before retiring in 1994; a Hunter pilot on 14 Squadron in the late 1950s and flight commander on the Phantom in the early 1970s, he commanded RAF Coltishall and was deputy C-in-C RAF Germany.
Hoole, Fg Off C.	Mosquito navigator. Cyril Hoole left 14 Squadron on release from the RAF in September 1946.
Hornsey, Flt Lt R.	Canberra pilot. Flt Lt Rod Hornsey retired from the RAF in 1972.
Howe, Fg Off K.D.	Vampire pilot. Keith Howe was 20 years-old when he was killed in a flying accident on 23 Feb 1953.
Howell, Flt Lt R.A.	Tornado navigator. Richie Howell, a well-respected QWI, died of cancer in 2013.
Hoyle, Fg Off R.F.	Hunter pilot. Raymond Hoyle transferred to the reserve in 1957 and later served in the RAFVR(T).
Huckins, Flt Lt N.M.	Jaguar Pilot. Gp Capt Nigel Huckins, MBE who retired from the RAF in 2006 became a QWI on 226 OCU and was the first QWI in the Tornado force. He was awarded QCVSA for his work on 617 Squadron's successful USAF SAC Bombing Competition and was as flight commander on 17 Squadron. He commanded 208 Squadron Buccaneers.
Jacks, PII	Mosquito pilot.
Jeremy, Flt Lt A.P.	Tornado pilot. Andrew Jeremy left the RAF in 1989 to join British Airways. He flew the Boeing 757 and 747 before becoming a captain on the Airbus A320, Boeing 767 and later Boeing 777.
Jevons, Fg Off P.	Hunter pilot. Wg Cdr Peter Jevons retired to Norway.
Johnson, Flt Lt S.	Phantom pilot. Steve Johnson later joined the Red Arrows and famously had to eject from his aircraft during a display at Brighton in 1979. After leaving the RAF he joined British Airways.
Jones, Flt Lt A.	Phantom pilot. Adrian Jones.
Jones, Flt Lt E.A.	Canberra pilot. Wg Cdr 'Ed' Jones left the RAF in 1993 and became the chief instructor at Cabair at Cranfield.
Jones, Wg Cdr R.I.	Mosquito pilot and OC 14 Squadron. An armament specialist, AVM Richard Jones, CB, AFC (1915-1993) retired from the RAF in 1970. He held appointments as SASO at HQ Fighter Command and AOC 11 Group.
Jordan, Flt Lt D.A.	Canberra pilot. Derek Jordan left the RAF in 1967 and after a few years flying with the Uganda Police Air Wing and later in Nigeria, he joined corporate aviation, eventually amassing over 10,000hrs on the HS125.
Joy, Fg Off R. M.	Canberra pilot. Sqn Ldr Bob Joy, MBE who retired from the RAF in 1996 was the manager of the Red Arrows before becoming a flight commander on IX Squadron (Tornado).
Kean, Flt Lt A.M.	Phantom pilot. Sqn Ldr Mike Keane, who retired from the RAF in 1980, was awarded a Queen's Commendation for Valuable Service in the Air for his handling of a Phantom emergency.
Kennedy, Flt Lt J.A. (DFM)	Marauder pilot. Retiring with the rank of Gp Capt in the air-traffic control branch of the RAF, James Kennedy had flown Marauders with 14 Squadron during the Second World War.
Kerr, Sqn Ldrs R.G.	Canberra pilot. Sqn Ldr Robert Kerr retired from the RAF in 1973.

Kerss, Flt Lt T.J.   Jaguar pilot. Wg Cdr Tim Kerss, MBE commanded 54 Squadron and left the RAF in
                            1996. He joined British Airways where he was a captain on Airbus A320 and Boeing
                            767 aircraft.

Keys, Fg Off D.   Hunter pilot. Flt Lt Dennis Keys retired from the RAF in 1966.

Kirby, Flt Lt R.A.   Jaguar pilot. Sqn Ldr Robert 'Rip' Kirby retired from the RAF in 1984.

Klein, Sqn Ldr J.B.   Tornado navigator. Gp Capt James Klein commanded 14 Squadron during his second tour
                            on the unit, overseeing its move to RAF Lossiemouth.

Kyrke, Fg Off R.T.V.   Canberra pilot. Richard 'Dick' Kyrke left the RAF in 1964 and joined British Airways.

Labouchere, Flt Lt C.M.   Canberra pilot. An engineering officer by trade, Wg Cdr Colin Laboucher, MA (b. 1938)
                            retired from the RAF in 1977.

Lane, Fg Off J.F.   Canberra pilot. Flt Lt Jeremy Lane left the RAF in 1976 and joined IBM. He later became
                            a director of Shearer Candles.

Lawrence, Sqn Ldr J.T.   Vampire and Venom pilot, also OC 14 Squadron. AVM John Lawrence, CBE, AFC was
                            commissioned 1941 and retired in 1975. During the war he flew Catalinas with 202
                            Squadron. Subsequent posts included station commander RAF Wittering and AOC
                            Scotland & Northern Ireland.

Lawton, Flt Lt J.V.   Jaguar pilot. Sqn Ldr James Lawton retired from the RAF in 1984.

Lee, Flt Lt B.R.   Phantom navigator. Gp Capt Brian Lee retired from the RAF in 1996.

Legg, Flt Lt D.A.C.   Tornado pilot. Wg Cdr Darren Legg, who was a flight commander on IX Squadron during
                            the Kosovo campaign, later commanded 100 Squadron Hawks.

Levy, Plt Off M.H.   Mosquito pilot. Sqn Ldr Michael Levy, MBE retired from the RAF in 1968 after
                            tours as a QFI on Meteors and a flight commander on 213 Squadron (Canberras) he
                            served as a staff officer at HQ 2ATAF. He subsequently worked in MoD operational
                            requirements on the SNEB rocket and the Nord AS30 and Martel missiles before
                            joining IBM.

Lewis, Flt Lt E.G.   Mosquito pilot. Edward Lewis was killed in a flying accident at Wahn on 30 Aug 1949,
                            aged 27 years-old.

Lindo, Flt Lt R.W.   Jaguar holding officer. Sqn Ldr Bob Lindo had to leave the RAF after damaging his back
                            after ejecting from a Jet Provost in 1986. Subsequently he became a vintner, running the
                            Camel Valley vineyard in Cornwall.

Linstead, Flt Lt A.S.   Tornado navigator. Gp Capt Andy Linstead commanded 12 Squadron; on retiring from the
                            RAF he joined Lockhead Martin.

Lloyd, Flt Lt S.J.   Tornado navigator. Steve Lloyd served two tours on 14 Squadron.

Loverseed, Flt Lt R.E.W.   Hunter pilot. Sqn Ldr 'Bill' Loverseed, AFC (1932-98), whose father had been a Battle of
                            Britain pilot, went on to lead the Red Arrows between 1970 and 1971 and was killed in a
                            flying accident in a DeHavllind (Canada) Dash 7 aircraft.

Lowe, Flt Lt H.H.   Mosquito pilot. Born in 1912, Sqn Ldr Harold Lowe retired from the air-traffic control
                            branch of the RAF in 1958. He originally joined the RAF as an apprentice in 1928
                            and qualified as a pilot in 1936, initially flying Wellesleys with 47 Squadron. He was
                            shot down while flying with 143 Squadron over Norway in March 1945 and rejoined
                            14 Squadron at Banff in July 1945.

Lumb, Flt Lt D.M.V.   Tornado navigator. Wg Cdr Mike Lumb's career has included three tours on 13 Squadron,
                            ground tours with the RN, Army and USAF as well as staff appointments, latterly with
                            DSTL.

Macpherson, Flt Lt J.A.   Vampire, Venom and Hunter pilot. Sqn Ldr Archie 'Mac' Macpherson was killed,
                            aged 32 years-old, in a mid-air collision flying a Seahawk from RNAS Lossiemouth
                            while on exchange with the Fleet Air Arm in 1959. As a Queen's University
                            Air Squadron student he had won the Hack Trophy for the best all-round UAS pilot
                            in 1948.

Maddison, Flt Lt J.K.	Hunter pilot. Sqn Ldr Joseph Maddison, AFC retired in 1979.
Madgwick, Fg Off D.F.	Venom and Hunter pilot. David Madgewick joined BOAC in 1958.
Madison, W/O	Mosquito navigator.
Magill, Wg Cdr G.R.	Mosquito pilot OC 14 Squadron. Originally from New Zealand, AVM Graham Magill, CB, CBE, DFC★ (1915-1998) won his first DFC while flying Wellesleys in the Eritrean campaign with 47 Squadron. He was later AOC 22 and 25 Training Groups.
Malone, Cpl J.	Phantom storeman. After working on Phantoms, Vulcans and Tornados, Sgt John Malone left the RAF to work at St Athan and later Bristol City Council Education Department, before starting his own printing business.
Malone, Flt Lt M.	Jaguar pilot. Sqn Ldr Mike Malone retired from the RAF in 1992.
Manville, Flt Lt C.P.	Canberra navigator. Clive Manville (1941-2002) retired as a Sqn Ldr in 1989.
Marriott, Fg Off J.F.H.	Hunter pilot. After his tour with 14 Squadron, Wg Cdr John Marriott flew the Hastings, Argosy and Hercules, becoming OC Operations Wing at RAF Lyneham and later serving as Naval & Air Attaché in Baghdad. He retired from the RAF in 1988 and worked for the chief executive of Gulf Air.
Marsh, Flt Lt P.	Canberra pilot.
Marsh, Flt Lt T.J.	Tornado pilot. Flt Lt Tim Marsh left the RAF in 1992 and joined British Airways and flew the Beoing 757 before becoming a captain on the Airbus A320.
Martin, Flt Lt P.N.	Jaguar pilot. Nick Martin left the RAF in 1988.
McAlpine, Flt Lt R. I.	Jaguar pilot. Air Cdre Bob McAlpine, DFC who commanded IX Sqn Tornados and RAF Marham, retired from the RAF in 2011.
McCairns, Sqn Ldr C.	Phantom and Jaguar pilot. Sqn Ldr Chris McCairns, who left the RAF in 1986 was both a Phantom pilot and a Jaguar Flt Cdr with 14 Squadron.
McDonald, Flt Lt F. J.	Phantom navigator. Forbes 'Mac' McDonald retired from the RAF in 1975.
McDonald, Sqn Ldr T.P.	Tornado pilot. Gp Capt Paul McDonald, OBE who retired from the RAF in 2005, had been chief instructor at RAF Linton-on-Ouse. In retirement he became a Tucano simulator instructor.
McElhaw, Wg Cdr T.J.	Canberra pilot OC 14 Squadron. Wg Cdr Tim McElhaw retired from the RAF in 1981. Flying a Spitfire, he shot down 2 Egyptian Spitfires during the Arab-Israeli war in 1948 before being shot down and captured by the Israelis. He also served on attachment to the USAF during the Korean War and had commanded 4 Squadron flying Hunters in the late 1950s.
McEntegart, Fg Off J.R.	Venom pilot. The son of AVM B. McEntegart, CB, CBE and the artist Anne McEntegart, John McEntegart was killed, aged 22 years-old, in a flying accident on 3 May 1955.
McLauchlan, Fg Off A.C.	Hunter pilot. Tony McLaughlan transferred to the reserve in 1963.
McVie, Fg Off J.	Hunter pilot. Sqn Ldr John 'Jock' McVie retired from the RAF in 1971.
Mellett, Flt Lt P.C.	Hunter pilot. Sqn Ldr Peter Mellett, MBE (d. 2013) retired from the RAF in 1973.
Meredith, Nav II G	Mosquito navigator. George Meredith.
Metcalf, Flt Lt M.J.	Jaguar pilot. Sqn Ldr Mike Metcalf was awarded two Queen's Commendations for Valuable Service in the Air.
Miller, Flt Lt G.A.	Jaguar pilot. Air Marshal Sir Graham 'Dusty' Miller, KBE (b.1951) joined the RAF as a Halton apprentice and flew two tours on Jaguars with 14 Squadron, the second as a flight commander. He commanded 17(F) Squadron (Tornado) and RAF Lossiemouth, and was AOC Training Group, Air Secretary and finally deputy commander at the NATO Joint Force Command Naples.
Moffatt, Flt Lt W.	Mosquito pilot. William Moffatt had served with 14 Squadron from April 1945-March 1946; he was awarded the DFC flying with 140 Squadron.
Moloney, Flt Lt J. P.	Tornado pilot. Gp Capt John Moloney commanded 6 Squadron (Jaguars).

Moon, Fg Off R.M.	Hunter pilot. Rod Moon transferred to the reserve in 1966.
Moore, Flt Lt R.	Canberra pilot. Originally a Vulcan pilot, Roger Moore subsequently became an air-traffic controller and served as CGI at Shawbury and as deputy station commander at Manston.
Morris, Flt Lt G.W.	Canberra pilot. After leaving 14 Squadron George Morris became a QFI, before flying Nimrods for 17 years. After retiring from the RAF he became a Nimrod simulator instructor and QFI at his local flying club.
Morris, Wg Cdr R.V.	Tornado navigator. Originally on Buccaneers, AVM Vaughan Morris, CBE, AFC was chief of staff at HQ PTC before he retiring from the RAF in 2002.
Morter, Flt Lt D.	Hunter pilot. Derek Morter amassed 6,500hrs of Hunter flying, latterly with FRADU which included leading the 'Blue Herons' aerobatic team. He had flown Meteors with 74 Squadron and was OC Stn Flt Oldenburg before joining 20 Squadron. After leaving 14 Squadron, he had tours at Chivenor and Aden and after leaving the RAF in 1968, he flew F-86 in Saudi Arabia, Canada and the US before returning to the Hunter.
Morton, Fg Off S.J.	Canberra pilot. Achieving just over 6,000hrs in fast-jets, 'Stu' Morton flew Buccaneers and Tornados before retiring from the RAF in 1996. He then spent 10 years as a Jaguar, then Tornado simulator instructor.
Moule, Sqn Ldr D.E.	Tornado pilot. Sqn Ldr Moule, DFC retired from the RAF in 1997 and flew with Monarch and Qatar Airways before joining EasyJet as flight operations manager at Gatwick.
Mullen, Flt Lt T.A.F.	Jaguar pilot. Flt Lt Thomas 'Paddy' Mullen, who retired from the RAF in 1991, flew Jaguars with the Sultan of Oman's Air Force.
Mumford, Wg Cdr A.	Jaguar pilot and OC 14 Squadron. Gp Capt Anthony Mumford CVO OBE (1936–2006) commanded RAF Benson and retired from the RAF in 1991.
Murtagh, Flt Lt M.J.	Tornado pilot. Mike Murtagh left the RAF in 1991 and joined British Midland Airways where he was a captain on the Airbus A320. He later became a CAA operations inspector.
Napier, Flt Lt M. J. W.	Tornado pilot. Mike Napier flew two tours with 14 Squadron and left the RAF in 1997 with the rank of Sqn Ldr. He joined British Airways and flew the DC10 and Boeing 777 before becoming a captain on the Airbus A320.
Nattrass, Fg Off T.	Hunter pilot. Air Cdre Trevor Nattrass, CBE, AFC★ retired from the RAF in 1991; he had commanded 16 Squadron (Buccaneers) and RAF Honington.
Needham, Flt Lt D.G.	Jaguar pilot. Sqn Ldr David Needham retired from the RAF in 1991 to become managing director of his family firm, the Needham Group, a company producing ink and printing materials.
Newby, Flt Lt B.W.	Jaguar pilot. Air Cdre Brian Newby, CBE AFC, who commanded 16 Squadron and RAF Valley, became Director of Flying Training.
Newland, SAC J.	Canberra radio technician. From 14 Squadron John Newland's career took him to Lyneham, Changi, and Odiham. On leaving the RAF he joined BA as an aircraft radio instructor and later spent 15 years instructing pilots at BA Flight Training Centre. After 'retiring' he became an aircraft radio instructor at the Defence College at Aborfield.
Newman, Fg Off R.A.	Canberra pilot. A QFI, Sqn Ldr Roderick Newman retired from the RAF in 2004.
Nichol, Fg Off	Mosquito pilot.
Noble, Flt Lt K.G.	Jaguar pilot. After pioneering the TIALD pod during the Gulf War, Sq Ldr Noble Kev Noble left the RAF in 1997 and joined British Airways, becoming an Airbus captain.
Norman, Flt Lt J.L.	Hunter pilot. Jeremy Norman transferred to the Photographic Interpretation Branch of the RAF in 1972.
Nottingham, Flt Lt J.	Phantom navigator. Sqn Ldr Jim Nottingham (b.1940) retired from the RAF in 1979.

O'Brien, Sqn Ldr F.C.StG.	Mosquito pilot OC 14 Squadron. A former Battle of Britain fighter pilot, Gp Capt Peter O'Brien, OBE, DFC★ (1918-2007) was born in Toronto and won the Sword of Honour at Cranwell in 1937. He retired from the RAF in 1959 and returned to Canada where he became vice president of the Southam Press.
O'Connor, Flt Lt P.	Hunter Engineering Officer. Originally from Trinidad, Patrick O'Connor left the RAF after 16 years' service in 1975 to join British Aerospace Dynamics. He later worked as an independent consultant on engineering management, reliability, quality and safety.
O'Shea, Flt Lt N.	Canberra navigator. Noel 'Paddy' O'Shea (1928-2010) retired from the RAF with the rank of Sqn Ldr; he subsequently served with the Sultan of Oman's Air Force.
Owen, AC1 E.	Mosquito flight mechanic. Originally from Liverpool, Ernie Own emigrated to Canada after leaving the RAF.
Oldham, Flt Lt M.G.	Tornado navigator. Gp Capt Mike Oldham, OBE was OC Ops Wg at RAF Marham.
Page, Flt Lt G.	Tornado navigator. Sqn Ldr Grant Page commanded 76 (R) Squadron Tucanos.
Parfitt, LAC W.	Mosquito flight mechanic. Wilf Parfitt played wing forward for the Garndiffaith and went on to captain Pontypool RFC against the Springboks in 1951.
Parker, Fg Off J.R.	Canberra pilot. Originally from Kenya, Jim Parker returned to his native country after leaving 14 Squadron (and the RAF) in 1967.
Parr, Sqn Ldr J.J.E.	Jaguar pilot. An ex-Lightning pilot before flying the Jaguar, Wg Cdr Jerry Parr was OC Flying Wing at Chivenor and retired from the RAF in 1996.
Parsons, Plt Off D.L.	Hunter pilot. Sqn Ldr David 'Snip' Parsons became a QFI on piston-engined and Jet Provosts. He served on the staff at CFS before an exchange tour with the RAAF. After tours as a multi-engine instructor and a staff officer at HQ Training Command he joined Britannia Airways in 1972 where he was a Boeing 737 and 767 captain. He retired in 1993.
Payne, Fg Off J. J.	Tornado navigator. After leaving the RAF in 1990, Jeremy Payne worked with BAe in Saudi Arabia before qualifying as a commercial pilot and flying for Maersk, Emirates and then Ryan Air.
Peacock, Fg Off P.G.	Venom and Hunter pilot. Air Cdre Peter Peacock, CBE BSc (d. 2013) retired from the RAF in 1984. After his tour on 14 Squadron he went on to command 43 Squadron and was later the station commander at RAF West Drayton.
Pearce, Flt Lt G.A.	Canberra navigator. George Pearce left the RAF in 1974.
Perks, Flt Lt G.D.	Mosquito pilot. Geoffrey Perks (1918-2012) won the DFC while flying Halifaxes with 434 (Canadian) Squadron. He later flew Dakotas on psychological warfare sorties in the Malayan Emergency and left the RAF in 1958. His subsequent careers included managing director of an engineering company and insurance brokerage.
Pettit, Fg Off B.D.	Vampire, Venom and Hunter pilot. After leaving 14 Squadron, Brian Pettit spent two tours flying Meteors before leaving the RAF in 1958. He rejoined the service shortly afterwards and over the next 24 years he became one of the few pilots to have flown all three V-bomber types: Valiant, Vulcan and Victor.
Pixton, Flt Lt G.W.	Jaguar pilot. Gp Capt Bill Pixton, DFC, AFC retired from the RAF in 2003. As OC 41 Squadron, he commanded the Jaguar Detachment at Muharraq during the 1991 Gulf War.
Platt, Fg Off C.	Tornado navigator. Wg Cdr Chris Platt served two tours on 14 Squadron and was OC Ops Wg at RAF Northolt.
Pluck, Fg Off M.F.E.W.	Canberra pilot. Malcolm Pluck subsequently flew Dominies and Vulcans with ground tours in Germany and the navigation school. He left the RAF in 1982 for a career in training and management within the finance industry.
Potter, Flt Lt D.J.A.	Tornado navigator. Wg Cdr Dougie Potter served three tours on 14 Squadron. After leaving the RAF he was the manager of the Scottish RFU for two seasons. He is the treasurer of the 14 Squadron Association.
Potter, Plt Off D.C.D.	Hunter pilot. David Potter transferred to the reserve in 1961.

Preece, Fg Off J.M.	Hunter pilot. Sqn Ldr John 'Pring' Preece retired from the RAF in 1975 after tours with CFS and the Malaysian Air Force. He had also flown Spitfires, Hurricanes and Me-109s during the making of the film *The Battle of Britain*. He joined Marshalls of Cambridge as a test pilot and deputy airport manager and later worked for the Mission Aviation Fellowship in Africa before returning to Cambridge to continue as a flying instructor with the Cambridge Aero Club.
Price, Sqn Ldr H.W.	Tornado pilot. Wg Cdr Hylton Price left the RAF in 2006 but was killed in a flying accident in a Grob Tutor in 2009.
Priestley, Sgt A.C.	Hunter radar & radio technician. Alan Priestley was 25 years-old when he was killed in a road accident on 15 August 1960.
Ramsey, Flt Lt F.N.	MRCP controller. Frederick Ramsey, AFC transferred to the Fighter Control Branch of the RAF and retired in 1974.
Rankin, Plt Off R.	Hunter pilot. Flt Lt Ronald Rankin (b.1933) retired from the RAF in 1971.
Read, Nav II G.	Mosquito navigator.
Reeves, Flt Lt S.E.	Tornado pilot. Gp Capt Steve Reeves later commanded 14 Squadron and RAF Leeming.
Reid, Sqn Ldr S.G.	Tornado pilot. After leaving 14 Squadron 'Stu' Reid became the CFS Agent for the Boeing E3 and also flew the Battle of Britain Memorial Flight Avro Lancaster.
Rhodes, Flt Lt K.D.	Phantom pilot. Wg Cdr Ken Rhodes retired from the RAF in 1994. He later built, and flew, his own autogyro.
Richardson, Sqn Ldr K.E.	Hunter pilot OC 14 Squadron. Gp Capt Ken Richardson, OBE retired from the RAF in 1982. He commanded RAF Neatishead.
Ridland, Plt II	Mosquito pilot.
Rimmer, Sqn Ldr J.A.J.	Tornado pilot. After serving as OC Ops Wg at RAF Coltishall, Wg Cdr Jerry Rimmer retired from the RAF in 2004, eventually joining SerCo as a contract director.
Ritch, Flt Lt D.N.S.	Tornado pilot. After loan service in Saudi Arabia, Don Ritch joined Virgin Atlantic Airways in 2001.
Roberts, Sqn Ldr G.	Phantom pilot. Previously a night-fighter pilot on Meteors and Javelins, Geoff Roberts had converted to the Phantom in the US. He later became an instructor at the Tri-National Tornado Training Establishment and also flew Spitfires and Hurricanes with the Battle of Britain Memorial Flight.
Rochelle, Sqn Ldr S.P.	Tornado navigator. Air Cdre Peter 'Rocky' Rochelle, DFC later commanded 617 Squadron and RAF Marham.
Rogers, Flt Lt P.C.H.	Jaguar pilot. Paul 'Buck' Rogers later joined the Red Arrows and also flew for the Royal Flight before leaving the RAF in 1999.
Rogers, Sqn Ldr P.F.	Canberra pilot. Originally a national serviceman, Gp Capt Peter Rogers, OBE retired from the RAF in 1986; he had previously flown Meteors and went on to command 208 Squadron Buccaneers in 1974, before staff tours in the USA and UK.
Rogers, Wg Cdr K.B. (DFC, AFC)	Canberra pilot. A New Zealander who won the DFC while flying Wellingtons with 150 Squadron in 1944, Keith Rogers (1922-2010) retired from the RAF in 1966.
Rossie, Fg Off M.D.	Canberra navigator. Maurice Rossie became specialist aircrew in 1976.
Rothwell, Fg Off I.P.	Hunter pilot. Flt Lt Ian Rothwell retired from the RAF in 1971.
Roxburgh, Flt Lt D.K.	Tornado pilot. Flt Lt Dougie Roxburgh transferred to the VC10 and flew tanker support for 14 Squadron crews during 'Operation Engadine'. After leaving the RAF he joined Virgin Atlantic Airways to fly the Boeing 747.
Rumens, Flt Lt K.R.	Tornado pilot. A pilot with Virgin Atlantic Airways, 'Kev' Rumens has also been a display pilot for the 'Vulcan to the Skies' project.
Rusling, Sqn Ldr N.C.	Jaguar pilot. Gp Capt Nick Rusling, who had commanded 226 OCU, retired from the RAF in 2002.

Russell, W/O D.H.	Mosquito navigator. Denis Russell (d. 2014) had served operationally with 128 Squadron during the war and was demobbed in December 1946.
Salter, Flt Lt A.	Canberra pilot. Later a helicopter specialist, Gp Capt Tony Salter was Mentioned in Dispatches while commanding RAF Aldergrove.
Sanderson, AC1 D.	Vampire engine mechanic. After leaving the RAF David 'Sandy' Sanderson joined the Post Office. He subsequently spent 27 years working in the cabinet office, rising to the level of higher executive officer.
Saxby, Nav III M.	Mosquito navigator. Michael Saxby had flown with 35 Squadron during the Second World War.
Sayer, Fg Off F.	Hunter Engeering Officer. Frank 'Lofty' Sayer, a former Engineering Warrant Officer, retired from the RAF in 1969.
Sayers, Flt Lt S.R.	Tornado navigator. Flt Lt Steve Sayers retired from the RAF in 2013.
Selka, Flt Lt J.A.	Mosquito pilot. After service in the RAF Joseph Selka (1915-2005) was the managing director of a textiles company in Bradford.
Sewell, Flt Lt J.	Canberra pilot. After tours as a QFI, Jim Sewell, BA specialized in Surface-to-Air Missiles and later commanded 85 Squadron (Bloodhounds). He retired from the RAF as a Wg Cdr 1993.
Sharp, Sgt K.	Mosquito and Vampire pilot.
Sharp, Flt Lt M.J.	Tornado pilot. Mark Sharp, who flew Buccaneers, Tornados and Harriers. He left the RAF to join British Airways as a Boeing 777 pilot.
Sheppard, Flt Lt R.I.	Phantom navigator. Sqn Ldr Reece Sheppard retired from the RAF in 1986.
Sim, Wg Cdr J.K.	Jaguar pilot and OC 14 Squadron. A former Javelin navigator, Gp Capt Joe Sim, OBE, AFC commanded RAF Bruggen and retired from the RAF in 1987.
Simpson, Flt Lt R.C.	Vampire pilot. Gp Capt Robert 'Bob' Simpson, CBE retired from the RAF in 1980.
Sinclair, Sgt A.H.	Vampire and Venom pilot. Andy Sinclair.
Skinner, Flt Lt A.H.	Canberra pilot. After tours at CFS and as OC Flying at RAE Llanbedr, Sqn Ldr Hugh Skinner retired from the RAF in 1977 and became a management consultant specializing in setting up small businesses.
Slessor, Fg Off J.A.G.	Mosquito pilot. The son of MRAF Sir John Slessor, Gp Capt John Slessor (1926–2008) commanded 83 Squadron and RAF Odiham.
Smith, Flt Lt D.C.	Phantom navigator. Gp Capt David 'Kip' Smith, OBE later commanded RAF West Raynham.
Smith, Flt Lt H.F.	Tornado pilot. Later, Gp Capt Hugh Smith.
Smith, Fg Off H.R.	Mosquito navigator. Henry Smith retired on medical grounds from the RAF in 1960.
Smith, Flt Lt K. A.	Tornado navigator. Wg Cdr Ken Smith, who commanded 39 Squadron Canberras left the RAF in 2005 and joined FRA Ltd.
Smith, Fg Off M.	Canberra navigator. Flt Lt Martin Smith was killed in a flying accident in a Phantom during 1972. He was 26 years-old.
Smith, Flt Lt M.P.S.	Tornado pilot. On 13 Jan 1989, Mike Smith was killed in a flying accident aged 37 years -old. He had previously flown Vulcans and Jaguars.
Smith, Flt Lt P.	Canberra pilot.
Smith, Sgt R.R.	Venom and Hunter pilot. Ralph 'Smudge' Smith was a QFI on Jet Provosts and Gnats before leaving the RAF to join BOAC in 1967. After qualifying as a captain on both Boeing 707 and 747 aircraft with BOAC (BA), he was amongst the first Boeing 747 training captains to join Virgin Atlantic Airlines when the company started up.
Smith, Wg Cdr W. A.	Vampire pilot, wing leader at Fassberg. Wg Cdr Bill Smith, DFC, AFC retired in 1962; he had been awarded the DFC while serving with 229 Squadron in 1942.
Spinelli, Capt A.	Tornado pilot. Andrea Spinelli was an Italian exchange officer.

Stanley, Flt Lt I.G.	Hunter pilot. Ian Stanley left the RAF in 1956.
Stanway, Flt Lt M.I.	Hunter pilot. Wg Cdr Ian Stanway, who retired from the RAF in 1985, had joined the squadron when 26 Squadron disbanded. He later commanded 28 Squadron flying Hunters in Hong Kong.
Stapleton, Gp Capt D. C.	Station commander at Oldenburg. AVM Deryck Stapleton, CB, CBE, DFC, AFC had joined 14 Squadron as a Plt Off in 1937 and left 40 years later as a Wg Cdr commanding the squadron. He retired from the RAF in 1968 having been AOC 1Group and subsequently worked for British Aerospace in Iran and China. Stapleton was the president of the 14 Squadron Association from 2001-2009.
Stead, Flt Lt J.C.	Mosquito pilot. Sqn Ldr John Stead commanded 31 Squadron (PR Canberras) and retired from the RAF in 1958 to work in Flight Safety at the Ministry of Aviation; he won the DFC with 100 Squadron in 1943.
Steggall, Fg Off G.	Venom and Hunter pilot. Geoff Steggall later flew Hunters and Lightnings with 74 Squadron and retired in 1984 after instructional tours on the Lightning Conversion Squadron/OCU, in Ghana, at the Tactical Weapons Units and the Air Navigation School.
Steward, Flt Lt M.J.	Canberra navigator. Malcolm Steward (b.1937) retired from the RAF in 1978.
Stilwell, Fg Off M.S.E.	Vampire and Venom pilot. Captain Maurice 'Mo' Stilwell was killed when his Viscount, OD-ADE of Middle East Airlines, collided with a C-47 over Ankrara on 1 February 1963.
Stoate, Fg Off L.C.M.	Vampire pilot. Shortly after completing his National Service, Len Stoate rejoined the RAF, but was killed in a flying accident at Wadhurst, Sussex, in 1956.
Stockley, Flt Lt T.P.	Canberra pilot. Sqn Ldr Terry Stockley retied from the RAF in 1979.
Stone, Sgt P.M.	Venom and Hunter pilot. Phillip 'Ginger' Stone, a somewhat accident-prone pilot, had previously served with 118 Squadron.
Strange, Wg Cdr G.	Canberra pilot, OC 14 Squadron. George Strange was commissioned in 1943 and retired from the RAF in 1974.
Stringer, Flt Lt S.I.	Canberra navigator. Stuart Stringer later flew Buccaneers but resigned from the RAF in 1980.
Stubings, Sqn Ldr R.A.	Canberra navigator. Sqn Ldr Robin Stubings, who commanded RAF Burtonwood, retired from the RAF in 1976.
Sutherland, Sqn Ldr R.A.	Vampire pilot OC 14 Squadron. Ronald 'Max' Sutherland, who retired from the (DFC★) RAF with the honorary rank of Wg Cdr in 1952 was a legendary wartime fighter pilot. He won two DFCs while serving with 602 Squadron which he commanded, and he appears in Pierre Closterman's book *The Big Show*. Although he could be unpredictable and violent, Sutherland was also a charismatic leader who was revered by his subordinates.
Sutton Wg Cdr J.M.D.	Phantom pilot OC 14 Squadron. Air Marshal Sir John Sutton KCB (b. 1932) was AOC-in-C RAF Support Command before retiring from the RAF in 1989. He subsequently served as the Lieutenant Governor of Jersey. Sutton had previously commanded 249 Squadron (Canberras) in 1964.
Swann, Fg Off R.N.	Canberra pilot. Sqn Ldr Ron Swann (b. 1941) retired from the RAF in 1979. He became the chief instructor at the BAe Flight Training School at Prestwick and later flew with City Flier airline.
Taylor, Sqn Ldr E.A.	Canberra navigator. Wg Cdr Tony Taylor who left 14 Sqn to be chief instructor at South Cerney. He retired from the RAF in 1980.
Taylor, Flt Lt G.A.	Canberra navigator. A Canadian ex-paratrooper, Flt Lt George Taylor was killed in Hastings crash at Abingdon on 6 July 1965 while on a parachute course from Finningley.
Taylor, Flt Lt R.	Phantom navigator. Roly Taylor
Tebb, Fg Off B.A.	Canberra navigator. Sqn Ldr 'Bernie' Tebb left the RAF in 1983 to join BAe Systems and later managed a leisure resort in Thailand.

Timilty, Flt Lt J.	Vampire pilot. A rugby player who frequently played for the station side, John 'Tim' Timilty, commissioned in 1944, had previously served with 3 Squadron. He retired as a Flt Lt in 1963.
Titchen, Flt Lt B.	Phantom navigator. Barry Titchen, ex-RN Buccaneers commanded 56 Squadron and retired as a Gp Capt in 2000.
Tite, Fg Off I.D.C	Hunter pilot. Sqn Ldr Iain Tite, AFC retired from the RAF in 1975.
Toal, Fg Off K.G.	Canberra navigator. Kevin Toal (1943-2005) retired from the RAF in 1981.
Tonkinson, Fg Off B.J.	Hunter pilot. Flt Lt Barrie 'Tonk' Tonkinson retired from the RAF in 1969.
Trotter, Fg Off R.W.D.	Canbera navigator. Wg Cdr Roy Trotter commanded 29 Squadron Tornado F3.
Tuhill, Flt Lt P.J.	Mosquito navigator. Flt Lt Pat Tuhill, DFC, had been Foxley-Norris's navigator on 143 Squadron and moved to 14 Squadron with him; he retired from the RAF in 1962.
Turner, Flt Lt F.L.	Jaguar and Tornado pilot, OC 14 Squadron. A Jaguar and Tornado QWI, Gp Capt Frank Turner left the RAF in 2007 from RAF Innsworth where he had been Gp Capt Flying Training.
Turner, Flt Lt H.S.	Tornado pilot. Steve Turner left the RAF in 1993 to join Cathay Pacific Airlines.
Turner, Flt Lt R.J.	Tornado navigator. Sqn Ldr 'Russ' Turner retired from the RAF in 2005.
Turnill, Flt Lt R.G.	Phantom pilot. Standing over 6ft tall, 'Rog' Turnill, was described by his contemporaries as 'one of the stars on 14' and 'a brilliant and dedicated fighter pilot.' He had previously flown Hunters with 1 and 8 Squadrons and became a well-respected Phantom pilot. After his tour with 14 Squadron he was posted to Coningsby. Tragically he died of cancer in 1974 aged 30 years-old.
Vacha, Flt Lt I.D.	Phantom navigator. Gp Capt Iain Vacha retired from the RAF in 2003.
Valentine Fg Off R.G.	Canberra pilot. Sqn Ldr Robert Valentine retired from the RAF in 1972.
Vernon, Flt Lt J.C.	Canberra pilot. Sqn Ldr John Vernon commanded the RAF Survival School at Mountbatten; he was also a member of the RAF Mountain Rescue Service.
Vosloo Flt Lt A.	Phantom navigator. Sqn Ldr Al Vosloo (1927-1997) retired from the RAF in 1981.
Wagstaff, Flt Lt L.E.	Hunter pilot. Laurence 'Mike' Wagstaff retired from the RAF in 1965.
Wain, Fg Off S.	Tornado navigator. Wg Cdr 'Stu' Wain left the RAF in 2007 and joined the CAA airspace management branch.
Walker, Flt Lt I. B.	Jaguar and Tornado pilot. A QFI, Ivor Walker, who retired from the RAF in 2004 with the rank of Wg Cdr, flew two tours with 14 Squadron. He was injured in a flying accident during the Gulf War.
Walker, Flt Lt S.	Tornado navigator. Simon Walker.
Walker, Gp Capt J.R.	Station commander Bruggen. Air Marshal Sir John 'Whisky' Walker KCB CBE AFC (b.1936) was SASO at RAF Strike Command and Deputy Chief of Staff COMAAFCE. He retired from the RAF in 1991.
Walliker, Flt Lt J.A.	Phantom pilot. Sqn Ldr John Walliker retired from the RAF in 1985 to run a hotel in Nuneaton.
Walton, Flt Lt I.R.	Tornado pilot. Sqn Ldr Ian Walton flew Mirage 2000 on exchange with the French Air Force. He later flew the Airbus A320 and A380 with British Airways.
Ward, Sqn Ldr D. J.	Canberra pilot. Wg Cdr Denis Ward retired from the RAF in 1983.
Ward, Flt Lt K.A.	Tornado pilot. After instructional tours, Kev Ward left the RAF in 1999 to become an airline pilot.
Ward, Flt Lt P.L.	Tornado navigator. After a tour as a Flt Cdr on IX Sqn, Sqn Ldr Pete Ward spent much of his post-Bruggen career at RAF Marham.
Wardell, Flt Lt G.A.	Jaguar pilot. After instructing at the TWCU, Graham Wardell (1954-1999) flew the F-117 on exchange with the USAF. He left the RAF in 1996 as a Sqn Ldr and joined BAe. He was killed while displaying a Hawk 2000 at the Bratislava Air Show.

Watson, Flt Lt J.	Phantom pilot. A former Hunter pilot, John 'Jock' Watson served with 14 Squadron throughout its days as a Phantom unit. He was awarded the AFC at the end of his tour, during most of which he had been the RAFG Phantom display pilot. He retired from the RAF in 1979 and continued to fly with a number of airlines. He holds the world-speed record for playing the bagpipes, having played while supersonic in a Phantom.
Wellings Flt Lt IG.	Phantom navigator. Wg Cdr Ian Wellings retired from the RAF in 1996.
Wells, Sqn Ldr R.J.	Canberra navigator. Robert 'Binky' Wells retired from the RAF in 1977.
Wesley, Fg Off R.J.	Tornado navigator. Sqn Ldr Richard 'Wes' Wesley (1961-1999) from Bozeat, Northants, died in an accident at RAF Henlow.
Wheeler, Fg Off R.	Canberra pilot. Roy Wheeler.
Whitfield, Wg Cdr J.J.	Tornado pilot and OC 14 Squadron. An former QFI, member of the 'Linton Blades' display team and Jaguar pilot, Gp Capt Joe Whitfield commanded RAF Honington and after leaving the RAF in 1994 he flew Hawks with FRADU.
Whitley, Flt Lt B.A.	Canberra pilot. Flt Lt Brian Whitley retired from the RAF in 1968 and returned to his native South Africa.
Wilkinson, Flt Lt P.J.	Canberra pilot. Air Cdre Phil Wilkinson, CVO, MA, FRAeS, FRSA later commanded 237 OCU (Buccaneers), was station commander at RAF Gatow when the Berlin Wall came down and later served as Defence and Air Attaché to Moscow.
Williams, Sqn Ldr E.H.C.	Hunter pilot and OC 14 Squadron. Sqn Ldr Edwin Williams retired from the RAF in 1968; he was commissioned in 1952 having been a Sgt pilot.
Williams, Fg Off L.P.	Tornado navigator. After serving with II (AC) Squadron, Flt Lt Larry Williams retired from the RAF in 2004
Williams, Fg Off R.H.	Vampire and Venom pilot. Sqn Ldr Ron Williams retired from the RAF in 1976.
Williams, Flt Lt R.L.	Mosquito navigator. Robert Williams was killed in a flying accident on 30 Oct 1948 aged 25; he won the DFC while serving with 35 Squadron in 1944.
Wilson, Fg Off D.S.	Canberra navigator. Doug Wilson left 14 Squadron to convert onto the Buccaneer and was the first RAF navigator to go straight to the RAF Buccaneer force. He set up 12 Squadron and 237 OCU and was awarded the Queen's Commendation for Valuable Service in the Air for his work. He retired from the RAF in 1985 with the rank of Squadron Leader.
Wilson, Fg Off J.A.	Canberra pilot. After leaving the RAF in 1969, Johnnie Wilson embarked on a highly-successful career in retailing. Having spent 13 years with Marks & Spencer, he helped to establish 'Tie Rack' as an international retailer, opening their head office in the US and eventually heading central operations team. He later became involved in local politics, serving as a cabinet member on Maidstone Borough Council.
Wingate, Flt Lt P.F.	Vampire pilot. On 8 Jun 1951, Peter Wingate was killed in a flying accident aged 31. He was commissioned in 1942 and won the DFC with 619 Squadron; before joining 14 Squadron he had been a QFI at the Empire Test Pilots' School.
Wintermeyer, Flt Lt M.J.	Tornado navigator. Flt Lt Martin Wintermeyer became a primary school teacher before rejoining the RAF as a navigator and later CRM instructor.
Wright, Fg Off M.C.	Canberra navigator. Matthew Wright retired from the RAF in 1970.
Wright, Fg Off R.M.	Canberra navigator. After tours on the Vulcan and as a ground instructor at RAF Valley, Dick Wright retired from the RAF in 1997.
Yates, Flt Lt W. H.	Canberra navigator. Bill Yates, who had previously flown Valiants and PR Canberras, transferred to the General Duties (Ground) branch in 1974 and retired from the RAF in 1982.

Appendix 2

Aircraft Operated by 14 Squadron 1945–2015

A/C Type	Serial No	Sqn Code	Date On	Date off	Comments	Crew
Mosquito FBVI	HR405	A	25 May 1945		scrapped	
Mosquito FBVI	HR414	L	25 May 1945		Transferred to Turkish AF	
Mosquito FBVI	HR436	J	25 May 1945		Transferred to Turkish AF	
Mosquito FBVI	HR604	V	25 May 1945	4 Dec 1945	Lost power on overshoot and crash-landed Sylt	WO B.J. F.Barlow, WO Madison – minor injuries
Mosquito FBVI	PZ417				Transferred to 21 Sqn	
Mosquito FBVI	PZ435				scrapped	
Mosquito FBVI	PZ439	C				
Mosquito FBVI	PZ446	T	25 May 1945		Transferred to RNZAF	
Mosquito FBVI	PZ451	B	25 May 1945		Transferred to RNZAF	
Mosquito FBVI	PZ466	Q	25 May 1945		Transferred to Turkish AF	
Mosquito FBVI	PZ473				Transferred to 228 OTU	
Mosquito FBVI	RF608	Y	25 May 1945		Transferred to *Armee de l'Air*	
Mosquito FBVI	RF618	G	25 May 1945		Transferred to 21 Sqn	
Mosquito FBVI	RF622	K	25 May 1945	6 Dec 1945	Wing hit sea during low-level bombing practice and aircraft broke up 1½ miles northeast of Sylt	Flt Lt M.J.C. Gooch, Fg Off M. Holme – both killed
Mosquito FBVI	RF640				Transferred to 25 APC	
Mosquito FBVI	RF645				Transferred to Lubeck	
Mosquito FBVI	RF646	X	25 May 1945		Transferred to *Armee de l'Air*	
Mosquito FBVI	RF897				Transferred to 21 Sqn	
Mosquito FBVI	RS559		22 Dec 1945	2 Apr 1946	Transferred to 19 MU	
Mosquito FBVI	RS606	O	25 May 1945	7 Apr 1946	Transferred to 107 Sqn	
Mosquito FBVI	RS607	F	25 May 1945	17 Jan 1946	On Navex – poor wx, VHF & 'Gee' both failed, ran out of fuel and crashed in forced landing nr Dunkirk	Sgt A.J. Bonsoni, Flt Sgt Brewer – both OK
Mosquito FBVI	RS625	D	25 May 1945	2 Apr 1946	To 19 MU	
Mosquito FBVI	SZ958		28 Sep 1945		Transferred to *Armee de l'Air*	
Mosquito FBVI	SZ962		13 Sep 1945	1 Apr 1946	To 151 RU	
Mosquito FBVI	TA589		2 Jan 1946	28 Mar 1946	Transferred to 21 Sqn	
Mosquito FBVI	TA593	CX-H	2 Jan 1946	17 Jan 1946	On Navex – poor wx, VHF & 'Gee' both failed, ran out of fuel and crashed in forced landing 8 miles west of St Pol-sur-Ternoise	Sgt J.F. Barrett, Fg Off C. Hoole – both OK
Mosquito B XVI	MM192		1 Apr 1946		scrapped	
Mosquito B XVI	MM204		1 Apr 1946		scrapped	
Mosquito B XVI	PF410		1 Apr 1946		scrapped	
Mosquito B XVI	PF413	CX-E	1 Apr 1946		scrapped	
Mosquito B XVI	PF415		1 Apr 1946		scrapped	
Mosquito B XVI	PF443	M5-M	1 Apr 1946		scrapped	
Mosquito B XVI	PF449		1 Apr 1946		Transferred to RN	
Mosquito B XVI	PF457		1 Apr 1946		scrapped	
Mosquito B XVI	PF461		1 Apr 1946	31 May 1946	Overshot single-engined landing and undercarriage leg collapsed Wahn – Damaged beyond repair	Fg Off K.R. Hughes
Mosquito B XVI	PF462		1 Apr 1946		scrapped	
Mosquito B XVI	PF525		1 Apr 1946		scrapped	
Mosquito B XVI	PF544	CX-F	4 Mar 1948	28 Jun 1948	Transferred to 27 MU	
Mosquito B XVI	PF545		4 Mar 1948	28 May 1948	Transferred to 9 MU	
Mosquito B XVI	PF548		1 Mar 1948	25 Apr 1947	Sank back and hit runway on take-off belly-landed El Adem 'Operation Sunshine' deployment to North Africa	Fg Off A.deL. Greig, Flt Lt F. Belfitt – both OK

A/C Type	Serial No	Sqn Code	Date On	Date off	Comments	Crew
Mosquito B XVI	PF555		2 Feb 1948	4 Aug 1948	Transferred to 98 Sqn	
Mosquito B XVI	PF557		5 Nov 1947	6 Jul 1948	Transferred to RN	
Mosquito B XVI	PF558		29 Jul 1947	22 May 1948	Transferred to RN	
Mosquito B XVI	PF561		4 Apr 1947	18 Dec 1947	Transferred to RN	
Mosquito B XVI	PF575	CX-Y	19 Jun 1947	28 Dec 1947	Transferred to RN	
Mosquito B XVI	PF579		4 Mar 1948	28 May 1948	Transferred to 9 MU	
Mosquito B XVI	PF607		2 Feb 1948	4 Mar 1948	Transferred to 98 Sqn	
Mosquito B XVI	PF609		11 Sep 1947	16 Dec 1947	Transferred to RN	
Mosquito B XVI	PF612	CX-G	5 Nov 1947	21 Jan 1948	Transferred to RN	
Mosquito B XVI	PF614		4 Mar 1948	11 Jun 1948	Transferred to 9 MU	
Mosquito B XVI	PF616	CX-T	7 Jun 1947	20 Jan 1948	Transferred to RN	
Mosquito B XVI	PF617		2 Feb 1948	4 Mar 1948	Transferred to 98 Sqn	
Mosquito B XVI	PF618		29 Mar 1947	19 Jul 1948	Transferred to 9 MU	
Mosquito B XVI	RV302		4 Apr 1946	16 Sep 1946	Brakes failed while taxying and undercarriage collapsed at Manston	Flt Lt C.D. Owen
Mosquito B XVI	RV313		4 Apr 1946	23 May 1947	To Squires Gate Exhibition	
Mosquito B XVI	RV319		4 Apr 1946	7 Nov 1946	to 151 RU	
Mosquito B XVI	RV345		4 Apr 1946	19 Nov 1946	to 151 RU	
Mosquito B XVI	RV354		4 Apr 1946	27 Oct 1947	soc	
Mosquito B 35	RS704	CX-B	26 Jan 1950	28 Feb 1951	Transferred to 22 MU	
Mosquito B 35	RS706	CX-G	24 Jun 1948	2 Aug 1949	Transferred to Brooklands	
Mosquito B 35	RS708	CX-Z	28 Jun 1948	5 Mar 1951	Transferred to 48 MU Hawarden	
Mosquito B 35	RV354		4 Sep 1946	27 Oct 1947	soc	
Mosquito B 35	TA694	CX-S	28 Jul 1949	28 Feb 1951	Transferred to 19 MU	
Mosquito B 35	TA695	CX-W	12 Jul 1948	27 Feb 1951	Transferred to 22 MU	
Mosquito B 35	TA706		30 Jan 1951	19 Feb 1951	Transferred to 27 MU	
Mosquito B 35	TA707		28 Sep 1949	28 Oct 1949	Hood disintegrated and hit tail during dive at max. permitted IAS 370kts - not repaired	Plt Off M.H. Levy, Flt Lt D. Coleman – both OK
Mosquito B 35	TA714		3 Jul 1948	25 Sep 1949	Swung on take-off and damaged undercarriage, belly-landed on return at Celle	Plt III Harding
Mosquito B 35	TH999	CX-A	28 Apr 1949	1 Feb 1951	Swung on take-off and undercarriage raised to stop, Fassberg	Sgt W. M. Crellin, AC Jennings – OK
Mosquito B 35	TJ141	CX-Y	30 Sep 1948	30 Oct 1948	Starboard engine caught fire - dived into sea off Gozo, Malta	Fg Off N.O. Cornwall, Flt Lt R. L. Williams – both killed
Mosquito B 35	TJ143	CX-A	28 Apr 1949	2 Apr 1949	Caught fire during Met Climb and abandoned nr Wahn.	Plt III R.L. Cocks – OK, Nav II Bolton - injured
Mosquito B 35	TK594		20 Apr 1948	8 Jun 1948	Crashed on take-off at Wahn	PII Clarke, Nav II Cooper – OK
Mosquito B 35	TK602		3 May 1949	11 Jul 1949	Swung on landing and undercarriage collapsed Wahn	Sgt F. Myhill, Sgt W.D.R. Bond – OK
Mosquito B 35	TK617	CX-D	3 May 1950	28 Sep 1950	Port undercarriage damaged on take-off, aircraft subsequently landed with port wheel partially retracted at Celle.	Flt Lt G.D. Perks, injured leg, Flt Lt B.J. Fry – OK
Mosquito B 35	TK625		13 Nov 1948	30 Aug 1949	Flew into ground in bad visibility during Met climb 8 miles East of Wahn.	Flt Lt E.G. Lewis, Nav II A.A. Fulker – both killed
Mosquito B 35	TK629	CX-Y	23 Dec 1947	19 Apr 1948	Transferred to 15 MU	
Mosquito B 35	TK656		22 Dec 1947	16 Apr 1948	Transferred to 15 MU	
Mosquito B 35	VP178		22 Jan 1948	4 Mar 1948	Transferred to Wahn Wing	
Mosquito B 35	VP180	CX-O	20 Apr 1948	15 Feb 1951	Transferred to Brooklands	
Mosquito B 35	VP189		22 Sep 1950	3 Mar 1951	Transferred to 22 MU	
Mosquito B 35	VP191	CX-X	1 Oct 1949	14 Jun 1950	Transferred to Brooklands	
Mosquito B 35	VP202	CX-B	2 Jul 1948	29 Apr 1949	Practice single-engine landing at Wahn – undershot and belly landed	Plt III R.L. Cocks; Nav II Shepherd – OK
Mosquito B 35	VR793		3 Nov 1949	13 Jan 1950	Transferred to Brooklands	
Mosquito B 35	VR799	CX-C	23 May 1949	15 Jan 1951	Transferred to Brooklands	
Mosquito B 35	VR802		19 Jan 1951	20 Feb 1951	Transferred to 27 MU	
Mosquito B 35	VR806		19 Apr 1948	30 Apr 1948	Transferred to 9 MU	
Mosquito TIII	LR554				Station Flight Wahn & Celle, transferred to 204 AFS	
Mosquito TIII	VA890			16 Sep 1949	Station Flight Wahn & Celle, swung on landing at Celle; written off	Sgt F. Myhill, Sgt W. D. R. Bond – OK
Vampire FB 5	VV219		19 Nov 1953	15 Jun 1954	Transferred to 10 MU, Hullavington	

A/C Type	Serial No	Sqn Code	Date On	Date off	Comments	Crew
Vampire FB 5	VV443	B–U	9 Mar 1951	21 Jan 1952	Spun into the sea during air-to-air gunnery pass at Sylt	Fg Off E.S. Harbison – killed
Vampire FB 5	VV538	B–V	9 Mar 1951	8 Jun 1951	Ammunition-bay door opened during rocket pass, half rolled and hit ground Fassberg range	Flt Lt P.F.Wingate – killed
Vampire FB 5	VV542	Y	26 Sep 1952	20 Aug 1953	Transferred to 130 Sqn	
Vampire FB 5	VV561		20 Aug 1952	10 Aug 1953	Transferred to 130 Sqn	
Vampire FB 5	VV563		16 Mar 1953	10 Aug 1953	Transferred to 130 Sqn	
Vampire FB 5	VV628	B–C	7 Jul 1951	22 Jun 1953	Multiple birdstrike during low-level airfield attack at Hesepe	Fg Off S.H.R.L. D'Arcy – OK
Vampire FB 5	VV639		Apr 1954		On loan from 118 Sqn	
Vampire FB 5	VX464	B–F	12 Jun 1952	10 Aug 1953	Transferred to 130 Sqn	
Vampire FB 5	VX976	B–X	9 Mar 1951	10 Aug 1953	Transferred to 130 Sqn	
Vampire FB 5	VZ262		10 Jul 1952	19 Aug 1952	Transferred to 266 Sqn	
Vampire FB 5	VZ277		23 Sep 1952	27 Sep 1952	Transferred to 234 Sqn	
Vampire FB 5	VZ318	B–Z	20 Jun 1952	10 Aug 1953	Transferred to 130 Sqn	
Vampire FB 5	VZ343		12 Jun 1952	9 Jul 1952	Transferred to 112 Sqn	
Vampire FB 5	VZ344	B–T	9 Mar 1951	21 Jun 1951	Transferred to 98 Sqn	
Vampire FB 5	VZ346		18 May 1953	10 Aug 1953	Transferred to 98 Sqn	
Vampire FB 5	VZ832	E	12 Jun 1952	28 Oct 1953	Transferred to 130 Sqn	
Vampire FB 5	WA109	B–A	9 Mar 1951	26 Nov 1951	Mid-air collision with WA169, landed at Wunsdorf	Sgt A.H. Sinclair – OK
Vampire FB 5	WA113	T/W	16 Jun 1952	20 Aug 1953	Transferred to 130 Sqn	
Vampire FB 5	WA128	Q	28 Feb 1953	10 Aug 1953	Transferred to 130 Sqn	
Vampire FB 5	WA144		26 Jun 1952	2 Jul 1952	Transferred to 98 Sqn	
Vampire FB 5	WA149	P				
Vampire FB 5	WA169	B–D	9 Mar 1951	26 Nov 1951	Mid-air collision with WA109 lost starboard drop tank & aileron; belly landed at Fassberg	Fg Off S.H.R.L. D'Arcy – OK
Vampire FB 5	WA185	G	9 Jun 1952	11 Aug 1953	Transferred to 118 Sqn	
Vampire FB 5	WA193	B–H	9 Mar 1951	18 Jun 1953	Belly-landed after engine failure at 2,000ft after take-off	Fg Off P.J. Fitzgerald – OK
Vampire FB 5	WA199	B–P	9 Mar 1951	10 Aug 1953	Transferred to 130 Sqn	
Vampire FB 5	WA206	Q	9 Jun 1952	23 Feb 1953	Engine failed, broke up during forced landing 4 miles south of Uelzen	Fg Off K. D. Howe – killed
Vampire FB 5	WA221		3 Jul 1951	29 Aug 1951	Cat 4 to 98 Sqn	
Vampire FB 5	WA234		21 May 1957	29 May 1951	Transferred to 118 Sqn	
Vampire FB 5	WA283		23 Jun 1952	2 Jul 1952	Transferred to 112 Sqn	
Vampire FB 5	WA293		19 Mar 1953	30 Aug 1954	Transferred to 5 MU	
Vampire FB 5	WA306		Apr 1954		On loan from 118 Sqn	
Vampire FB 5	WA317		Apr 1953		On loan from 118 Sqn	
Vampire FB 5	WA355	B/D	7 Jul 1951	16 Aug 1952	Hit trees during instrument approach to Fassberg; undercarriage would not lower	Plt Off R.J.Adams
Vampire FB 5	WA374		19 Nov 1953	13 Jun 1954	Transferred to 10 MU, Hullavington	
Vampire FB 5	WA391	B–R	23 Jun 1951	28 Oct 1952	Transferred to 5 Sqn	
Vampire FB 5	WA396		Apr 1954		On loan from 118 Sqn	
Vampire FB 5	WE844	B–A	12 Dec 1951	1 Sep 1953	Transferred to 130 Sqn	
Vampire FB 5	WE854	A				
Vampire FB 5	WG832					
Vampire FB 5	WG841					
Vampire FB 5	WG845	B–B	12 Dec 1951	25 Jun 1953	Brake failure – ran into overshoot area – Cat 5	Plt Off E.J. Cross
Vampire FB 5	WG847		19 Nov 1953	22 Apr 1954	Engine failure on take-off; force landed 1 mile east of Fassberg	Fg Off M. Stilwell – OK
Vampire FB 5	WL493	R	8 Feb 1952	2 May 1952	During special trial, drop tanks fell from aircraft at high speed	Sqn Ldr R.A. Sutherland, DFC
Vampire T 11	WZ454	A	23 Oct 1958	19 Dec 1958	Transferred to 27 MU	
Vampire T 11	WZ516		26 Oct 1953	15 Jun 1955	Transferred to 107 MU, Kasfareet	
Vampire T 11	WZ518		14 Sep 1953	7 Sep 1955	Transferred to Oldenburg Station Flight	
Vampire T 11	WZ555		7 Dec 1953	31 Oct 1955	Transferred to Oldenburg Station Flight	
Vampire T 11	WZ620		18 Nov 1958	13 May 1959	Transferred to RAF Benson	
Meteor T7	WF779		21 Apr 1951	20 Oct 1953	Transferred to 541 Sqn	
Venom FB 1	WE270					
Venom FB 1	WE278		26 May 1953	28 Oct 1953	G-limited, Transferred to 22 MU Silloth	

A/C Type	Serial No	Sqn Code	Date On	Date off	Comments	Crew
Venom FB 1	WE283		5 Apr 1955	17 Jun 1955	Transferred to 5 Sqn	
Venom FB 1	WE288	Y	17 Aug 1953	8 Jul 1955	Transferred to 22 MU Silloth	
Venom FB 1	WE304	B	30 Jun 1953	26 Aug 1953	Engine failure – (oil-pump quill drive) force landed in field	Fg Off S.H.R.L. D'Arcy – OK
Venom FB 1	WE305					
Venom FB 1	WE349	B-E	26 Jun 1953	11 Jul 1955	Transferred to 48 MU, Hawarden	
Venom FB 1	WE354		21 Jul 1953	2 Dec 1953	Starboard undercarriage failed up, wheels-up landing carried out on grass at Fassberg	Fg Off W. Deluce – OK
Venom FB 1	WE355	B-D	17 Jun 1953	11 Jul 1955	Transferred to 48 MU, Hawarden	
Venom FB 1	WE356	B-X	28 Sep 1953	23 Feb 1955	Starboard fuselage and intake struck by debris during recovery from rocket attack, Fassberg range	Fg Off B. Pettit – OK
Venom FB 1	WE357	B-F	1 Jul 1953	3 May 1955	No 2 of a 4-ship practising low-level battle formation. Passed low over a Centurion tank and hit trees, impacted ground & exploded. 6 miles northwest of Munsterlager	Fg Off J.R. MacEntagert – killed
Venom FB 1	WE358	C	26 Jun 1953	11 Jul 1955	Transferred to 22 MU Silloth	
Venom FB 1	WE359	B-W	27 Jul 1953	19 Nov 1954	Landing as No 4 in 7 ship stream, swung to right due to uncommanded brake application. Left the runway and nose gear collapsed	Fg Off G. Steggall – OK
Venom FB 1	WE362	B-P	27 Jul 1953	11 Jul 1955	Transferred to 22 MU Silloth	
Venom FB 1	WE363	B-A	26 Jun 1953	5 Aug 1955	Transferred to 48 MU Hawarden	
Venom FB 1	WE367		30 Jul 1953	15 Aug 1953	Engine failed at 41,000ft, force landed at disused airfield Boulmer	Fg Off T.J. Bolger – OK
Venom FB 1	WE368	B-W	6 Aug 1953	23 Mar 1954	Structural failure of port wing spar during high-angle dive bombing at Fassberg range, aircraft exploded, pilot ejected	Fg Off S.H.R.L. D'Arcy – OK
Venom FB 1	WE371	B-T	26 Aug 1953	30 Dec 1953	Stalled at 50ft on finals and crashed into runway undershoot	Sgt P.M. Stone – OK
Venom FB 1	WE379	B-F				
Venom FB 1	WE399					
Venom FB 1	WE405	Q	11 Jan 1954	15 Jul 1955	Transferred to 22 MU Silloth	
Venom FB 1	WE407		6 Jan 1954	15 Jan 1954	Transferred to 118 Sqn	
Venom FB 1	WE410	B-G	31 Dec 1953	26 Oct 1954	Engine vibration during tail-chase, engine failed during recovery. Force-landed wheels up on crash strip at Fassberg	Fg Off D. Madgewick – OK
Venom FB 1	WE419					
Venom FB 1	WE425	B	7 Apr 1954	14 Sep 1954	Wing hit runway during overshoot from night GCA, aircraft stalled and crashed – ejection seat fired as aircraft broke up	Fg Off E.J. Cross – injured
Venom FB 1	WE438	B-P(B?)	22 Dec 1953	8 Jan 1954	Heavy landing and swung into snow drift	Fg Off J.K. Bancroft
Venom FB 1	WE445					
Venom FB 1	WE476	R	3 Mar 1954	5 Aug 1955	Transferred to 27 MU Shawbury	
Venom FB 1	WK397	T	15 Jan 1954	13 Jun 1955	Transferred to 27 MU Shawbury	
Venom FB 1	WK413	B-Z	6 May 1954	13 Jun 1955	Transferred to 27 MU Shawbury	
Venom FB 1	WK499	H	15 Jun 1954	13 Jun 1955	Transferred to 27 MU Shawbury	
Venom FB 1	WR298	B	8 Oct 1954	15 Jul 1955	Transferred to 22 MU Silloth	
Venom FB 1	WR350		4 Mar 1955	17 Jun 1955	Transferred to 22 MU Silloth	
Hunter F 4	WT711	A	8 Jun 1955	24 Aug 1957	To 5 MU for Disposal	
Hunter F 4	WT712	D	3 Jun 1955	31 May 1957	To 5 MU for Disposal	
Hunter F 4	WT714	F	13 Jun 1955	18 Aug 1955	Mid-air collision with WT806 at 40,000ft, 3 miles northeast of Bremen	Fg Off W. Deluce – killed
Hunter F 4	WT723	T	13 May 1955	18 Apr 1957	To 5 MU for Disposal	
Hunter F 4	WT724	E	13 May 1955	12 Apr 1957	To 5 MU for Disposal	
Hunter F 4	WT749	P	13 May 1955	15 Apr 1957	To 5 MU for Disposal	
Hunter F 4	WT755	Q	23 May 1955	18 Apr 1957	To 5 MU for Disposal	
Hunter F 4	WT761	O	16 May 1955	1 May 1957	To 5 MU for Disposal	
Hunter F 4	WT767	C	19 May 1955	9 Apr 1957	To 5 MU for Disposal	
Hunter F 4	WT797	Z	17 Jun 1955	9 Apr 1957	To 5 MU for Disposal	

A/C Type	Serial No	Sqn Code	Date On	Date off	Comments	Crew
Hunter F 4	WT806		20 May 1955	17 Jun 1955	Overstressed (14g) during high-speed manoeuvring	Fg Off C.P. Field – OK
Hunter F 4	WT807		3 Jun 1955	18 Aug 1955	Mid-air collision with WT714 at 40,000ft, 3 miles northeast of Bremen	Sgt P.M. Stone – OK
Hunter F 4	WV259	B	19 Jul 1955	26 Apr 1957	To 5 MU for Disposal	
Hunter F 4	WV267		24 Sep 1955	18 Jan 1956	Transferred to 93 Sqn	
Hunter F 4	WV277	K	19 Sep 1955	17 Jan 1956	Transferred to 93 Sqn	
Hunter F 4	WV318		16 Sep 1955	27 Mar 1956	Transferred to 93 Sqn	
Hunter F 4	WV377	W	10 Sep 1955	7 Nov 1955	Transferred to 26 Sqn	
Hunter F 4	WW663	H	24 May 1955	18 Apr 1957	To 5 MU for Disposal	
Hunter F 4	XE657	Y	13 Jun 1955	12 Apr 1957	To 5 MU for Disposal	
Hunter F 4	XE708		18 Oct 1955	15 Apr 1957	Transferred to 229 OCU	
Hunter F 4	XE710	R	18 Oct 1955	25 Apr 1957	To 5 MU for Disposal	
Hunter F 6	XE530		9 May 1958	9 Jun 1958	Transferred to 26 Sqn	
Hunter F 6	XF417		9 May 1958	9 Jun 1958	Transferred to 26 Sqn	
Hunter F 6	XG131	N	7 Jun 1957	7 Mar 1963	To 19 MU for Disposal	
Hunter F 6	XG166	K	29 Jul 1957	17 Dec 1962	To 19 MU for Disposal	
Hunter F 6	XG210	A	9 Apr 1957	17 Feb 1958	Canopy shattered on take-off at Sylt	Fg Off J. McVie – OK
Hunter F 6	XG251	E	21 Sep 1959	17 Dec 1959	To 5 MU for Disposal	
Hunter F 6	XG274	P	18 Apr 1957	17 Dec 1962	Transferred to 229 OCU	
Hunter F 6	XG291	Q	1 May 1957	17 Dec 1962	To 5 MU for Disposal	
Hunter F 6	XG292	R	1 May 1957	9 Jun 1958	Transferred to 26 Sqn	
Hunter F 6	XG295	S/C	8 Apr 1957	5 Jan 1961	To 5 MU for Disposal	
Hunter F 6	XJ636	S	2 Jan 1961	17 Feb 1962	To 19 MU for Disposal	
Hunter F 6	XJ642	A	8 Apr 1957	17 Dec 1962	To 19 MU for Disposal	
Hunter F 6	XJ643	B	8 Apr 1957	22 Apr 1957	Hit by XG295 while attempting to give visual inspection after nosewheel red light, top of aircraft and control runs badly damaged	Flt Lt R.E.W. Loverseed – OK
Hunter F 6	XJ644	C	9 Apr 1957	17 Dec 1962	To 19 MU for Disposal	
Hunter F 6	XJ646	D	15 Apr 1957	17 Dec 1962	To 19 MU for Disposal	
Hunter F 6	XJ673	E	15 Apr 1957	18 Aug 1959	Starter bay explosion due to Avpin leak	Fg Off A. C. McLauchlan
Hunter F 6	XJ689	F	1 May 1957	17 Dec 1962	To 19 MU for Disposal	
Hunter F 6	XJ690	H	8 May 1957	17 Dec 1962	To 5 MU for Disposal	
Hunter F 6	XJ691	M	1 May 1957	17 Dec 1962	To 19 MU for Disposal	
Hunter F 6	XJ695	L	7 Feb 1961	17 Dec 1962	To 19 MU for Disposal	
Hunter F 6	XJ712	B	2 Jan 1961	14 Feb 1963	Transferred to 1 Sqn	
Hunter F 6	XJ713	G	2 Jan 1961		Transferred to 1 Sqn	
Hunter F 6	XJ717	R	12 Jan 1961	14 Feb 1962	Transferred to 54 Sqn	
Hunter F 6	XK138	Y				
Hunter F 6	XK149	T	Jan 1962	18 Dec 1962	Transferred to 1 Sqn	
Hunter T7	XL618		12 May 1959	27 Nov 1961	Transferred to 5 MU	
Hunter T7	XL619		1 Jan 1961	28 Mar 1961	Transferred to 19 MU	
Canberra B(I) 8	WT336	C	3 Dec 1962	11 Mar 1969	Transferred to 3 Sqn on disbandment	
Canberra B(I) 8	WT337	A	28 Apr 1966	11 Jun 1970	Transferred to 16 Sqn on disbandment	
Canberra B(I) 8	WT339	D	24 Feb 1966	9 Jun 1970	Transferred to 3 Sqn on disbandment	
Canberra B(I) 8	WT341	X	9 Aug 1967	18 Aug 1967	Transferred to 16 Sqn	
Canberra B(I) 8	WT345	ET	1 Apr 1964 / 5 Sep 1968	24 Feb 1967 / 14 Nov 1968	Transferred to 16 Sqn / Transferred to 16 Sqn	
Canberra B(I) 8	WT346	F	17 Dec 1962	7 Oct 1970	Transferred to 3 Sqn on disbandment	
Canberra B(I) 8	WT347	N	18 May 1965	11 Jun 1970	Transferred to 3 Sqn on disbandment	
Canberra B(I) 8	WT362	G	1 Jul 1963	3 Jun 1970	Transferred to 3 Sqn on disbandment	
Canberra B(I) 8	WT363	H	19 Nov 1962	11 Jun 1968	No2 of a 4-ship close formation. Slipped back and collided with No 4 (XM278). Crew ejected successfully over Annendaal NL	Flt Lt G. Morris, Flt Lt S. Stringer – OK
Canberra B(I) 8	WT365	J	29 Apr 1963	9 Jun 1970	Transferred to 16 Sqn on disbandment	
Canberra B(I) 8	WT366	K	17 Dec 1962	3 Jun 1970	Transferred to 16 Sqn on disbandment	
Canberra B(I) 8	WT368	L	17 Dec 1962	3 Jun 1970	Transferred to 16 Sqn on disbandment	
Canberra B(I) 8	XK951	M	22 Feb 1963	9 Jun 1970	Transferred to 16 Sqn on disbandment	
Canberra B(I) 8	XK952		14 Oct 1969	12 Feb 1970	Transferred to 16 Sqn	
Canberra B(I) 8	XM264	B	6 Nov 1964	11 Jun 1970	Transferred to 16 Sqn on disbandment	
Canberra B(I) 8	XM269		17 Dec 1962	19 Jun 1964	Transferred to 16 Sqn	
Canberra B(I) 8	XM273		17 Dec 1962	25 Mar 1964	Transferred to 3 Sqn	

A/C Type	Serial No	Sqn Code	Date On	Date off	Comments	Crew
Canberra B(I) 8	XM277	P	17 Dec 1962	3 Jun 1970	Transferred to 3 Sqn on disbandment	
Canberra B(I) 8	XM278	O	9 Mar 1965	4 Jun 1970	Transferred to 3 Sqn on disbandment	
Canberra T4	WD944		6 Jul 1966	23 Nov 1966	Transferred to 23 MU Aldergrove	
Canberra T4	WE194		29 Apr 1963	7 Oct 1963	Transferred to 31 Sqn	
Canberra T4	WH840					
Canberra T4	WH850	Z	17 Dec 1962	10 Sep 1969	Wildenrath Station Flight	
Canberra T4	WJ881					
Canberra T4	WT479					
Canberra T4	WT486	Y	26 Sep 1963	16 Oct 1969	Wildenrath Station Flight	
Phantom FGR 2	XT900	900			Transferred to 31 Sqn	
Phantom FGR 2	XT912	912	1 Jun 1970		Transferred to 111 Sqn	
Phantom FGR 2	XT914	914	1 Jun 1970		Transferred to 228 OCU	
Phantom FGR 2	XV399	399			Transferred to 228 OCU	
Phantom FGR 2	XV411	411	Jul 1970		Transferred to II Sqn	
Phantom FGR 2	XV413	413			Tansferred to II Sqn	
Phantom FGR 2	XV417	417			Transferred to II Sqn	
Phantom FGR 2	XV419	419			Trasnferred to 29 Sqn	
Phantom FGR 2	XV421	421	Jul 1970		Transferred to 23 Sqn	
Phantom FGR 2	XV425	425			Transferred to 17 Sqn	
Phantom FGR 2	XV432	432			Transferred to 228 OCU	
Phantom FGR 2	XV434	434			Transferred to 23 Sqn	
Phantom FGR 2	XV435	435	2 Aug 1970		Transferred to 23 Sqn	
Phantom FGR 2	XV439	439	Jul 1970		Transferred to II Sqn	
Phantom FGR 2	XV441	441		21 Nov 1974	Engine fire on take-off from Bruggen, crashed at Lang Hent, NL. crew ejected	Flt Lt A.M. Keane, Flt Lt I.D. Vacha - OK
Phantom FGR 2	XV460	460	Jul 1970		Transferred to 31 Sqn	
Phantom FGR 2	XV463	463	Jul 1970		Transferred to 41 Sqn	
Phantom FGR 2	XV464	464	Jul 1970		Transferred to II Sqn	
Phantom FGR 2	XV466	466			Transferred to 228 OCU	
Phantom FGR 2	XV470	470			Transferred to 17 Sqn	
Phantom FGR 2	XV473	473			Transferred to II Sqn	
Phantom FGR 2	XV484	484			Transferred to 23 Sqn	
Phantom FGR 2	XV485	485			Transferred to 29 Sqn	
Phantom FGR 2	XV486	486			Transferred to 31 Sqn	
Phantom FGR 2	XV496	496			Transferred to 17 Sqn	
Phantom FGR 2	XV501	501	Jul 1970		Transferred to 31 Sqn	
Jaguar GR 1	XX744				Transferred to 6 Sqn	
Jaguar GR 1	XX748	AA	1983	Oct 1985	Transferred to 54 Sqn	
Jaguar GR 1	XX750			7 Feb 1984	Crashed during Ex Red Flag, Nevada, USA	6 Sqn pilot killed
Jaguar GR 1	XX751		Apr 1975		Transferred to 226 OCU	
Jaguar GR 1	XX755		Apr 1975		Transferred to 226 OCU	
Jaguar GR 1	XX756		Apr 1975	Oct 1975	Transferred to 226 OCU	
Jaguar GR 1	XX757		May 1975		Transferred to 226 OCU	
Jaguar GR 1	XX758		May 1975	Oct 1975	Transferred to 226 OCU	
Jaguar GR 1	XX759		2 May 1975	Oct 1975	Transferred to 226 OCU	
Jaguar GR 1	XX760	AA	20 Nov 1975	13 Sep 1982	Transferred to 226 OCU Engine fire, crashed nr Braegudie, Sutherland - pilot ejected	Flt Lt D.S. Griggs - OK
Jaguar GR 1	XX761			Nov 1975	Transferred to 226 OCU	
Jaguar GR 1	XX762	H		30 Mar 1976	Transferred to 226 OCU	
Jaguar GR 1	XX764			Nov 1975	Transferred to 226 OCU	
Jaguar GR 1	XX765			Dec 1975	Transferred to 226 OCU	
Jaguar GR 1	XX766			Dec 1975	Transferred to 226 OCU	
Jaguar GR 1	XX767	AY/AN	29 Nov 1976		Transferred to 31 Sqn	
Jaguar GR 1	XX768				Transferred to 17 Sqn	
Jaguar GR 1	XX821				Transferred to 41 Sqn	
Jaguar GR 1	XX822	AA	By Nov 75	2 Jul 1976	Crashed north of Alhorn during low-level navigation exercise	Flt Lt T.M. Bushnell - killed
Jaguar GR 1	XX824	AB		Aug 1978	Transferred to 17 Sqn	
Jaguar GR 1	XX825	AC	16 Oct 1975			
Jaguar GR 1	XX826	AD			Transferred to 20 Sqn	

A/C Type	Serial No	Sqn Code	Date On	Date off	Comments	Crew
Jaguar GR 1	XX827	AE	By Jan 1976	Mar 1977	Transferred to 20 Sqn	
Jaguar GR 1	XX955	AF	6 Oct 1976	Oct 1983	Transferred to 17 Sqn	
		AN	Oct 1984	Oct 1985	Transferred to 54 Sqn	
Jaguar GR 1	XX956	AB	21 Nov 1975 Oct 1978	Mar 1979	Transferred to 17 Sqn	
Jaguar GR 1	XX957		24 Oct 1975	Mar 1977	Transferred to 20 Sqn	
Jaguar GR 1	XX958	AH	By Jan 1976	Dec 1983	Transferred to 17 Sqn	
Jaguar GR 1	XX959	AJ	By Jan 1976	Jun 1977	Transferred to 20 Sqn	
Jaguar GR 1	XX960	AK		18 Jul 1979	Hit mast, crashed nr Iserlohn, Germany – pilot ejected	Flt Lt G.A. Wardell – OK
Jaguar GR 1	XX963	AL	By Dec 1975	25 May 1982	Accidentally shot down with AIM 9 missile by RAF Phantom – pilot ejected	Flt Lt D.S. Griggs – OK
Jaguar GR 1	XX965	AM	By Jan 1976	1983	Transferred to 54 Sqn	
Jaguar GR 1	XX967	AC	Oct 1983	Oct 1985	To Shawbury	
Jaguar GR 1	XX968	AJ	Dec 1983	Oct 1985	To Shawbury	
Jaguar GR 1	XZ356		Apr 1985	Oct 1985	Transferred to 41 Sqn	
Jaguar GR 1	XZ369	AP				
Jaguar GR 1	XZ371	AP	Aug 1984	Nov 1985	To Shawbury	
Jaguar GR 1	XZ372	AQ/AK		Oct 1983	Transferred to 20 Sqn	
Jaguar GR 1	XZ374		Oct 1983	Aug 1985	To Shawbury	
Jaguar GR 1	XZ375	AD	Oct 1983	Feb 1981	Transferred to 54 Sqn	
Jaguar GR 1	XZ376	AE		Aug 1978	Transferred to 17 Sqn	
Jaguar GR 1	XZ382	AE	17 Aug 1978	Sep 1978	JMU	
Jaguar GR 1	XZ383	AF		Nov 1983	To Cosford	
Jaguar GR 1	XZ385	AG		Jun 1983	Transferred to 17 Sqn	
Jaguar GR 1	XZ386	AJ		Dec 1983	Transferred to 31 Sqn	
Jaguar GR 1	XZ388	AH		1 Apr 1985	Pilot disorientated, flew into the ground nr Rebberleh, Germany – pilot ejected	Fg Off G. Brough – OK
Jaguar GR 1	XZ399			Feb 1984	Transferred to 6 Sqn	
Jaguar T2	XX833	AY	1984		Transferred to RAE Farnborough	
Jaguar T2	XX834				Transferred to II Sqn	
Jaguar T2	XX835				Transferred to 17 Sqn	
Jaguar T2	XX836	AZ	7 Apr 1975	15 Aug 1980	Transferred to 17 Sqn	
Jaguar T2A	XX845	AZ			Transferred to 226 OCU	
Jaguar T2A	XX847	AY				
Tornado GR1	ZA375	BN	by 1990			
Tornado GR1	ZA393	BE	1988	2001		
Tornado GR1	ZA406	CI	2000			
Tornado GR1	ZA452	BP	1991			
Tornado GR1	ZA462	BV	1988	2001		
Tornado GR1	ZA470	BQ	1988	2001		
Tornado GR1	ZA490	BR				
Tornado GR1	ZA544	BX	by 1990		Trainer variant	
Tornado GR1	ZA564	CK	2000			
Tornado GR1	ZD707	BK BU	1985		2001	
Tornado GR1	ZD710	BJ	1985	14 Sep 1989	Crashed on take off from Abingdon after multiple birdstrike – IX Sqn crew ejected	IX Sqn
Tornado GR1	ZD712	BY	1985		Trainer variant	
Tornado GR1	ZD714	BE	by 1990			
Tornado GR1	ZD718	BH	1985	13 Jan 1991	Flew into ground during ultra-low flying practice 140 miles west of Masirah, Oman	Flt Lt K.J. Duffy, Flt Lt N.T. Dent – both killed
Tornado GR1	ZD739	BI	2000			
Tornado GR1	ZD744	BD	1985			
Tornado GR1	ZD745	BM	by 1990			
Tornado GR1	ZD749	BG	2000			
Tornado GR1	ZD788	BT	1988	2001		
Tornado GR1	ZD790	BB				
Tornado GR1	ZD791	BG	1985	17 Jan 1991	Shot down by SAM at Ar Rumayah, Iraq – XV Sqn crew ejected	XV Sqn
Tornado GR1	ZD809	BA	by 1990	14 Oct 1999	Crashed near Inghoe, Northumberland	XV Sqn

A/C Type	Serial No	Sqn Code	Date On	Date off	Comments	Crew
Tornado GR1	ZD812	BW	2000			
Tornado GR1	ZD842	BZ	1985		Trainer variant	
Tornado GR1	ZD845	BA	1985			
Tornado GR1	ZD846	BL	1985	11 Jan 1996	A/c departed during high AOA manoeuvring at low level, southwest of Munster; crew ejected	Capt A. Spinelli (ItAF) OK, Sqn Ldr C.J. Donovan injured
Tornado GR1	ZD848	BC	1985			
Tornado GR1	ZD849	BT	CM	1995?	2000	
Tornado GR1	ZD851	BO	2000			
Tornado GR1	ZD891	BB	1985	13 Jan 1989	Mid-air collision with *Luftwaffe* Alphajet near Wiesmoor, approx 10 miles south of Jever	Flt Lt M.P.S. Smith, Flt Lt A.G. Grieve – both killed
Tornado GR1	ZD892	BJ	by 1990			
Tornado GR1	ZD894	BE	1985	30 Jun 1987	Starboard taileron failed to full deflection at low level 5 miles east Wesel. Crew ejected	Flt Lt J.P. Moloney, Flt Lt J.A. Hill – both OK
Tornado GR1	ZD895	BF	1985	2001		
Tornado GR1	ZG756	BX		2001		
Tornado GR1	ZG794	BP	2000			
Tornado GR4	ZA371	005	2004			
Tornado GR4	ZA404	BT/013	2004			
Tornado GR4A	ZA405	014	2009			
Tornado GR4	ZA470	BQ	2003			
Tornado GR4	ZA473	BH/032	2003			
Tornado GR4	ZA492	BO	2003			
Tornado GR4	ZA554	BF/046	2002			
Tornado GR4	ZA560	BC/050	2001			
Tornado GR4	ZA588	BB/056	2001			
Tornado GR4	ZA592	BJ/059	2001			
Tornado GR4	ZA596	BL/062	2000			
Tornado GR4	ZA602	BY	2000	2002		
Tornado GR4	ZA604	068	2009			
Tornado GR4	ZA606	BD	2001			
Tornado GR4	ZD707	077	2009			
Tornado GR4	ZD712	BX	2000			
Tornado GR4	ZD719	BS	2001			
Tornado GR4	ZD740	BG	2003			
Tornado GR4	ZD741	BZ	2000			
Tornado GR4	ZD747	095	2009			
Tornado GR4	ZD788	BE/098	2000			
Tornado GR4	ZD792	BE	2001			
Tornado GR4	ZD810	102	2011			
Tornado GR4	ZD811	BK/BU	2001			
Tornado GR4	ZD847	108	2009			
Tornado GR4	ZG709	120	2004			
Tornado GR4	ZG727	126	2003			
Tornado GR4	ZG756	BX/131	2003			
Tornado GR4	ZG775	134	2008			
Tornado GR4	ZG777	BS	2000			
Tornado GR4	ZG791	BI	2001	2002		
Shadow R1	ZZ416		14 Oct 2011			
Shadow R1	ZZ417		14 Oct 2011			
Shadow R1	ZZ418		14 Oct 2011			
Shadow R1	ZZ419		14 Oct 2011			
Shadow R1	ZZ504		12 Dec 2011			
KingAir 350C	G-LBSB		July 2013			

Appendix 3
14 Squadron Aircraft Markings 1945-2015

De Havilland Mosquito (1945-51)

The Mosquito FBVIs (1945-46) were inherited when 143 Squadron was renumbered 14 Squadron and these aircraft were painted in standard Coastal Command Mosquito camouflage. The squadron codes 'CX' were used.

The Mosquito BXVIs (1946-47) were inherited when 128 Squadron was renumbered 14 Squadron. These aircraft were finished in standard dark grey/dark green camouflage with grey undersides; the 128 Squadron code letters 'M5' were slowly replaced by 'CX' in yellow, edged in black. Propeller spinners were painted yellow.

Mosquito B35s (1947-51) were either camouflaged (minority) or finished all-over in silver (majority). In all cases, spinners were painted yellow and squadron code letters 'CX' and individual aircraft letters were painted in yellow with black edging. The squadron crest was painted on both sides of the fin.

De Havilland Vampire (1951-54)

Like most of the later Mosquitoes, the 14 Squadron Vampires were initially painted in an all-over silver finish. The 'Fassberg Flash' was painted in blue on either side of the nose and the original squadron badge (i.e. winged shield rather than plate) was painted just below the cockpit on the port side of the fuselage. Aircraft individual letters were painted in yellow with black edging ahead of the roundel on the tail boom, and the squadron code letter 'B' was painted on the opposite side of the roundel. However, by February 1953, aircraft had been camouflaged in dark green/dark sea grey disruptive pattern upper surfaces and sides with silver undersides. The 'Fassberg Flash' was light blue with a white outline. Aircraft individual letters and the squadron code letter 'B' were painted in black. The T11 trainer variant carried a white 'Flash' outlined in red.

De Havilland Venom (1953-55)

The Venoms were camouflaged with a high-gloss dark green/dark sea grey disruptive pattern upper surfaces and sides and 'PR Blue' undersides. The 'Fassberg Flash,' squadron badge and squadron code letters were all as per the Vampire.

Hawker Hunter (1955-62)

Like the Venoms, the Hunters were painted in the high-gloss dark green/dark sea grey disruptive pattern camouflage on the upper and side-surfaces with grey undersides. Bars comprising three blue diamonds on a white background were applied on either side of the roundel on the aft fuselage. [The squadron had originally wanted to have blue and white chequerboard reflecting markings that were supposedly used on the tailfins of some squadron aircraft during the 1920s, but the chequerboard had already been officially approved for 19 Squadron.]

On the F4 variant, the aircraft individual letter was painted on the tail in white and repeated in blue, along with three blue diamonds, on the nose wheel door. The squadron badge was painted in a white disc either side of the nose (a blue disc was used initially, but this was quickly replaced by a white disc).

The markings of the F6 variant were similar to the F4, except that the aircraft individual letter was painted on the tailfin in black on a white disc and the squadron badge was deleted; additionally, from late 1959, pilots' names were painted in white under the cockpit on the port side. The colours of the disc and letter on the tail were reversed in late 1960, at which time the aircraft serial number was also painted in white on the rear fuselage. A smaller version of the squadron badge was painted on the side of the nose. From late 1961, the roundel bars were moved upwards to align with the top half of the roundel.

English Electric Canberra (1962-70)

The Canberras of 14 Squadron were finished in dark green/dark grey disruptive camouflage with black undersides. Until approximately 1964, the aircraft serial number was stencilled in large letters/numbers in white on either side of the rear fuselage. After that date, the undersides were finished in light grey and the aircraft serial number in black. The squadron crest (i.e. winged plate) was painted on the tailfin above the black-painted aircraft individual letter. On some aircraft the squadron crest, flanked by the blue-and-white diamond bars was painted on the nose above and forward of the crew entry door.

McDonnell Phantom (1970-75)

Phantom aircraft were painted in dark green/dark grey disruptive camouflage, with light grey undersides and a black nose-cone. The roundel was painted on the engine intake and the 'last three' numbers of the aircraft serial number were repeated in white on the tailfin above the tail flash. The 'Crusader badge', a stylized squadron crest flanked by blue-and-white diamond bars was painted on each side of the forward fuselage. From mid-1972, the red/white/blue national markings were 'toned down' to red/blue.

SEPECAT Jaguar (1975-85)

Jaguar markings were similar to those carried on the Phantom, with the exception that the 'Crusader badge' was applied to the engine intakes and the roundel was carried on the forward fuselage. From Jun 1976, the squadron letter 'A' prefixed an individual aircraft letter and both were painted on the tailfin in black with white edging. From Oct 1976, the disruptive camouflage scheme was progressively repainted as a 'wraparound', including the under-surfaces.

BAe (Panavia) Tornado (1985-2011)

14 Squadron Tornado GR1s were painted in 'wraparound' dark grey/dark green disruptive camouflage with black nose-cones. The 'Crusader badge' was painted on the forward fuselage and the roundel was painted on the engine intake. A row of nine blue diamonds was painted across the top of the fin between the RHWR aerial fairings. The squadron code letter 'B' prefixed the individual aircraft letter, in black with white edging on the tailfin ahead of the tail flash. From 1987, the tail diamonds were highlighted with white along the leading edges, and from c.1989 the tail diamonds were reduced in number to seven.

During operations in the Gulf War, aircraft were painted in an overall 'Desert Pink' finish. All squadron markings were deleted, but the aircraft tail letters were retained.

From 1998, an all-over grey colour scheme was introduced, and the nose-cone was repainted grey. The 'Crusader badge' was reduced in size and moved to the panel-access door on each side of the lower forward fuselage, the squadron code and aircraft letters were reduced in size and moved to the rear topmost corner of the tailfin. The seven tail diamonds were retained.

This latter scheme was also applied to the Tornado GR4 variant. The individual tail letters were replaced from c.2006 by a 'fleet number,' allocated on a Tornado GR4 fleet-wide (rather than individual squadron) basis, which was painted on the tip of the tailfin.

It is worth noting that aircraft were routinely shared amongst squadrons and that the aircraft allocated to major Tornado Force detachments (either for training or operations) were provided from across the entire Tornado Force. Thus it was common for 14 Squadron crews to fly aircraft which carried the markings of other units.

Beechcraft Shadow (2011-present)

The Shadow R1 is painted all over grey finish with no squadron markings

Appendix 4
14 Squadron History References 1945-2015

National Archives Files:

Air 16/1408	Day combats against Canberras in Exercise MOMENTUM
Air 24/1804	BAFO Operations Record Book :January-December 1946
Air 24/1825	BAFO Operations Record Book :Appendices April-June 1946
Air 25/49	2 Group Operations Record Book :Appendices October 1945-April 1947
Air 25/1405	No. 2 Group: July - December 1951
Air 25/1406	No. 2 Group: January - June 1952
Air 25/1407	No. 2 Group: July - December 1952
Air 25/1408	No. 2 Group: January - June 1953
Air 25/1409	No. 2 Group: July - December 1953
Air 25/1410	No. 2 Group: January - June 1954
Air 25/1411	No. 2 Group: July - December 1954
Air 25/1412	No. 2 Group: January - June 1955
Air 26/199	138 Wing Operations Record Book: November 1943-April 1946
Air 27/2398	14 Squadron Operations Record Book: June 1945-December 1950
Air 27/2600	14 Squadron Operations Record Book: January 1955-December 1955
Air 27/2905	14 Squadron Operations Record Book: January 1961-December 1965
Air 27/3021	14 Squadron Operations Record Book: January 1966-December 1971
Air 27/3283	14 Squadron Operations Record Book: January 1972-December 1975
Air 27/3409	14 Squadron Operations Record Book: January 1976-December 1980
Air 27/3541	14 Squadron Operations Record Book: January 1981-December 1982
Air 28/49	Banff Operations Record Book: September 1944-August 1945
Air 28/297	Gatwick Operations Record Book: July 1940-August 1946
Air28/1646	Tengah (including RAF Detachment Kuantan) Operations Record Book 1961-65
Air 29/1298	Armament Practice Station, Sylt, Germany: August 1945 - December 1950
Air 55/1	BAFO Order of Battle: July 1945-June 1950
Air 55/92	Annual Training Scheme Mosquitoes 1946
Air 55/221	Annual Training Scheme Mosquitoes 1945
Air 55/352	Note on Recent Demonstration of Napalm attacks by Vampire V aircraft of 2TAF
Air 55/358	Low Level Detection and Control Trials Exercise HARGIL
BT 233/54	Accident to Vampire VV538
DEFE 56/145	Phantom Missile Firings: March 1973-November1974
DEFE 58/57	Missile Firing Report 14 Squadron: 3-12 February 1972

Log Books:

Air Marshal T.M. Anderson	Gp Capt M.W. Ball	Sqn Ldr R.N. Broad
Sqn Ldr N.P. Bury	Gp Capt S.H. Cockram	Flt Lt T.J.B. Dugan
Sqn Ldr A.R. Fisher	Wg Cdr J.A. Freeborough	Flt Lt K. Gambold
Flt Lt M.A. Gibson	Flt Lt A.D. Glover	Flt Lt J.H. Hanson
Gp Capt N.M. Huckins	Gp Capt J.B. Klein	Sqn Ldr M.H. Levy
Sqn Ldr R. Mannering	Flt Lt T.J. Marsh	Sqn Ldr D.E. Moule
Sqn Ldr M.J.W. Napier	Wg Cdr D.J.A. Potter	Gp Capt S.E. Reeves
Sqn Ldr J.A.J. Robins-Walker	Air Cdre S.P.Rochelle	Flt Lt P.T. Rossiter
Flt Lt D.K. Roxburgh	Flt Lt C.J. Stradling	Flt Lt M.J. Wintermeyer

Unpublished Memoirs:

Memoirs of a Sprog Mosquito Pilot on 14 Squadron - Mike Levy
Memoirs of a Venom Flight Commander - Bob Broad
Memoir - Ron Burgess
The Real Blue Diamonds - Chris Golds
No. 14 Squadron, 1959 – 63 - John Preece
Spreading My Wings - Patrick O'Connor
Tornado over the Tigris – Michael Napier
Diary Extracts – Jameel Janjua
Spring in Deid – diary extracts – Ian Davis
14 Sqn Participation In Op Granby/Desert Storm – Douglas Moule & Chris Coulls
14 Squadron Notes: 1993-1995 and 2000-2003 – Gp Capt J. B. Klein

Books:

Aircraft of the RAF - Owen Thetford, Putnam 1979
Aircraft Camouflage & Markings 1907-1954 - Bruce Robertson, Harleyford 1961
Aircraft of the Royal Air Force Since 1918 - Owen Thetford, Putnam 1979
A Lighter Shade of Blue - Christopher Foxley-Norris, Ian Allan 1978
The Big Show - Pierre Clostermann, Chatto & Windus 1951
De Havilland Mosquito an Illustrated History Vol 2 - Ian Thirsk, Crecy 2006
Jet Jockeys - Peter Caygill, Airlife 2002
RAF Hunters in Germany – Gunther Kipp & Roger Lindsay, Lindsay 2003
Royal Air Force Germany - Bill Taylor, Midland 2003
The Squadrons of the Royal Air Force - James J. Halley, Air Britain 1980
Thunder and Lightning – The RAF in the Gulf War - Charles Allen, HMSO 1991
TIALD – The Gulf War - GEC Ferranti 1991
Venom - de Havilland Venom and Sea Venom the Complete History - David Watkins, The History Press 2009
Winged Warriors - Paul McDonald, Pen & Sword Books 2012

Miscellaneous Documents:

Aircraft Accident Cards - RAF Museum
Aircraft Movement Cards - RAF Museum
14 Squadron Crewroom Diaries: 1958-Oct 1964
14 Squadron Crewroom Diary: 1970- 2011
14 Squadron 90th Anniversary booklet
Iraq: No Fly Zones, MoD 2009 via Iraq Inquiry website
MoD Gulf War History, via MoD website
A Short History of the RAF, Chapter 6 – Return to Expeditionary Warfare, via MoD website
RAF Operational Update - Op Herrick, via MoD website
Counterinsurgency In Kandahar - Evaluating The 2010 Hamkari Campaign – Carl Forsberg, Institute for the Study of War 2010

Correspondence (letter and/or e-mail):
All individuals named in the Acknowledgements.

Periodicals:
Air Forces Monthly, February 2008 – "Operational CAS over Iraq"
Air Forces Monthly, April 2013 – "Out of the Shadows" - Tim Ripley
Air Pictorial, Vol 30 Issue 10 – "Striking Saddam" – Sqn Ldr M.J.W. Napier
British Roundel, January/February 2006 – "14 Squadron 1951-1970" – Geoff Cruikshank
Threshold HQ PTC Flight Safety Magazine, Issue 2/97 – "You Ave Keel-ed Two Orses" – Sqn Ldr M.J.W. Napier

Flight,	various via website - see below
The London Gazette,	various via website - see below
The Weekly Standard,	20 June 2008 – "The Battle for Basra" - Marisa Cochrane

Websites:

Air of Authority	http:www.rafweb.org
London Gazette	http://london-gazette.co.uk
Flight Magazine Archive	http:flightglobal.com
Jever Steam Laundry	http://www.rafjever.org
UK MoD/RAF	http://www.raf.mod.uk/history
Iraq Inquiry	http://www.iraqinquiry.org.uk
NATO	http://www.nato.int

Index